Acknowledgements:

Special mention is due to Dr. Derek L. Smith for his perceptive critiques during proofing and editing.

Another colleague, P. L. Housley, volunteered skilled assistance by directing and preparing this work for publication, then capped that performance by producing an inspired portrait of Joseph's death mask for the book's front cover.

Due to their cheerful yet longsuffering patience I am indebted to Aggie and Debbie.

The
Make-Believe
Martyr

An Introduction to Literary
Excellence in the Book of Mormon

Lofte Payne

© Copyright 2005 Lofte Payne.
All rights reserved. No part of this publication may be reproduced, stored in a retrieval system, or transmitted, in any form or by any means, electronic, mechanical, photocopying, recording, or otherwise, without the written prior permission of the author.

Cover illustration: *The Martyr's Masque*, acrylic on canvas by P.L. Housley. © 2005
Used by permission.

Note for Librarians: A cataloguing record for this book is available from Library and Archives Canada at www.collectionscanada.ca/amicus/index-e.html
ISBN 1-4120-4945-8

Offices in Canada, USA, Ireland and UK
This book was published *on-demand* in cooperation with Trafford Publishing. On-demand publishing is a unique process and service of making a book available for retail sale to the public taking advantage of on-demand manufacturing and Internet marketing. On-demand publishing includes promotions, retail sales, manufacturing, order fulfilment, accounting and collecting royalties on behalf of the author.

Book sales for North America and international:
Trafford Publishing, 6E–2333 Government St.,
Victoria, BC v8t 4p4 CANADA
phone 250 383 6864 (toll-free 1 888 232 4444)
fax 250 383 6804; email to orders@trafford.com

Book sales in Europe:
Trafford Publishing (uk) Limited, 9 Park End Street, 2nd Floor
Oxford, UK ox1 1hh UNITED KINGDOM
phone 44 (0)1865 722 113 (local rate 0845 230 9601)
facsimile 44 (0)1865 722 868; info.uk@trafford.com

Order online at:
trafford.com/04-2753
10 9 8 7 6 5

Contents

Introduction ix
    The Make-Believe Martyr, x

Chapter 1: **An Unlikely Martyr** 1
    Life Too Intense for the Biographer's Art, 3; Correcting for Magnification and Focus, 6

Chapter 2: **Zion's Camp: Launching the Apotheosis** 9

Chapter 3: **Coming to Grips with a Tale Twice Told** 16
    "Let the Language of the Book Speak for Itself," 18; "I have Spoken Plainly That Ye Cannot Err," 19; Opposition in All Things…Pervasive Ambiguity, 20; Four More Keys to the Kingdom, 23

Chapter 4: **Capturing the Scene with a Mormon** 25
    Like Mormon, "Quick to Observe," 26; "A Good Name is Rather to Be Chosen than Great Riches," 28

Chapter 5: **Nephi, Part 1: A Journey Too Far for St. Paul** 31
    A Small Roast for Twelve, 33; Joseph, Ignorant and Learned Son, 35

Chapter 6: **Nephi, Part 2: The Two-Story Myth of Nephi** 37
    Nephi as Black Smith, 38; Wresting a Smith from the Bible, 39; 1805—It Was a Very Good Year, 40

Chapter 7: **Lehi and Sariah as Joseph and Lucy** 42
    Sariah: Just Another Day's Work for a New World Mom, 44; Lucy on the Move—at Onidah (Oneida), New York, 45; "My Mother Complained Against My Father," 46; Lucy Knew the Truth: Family Comes First, 47

Chapter 8: **Lehi's Dream of the Tree of Life** 51
    A Little Something *Fresh* from the Garden, 51; In a Dark and Dreary Waste, 53; Wave to All the Nice People, Darling, 55; Nephi's Confirmation, Another Witness of Jesus, 56; Lehi's Corroboration—Practice Makes Perfect, 58; Follow up: Adam's Desperation Prayer, 58

Chapter 9: **Troubles with Three Good Bad Guys** 63
Laman: As a Humble Amateur, He Was a Much Loved Brother, 66;
Lemuel: "A Man's Enemies are the Men of His Own House," 68;
Laban: The Uncle Who Made All the Difference, 70

Chapter 10: **Painful Origins on Plates of Brass** 73
Uncle Jesse, Salem, 1813, 75; In an Age of Reason the Atonement
Becomes Infinite, 77; Bitter Pain, Exquisite Paine, 81; To Voltaire, a
Grateful Adieu, 82

Chapter 11: **Samuel, Jacob and Joseph—How Team Players Engineered the Great Media Coup** 86
With a Name Like Joseph, 89; Realize All Your Dreams,
Line upon Line, 90; Onward to Glory—with Help
from Two Friends, 94; Jacob, the Stumblingblock, 96

Chapter 12: **Zenos' Wild Allegory** 98
Haven't We Met the Zenos Brothers Somewhere Else? 99; Casting
Call for Three: Vineyard, Servant, Master, 100; Old Wine, New Bottle,
New Wine, Old Bottle, 102; Getting Digged, Pruned and Dunged, 103;
In Its Latter Days, a Fruitful Bough, 104

Chapter 13: **Omni: One for All, All in Fun** 107
Chemish, 109; Abinadom, 109; Amaleki, 109; Benjamin, 110

Chapter 14: **Mosiah, the Prophet-Savior Combo** 112
Abinadi, the *Other* Cantankerous Martyr, 114; Parody from Head to
Foot, 115; Abinadi: Fiery Prophet, Model Martyr, 116; As a Relentless
Political Paradigm, Amulon Grinds the Mill, 119

Chapter 15: **Zarahemla—One City, Two Tales** 122
Coloring the Law, 125; It's No Place Like Home, 127; Palmyra—
a Model for Zarahemla? 127

Chapter 16: **Alma, Part 1: Portrait of a Mormon Soul** 131
If Not *the* Vision, at Least the *Ideal* Vision, 131; "If thou Wilt of
Thyself Be Destroyed…," 132; Tainting the Experiment, 134; With
Korihor's Curse, One Saving Grace, 135; Alma's Confession, 137

Contents   vii

Chapter 17: Alma, Part 2: As Mormon As it Gets 139
   Helaman, Firstborn of the Father, 139; Corianton and Isabel—Two
   Heavy Hearted Lovers, 140; An Attaboy for Shiblon, 142; When
   Humor Runs in the Family, 144; Gazelem, 146; Amalickiah, the King 147

Chapter 18: Alma, Part 3: Alma's Quasi Chiasmi
   Find Their New Literary Heritage 149
   Matthew's Good Fruit Chiasmus, 151; When Words Fail, Say It
   With an X, 152; Alma's Great Geographical Chiasmus, 154; Alma's
   Triple Crucifixion Chiasmus, 156; Alma's Six-Chain-Linked Chiasmus, 161

Chapter 19: A Hostile but Faithful Witness, Part 1:
   The Descent of Jesus Christ 168
   The Mother Hen Parody, 170; Old Things Done Away, 171;
   Miracles (and Parody) on a Budget, 173; Now I Know Where Bad
   Comes from, 173; Bringing About the Bowels of Mercy, 175; Taking
   a Narrow Path Less Traveled, 175

Chapter 20: A Hostile but Faithful Witness, Part 2:
   Spotting A Host of Dubious Gods 177
   An Accountable, Unchangeable, Semi-Supreme Being, 179; A God
   of Miracles...Don't Hold Your Breath, 180; A God Meaner than
   the Junkyard Dog, 181; A Genie in Your Lamp, 181; The God Who
   Should Have Known Better, 182; A Trinity, Plus or Minus One, 183;
   Fatherandson, 185; The Shadow God, 186; The Adam-God Doctrine, 187

Chapter 21: A Stratospheric Genealogy—Capped by Ether 190
   Escape from a Tower of Babel, 193; Joseph and Lucy Revisited, 195

Chapter 22: Martyr's Journal, Part 1:
   A Pause for Breath...Then Immortality 201
   The Mental Side of Martyrdom, 203; The Die is Cast, 205

Chapter 23: Martyr's Journal, Part 2:
   Winning Position in a War of Words 208
   Meeting Shiz Half Way, 210; Ether, Gilead, Lib and Coriantumr, 212

Chapter 24: Martyr's Journal, Part 3:
   Such a Short Lifetime, Only Nine Moons 217

Chapter 25: **The Polygamy Plot, Part 1: Essentials** 224

Chapter 26: **The Polygamy Plot, Part 2:
Opposition from a Chosen Few** 231
    William and Wilson Law, 232; Robert and Charles Foster, 233; Francis and Chauncy Higbee, 235; Stirring the Opposition, 237; "Little Foxes Spoil the Vines," 239; Dissidents Coalesce, 242

Chapter 27: **The Polygamy Plot, Part 3: Testing Games** 249
    Edwin's Test, 250; Heber's Test, 251; Brigham's Test, 252; Sidney's Test, 254; Hyrum's Test, 256

Chapter 28: **Moroni, Last of the Mormons** 260
    Moroni I, 261; Moroni II, 262; Moroni's First Corinthians Cameos, 264

In Conclusion—Introducing
the Seventh Literary Wonder of the World 267

Notes 274

Index 299

Introduction

A couple of auspicious "arrivals" enlivened America's prospects during the final weeks of 1805: in November, Lewis and Clark were able to celebrate completion of their overland route to the Pacific. Not too much later a humble village in Vermont produced one of our nation's more remarkable citizens, Joseph Smith, Jr. Although born into severe poverty, this man eventually gathered so much success and popular support that, prior to his assassination in 1844, he'd announced himself as candidate for President of the United States. During the previous fourteen years he had been acting as the prophet for one of the nation's fastest growing religious groups where attendance at his public sermons could be expected to number as many as twenty thousand. He simultaneously held office as mayor in one of the largest cities on America's western frontier and wore higher military rank (Lieutenant General) than any officer in the nation.

What isn't generally known is that Joseph Smith also composed some of the most marvelous literature of his time—or *any* time. Drama sketches he penned during the 1840s continue with daily encore performances throughout the world. Okay, so the show is for members only; I won't lie. But there is one thing more and you'd never have guessed it—before turning 24 he finished writing his first fictional novel and it well deserves consideration as America's earliest literary masterpiece. Historians often set Joseph Smith aside as a marginal character in our nation's history because of unsettled mysteries in both his conduct and writings—his profound, all but perfect, *Book of Mormon*. That such a prominent man of affairs had become so entirely misunderstood by the end of his life is quite unfortunate; yet, for this particular individual the puzzle he's become is nothing other than as he designed it, and that leads to an even more curious story.

Rather than suppose his reliance upon mystery a disingenuous strategy, first appreciate the fact that by over-utilizing the most common errors of perception one man successfully spawned a religion, now world wide, that continues thriving long after earliest critics projected its demise. Also, among followers, Joseph continues receiving higher praises than anyone "save Jesus only" for his efforts at saving mankind. However, the legacy he left for them is really quite clouded—a problem that never ceases to provoke frustrations for those who investigate his life—and likewise inviting new theories of what motivated him and ignited his imagination, even as upwards of eleven million members proceed under assumptions of validity for his religious teachings.

The Make-Believe Martyr

By referring to him as the Make-Believe Martyr, it would make no sense to imply that Joseph Smith, Jr. never existed; neither would I dare suggest that he doesn't quite deserve status as a martyr. While my title choice admits an ambiguous element, no pejorative purpose has been intended. Rather, I selected those words to help in capturing something of his essence—they are more respectful than may appear. I might just as appropriately have chosen as a title, *The Riddlemaster*, because Joseph had a genius for speaking two ways or telling two stories simultaneously. Some double messages from his book don't simply deliver two meanings that differ, but establish ideas standing highest in contrast to one another. One thing you'll discover from this inquiry into his *Book of Mormon* is that realities aren't always as they appear, and they sometimes turn out most contrary to one's earlier anticipations.

Throughout our examination of his book, we'll often want to reflect on characteristics that may bestow superior grace to works of literature. Does Joseph's work demonstrate any of them? If we were to momentarily set aside its religious dimension, we'd quickly recognize that Joseph's book is a formidable piece of writing simply because large numbers of people have come to believe its fiction represents historical realities. That's not bad fiction. Over and above that, rather than being driven by plot/subplot, this piece shows an abundance of exquisite symbolism and

☙ Introduction ❧

that's what really transforms it into literary gold. On its down side, the nuance of symbolism common to good literature has never been so easy to grasp. Readers who are unfamiliar with a particular subject can benefit from guidance by someone intimate enough with the author and his topic that they are able to suggest insights to elucidate complex passages. That is no less true for Joseph and his book; in fact, due to his rare ability for delivering the unexpected, his book demonstrates the following literary qualities that have *never* yet received adequate notice:

- Humor
- Parody
- Riddles
- Autobiography
- Poetry
- Social satire
- Religious critique
- Double entendre

Joseph lived a one-of-a-kind life by combining his extremely high intelligence with rich imagination, quick wit, infinite creativity, conscientiousness and the rigid discipline of total commitment. You may disagree with his philosophy, or you may well bristle at his unconventional ethics, but he employed his facility for make-believe in ways that deserve appreciation throughout a much broader audience than presently constituted. One of the things I'll propose showing is how he successfully cultivated abilities for framing a make-believe world in order to achieve one of his prime ambitions—that of becoming a religious martyr.

This volume competes with at least a dozen other good books that have been written concerning the life and ideals of Joseph Smith, founder of Mormonism. Both my method and conclusions will vary considerably from any of those previous biographies but in so doing will allow readers to get nearer to Joseph and his precepts than with any other book. My course proposes incorporating elements of his life's story as he intended preserving them in his fictional tale, the *Book of Mormon*. I believe this study to be the first to achieve such a degree of perceptual breakthrough.

While the same strategy of searching their fictional works has always been standard and prudent practice for studying the life story of any other author, Joseph intentionally introduced several roadblocks for recognizing those relationships between himself and his book. For starters, he presented himself very convincingly as an unlearned backwoodsman. Secondly, he denied having authored his book, claiming only to have translated it by the gift and power of God. Third, he maintained that it presented a genuine account of historical characters and real events from antiquity. Most important, he used his book to found a church that has experienced constant expansion in its membership. With at least 99% of his readers either being or becoming true believers, interpreting his book though its autobiographical markers would have cost them an unacceptable sacrifice of integrity and faith.

Honestly, the overwhelming majority of that remaining *one* percent of its readers are not only non-believers but scoffers who view the book skeptically as product of an unskilled but imaginative dreamer; they don't view it anywhere close to being authentic but suspect Joseph intended a hoax by it, and most of them will readily admit how disappointed they have been by its abysmal performance as literature. In truth it seems as though one established prerequisite for assembling a successful anthology of American literature has been to shun Joseph and his book. The excellence of his story has been buried under a bushel.

While others have resisted analyzing its author-book relationships, or have found that proposition difficult or unproductive, my study of the Book of Mormon and Joseph's life reveal that its fictional stories represent his deepest intimacies. Here, you'll take a trip behind the scenes to learn of secrets he never told his mother, his wife nor any of his twelve apostles. Not only did he compose his literature to mark significant episodes recalling his youth but also included a blueprint in it for *future* plans stretching out beyond its publication date of 1830, all the way to his martyrdom fourteen years afterward. While he may have begun it as a make-believe tale, that is where he chose to carry its myth.

Through his eyes we can also discover a critical portrait showing how early America's struggle for success has been hindered by hopeless burdens of inherited religious superstition. His book illustrates how man's haughty pride combines with a morally flawed nature to carry civilization along cyclical paths of conflict, rise and fall.

Aside from showing that very literary quality of autobiography, its symbolic richness exhibits much greater evidence of genius than anyone has previously imagined. I'd like to think that my view differs from all others in how it reveals Joseph's book, not just as make-believe, but *haut* literature, the best. If I am not incorrect, there seems to be no good reason why we shouldn't reincarnate Joseph's work as the once coveted "Great American Novel," now considered a sign of our early nation's unfulfilled intellectual promise.

Perhaps the next reasonable thing would be to flip to the opening chapter and begin, for, they say, the proof of the pudding is in the eating, and I am very confident that Joseph's story will sell itself with only the necessary orientation to guide objective, open-minded readers to the treasure. My intent has been to enlarge access to the meaning of an American original, a man with a great mission burning in him to change the world—but who realized that his effectiveness might be substantially improved by taking an indirect route.

In this study, after briefly exploring material intended to familiarize readers with the uniqueness of Joseph's character, we'll pursue his philosophical tale along a sequence generally paralleling his book. The *Book of Mormon*, by the way, has never gone out of print, although it receives widest distribution through private channels, at little or no charge, with popular give-away programs being advertised periodically on radio and television. Inexpensive copies are often found at thrift stores, but don't feel too embarrassed about requesting a freshly minted volume from your local LDS church or Mormon neighbor. They can be had, *gratis,* from a website simply by entering "free Book of Mormon" on any popular search engine.

CHAPTER 1

An Unlikely Martyr

"The world always mistook false prophets for true ones." (Joseph Smith, 1842)[1]

Joseph's telling of his first visit by an angel reveals little difference from a business meeting between two partners:

> He called me by name, and said unto me that he was a messenger sent from the presence of God to me, and that his name was Moroni; that God had a work for me to do; and that my name should be had for good and evil among all nations, kindreds, and tongues, or that it should be both good and evil spoken of among all people.[2]

Justly told. Approaching that event's bicentennial year almost nobody speaks with equanimity concerning the name Joseph Smith. Those enchanted by his revelations seem capable of expounding only the man's merits, leaving the negative portion of Moroni's task to an unusually naive set of critics who squander their energies rehearsing Joseph's absurdities, nimbly pointing out his chicanery, inconsistencies and doctrinal contradictories. Laboring as hard as they do to expose him only proves Moroni's words prophetic, and, to the eyes of true believers, no gainsayer's list of facts can outweigh tribute from an angel so unerring in his predictions.

One recent promoter of Smith's mission suggests that Joseph fulfilled a Judaic prophecy from the Dead Sea Scroll era that foretold a *second* "messianic figure."[3] From there his reputation rises several levels as we find him "mingling with gods,"[4] and in the lead to gain the bid "even unto his exaltation and glory."[5] Can truth about the Great American Prophet only reside at one extreme or the other when one camp exalts him further above the clouds while counterpart critics bury him deeper into a pit? Today we might sympathize with many of Joseph's frustrated biographers, including faithful church members, who at times have characterized him as "an enigma defying normal historical explanation."[6]

Joseph himself joined efforts to throw future biographers off his tracks when he claimed, "You don't know me; you never knew my heart. No man knows my history. I cannot tell it; I shall never undertake it [...],"[7] when in fact he had already pieced together a record of his life that, annotated and published, extends well beyond three thousand pages. What was there not to tell? Had he forgotten the existence of his personal diaries, journals and serialized press articles detailing all his adventures? Or could those words have hinted his confession of some burden much too difficult to share with devoted followers? The best-known account Joseph gave of his life has become the basic text for all serious students of Mormonism, his *History of the Church, Period I, History of Joseph Smith, the Prophet, by Himself*, a mammoth six-volume resource that is loaded with autobiographical data. In it, time and again, Joseph set himself in the best possible light while exposing his persecutors to the glare of their malice and deep prejudices; he recounts his bravery during heroic exploits, is guided by the voice of God, becomes a bold negotiator, a wise teacher and counselor to his Saints. He represented himself as affable, loyal and supportive to friends, one who cemented himself to his family and showed emotions openly, often giving more consideration to followers than to himself. But then, too, he made it abundantly plain how he kept several steps ahead of onlooker subordinates.

Through the years Joseph suffered intolerable abuse from opponents, getting beaten, mobbed and covered with hot tar. He had to defend himself against dozens of vexatious lawsuits. Without judgment or trial he and several associates were held in shackles for several months while being insulted by cowardly jailers until further silence would no longer have constituted virtue. Two states drove him and his people into exile. Followers were bombarded and exiled once again after Joseph and Hyrum, his brother, were murdered by a furious mob.

What an enduring war of words this American Prophet stirred up for himself and his Saints, an army of followers now approaching a dozen million members, worldwide. Why he did it, his underlying reasoning and motivations, had little to do with revelations handed down by God. By his own admission, Joseph refused to expose his inner drives to anybody: "Would to God, brethren, I could tell you who I am! Would to God I could tell you what I know! But you would call it blasphemy [...]."[8] Since his public teachings already demonstrated potent blasphemy, what especially irreverent thought had he left to conceal? Evidently we'll need to review his life and works more closely while keeping within sight a level of reason that avoids judgmental extremes. Since complex circumstances have combined to make our task more difficult, we must constantly remind ourselves that appearances don't always reflect all the facts of a matter: "I don't blame anyone for not believing my history. If I had not experienced what I have, I would not have believed it myself."[9]

Life Too Intense for the Biographer's Art

Joseph's birth came just a couple of days shy of Christmas, on December 23, 1805, the fourth of nine children born to Joseph Smith, Sr. and Lucy Mack, who, for a short time had been living in Sharon, Vermont. His family kept slipping into poverty, struggling constantly to better themselves, but forced to move from place to place until some of the older children grew big enough to lend added support. By then they had moved to the township of Palmyra, then to Manchester, New York.

There, according to the most widely circulated version of his own story, Joseph, age fourteen, determined that the whole religious world around him exhibited such confusion that he solicited the Lord's advice in determining to which sect, if any, he should apply for membership. The Lord, rather than gently guiding the young man towards Methodism or Presbyterianism, visited him as he prepared himself to pray for direction. Both the Father and Son bodily appeared from above, with Jesus forbidding Joseph joining any existing sect, for they were all wrong and their creeds abominable to Him.

Three years elapsed before Joseph experienced his first visitation by the angel, a resurrected being with a message from God. Once as mortal as you and I, Moroni had lived and died some fourteen centuries earlier.

He claimed descent from a long line of religious pilgrims, *Nephites* who migrated from Jerusalem to America, and had, throughout several hundreds of years, established a form of Christianity, all the while preserving their somewhat narrow history of God's dealings with them. Their religious record, engraved onto thin plates of gold, revealed an account of Jesus' visit to the New World following his resurrection. It was that history-like saga that Joseph had been chosen to translate under God's influence and authority, into the *Book of Mormon*, named after Moroni's father, who had anciently edited the extensive records of his people.

Despite his meager writing experience, lack of resources necessary to meet publishing expenses, many trials, troubles and persecutions from local religionists who were among the first to ridicule his unusual tale, Joseph, at age twenty-four, finally got his book (self) published in 1830. Then, within weeks, gathered friends, family and converts together to establish his sect as the world's final gospel dispensation, hailing it the one true church—restored to a semblance of ancient Christianity. Its first few years witnessed development of a finely-tuned authoritarian structure encompassing two classes of priesthood that began ushering all its male members into active service through ecclesiastical offices, including: apostles, bishops, high priests, seventies, elders, priests, teachers and deacons. The church grew by leaps and bounds. To avoid sour contention and fragmentation among the brethren, God chose Joseph to serve as His authorized mouthpiece, or prophet, as had been the prudent rule in Old Testament times.

Assigned the seamless, revealed task of managing both spiritual and temporal church affairs, Joseph selected a gathering center for his Saints, named Zion, creating what began to take shape as a poor Mormon ghetto. That New Jerusalem idea quickly brewed a horrifying but predictable social disaster, the Missouri Mormon wars. In fact, during the last fourteen years of his life, Joseph led his followers through enough tribulation to drive St. Peter into therapy. Non-member neighbors often became fearful, suspicious of Mormon zeal, unity, and of the power those newcomers exercised in swaying local politics to their advantage.

Mormons naturally began perceiving themselves as victims of persecutions, sharply heightening their sense of just religious cause, though it would not be unfair to lay the root of every instance of suffering at their own doorstep, rather than assuming that malicious bigots pestered them everywhere they went. Joseph's group were run out of New York, then from Ohio and again out of Missouri, yet they showed great resilience while bearing opposition like the saints of ancient days, continuing as followers despite financial devastation, extraordinary labors and violence from frontier mobs. Early Mormon experiences effectively demonstrate how great faith may inspire a people to unite even throughout periods of rugged adversity. A deftly facilitated opposition may even have assisted Mormonism's rapid early ascent.

The Saints' prosperity improved dramatically beginning in 1839 as they began settling in western Illinois, building up a large town along the Mississippi's east bank. Joseph promoted his new venture by inventing a unique name for it—Nauvoo—then instructed his European missionaries to send converts back by the shipload. His new place of gathering soon became a thriving boomtown as large as Chicago, and Mormonism briefly enjoyed its new status as a success model of America's religious and economic freedoms. Left unchecked, Joseph's church might have eventually blossomed into a sprawling metropolis greater than Philadelphia. Obviously, that never happened.

Exactly *why* has become subject of controversy provoking an unending scramble for answers, but if you could have put yourself into Joseph's shoes during the first quarter of 1844, you'd probably have imagined the world had just been handed to you on a plate, for he had everything going his way:

- He had become the highly regarded spiritual leader of one of America's fastest growing religious sects.
- His people appointed him mayor of his own great city, Nauvoo, "the beautiful."
- He served as the "chief justice" of Nauvoo's municipal court.
- He'd been commissioned as a Lieutenant General of America's largest body of citizen militia.
- His followers had built him a large executive mansion.
- And he had just engaged a well-organized campaign to become the eleventh President of the United States.

By age 38, Joseph had edged to within inches of status as an American aristocrat. Then, at a quarter past five p.m. on June 27, 1844, while held in an upstairs jail room in a neighboring community, in protective custody under the governor's personal pledge of safety, an overwhelming force of raucous militiamen attacked him and his brother, assassinating both.

Correcting for Magnification and Focus

Mormonism represents a rare cluster of phenomena far beyond the unstable fervor induced by novel and seemingly sacred musings of its philosopher-leader. It embraces an extensive, complex collage of religious romance partnered with a pragmatism that became energized readily through America's pioneering spirit, and much more. Nevertheless, both origins and essentials are encompassed within those years, 1805 to 1844, and even today the LDS church continues its existence as an extension of an ever-expanding circle whose radius and circumference are metered through the life, thought and teachings of one single individual—Joseph Smith, Jr.

Whereas the remainder of Mormon history is informative and fascinating, our better understanding of its core is wholly dependent upon resolving issues laid down during those origins, for, as one modern historian has suggested: "The mystery of Mormonism cannot be solved until we solve the mystery of Joseph Smith."[10] It seems quite evident that most of our difficulties in understanding that era stem from barriers Joseph erected to prevent anyone getting to know him very well. Or, perhaps, as is often the case, our difficulty is caused by inherent perceptual limitations. Even though all that had been crystal clear to the Prophet has been obscured, I'll hypothesize that all the best clues and a majority of the solution we've been looking for have been available all along. Were he present today, surely he'd waste no time in getting us onto the right track.

> I combat the errors of ages; I meet the violence of mobs; I cope with illegal proceedings from executive authority; I cut the gordian knot of powers, and I solve mathematical problems of universities, with *truth—diamond truth; and God is my "right hand man."*[11]

One must get a feeling that extraordinary circumstances dictated Joseph's strategy, and that today he would more willingly explain each mystery and secret of doctrine, his reasons for condemning sectarianism, the psychology he devised for handling both followers and enemies, and all the precautions he employed for guarding against prompt exposure. Having quite briefly outlined the earliest years, skipping much, we'll need to resist the flaw of trying to introduce his essence to the general public through exhaustive, comprehensive narratives of his life. Catalogues of LDS history supply sufficient records witnessing the Prophet's behavior, his character and achievements. Critics have further expanded those resources, mainly in attempts at encouraging full disclosure, even at the expense of embarrassing the newly conservative sect with its past.

Let's simplify. During its beginnings, throughout the 1830s, Joseph acted as lawgiver to his followers. Nobody else produced the Book of Mormon, dreamed up new and outlandishly apocryphal works attributed to such as Father Abraham and the prophet Moses, nor, since his martyrdom, any substantive LDS doctrine. Mormon thought, though censored by his successors, has continued emphatically dominated by ideas generated solely from the mind of its founder. Despite a tendency some have for supposing that fate or serendipity controlled events in his life, Joseph maintained distinctive, impressive control throughout his adulthood; he ran the show every moment of every day. Not even polygamy became as much of a doctrinal anomaly as many must imagine, but served specific, logical functions during a limited and carefully scheduled segment of his program.

His works demonstrate examples of brilliant organizational strategy, goal-setting directed towards phenomenal church growth, Herculean achievements pushed forward with obvious agenda and a moral fortitude that exhibits immense discipline as well as intensity of spirit. As for his becoming a religious martyr, it hardly exhibits any randomness at all, but suggests a conspicuously public display that could have either been staged or manipulated to produce a terrifying emotional impact.

Somewhere in a life so charged with drama we must detect a well-defined plan. But to what end? What greater destiny might his assassination have terminated? Or *promoted*? His whole being evidences a man far too intelligent to let himself become set up for slaughter in a deadly, highly predictable, avoidable showdown. Or, could that martyrdom have been a strategic element essential to his ambitions, even from his earliest years? Do accepted facts allow such a conclusion?

Since his character continued essentially unchanged at least from his late teen years onward, it may be entirely unnecessary to exhaustively examine his life in minute detail in order to orient ourselves and comprehend his inner world quite accurately. By carefully selecting appropriate viewing windows, most of the good and evil in his soul can be assayed without inciting heated prejudices. While our main source reference will be Joseph's autobiographical account, we're going to begin by narrowing focus in order to spotlight one revealing but brief early episode, his Zion's Camp expedition.

CHAPTER 2

Zion's Camp: Launching the Apotheosis

The Mormon Expedition of Zion's Camp covered a 59-day period from May to July, 1834 and describes a failure that followed a case of apparent madness that had disaster written in from its inception; still, it may be true that almost nothing in his life caught Joseph entirely by surprise. His account of the march to rescue Zion includes unexcelled illustrations of the Prophet's *modus* and character.

Mormon problems began in July of 1831 when Joseph created a bind that irremediably sowed seeds of contention when he established Independence (today a suburb of Kansas City), Missouri as his holy city, gathering-place, or Zion:

> And thus saith the Lord your God [. . .] Behold, the place which is now called Independence is the center place; and a spot for the temple is lying westward, upon a lot which is not far from the courthouse.[1]

Carefully note that Joseph didn't live in that community, but made his home nearly 700 air miles eastward, in Kirtland, beyond Cleveland, Ohio. Understandably, local residents and Independence property owners felt threatened when Joseph applied his new name to their hometown, more so as he coveted their yards and house lots in the name of the Lord. They saw Mormons as an unstable "sect of fanatics,"[2] thus inciting hostility to Joseph's new gospel idea of making *their* town the center for *his* gathering.

By 1833 Zion's ten Mormon meeting-houses showed no signs of slowing in growth, for they had already amassed some twelve hundred followers. Mormon Elders began preaching to nearby Indian tribes, and the utopian community became characterized by an abundance of poor people.[3] Another upset entered the picture when church leaders seemed amenable to introducing free Mormon blacks within the slaveholding community. Instead of shrugging off the religious leader's revelations, Gentile townspeople began closely monitoring local events and thus began developing anxieties from Joseph's ambiguous plea that all their surrounding properties be procured for use by the Saints, "Wherefore, the land of Zion shall not be obtained but by purchase or by blood, otherwise there is none inheritance for you."[4] Non-Mormons were positively enraged by the upstart audacity of their neighbors, but it would be highly misleading to charge sectarian ministers with initiating the friction.[5] The one unfortunate choice making conflict inevitable was Joseph's insistence that the Saints encroach on an established community.

Original settlers of Independence felt justly threatened and although the church prepared its course to maintain compliance with current Missouri law, their plan to gradually wrest control began to dawn on earlier inhabitants.[6] Locals felt cornered with an undesirable choice to resist and expel intruding Mormons, or to expect gradual displacement for themselves. Wise to the abuses of liberality afforded by American freedoms fostering religious diversity, a unique situation demanded that Independence landholders apply extra-legal maneuvers to preserve a sense of stability and secular control over their community. By July of 1833 Zion's opponents had organized to dissipate those imminent, odious prospects. They met together in council, formulated clear demands for disbursing members of the unwanted sect and attempted peaceably entreating to find if the Saints wouldn't accede to demands that they take their Zion to any other location—within a reasonable time.

After Mormon leaders refused to bow out gracefully, the citizen committee formed itself into a force of at least four hundred, including eight prominent clergymen. First they destroyed the LDS printing house, *The Evening and Morning Star,* turning its residents out of doors; next they tarred-and-feathered two prominent Mormons. Nobody got killed, but when the mob reasserted itself three days later they were holding aloft a red flag on a pikestaff.[7] Suddenly more attentive, the Mormon community capitulated by agreeing to remove by the following January. Today that decision appears sound enough, except that Joseph attributed his revelations to God, thus imparting irrevocability to the call to enlarge Zion's borders. As with ancient Israel, Mormon opportunities for peaceful coexistence among modern-day Philistines began to wash out, "[...] and the brethren continued to remove to Zion and Kirtland."[8]

A couple of months afterward, having been ill-advised by Missouri Governor Dunklin,[9] the Saints of Independence swore out warrants against Gentile rioters, thus violating their covenant to remove. As soon as Mormon efforts at legal retaliation became publicized, the wrath of the local committee transformed the town into hostile territory. After several days' depredations and beatings, then destroying a couple hundred members' homes, they forcibly expelled the Saints from Independence, and then, with assistance from leaders of the local militia and Missouri's Lieutenant Governor, Liburn Boggs, confiscated all Mormon arms.[10]

At very best, Zion's Camp, originating at Kirtland, intended performing duty as a peaceful relief expedition, nevertheless its members took with them every form of armament available.[11] They planned on redeeming Zion from her enemies, so proclaimed themselves the "armies of Israel" as the Kirtland church council appointed Joseph its commander-in-chief.[12] The Prophet soon received a revelation from the Lord that ambiguously promised, "mine angels shall go up before you, and also my presence, and in time ye shall possess the goodly land."[13] It's quite possible that a few true believers were hoping to watch from a safe distance as heaven's fireworks swept the Independence Gentiles away to allow righteous habitation by their beleaguered brethren.

Joseph's actual quarry, one might perceive, was not redress against the over-powering citizen army of Independence, but marching in pursuit of a golden opportunity to more deeply cultivate and fire up the faith of two hundred choice volunteers who, it turned out, were willing to accompany him outside their secure surroundings and into the very jaws of hell. Along their way, Joseph took every moment afforded him to peddle his peculiar propaganda among members of the camp.

His first order of business was to organize into companies of twelve, insisting that each soldier hold morning and evening prayer at the sound of a trumpet. Day after day Joseph marched his men ragged, averaging more than twenty miles across hot, open prairies, simultaneously selling them further on the benefits of his counsel and prophetic gifts. When men questioned whether enemies had tainted their milk, Joseph advised,

"[. . .] if they would follow my counsel, and use all they could get from friend or enemy, it should do them good, and none be sick in consequence of it [. . .]."[14] While traveling through Indianapolis, "some of the brethren were afraid that we might have difficulty there. But I had told them, in the name of the Lord, we should not be disturbed [...]."[15]

Joseph daily counseled his troops, rebuffed, reproved and rebuked them, then dazzled them with sensational insights. Having crossed the scene of an old Indian burial mound, the Prophet envisioned the former life of one of the skeletons his men had unearthed. He "[…] was a white Lamanite…a man of God. His name was Zelph. He was a warrior and chieftain […]."[16] One awestruck marcher removed the arrow point that had ended Zelph's life, saving it as a souvenir to help certify Joseph's impressive credentials as seer.

Lacking sufficient vision for procuring the army's immediate needs, Joseph and his men had departed Kirtland without adequate provisions or suitable financing, consequently suffering painful deprivations: their sore feet bled; they suffered hunger and thirst. Dissension and rebellion soon began its descent over Zion's Camp. Joseph explained, "[...] the Lord had revealed to me that a scourge would come upon the camp in consequence of the fractious and unruly spirits that appeared among them."[17] Their arduous marching caused a danger of dehydration so severe that it reduced many of the men to sucking water from mud holes in the road or from sloughs crawling with wiggling crud. Within four days a plague of cholera swept over the camp, striking even at Joseph.[18] Exhausted and malnourished, fourteen members of the camp died. Joseph admonished survivors that,

> […] in consequence of the disobedience of some who had been unwilling to listen to my words, but had rebelled, God had decreed that sickness should come upon the camp, and if they did not repent and humble themselves before God they should die like sheep with the rot."[19]

One particular Zion's Camp incident stands above the rest in helping gauge the Prophet's method and character. This somewhat charming episode enters the record about three weeks into the trek to redeem Zion:

> Monday, May 26.—A very hot day [. . .] we were almost famished, and it was a long time before we could, or dared to satisfy our thirst. We crossed the Embarras river [in eastern Illinois] and encamped on a small branch of the same about one mile west. In pitching my tent we found three massasaugas or prairie rattlesnakes,

which the brethren were about to kill, but I said, "let them alone—don't hurt them! How will the serpent ever lose his venom, while the servants of God possess the same disposition, and continue to make war upon it? Men must become harmless, before the brute creation; and when men lose their vicious dispositions and cease to destroy the animal race, the lion and the lamb can dwell together, and the sucking child can play with the serpent in safety." The brethren took the serpents carefully on sticks and carried them across the creek. I exhorted the brethren not to kill a serpent, bird, or an animal of any kind during our journey unless it became necessary in order to preserve ourselves from hunger.

I had frequently spoken on this subject, when on a certain occasion I came up to the brethren who were watching a squirrel on a tree, and to prove them and to know if they would heed my counsel, I took one of their guns, shot the squirrel and passed on, leaving the squirrel on the ground. Brother Orson Hyde, who was just behind, picked up the squirrel, and said, "We will cook this, that nothing may be lost." I perceived that the brethren understood what I did it for, and in their practice gave more heed to my precept than to my example, which was right.[20]

In the end Joseph's army disbanded without having engaged the battle to secure Zion, suggesting that it wasn't his highest priority. He returned to Kirtland having consolidated a position further above all his followers, likely his more immediate objective. His antics along the way yielded all the headway actually intended—to promote himself while disciplining and testing the commitment of as many of his believers as possible. Members of Zion's camp later comprised the great bulk of future Mormon leadership, including two of his successors as church president, nine of its first twelve apostles and dozens of missionaries whose names later became synonymous with Mormonism's soaring early growth.

Here his brethren might have learned to appreciate and indulge one of Joseph's strategic specialties—for he baffled and caught them off guard by the infinite facility of his imagination. For those able to savor the unexpected, Joseph became a perpetual entertainment, for it seems they'd discovered a man built on the scale of Abraham or Moses. If the picture may not yet be perfectly clear, we can still view him with some of the same awe his soldiers experienced—close to incomprehensible from mortal vantage. Still, one might receive no finer perception of Joseph than from his own record of events, and we must recognize his candor while enjoying this preview of its contents. His imagination, quick wit, task focus and insistence on organization are noteworthy signs of admirable intellectual resources. Has he not forthrightly presented himself as being calculating and ingenuous while displaying a gifted mastery of psycho-conditioning techniques? Some might go so far as to note that scientists wouldn't accomplish the like for more than a century. If not unequivocally brainwashing, the Prophet was bearing down hard on the craft—and he was proud enough of it to submit that fact into his record.

We should mark this episode of Zion's Camp for future reference as we continue our study of Joseph, for it preserves valuable instances of his style of thinking and key behaviors. His account will provide useful points of comparison to his Book of Mormon, both works supposedly initiated by command—revelations from God.[21] By now we have a few key questions to guide our study. What notable parallels from his book will catch our eye—perhaps suggesting similar levels of ambition, strategy or intellectual accomplishments? Are we able to witness that propaganda campaign of self-promotion continuing within his book of scripture? If so, will strategies soliciting loyalty be engaged openly, or will it be necessary to summon his intentions only from behind incidental literary landscapes and symbolic markers? How much of the prophet's puzzle might be assembled from an accumulation of clues that Joseph intentionally inserted into his Nephite account?

Although getting at the ultimate mystery of his "why" will take a good bit more investigating, what seems so evident during our Zion Camp encounter is the degree of Joseph's intensity and the level of his mental involvement. He shows no signs of waiting idly for heaven's promptings but rather has taken the bit between his teeth. If we could continue watching from day to day for the remainder of his life we would find him likewise charging ahead with similar patterns of assertive behavior. We'd be able to pick him out of any crowd by his characteristic total commitment as he courts an expanded, more devoted following. His mysteriousness and intensity of soul combine to produce a truly absorbing historical study in character.

If the glimmering of his genius seems too genuine to justify an accusation of fakery, his cover as a simple seeker of truth, driven by native spiritual inquisitiveness, may be seen as quite a different matter. Toward the end of his life he tried setting aside that incorrect assumption: "I am not so much a 'Christian' as many suppose I am,"[22] then admitting, "I do not want you to think that I am very righteous, for I am not."[23] Judging that he used his façade as religious leader to conceal a complex but urgent cause, how much of it might we expect to uncover? Early inspiration from some hard-to-pinpoint source seems to have set him on a single-minded personal crusade to gather his own band of followers from within the most popular religion of his day, making it necessary for him to piggyback his unspoken agenda upon beliefs that had long since percolated through society's consciousness.

Plunging into Joseph's thinking, into his mind, may seem impossible, even undesirable, yet it just might also empower us to begin understanding a conundrum so vital to his success that it became impossible for him to elucidate freely, thereby forcing him to carry his most closely guarded secret with him to the grave. To open and enter that doorway into his soul we'll need to exercise an even higher power of magnification and attempt a method that has been relatively untried with Joseph.

Our scheme will be to inspect the Book of Mormon from cover to cover while interpreting it as we would any intelligent work of literature—in this instance a book representing the life, projecting the death and revealing the incomparable imagination of Joseph Smith, Jr. This procedure follows standards that have proven effective when attempting to discern the innermost intents and affections of many other figures in the literary world. Our mission will be to reconstruct a view that is reasonably consistent, yet relying primarily on Joseph and other accepted sources for the bulk of our evidence. We can hopefully diminish the error had we otherwise depended on prejudicial works or maundering speculation.

What comes of this new view will be noted for its admitted radical departures from orthodox *pro* or *con* interpretations. Modern Saints have labored since the beginning to develop explanations for the phenomenology of Mormonism that would distance themselves from the fringes of irrational thought. Hopefully, future judgments will warrant that a redirecting assist bears sound reason and is in good order. If it shall ever stand the world on its ear, much credit will be due to a wonderful ability Joseph had for exemplifying his rule of "opposition in all things,"[24] for, while millions of readers consider his book a work of God, Joseph methodically crafted it with simultaneous contradictories in expectations of leading followers toward the ultimate mystery of his heartfelt philosophical position, one that is most skeptical of God. Never has a story been more two-sided than Joseph Smith's, and thus it is with the Book of Mormon and Mormonism's true origins.

CHAPTER 3

Coming to Grips with a Tale Twice Told

> We want a national literature commensurate with our mountains and rivers [...]. We want a national epic that shall correspond to the size of the country [...]. In a word, we want a national literature altogether shaggy and unshorn, that shall shake the earth, like a herd of buffaloes thundering over the prairies.
> (Henry Wadsworth Longfellow, *Kavanagh*, 1849)

Regardless of whether it is of God or man, the book falls (per Longfellow's request, somewhat shaggy and unshorn) into the category of American literature. The highly unconventional method by which the Book of Mormon received its introduction certainly bespeaks an artful achievement, and, as Joseph Conrad once pointed out, "[…] art itself may be defined as a single-minded attempt to render the highest kind of justice to the visible universe, by bringing to light the truth […];"[1] and that is the manifest purpose Joseph sought to portray, not just in producing his book, but also in having lived.

Once we begin to treat his book as a respectable work of art; searching out distinctive literary qualities, comparing our findings against its perceived messages; we'll discover either consistency or confusion in the author's work. Quite surely we'd prefer consistency that, once settled, might be useful in reconstructing its author's intent and there unravel his wonderful secret. Regrettably, though, no work of American fiction has become so widely published only to be snubbed so thoroughly within even the most comprehensive collections of American Literature: it has been scorned, rebuffed and left untouched by nearly everyone who enjoys reading the best books. Both benumbed and beguiled, its highly regarded critics prematurely dismissed a work they might have loved had they understood Joseph's objectives better.

Foremost among reasons why the Book of Mormon has never achieved recognition as one of the world's finest literary gems is that Joseph devised it with no consideration for high literary art, nor any art at all. Quite to the contrary, even its title page modestly acknowledges that some faults may be present, as if making an apology in advance for endless flaws due to a crude translation that would only occur some fourteen centuries after the Nephite record had been secured within a hillside vault for posterity: "And now, if there are faults they are the mistakes of men; wherefore, condemn not the things of God [...]."[2]

In its first edition the Book of Mormon weighed in at a stout 588 pages of dense reading material. It is still heftier and has more genuine density than most books its size. We might even think of the Book of Mormon as if it were *two* books. First is the one accepted and disseminated by the LDS Church, often billed as "Another Testament of Jesus Christ." The other book, or its second channel, will be discovered as a literary *magnum opus* residing there in the very same words, the same tales and allegories, entirely the same fabrication as in the first. Its channel two manifests opposing interpretations that seem at least as consistent, end-to-end, but which resonates better with an irreverent nature formed for it by the author. The more completely you are able to separate your Book of Mormon from theirs perhaps the less offensive our study will be to them as we probe its beguiling contents. As one old BYU professor once said, "There are many levels of revelation in the Book of Mormon; it's a very interesting thing."[3]

While we can recognize religion as a subject that evokes great emotional response, the whole logic of Mormonism seems originally intended as a course leading toward truth. Partly because its truth is judged too obscure, and its literacy level has typically been seen as inferior and inconsequential, accepted interpretations for the Book of Mormon have almost universally been abandoned to those enthusiasts who suffer delusions of its grandeur, viewing it mostly as a supernatural, spiritual phenomenon. Whenever any book has come to be considered scripture, or word of God, its status metamorphoses into an extension of the infallible Supreme Author being worshipped. Due respect persuades readers to mentally soften any supposed faults within its text—"Prepare ye the way of the Lord, make his paths straight."

Such high esteem may be acceptable for scripture. Literature, on the other hand, as an acknowledged artifice of man, encourages more thorough critical analysis for the sake of evolving a suitable cultural heritage that we desire to pass along to succeeding generations. The Book of Mormon has never really endured the close academic, public scrutiny necessary to fairly evaluate its merits as literature or scripture. Almost never do we find a work so dependent upon reader subjectivity to achieve a specific set of desired effects: many structural and contextual weaknesses prejudice the minds of non-believers, while a sense of obligatory esteem has so entirely predisposed the thinking of those who have linked themselves with it through an assortment of emotional forces that are not entirely understood by anyone.

"Let the Language of the Book Speak for Itself"[4]

The bulk of the Book of Mormon records just over one thousand years of history as shaped by two warring factions of a single family, Nephites and Lamanites, but from an arrogant perspective taken by the Nephite clan that very gradually experienced a most humiliating downfall. As we discover why that calamity took place we'll realize how its story encompasses no dismal tragedy of history but, rather, rises above it to become a highly positive, upbeat work of fiction. One's interpretation will depend upon which side they've chosen to urge on to victory. A balanced view in opposition to its Nephite writers would improve the book's stature as literature while cutting down on much of the polarized glare generated from portraying themselves as good guys.

Readers haven't considered the possibility that its author perfected uniquely specialized stylistic effects. To help establish an impression of innocent, almost raw history, Joseph gave his work an awkward pair of artificial linguistic façades and an entirely unexpected writer's point of view. He suffused his story with discontinuities as if from the pens of a number of ancient record keepers totally lacking consciousness of essential writing skills, such as organization of thought, clarity, directness or purpose. An abundance of ambiguity, repetition and stammering clutter its sentence structure throughout.

Layered over that, Joseph added a more familiar but uncomfortable voice that appears to imitate language in the Authorized, or King James Bible. He even had to engineer such expressions as, "hinderment," "Rabbanah," "beginneth," "swellest," "sproutest," "casting about your eyes," "methought," "mattereth," "atoneth," and a number of others that look as though they might have been lifted directly from the Bible but aren't to be found there.[5] That false front was made to simulate the real thing so poorly that no more than one in a hundred readers who begin cares enough to continue beyond its first few chapters. If written using then current (1830) standards of English, the substance of its message would have been detected very shortly. Perhaps then it would have endured as a classic on more genuine merits—except that Joseph's objectives seem to have been more ambitious and noteworthy.

Concerning the writer's perspective (not Joseph's, but that of its supposed original authors), we are accustomed to having history conveyed to us by those who have analyzed complex events they wish to chronicle for the purpose of transmitting a positive message. That is so because members of the winning side usually write the history that achieves acceptance, not its losers who have many complaints of foul play, desertions, unfortunate timing or miserable fortune. Our view of the past is often contaminated by a one-eyed view of history.

"I Have Spoken Plainly That Ye Cannot Err"

Should you choose to debate the meaning of any passage within the Book of Mormon with someone whom you're afraid may understand it as well as you, you can still score an important point by remembering to include as part of your argument this one irrefutable fact: the Book of Mormon is so congested with ambiguity that its intended messages are not that easy to deduce. One favorite classic example from the book says, "And now, my brethren, I have spoken plainly that ye cannot err."[6] The humor of Nephi's statement follows from realizing that he seems to boast of clarity in his words while showing intent so vague and obscure that he may be interpreted going in at least three different directions.

Furthermore, each separate expression or explanation of the passage has complete legitimacy within LDS teachings:

1.) Perfection is demanded: "I have told you plainly that it is forbidden for you to slip up; don't err; don't even think wrong."

2.) Subscribing to the "New and Everlasting Covenant" will permit exceptional latitude in one's ethics and behavior: "You are at liberty to do as you please because no sin will exclude you from exaltation—you cannot err."

3.) Simple, clear and unambiguous communication has eliminated all possible misconstructions of the message from the book: "The reader cannot misunderstand what I have just written." In other words, Nephi built into his own words the exact error he seems to have opposed while denying any flaw.

In acknowledging the book's literary imperfections, Moroni, last of its writers, actually endorsed thorough criticism and showed its absolute necessity—"Condemn me not because of mine imperfection [...] neither them who have written before [...] but rather give thanks unto God that he hath made manifest unto you our imperfections, that ye may learn to be more wise than we have been."[7] So now it looks as though scrounging through the book for imperfections will be the only sure way to wring wisdom from it.

Opposition in All Things...Pervasive Ambiguity

Clues to its intended meanings do not merely appear in the book as if through accident or chance, perhaps being left behind as subconscious slips, errors of coincidence or author's oversights that we are privileged to manipulate through random guesses or flighty conjectures; they are sufficiently frequent, consistent, very deliberate and highly conscious. The fact that he supplied a system of clues to assist in the understanding of his work adds to our assurance that it wasn't written for Joseph's private amusement. Also, if conclusions from his book were going to accomplish their ultimate effect, a certain amount of time must have been expected to pass before any breakthrough into its extraordinary significance might secure recognition. Intellectual capacity of his early followers kept Joseph leery of moving forward in a bid to dismantle patterns of thought when the power of tradition had rendered them very resistant to logic. After flooding his people with scores of revelations, he still had to confess,

> I have tried for a number of years to get the minds of the Saints prepared to receive the things of God; but we frequently see some of them, after suffering all they have for the work of God, will fly to pieces like glass as soon as anything comes that is contrary to their traditions; they cannot stand the fire at all.[8]

Here Joseph has made it clear that all efforts to reform religious traditions, despite his great strides, left that task far from completed. We detect agonizing barriers preventing him from unburdening himself of his ultimate mystery, "[…] It is not always wise to relate all the truth."[9]

New interpretations of his work need not be regarded as systematic mis-directions being diverted from actual context in order to achieve some cunning or sinister purpose. During our study we'll frequently return to the fact that one of the most under-noticed, understated wonders of the Book of Mormon is its exquisite balance of equivocal expression, both stamp and seal of Joseph's literary brilliance. By charting an unremitting course of ambiguity, he knew his book could someday be understood—just not easily, nor too soon.

Understand also that his ambiguous course is not representing a simple vagueness of expression, but what we might refer to as a *loaded duality*. Joseph perceived the fact that readers generally impose impressions of their own (*schema*) upon such works—whether favorable or unfavorable—that are pre-conceived, or loaded, and which are emotionally generated. Study, reflection and reasoning are all that are needed to realize and explore its alternate meanings.

In order to urge readers in perceiving the existence of his second channel of interpretation, Joseph inserted symbolic prompts to give advance warning that literary forks should be expected along the journey: deciding which path to take would not be automatic. His first great indicator received its introduction when Father Lehi found a remarkable, magical brass compass, the *Liahona*:

> And it came to pass that as my father arose in the morning, and went forth to the tent door, to his great astonishment he beheld upon the ground a round ball of curious workmanship; and it was of fine brass. And within the ball were two spindles; and the one pointed the way whither we should go into the wilderness.[10]

Needless to say, a compass bearing two pointers could easily direct lost pilgrims toward even more hopeless confusion. Might a *pair* of spindles suggest conflict, rather than its resolution? Father Lehi soon tried once more to signal how those approaching crossroads would require readers to choose between opposing directions. Furthermore, those conflicts represented contrasting moral positions:

> For it must needs be, that there is an opposition in all things. If not so, my first-born in the wilderness, righteousness could not be brought to pass, neither wickedness, neither holiness nor misery, neither good nor bad [...]."[11]

Note that Lehi offered no value judgment favoring righteousness above wickedness, or vice versa, but continued, "Wherefore, all things must needs be a compound in one."[12] According to Lehi, unless both good and evil were placed equally before him, no man could truly exercise his volition or agency, "Wherefore, man could not act for himself save it should be that he was enticed by the one or the other."[13]

Much later, Joseph, while incarcerated in a Missouri jail, amplified that kernel of Lehi's thought when writing an epistle to the church: "Thy mind, O man! If thou wilt lead a soul unto salvation, must stretch as high as the utmost heavens, and search into and contemplate the darkest abyss."[14] Since our culture has long established its bias favoring a "good" set of behaviors and "righteous" judgments, Joseph knew that any teachings (i.e., "the darkest abyss") contrary to those that had previously been settled within our common consciousness would need to be presented using utmost subtlety by teasing the mind with ambiguity and suggestion rather than bringing new ideas forward with precise clarity. Then, using propaganda efficiently, writing as if by an assortment of authors with a one-eyed view—historians who were self-serving, self-justifying scandal-mongers—Joseph got his readers to cheer on and adopt the side opposite to the one they probably would have chosen if inspired by an alternate set of clues.

Before continuing let me here emphasize one of the more essential points of my argument: any new interpretations being forwarded are not proposed for the purpose, or with necessary expectations, of superseding the conventional, orthodox rendering but only for demonstrating the fullness, consistency and intent or design of a radically opposing view—channel two. Readers should feel completely at liberty to choose their own interpretive preferences. However, I do expect to make an adequate case for exquisite ambiguity, the flair that helps turn Joseph's book into a literary marvel.

Four More Keys to the Kingdom

A.) Joseph Employed Character Symbol Names. One of the prime indicators Joseph used throughout the Book of Mormon, well known within works of good literature, even since antiquity, is his use of character symbol names chosen by the author for guiding readers to underlying meaning. An author may give one of his characters the name of Snidley Whiplash, for example, to suggest a perceived position as the villain in a drama. For quickly developing the hero's character, he might choose something less menacing, such as Dudley duRite. We'll want to watch for possible character symbol names as we work our way through Joseph's book, first acknowledging the admitted inadequacy of LDS studies concerning this phenomenon.[15] Furthermore, if one or more of those symbolic names should be shown as significant reference to Joseph, that will weaken any suspicion that some ghostwriter may have surreptitiously written the book. An author seems much more likely than a ghostwriter to include genuine, useful autobiographical detail.

B.) The Book of Mormon is Intimately and Thoroughly Autobiographical. Another generally recognized characteristic of good literature has always included the intimate relationship of the story, its events and symbols to its author. Many great works of fiction are fundamentally autobiographical: we might consider various novels of Herman Melville, Louisa May Alcott or Ernest Hemingway as prime examples. While sailing through the Nephite record, we must take special note of issues and events that either resemble or cause us to note and expand on significant events in Joseph's life. Whenever we can detect an attitude particular to Joseph's view, it, too, will be considered evidence that something autobiographical is in process. Along with our quest to find out *what* the Book of Mormon is all about, we can also expect to identify the *who* it was created to glorify.

C.) Joseph is the Riddlemaster. Riddling preserves a folk tradition descended from ancient times, achieving its height of popularity during the Middle Ages. Without explicitly asking the question, riddles test one's ingenuity with an absurdity, an associated symbol or *non sequitur* that must be solved by clues provided by the riddler. Joseph posed an extensive series of riddles throughout his book, then, just as subtly disbursed a set of clues within his subsequent speeches and writings.

D.) It's An Intelligent Work. Logic allows that if our key statements A, B and C are shown to have validity, statement D becomes ever more probable, although certainly dependent upon the quantity, quality and richness of the underlying fabric and the net effect Joseph's book has upon those reading it.

Absolutely no advance in one's understanding of the Book of Mormon can be made by readers too set in their ways. Some, like those Zion Campers, feel that the Book of Mormon is too sacred to be savaged by common literary criticism. Others, like those earlier settlers of Independence, are put off by the certainty that, although highly imaginative, it is still too dull—a non-edifying production from Joseph's own mind, and in either case that it falls outside the realm of serious consideration by respected critics. For a book to be held in such opposite extremes of esteem we're reminded of the angel's words to Joseph: "[…] that it should be both good and evil spoken of among all people."

Both "Zion's Campers" and viewers aligned with "Independence" are, perhaps, being crippled by the same underestimation of Joseph Smith's intellectual stature. Believers are too willing to forgive him his occasional grammatical error and lack of polish because God held him in such high esteem. They consider that he must have been chosen as one who had not been tampered with by worldly sophistications. Non-believers shrug him off too flippantly as a glib, ignorant rustic with too much charisma for the common good. Those who are wise will suspend their judgments until adequate evidence suggests an appropriate resolution.

When we're ready to assess the power each aspect his book has for divulging its author's true purposes, the Book of Mormon stands crammed with an abundance of useful evidence and direction. The reader, having secured a proper orientation, can then read the mind of Joseph Smith in a way quite superior to any understanding dependent upon spiritual insights of others. Joseph's composition purposely appears as an unpalatable and crude literary flop to function as a blind for things he found necessary to say but deemed unwise for anyone to recognize while he was still alive. Hopefully, sufficient time has passed so that we may breathe new life into the essentials of his creativity and underlying thought.

CHAPTER 4

Capturing the Scene with a Mormon

> In short, every secret of a writer's soul, every experience of his life, every quality of his mind is written large in his works, yet we require critics to explain the one and biographers to expound the other.
> (Virginia Woolf, *Orlando*)

The Book of Mormon both begins and ends with the writings of Mormon. He's been brought forth as its chief editor, the man who compiled the extensive Nephite records, then abridged the entire work into the form Joseph would take possession, upon gold plates, ready for translation from "Reformed Egyptian" into English. He is given credit for the composition of its title page plus two of its segments or books, both written under his own name. Just prior to the end of Nephite civilization, supposedly in 421 CE, Mormon's son Moroni took over to conclude his nation's journal, yet three out of the last four chapters of Moroni's book were compositions undertaken by Mormon.

Cautioning readers not take his material too seriously, Mormon inserted a brief but ambiguous confession that nothing he wrote need be taken at face value: "[…] behold there are records which do contain all the proceedings of this people; and a shorter but true account was given by Nephi."[1] Note how the qualifier word "but" develops a comparison between Nephi's shorter but true account and Mormon's record—which by inference now seems longer and of questionable veracity.

Like Mormon, "Quick to Observe"

Mormon claimed lineal descent from Nephi, the book's first author.[2] Though chronologically separated by a millennium within the story's timeline, both characters show indications of a more than passing relationship to one another—and to Joseph. Both Nephi and Mormon regarded themselves as being "large of stature," a feature contemporaries couldn't help but notice about the charismatic young prophet.[3] Mormon showed further similarity with Nephi in how he began his book by admitting, "I began to be learned somewhat after the manner of the learning of my people."[4] Likewise opening his earliest journal account, Joseph established the "somewhat" manner of his education: "I was merely instructed in reading, writing, and the ground rules of Arithmetic which constituted my whole literary acquirements."[5] As to the limited extent of his own education, Joseph never hinted of embarrassment that he had little formal schooling; basics provided sufficiently for his needs. People are quite often deceived by the impoverishment of his upbringing into thinking that he somehow avoided or neglected the discipline of educational pursuits. The fact that he became a respected member of Palmyra's local debating society during his late teens doesn't seem to register as any significant inconsistency.[6]

College education throughout early America often centered upon a core curriculum of divinity studies; most colleges were established and run under the auspices of religious foundations, led by clerics—not quite to Joseph's taste. Still, his hunger for knowledge became insatiable, and even critics describe him as an avid reader.[7] Subtle fruits of his study and deep thinking are readily evident throughout his works. In his generation public secular schools weren't yet the norm, and expenses of higher education made it nearly prohibitive among the lower classes. Those destined to make their living off the land never judged it too essential, while wise men of that era could rightly boast of being self-taught and having common sense, as did Thomas Paine, Benjamin Franklin and numerous other successes.[8]

Although Joseph admitted to being "unlearned," he approached knowledge and truth with a sacred determination, "reflection and deep study," as his mother wrote of him.[9] Joseph's father actually worked as a schoolteacher for several years, so his family did not suffer altogether from intellectual impoverishment.[10] Indeed, a father-teacher/son-student relationship enjoyed by Joseph has been symbolized through Nephi: "I was taught somewhat in all the learning of my father." [11] Furthermore, within half a dozen years of authoring his book, we find Joseph lecturing on grammar while taking up the serious study of Hebrew and Greek, so, despite any apparent lack of time spent in the classroom he demonstrated considerable initiative in gaining understanding.[12] Intelligence, rather than the flourish of academic credentials, became the quality that he felt epitomized the glory of God.[13]

Another fact often overlooked is that Joseph possessed an excellent memory—perhaps approaching the phenomenal. Joseph seems finally to have revealed this exceptional gift almost by accident. During August, 1843, while reporting his revelation concerning the New and Everlasting Covenant (Plural Marriage, or polygamy),

> Hyrum very urgently requested Joseph to write the revelation by means of the Urim and Thummim, but Joseph in reply, said he did not need to, for he knew the revelation perfectly from beginning to end.[14]

His revelation introducing celestial marriage, consisting of 66 stout and pithy verses, consumes a good six pages of print, thus requiring a feat of recall so extraordinary that few Mormons since have attempted committing it to memory.

In a word, Joseph's cover of ignorance, his own creation, may have been planted intentionally as useful disinformation. While he never claimed to having had a photographic memory (neither the term photographic memory nor *eidetic* memory were invented until many years later), he could have put such an extraordinary gift to excellent use, especially while translating lengthy material from the gold plates for his scribe to record. We must also appreciate the fact that in his day to boast of one's own superior intelligence would have been condemned as a haughty act of vanity and excess pride: "For not he that commendeth himself is approved, but whom the Lord commendeth."[15]

Lucy, his mother, recorded a second instance in which he seems likely to have suggested how his mental abilities provided him a great advantage in understanding more while studying less. Once, when urged to attend church with his family, Joseph replied, "...I will take my Bible and go out into the woods and learn more in two hours than you could if you were to go to meeting for two years."[16] If only half correct he would have been admitting his quite substantial intellectual gifting.

Later in his book Joseph preserved a third instance wherein he briefly acknowledged his prodigious mental acuity. His clue is so subtle as to be overlooked by all readers unable to allow Joseph's representation of himself through symbolic devices. His character Mormon noted how old Ammaron, the previous keeper of Nephite records, admired his intellectual capacity, saying, "I perceive that thou art a sober child, and art quick to observe."[17] Ammaron's observation bolsters the report preserved by a contemporary Palmyra resident who remembered Mr. Smith, the father, boasting with pride of his young Joseph, as "genius of the family."[18]

Joseph's abilities for quick, creative thinking were characteristic assets that become readily recognizable by all who study his life, but, since he never pounded his shoe on the table while stating the fact, readers must also be quick to observe if they'll ever recognize to whom he's referring in his fiction.

"A Good Name is Rather to be Chosen than Great Riches"[19]

Usually we don't expect someone who is unlearned to have enough subtlety to invent such wonderful deceptions, to devise intricate story lines and to keep the names, dates, authorship, geography facts and many other details in line, as Joseph was able to do for a book of this length. That argument has been used without much further comment in supporting the book's claim to (presumed) authenticity. Alongside having completed a work that is structurally quite sophisticated, Joseph seems to have developed impressive skills for employing a widely recognized literary device known as character symbol names. In truth not many works of fiction in a public library contain quite as constant a supply of proper names used to support and direct the story, fewer still that utilize them so frequently to help identify its author. Hardly anyone understands where Joseph came up with the name Mormon, for instance. It is one of the most insightful and intelligent symbol names found in any work of literature, ancient or modern, made to distinguish its author, and which dispels most doubt that anyone else might have written Joseph's book.

Mormon writes how, as a young lad of about ten years, Ammaron instructed him to fetch gold plates containing the full history of his people from a hill, appropriately named Shim, after he turned twenty-four.[20] Joseph, of course, had only passed his twenty-fourth year shortly prior to the publishing of his book, having obtained the gold plates, according to his testimony, from a repository in a nearby prominent mount, subsequently given the name "Hill Cumorah," located convenient to his family's home at Palmyra, New York. Mormon also tells his readers: "my father's name was Mormon."[21]

Joseph Smith was likewise a junior, but what so strongly suggests his insertion of an autobiographical cue is shown by the manner in which Mormon received his name. When first introducing himself, Mormon the younger didn't attribute inheriting the name from his father, but says, "behold, I am called Mormon, being called after the land of Mormon, the land in which Alma did establish the church among the people [...]."[22] Why be named after a spot of ground? Yet isn't that the same as we've sometimes done for persons who migrate from distant regions, supplying such popular nicknames as "Tex," "Montana" and "Cal"? So, following our hunch, let's turn backwards through the book to find origins of the Mormon idiom, perhaps to discover what significant fact, if any, it offers for establishing a connection between Mormon-land and Joseph.

Alma (the first) lived much earlier than Mormon. A refugee priest who had been exiled from a corrupt priesthood, he met clandestinely with other oppressed outcasts, organized a new church, and,

> [...] all this was done in Mormon, yea, by the waters of Mormon, in the forest that was near the waters of Mormon; yea, the place of Mormon, the waters of Mormon, the forest of Mormon, how beautiful are they to the eyes of them who there came to the knowledge of their Redeemer [...].[23]

Now that we're able to recognize the place and event his name commemorates, Mormon seems somewhat more distinguished, even though the book has already given him high prominence by incorporating his name into its title. Might Joseph have exaggerated repetition of the place-name Mormon in order to urge readers to envision a very particular locale? So now, try picturing in your mind what that "place of Mormon" looks like. Specifically, what colors seem to predominate throughout the landscape of Mormon-land? Is it so bleak and dreary? Perhaps a dry canyon or desert? Or is it a lush and green, well-watered forest? What, then, might be the specific map-able location, a point of origin that gave rise to his name, to his book, the nickname of the church Joseph would establish, and again, the name eventually applied to each of his followers? Without giving away the answer to his riddle, Joseph shared one more clue to help pinpoint the derivation of Mormon's name:

> I was born in the year of our Lord one thousand eight hundred and five, on the twenty-third day of December, in the town of Sharon, Windsor county, State of Vermont.[24]

Vermont is known as the "Green Mountain State," so named from the evergreen (well-watered) forests of its mountains, which is exactly what the name means (it's French: *verd mont*). The state is almost two-thirds surrounded by rivers and lakes; so perfect. But even though green is suggested within Alma's description of the place of Mormon, that still doesn't say anything about mountains, does it? Actually, it says more about mountains than it does about how green they were. Mormons is a symbol name made up of two words, "more," + "mons." *Mons* is Latin for mound or mountain. Quite likely, Joseph had just attached the name Mormon forever to his own birth state of Vermont.

Over the years several competing theories have been promoted suggesting sources for several character names in Joseph's fiction. Most frequent choice for the word Mormon is the surmise that he may have been playing with the word "moron," of Greek derivation, indicating "foolish," even though in Joseph's day that word hadn't yet entered use as a clinical description for someone with retarded mental capacity. The name Moron had, however, been applied to one of Joseph's other characters. Moron represents one of the final monarchs among the Jaredite tribes, a minor figure who twice [foolishly] lost control of his kingdom, resulting in his being held in lifetime captivity.[25]

Another favorite among his critics who speculate on the origin of the word Mormon is that Joseph adapted it from an extremely obscure Greek myth. There, it is said, Mormo is the name of a hideous she-monster: Mormo…Mormon. While the earlier theory may exhibit a certain appeal, yet it takes distant second place in the test for reason because no apparent relationship with the author is apparent. Such randomness would have been useless to Joseph. If we can picture the overdrawn description of Mormon-land as a riddle we'll be well on our way to capturing the scene as he intended.

CHAPTER 5

Nephi, Part 1:
A Journey Too Far for St. Paul

"The Salutation of me Paul with mine own hand." (1 Corinthians 16:24)

Many consequential Book of Mormon roots cannot be detected unless you are at least familiar with the Bible, and especially with Christian origins extending beyond the character and teachings of one Jesus of Nazareth, son of Mary, as opposed to the familiar Christianity of modern day. More specifically it can be a challenge to reach agreement on how extensively our experience with Christianity has been influenced by Saint Paul. Without his forceful leadership, missionary zeal, doctrinal interpretations and innovations, today's Christianity would have had an entirely different cast. Without Paul, the nucleus of thought from the earliest Jerusalem followers of Jesus, Jews who were called Christians to distinguish them from the more calcified followers of the Torah, might not have survived to flourish beyond the second century of the common era; indeed, Paul's changing of its course assured that it wouldn't. He is widely regarded as Christianity's most creative exponent. More than a third of the New Testament involves what he said and did, his many travels, afflictions and the letters he wrote. Some of his original letters Paul signed personally, "With mine own hand."[1]

Saint Paul, born into a Jewish family, grew up in Tarsus, a self-governing free port city of Celicia at the center of the eastern Mediterranean coast, but within the extended Roman Empire. Tarsus is situated about 360 miles north of Jerusalem with Damascus between them. Although he claimed Roman citizenship, Paul can be recognized as product of the Hellenist culture and learning of Greece. In addition to being familiar with Jewish learning, in a city as prominent as Tarsus it would have been impossible for him not to have imbibed some sense of the local philosophers, for there it became fashionable to publicly teach, proselyte and debate. In his day pedagogues were afforded a welcome, as well as charlatans, mystery cults and wonder workers. Paul followed suit, addressing himself as one of the "stewards of the mysteries of God."[2] Whether brought in directly by Paul or those who followed, influences in Christianity of Hellenist and Roman paganism are readily evident. However, Saint Paul persisted in opening its intellectual gates, making conversion of Gentiles into the early church so much easier.

In writing his Book of Mormon, then, Joseph took stock of Saint Paul's prominent, pervasive imprints. One of its chief premises can be stated in the following question: How far afield of primitive Christianity might we have come had it been invented by a zealous Jerusalem Jew, somewhat like Paul, but who brought with him influences from some other great empire along the Mediterranean coast, say from an *Egyptian* heritage? Thus begins Nephi's narrative in the Book of Mormon—

> 1. I, Nephi, having been born of goodly parents, therefore I was taught somewhat in all the learning of my father; and having seen many afflictions in the course of my days, nevertheless, having been highly favored of the Lord in all my days; yea, having had a great knowledge of the goodness and the mysteries of God, therefore I make a record of my proceedings in my days.
> 2. Yea, I make a record in the language of my father, which consists of the learning of the Jews and the language of the Egyptians.
> 3. And I know that the record which I make is true; and I make it with mine own hand; and I make it according to my knowledge.[3]

From its very beginning, several parallels with St. Paul are begging acknowledgement, and it is here that we receive our initial, though as yet faint suspicion that somebody may have devised a mild but clever parody of the Holy Bible. In telling of his famous vision on the road to Damascus, Paul imparts such distinct approval of mystical experience that his episode, with adaptations, characteristic repetition and elaboration, got placed into Alma's narrative.[4] Now you may wish to ask, "Is this Book of Mormon supposed to be on the level?" And you'll probably ask the same question many dozens of times before you finish reading it or the answer gets a firm hold within your consciousness. During one of his subsequent attempts at fabricating unique scripture, Joseph allowed just a brief hint of the irony in his design: "[...] Egypt, which signifies that which is forbidden."[5]

Back in the Book of Mormon you'll get introduced to one of its notable heroes, a curious young man of invincible might, miraculous gifts, and who, with evident purpose, became mistaken for a god. His name, Ammon, corresponds to the ancient Egyptian God Amon.[6] The wonderful mysteries of godliness being examined through the portals of this newly postulated premise will become deeper and more screwed up than Saint Paul could ever have gotten them. The resulting work, with all its sheer irreverence and blasphemy must be ranked among the most stunning, surreal and humorous events throughout literary history and modern theology. In fact, the reader should be forewarned that some of the humor Joseph Smith intended within his book will come to the surface and make sense only for those able to conceive thoughts that are generally forbidden within the ordinarily perceived contexts of religion, of reverence and the usual solemnities associated with more conventional theological writings.

Its actual irreverence is poles apart from the sober esteem held for it by LDS believers, but that merely heightens pungency of its humor. One major reason that the opposite side of Smith's book has never made a strong public appearance is because the necessity for preserving a unified cosmological view demands that believers repress much of what they've been commissioned to broadcast throughout the world. Essentially, they have stolen Joseph's book away from the literary crowd without even being conscious of what they do. They deem themselves its conservators, so commandeer the interpretation of its mythology while assuming monopoly over its editing, publication and distribution.

A Small Roast for Twelve

Even on its second page there is an irreverent allusion to Christ's twelve apostles, a mildly humorous insult that one cannot fully appreciate without referring to later LDS teachings in order to discover the amusement intended by its author. First, Nephi, the heroic main character at the opening of the record, 600 BCE, tells concerning a vision his father Lehi had concerning the soon-to-come destruction of Jerusalem, which actually did occur fourteen years later, in 586. Early in that vision, Lehi viewed "God sitting upon his throne" in heaven. Then he "[...] saw One descending out of the midst of heaven, and he beheld that his luster was above that of the sun at noon-day."[7] We're confident that personage signifies Jesus because Lehi, directly afterward, "[...] also saw twelve others following him, and their brightness did exceed that of the stars in the firmament."[8] Not only are stars so much dimmer than the sun around mid-day, but Lehi's out-of-balance comparison refers to a particular doctrine which only Mormons believe, one calculated to severely diminish the eternal status of Peter, James, John and the rest of the twelve disciples once chosen by Jesus to succeed him in shepherding his followers. Mormons believe in three heavens, or, "degrees of glory," following the judgment. First to rise in the resurrection will be those who have been made perfect:

> 70. These are they whose bodies are celestial, whose glory is that of the sun, even the glory of God, the highest of all, whose glory the sun of the firmament is written of as being typical.[9]

We might all agree that Jesus deserves his exalted position in Lehi's vision. One could also imagine that the twelve apostles, eye-witnesses for Jesus, had earned a prestigious place of honor above common sinners, and thus would have received a significant measure of glory in the same vision, but no. Neither did they receive glory within the lesser, terrestrial kingdom, "[...] whose glory differs [...] even as that of the moon differs from the sun in the firmament."[10] Lower still, the twelve apostles of Jesus, through connotation within Lehi's dream, secured,

> 81. [...] the glory of the *telestial*, which glory is that of the lesser, even as the glory of the stars differs from that of the glory of the moon in the firmament [...].
> 84. These are they who are thrust down to hell.[11]

The humor of it isn't easy to define, nor is it in very good taste, though not virulently diabolical. Its wit only receives recognition by those who can associate together two distant segments of Joseph's teachings. Even after acknowledging what has taken place, the mischievous put-down remains not especially welcome. Conversely the discovery of one's subtle intent to give an unforeseen tweak to an idea usually held on a different level of consciousness may be precisely what causes humor to register. His insult to the sacred twelve apostles of the Lamb of God, wrought only through nuance, is too rude even for Mormons to brook, yet so far we've encountered three fairly simple segments suggesting potentially humorous content, all within the book's first *two* pages.

Again you may wish to ask, "This book can't be for real, can it?" To assist in getting to your answer, Joseph left a particularly pertinent clue when he wrote a brief biographical sketch to accompany the account of his earliest angelic visions. In it he confessed his youthful imperfections—nothing too "great or malignant"—and, moving on to specifics, the worst fault he could admit to: "I was guilty of levity."[12] When able to view and appreciate the unexpected depth within his book you may begin to wonder if it's possible Joseph ought to be awarded long overdue recognition as that early "Great American Author" we've searched for so long to establish our nation's intellectual stature—and missed entirely.

Joseph, Ignorant and Learned Son

His sometimes tart, very dry Yankee humor is but one unrecognized gift Joseph's book offers to the reader willing to set aside previous notions of what Mormonism brings to our expanding intellectual marketplace. The Book of Mormon also suggests an extraordinarily rich menu for philosophical, social, political—as well as religious thought, yet without necessarily trying to establish its author's preferences in a perfectly black-and-white format. Although the author has definite ideas for the reader to consider, masking his book as an ancient history and the amazing pains he took to dress it in the rough garb of an illiterate, stammering translation require the reader to look more deeply in order to determine the author's true objectives. That is exceptional literature if for no other reason than because it has been working flawlessly since first published.

Within his book Joseph actually referred to himself as "him that is not learned," while selling himself elsewhere, and pretty convincingly, as "an uneducated, obscure and ignorant youth," that is, until he later boasted, "I am learned, and know more than all the world put together"[13] Although his boast probably held more merit than you'll at first want to credit him, Joseph's whole life was so full of contrast, opposition and even contradiction that we may be forced to conclude that part of his intent in much of what he wrote for posterity may have been to keep the majority of his readers confused, or at least uninformed.

Placing terse autobiographical elements into his book served another of Joseph's essential purposes: to bring his identity into wide public recognition, so I may as well tell you now that he placed both his first and last names, along with many other facts about himself, into the Book of Mormon well upwards of two dozen times. Yet today only one single reference to Joseph Smith is listed following his name in the book's massive 242 pages of index (listing: Smith, Joseph, Jr.). Might we quite naturally suspect that he had conflicting (self) interests? Could he have been trying to build his stature with self-fulfilling prophecies? Or could it be that he purposely devised unmistakable signatures throughout his book by which indisputable evidence would later be preserved should anyone doubt who had actually authored the entire work? What slim chance is there that he designed it so that, by continually placing evidence of himself in amongst all its characters, his book would eventually get discovered as a better-than-average work of fiction?

The facts will now become yours to debate as well as to enjoy. With that special touch of wonder that characterizes only the best works of literature, not only does its future get placed into your hands, but you may also discover something of yourself that will likewise be revealed somewhere between its lines.

CHAPTER 6

Nephi, Part 2:
The Two-Story Myth of Nephi

Aptly chosen as an appellation for the Book of Mormon's introductory protagonist, Nephi's name has also been applied to the white-skinned, predominant, seemingly more righteous race, the Nephites. But then, supposedly, Nephi was the one writing the story. To ascertain the reasoning for their grand stature, we must turn to the Bible. Original text of Genesis refers to a tribe of giants named *Nephilim*, taking the Hebrew plural form of Nephi. From its earliest days the LDS have exclusively used and quoted the Authorized, or King James Version, which doesn't utilize the term Nephilim but, simplifying meaning for its readers, substituted the word "giants."[1] Newer translations help get at the root.

Joseph fitted Nephi with a suitable character that registers even more colorful origins. The Hebrew dictionary associates the word (in English, spelled nᵉphil, pronounced *nef-eel*) with "bully" or "tyrant," exactly the role adopted for Nephi's character—and Joseph Smith's, also, according to scattered reports within his more popular autobiography.[2] Nephi used intimidation, electric shock, coercion and even murder to get his way.[3]

In turn, the word nᵉphil refers to another Hebrew word, *naphal*, meaning "to cast down" or "fall away."[4] As his book progresses the Nephites do indeed fall away from the orthodoxy of their parent religion. Nephites, not Lamanites, were guilty of persisting in the unaccepted practice of polygamy.[5] In a symbolic sense, *Nephites* represent a body of self-hallowing religious purity ("white and delightsome"), large of stature (perhaps to suggest an imposing political presence), and forceful in bringing others into service to accomplish their formidable aspirations.

More general to his purpose, might Joseph have borrowed the name as metaphor to represent the dominant role taken by European (white) man in America? Nephi and his followers are constantly appearing in their function as self-righteous, self-appointed authoritarian buffs, maintaining opposition to the Lamanites, initially seen as participants at the lower end of the moral world, and constantly in rebellion against Nephi's descendants. Might Joseph have designed his story to question a prominent but flawed system of virtues and moral notions?

Nephi as Black Smith

Both Nephi and Mormon grew to be "large of stature."[6] Although Joseph was six feet tall, his robust physique gave him the appearance of being even larger. He weighed in at about 210 pounds and boasted of great strength, especially his ability as a wrestler.[7] Joseph was a champion, both mentally and physically, so Nephi didn't merely serve as a hero in fantasy but became a model whom Joseph justified through his own living. Nephi, like Joseph, was positioned as the fourth-born child in a family of six boys.[8] Joseph, like Nephi, felt he deserved to be chosen as a "ruler and teacher" over his brethren, influenced in no small degree by the Bible's story of the famed *Joseph* of Egypt.[9] Nephi kept his less righteous brothers in line while crediting himself with single-handedly transporting his whole family over to the New World. The true story shows Joseph likewise keeping his family together despite occasional eruptions. Each of them followed his lead into the religion he intended to help restructure that world anew.

A self-taught young man with great ambition, Nephi blossomed into a talented ship-builder. Not least among his technological gifts were metalworking skills so uncommon upon the shores around Arabia that even today they are quite scarce. Nephi established a metal foundry and blacksmith shop for fabricating the necessary tools to construct his ship:

> And it came to pass that I, Nephi, did make a bellows wherewith to blow the fire, of the skins of beasts; and after I had made a bellows, that I might have wherewith to blow the fire, I did smite two stones together that I might make fire.[10]

With bellows, fire and a smite, Nephi, *as blacksmith*, was Joseph's effort to forge a link between his leading man and himself through the family name. The two stones that sparked his fire must refer to a pair of magical seer stones that Joseph, in real life, devised for producing the book's translation.[11] "Fire" represents the incendiary effect that Mormonism brings against orthodox Christianity. An LDS publication explains, "Lorenzo Snow records a day when someone came and said to Joseph, and it happened hundreds of times, 'Who are you?' And he replied, 'Noah came before the flood; I have come before the fire.'"[12]

Wresting a Smith from the Bible

Given such an adaptable name, Joseph didn't have to search very hard to find an advantageous reference to the word "smith" in the Bible. He had been pulling chapter after chapter out of Isaiah, changing a word or two to suggest to the reader that the original had been imperfectly translated or copied [by wicked priests] into a book he needn't necessarily trust.[13] For his own part Joseph had seldom appropriated an entire segment from Isaiah into the Book of Mormon with so few alterations as he did its 54th chapter. Nevertheless, hidden within, you'll find the word "smith" in exactly the context he needed to match the symbol introduced by Nephi, the blacksmith.

(From Isaiah, as recorded in the Book of Mormon)
15. Behold, they shall surely gather together against thee, not by me; whosoever shall gather together against thee shall fall for thy sake.
16. Behold, I have created the smith [Smith] that bloweth the coals in the fire, and that bringeth forth an instrument for his work; and I have created the waster to destroy.
17. No weapon that is formed against thee shall prosper; and every tongue that shall revile against thee in judgment thou shalt condemn. This is the heritage of the servants of the Lord, and their righteousness is of me, saith the Lord.[14]

Calling attention to his clue and understanding that his purposes would otherwise be difficult for anyone to ascertain afterwards, Joseph followed up in the very next verse by instructing readers to concentrate and persevere when studying those words from Isaiah, "And now, behold, I say unto you, that ye ought to search these things. Yea, a commandment I give unto you that ye search these things diligently; for great are the words of Isaiah."[15] Yet even today recognition of any hint of conceit in the author's intentions, even when accompanied by this dead give-away devised specially for urging readers to focus more intently upon its meaning, presents a stiff challenge for true believers.

1805—It Was a Very Good Year

Nephi commenced writing his record at 600 BCE, or, "[...] the first year of the reign of Zedekiah, king of Judah [...]."[16] That date could have been earlier or later except that with it Joseph was able to capitalize on a unique historical timeline to signify his own birth year. Why not? If he'd commemorated only Vermont, his birth state, the true target he intended celebrating would have maintained a safe margin of obscurity.

The book's timeline of years is kept in careful sequence from beginning to end, appearing integrated continually within the story and showing few, if any, internal inconsistencies. Estimated dates are carefully fixed and noted at the lower corner of each page (excluding the Book of Ether). Those dates would have been quite difficult to keep in proper sequence, especially if Joseph needed to hold them in memory because he continuously composed his story during its writing. The book's claim to authenticity is made more convincing to many of its readers by both the continuity and consistency in its timeline. Few believers question or try to imagine that any alternate significance may have been intentionally imported through the dates established within its framework of roughly 1021 years.

In order to visualize how Joseph put his birth year into the Book of Mormon through its dateline, you'll have to accept a couple of simple premises. The first should be easier for non-LDS to accept: the Book of Mormon is a work of fiction. The second proposition isn't all that difficult to sustain, if only for the fact that the resulting calculation is simple to make, clean and exact: Joseph configured history in his book to mark his birth year by having it coincide with a specific, highly significant event—the appearance of Jesus in the New World. It is possible thus to conclude that he tried positioning himself as a *second* savior, however, in order to fix his symbolic calculation so it would be only half as easy for readers to recognize, Joseph *doubled* his count of years, requiring division by two.

Rest assured that Joseph made *his* choice of calculations for *his* book. His simple formula wasn't especially intended to tax our mental abilities so much as one's credulity that such a feat might be imagined. Try realizing that if he didn't obscure his birth year in some simple fashion (i.e., multiplying it by two) his prominent vanity would surely have been pierced by early detection. Furthermore by beginning his Nephite history at 600 BCE, he helped build credibility by associating his book with a prominent moment in genuine Judaic history that would have otherwise been lost. You may judge validity for his mathematical method better once you see how the calculation takes place, and why. The fact that he implemented the math problem, division by two, relates to the fundamental character of the entire Book of Mormon. It carries its truth in black-and-white halves while supporting exceptional bifurcation throughout. It promotes distinctive patterns of "opposition in all things," while broadcasting simultaneously on *two* channels. Obviously the book can be viewed as a second witness for Jesus—or it can be legitimately interpreted as a literary denial of God and as an anti-Christ manifesto. Hence, division by two (or multiplication by one-half) becomes a logical math function Joseph used while helping defer premature exposure.

Therefore, leaving Jerusalem in 600 BCE, Lehi's family sojourned for eight years before they arrived in America, landing in 592.[17] Eight years is the only period mentioned separating the Nephite departure at Jerusalem from their landfall in America. As symbol the arrival of white Nephites represents the advent of white man in the New World—Europeans—Columbus—i.e., 1492. Then, according to the timeline given, the "Savior" who appeared in the New World came, following his crucifixion, at 34 CE.[18] Add 592 plus 34, giving 626 years from the arrival of Columbus until the symbolic advent of [the new] "Jesus" among the New World's Nephites. Finally, divide 626 by 2, allowing 313 years. 1492 plus 313 equals 1805. Not coincidently, that was Joseph's birth year.

This interpretation of course assumes that Joseph considered himself a *second* messianic figure intent on saving the world. Mormons will recognize how Joseph actually projected eventual godhood for his followers, so viewing himself as a savior should not really be outside anyone's conceptual reach. Can his final act of suffering as a religious martyr help preserve that disturbing view through a few more chapters until we can return to this fascinating theme for a more thorough investigation? That relationship will be investigated further in chapters 11 and 14.

CHAPTER 7

Lehi and Sariah as Joseph and Lucy

Lehi is portrayed as the earliest patriarchal figure to preside over both great civilizations, Nephite and Lamanite, carried from Jerusalem to America, and is seen as a visionary character contemporary with Jeremiah, the Bible prophet (c. 600 BCE). Despite that seemingly honorable role, Lehi's character never achieved full development before being eclipsed by his boldest, brightest son, Nephi. Whatever at the beginning suggests Lehi's incipient power as head of his family, he soon became reduced to figurehead status.

Observant readers might recognize how Joseph's characterization of Lehi suggests passive criticism by the way he is made to assign complex, difficult tasks to his four eldest sons while offering insufficient assistance or practical instructions. While the father's character helps Nephi's story get rolling, it isn't about Lehi at all. The old man acts as a necessary launching pad for his son's career, meantime modeling the serviceable concept that prophets act as God's mouthpiece by giving second-hand commandments to others. As symbol, Lehi could well operate as the *Holy Father*, or Vicar of God. And if we extend that perception just another step upward, the name itself lends potential as a mild slur poised against God's dwindling omnipotence (including a cute French accent), as in, "*le high and mighty.*" Will Joseph's further treatments of God confirm an unkindly disposition?

Nephi claimed in his narrative to have substituted an abridgement of his father's record.[1] No respect! You'll also note in the story that Lehi's character is not indelibly strong, for Nephi reports that Lehi "[...] began to murmur against the Lord his God."[2] Lehi, one might reflect, had been slipping out of touch with a changing, modernizing world as his influence faded prior to ever achieving the prominence anticipated for a leadoff prophet in such an epic. He becomes overshadowed and is soon replaced by his more spiritually resolute and technologically adept son, Nephi. Nephi, of course, becomes a mask for Joseph, whose strategy is to outshine and (symbolically) outmaneuver *the* Father by manipulating revisions to *His* record (i.e., the Bible).

Relying strongly upon his dreams and visions to bolster claims to authority, Lehi ordered his family to leave a good home in Jerusalem on short notice, somewhat reflecting the Smith family situation in 1816 when Joseph, Sr. arranged for them to move from Norwich, Vermont to Palmyra, New York. Joseph's father seems never to have garnered success in life, but avoided the specter of failure largely through dogged industry—mostly that of his wife and children. He settled on no permanent vocation, even though he plied a number of trades, such as cooper, market clerk, occasionally as a piddling entrepreneur and once as processor and exporter of ginseng root. If not wholly accurate to characterize the father as lazy, no argument can dispute that the family suffered dire poverty caused by *somebody's* lack of motivation, and it wasn't Lucy's. Prior to initiating a religious movement, the two Josephs—father and son—appear to have worked together on several hustles intent on finding buried treasure and, thus, making ends meet. They were known at various times as money-diggers, glass lookers or [dowsing] rodmen, although success eluded their efforts as practitioners in the occult arts.[3]

Joseph, Sr.'s highest life achievement came by appointment as first LDS church patriarch, the sinecure position handed him by Joseph in 1833. If not for Joseph, the elder Smith would certainly have died undistinguished, impoverished and soon forgotten. A typical opinion, offered by one of the Smith's Palmyra neighbors, cannot be successfully challenged: "Old Jo claimed to be a Cooper but worked very little at anything. He was intemperate." Father Smith admitted that wine had once been a weakness.[4] The fact that Mormons never sustained a popular biography of the elder Joseph tells almost too much; he so visibly fits the profile of uninspiring, unfulfilled potential. Although lacking obvious ambition—and next to nothing of lasting importance can be attributed him—we might add that science hadn't yet overturned a deeply superstitious spirit at that earlier age, and Joseph, Sr. earned no worse reputation than many average settlers, that of a peaceable individual, a seldom-conspicuous, generally inoffensive member of his community.

Following their exodus from Jerusalem, arriving at the Red Sea, Lehi commanded his sons to hike all of the way back to the holy city, hauling pack and tent, to obtain a record of the Jews ("brass plates"). Then, after they returned to camp, he bade them hike back a second time to enlist Ishmael and his family in their venture toward the land of promise.[5] Conservatively the trip would have been 150 miles on foot, each way. There is little wonder, then, that Nephi's older brothers murmured; Lehi (as God) proved himself preoccupied with less practical matters, lacked consideration and exhibited heavy-handedness while exercising family management skills.

The name Lehi, in the Bible, actually registers as a place name from the land of Judah but a part that had been taken over by the hated Philistines, uncircumcised worshippers of the false gods Dagon, Ashtaroth and Baalzebub. In Hebrew the word *Lehi* signifies "jawbone,"[6] possibly enlisted by Joseph as a mild insult to God, who some might view as a long-winded "chatterbox," especially when we consider His exhausting wordiness throughout portions of the Old Testament. While designing his father's church calling as a Patriarch, Joseph affirmed Lehi's symbol. Essentially the office demands little more than one's volubility in pronouncing blessings upon the heads of young Saints in search of inspired guidance, hence, Lehi/jawbone. Joseph may have viewed both God and his own father, then in his late fifties, as impotent, dependent figures having no genuine influence beyond that offered through society's feeble traditions.

Sariah: Just Another Day's Work for a New World Mom

It should be quite evident why Sariah obtained a prominent position in the Book of Mormon. Joseph's place for her may have been created chiefly from the fact that no other woman, not even his young wife Emma, influenced his life so significantly as did his mother. References to women occupy less than one percent of the book's written matter; while names of presumably important figures, such as Nephi's wife, are conspicuously omitted. Sariah, however, became an "Eve" to both New World nations simply by having borne and nursed Lehi's children. Her symbol name blends both forms of the name given to Abraham's wife, Sarah, the Bible's first true matriarch, who, previous to God's covenant was known as Sarai.[7] The name Sarah refers to "princess," whereas Sarai connotes a subtle but curious alternate—"dominative."[8] Although her part be ever so small, and in the same manner as Lehi may be perceived as silhouetting Joseph's father, Sariah seems to resemble Joseph's strong-willed mother, Lucy Mack Smith.

Lucy on the Move—at Onidah/Onieda, New York

Taking the liberty of viewing the Book of Mormon as a work of literature will open many opportunities for intuitive renderings heretofore unlikely or impossible. In his selection of unfamiliar symbol names, Joseph seems to have included a few *homophones*, words that sound like other words. One such, Onidah, might resemble Oneida, a town and county in New York State. Although he never lived there, Joseph and his family passed through while moving to their new home in Palmyra. If so, what could have occurred there that Joseph might have thought to commemorate? Little beyond the fact that he placed its name in his book suggests that Joseph may have intended Onidah as a biographical milepost, a clue. If that were his intent, not only did he honor his mother but also used that event to register his family's most significant move prior to visitations by heavenly beings and pushing his Book of Mormon through to publication.

We pick up the story in 1816, during his eleventh year as Joseph's father moved from Norwich, Vermont, three hundred miles inland to Palmyra, New York, then instructed his family to follow.[9] In her account of the route taken by the family, Lucy identified a stopping point along the way, "twenty miles west of Utica."[10] Her description placed the family in a locality then known as *Oneida*; it's an Iroquois word for "standing rock." Buried within the Book of Mormon, we'll find almost exactly the same place name, Onidah, applied to a hill upon which Alma stood while delivering a powerful sermon to a "great multitude." The people there were "poor in heart, because of their poverty as to the things of the world."[11] Onidah and Oneida are pronounced identically the same.

At Oneida, New York, the Smiths found themselves impoverished after several unproductive farming seasons. Having one-third of their journey left to travel they also felt downhearted, for their wagon driver had just abandoned them. To save her family from utter ruin and the necessity of walking the remaining one hundred miles, Mrs. Smith caught up with her driver at a local tavern and, speaking loudly enough for all patrons to take note, demanded return of her wagon, horse team and goods. She fired her dumbstruck driver and managed teamstering the remainder of the journey without his expertise—a dangerous and daunting task for any greenhorn skinner. Her "sermon at Oneida" may capture one unforgettable fragment from the very active imagination of her eleven-year old son. Previously Joseph had been roughly treated by the wagon driver, and, despite youth and lameness, had been required to walk throughout the journey. Oneida may have marked a welcome turn in relieving his suffering, a moment in which he, like Alma's gentle multitude, felt salvation drawing nigh.

"My Mother Complained Against My Father"[12]

How better could Joseph have mirrored his mother in literature? Sariah complained of Lehi having been a "visionary man" (ungrounded? impractical?). In her later writings about Joseph, Sr., Lucy included synopses of several of his purported visions or dreams,[13] yet didn't hold back from sharing details of the elder Smith's failures in business, farming speculations and careless economics.[14] Without seeming to cast blame, she testified how the family once lost ownership of their farm with its newly built home, becoming lowly renters because he neglected his mortgage payment.[15]

After surviving several more decades of an enormously volatile, seesaw existence, the earlier pain of her husband's incompetence had noticeably softened for Lucy. Living through such trying times, deep losses, notoriety, disappointments and failures, her hopes of maintaining stability required a substantial investment of faith; she held tenaciously to it until the end. Early in their marriage, perhaps as with most couples, Joseph Sr. and Lucy had to resolve differences in their attitudes concerning those matters of faith. Lucy had become most wrought up by the need to get religion, endeavoring to persuade her husband to attend church. Although the elder Joseph made a start, he quickly ceased going, requesting that Lucy also stop. She admitted how hurt she was by his lack of interest and prayed "[…] that he might become more religiously inclined."[16] If Joseph meant to suggest that Lucy exhibited a "dominative" character, Sariah became a logical choice as his symbolic vehicle.

Lucy Knew the Truth: Family Comes First

While Joseph facilitated our imagining Lehi's family by portraying life as it was experienced within the Smith household, Lucy's book shows all but conclusively that that's just what he was attempting. While writing her son's biography she proudly emphasized her husband's dreams and visions, suggesting quite appropriately how Joseph's father provided portrait material upon which her young son modeled Lehi's character. Among those visions, one stands out in particular, for she recorded it with so much detail that faithful Mormons have documented how markedly it parallels the Book of Mormon dream-parable identified as "Lehi's Vision of the Tree of Life." Their comparisons yield over thirty correlations between the two visionary incidents.[17]

Also among her recollections of young Joseph's early years, Lucy included the fact that her whole family spent many an evening listening to the prodigy spinning tales about ancient America's earliest inhabitants.

> In the course of our evening conversations, Joseph gave us some of the most amusing recitals which could be imagined. He would describe the ancient inhabitants of this continent, their dress, their manner of traveling, the animals which they rode, the cities that they built, and the structure of their buildings with every particular, their mode of warfare, and their religious worship as specifically as though he had spent his life with them.[18]

Those evening gatherings referred to a time approximately three to four years preceding Joseph's earliest possession of the golden plates. Thus Lucy helps generate at least three inferences for her readers. First is that the Book of Mormon develops issues that Joseph had already been addressing long prior to beginning his work of translation.

Second is an almost unavoidable reality that, after having read her son's book, Lucy recognized elements unexpectedly similar to tales held in her memory from those earlier "evening conversations." If today's readers are easily able to *recognize* those parallels, Mother Smith *lived* them, so there should hardly be any question that she also recognized them and considered them. She expressly included them in her book, most likely because she determined that they carried high relevance. She could not ignore them.

Third, Lucy determined that sufficient reason compelled her to insert those parallel segments into her memoir. Although she never spelled out private conclusions that she *may* have drawn regarding them, the parallels must have piqued her interest. She found them most curious and probably judged it best simply to supply readers with the most complete information, allowing them to infer suitable opinions on their own. One must only consider the strength of filial bonds between mother and child to realize why it became absolutely impossible for her to break faith with her son—and consequently with every remaining faction of the restoration movement. Her readers would need to exercise their intuition in order to follow where her lead might take them.

To see this better, let's first be assured that Lucy, as typical with any good mother, made it her business to become extremely intimate with all the habits and personality traits of each of her children—Joseph no less than the rest. She exhibited the behavior and character of a conscientious individual, a moral and intelligent, if troubled, woman. Lucy showed herself as a mother who remained keenly, superbly in tune with religious vibrations within her family. This mom in particular had invested heavily in her family, their health, welfare and most of all, their spiritual development. Certainly she became intimate with every one of Joseph's idiosyncrasies—his boldness, his huge imagination and intellect, but also his proclivity for fabricating fictions. The fact that Joseph had never developed lasting enthusiasm for any organized religious experience had never been lost on his mom, yet he soon began transforming himself, most stunningly, into the very religious figure of whom she could take greatest pride—and boast of to other mothers—a duty that never found her at a loss.

Joseph's close relationship with God simultaneously presented Lucy with potentially valuable assurances that she'd sought in meeting her salvation-security needs. To whatever degree she may have suspected

Joseph's work as fraud, she also saw him sincerely beginning to devote his substantial energies to a cause that suggested a capacity for delivering necessary revealed truth that could have led to the betterment, perhaps salvation, of all mankind. What mother might ever think to step between a child and his spiritual ambitions when *no* indicators implied that he had any other than rightful intentions?

Beyond everything that she might have understood about her son, she also comprehended one great truth that reaches to the core of every mother-child relationship: no matter to what age one's offspring develop, damage control remains a mother's womb-generated responsibility. Any failure there would jeopardize all the delicate realities she had constructed within her mind. If she ever imagined that her son devised a religious scam, she permitted him to pass inspection, mostly viewing his actions as having an overall positive impact. Joseph's testimony brought Jesus closer to the American homeland, thus imparting a nobler coloring to any hint of shadiness. Given that his aims showed pious promise, she found no ostensible cause for demanding repudiation of his work or his gifts. Further, her ability to conceive any harm being generated from his mischief dissipated in proportion to growth of Joseph's religious movement. Great success repelled her doubts while validating the assumption that her son exercised his gifts under God's tutelage and blessing.

Joseph, Jr., writing his religious saga, resolved any conflict between Lehi and Sariah by giving their son Nephi charge over the entire show. His parents were gently made to step into the background as he asserted leadership, built and captained the ship that carried them to the New World, then assumed position as lead political-religious figure over the Nephites after arrival. In actual respect to his family, Joseph founded a religion that appears to have brought peace to his mother's anxious heart, yet satisfied his father's objections against the puffery and insipid formality of established religions.

Although he set himself up as number one player and top authority in charge of directing the destiny of his great people, the Mormons, one particularly redemptive characteristic stands out: those bonds with family were paramount to Joseph and were permanent. Consequently, despite serious occasional frictions, he would never exclude any of them.

After hardy Lucy had endured seventy-nine harsh winters, she ended her days resenting the fact that tireless good works hadn't yielded consolations that she felt were entirely deserved. She stewed over deep injustices and losses greatly disproportionate to her contributions. As with Joseph, we sense Lucy hoping for remembrance, not as much from her notable righteousness so much as from having survived martyrdom. If highest significance in her life became an outgrowth of any intense spiritual relationship, it derived from the one shared with her famous son. She owed huge debts of loyalty to Joseph, not just for bringing repute to her family, but also for recovering the spiritual atmosphere she had once enjoyed in her childhood home and had sought ever since. The closing paragraph from her book seems almost unconsciously copied from the final verse of her son's: "I bid farewell until I shall appear before him who is the judge of both quick and dead […]."

To a garrulous, inept but kindly father, his instructor in various and sundry arts, no memorial could surpass tribute of borrowing the inspiration he rendered for Lehi's Dream of the Tree of Life.

CHAPTER 8

Lehi's Dream of the Tree of Life

[Man] has imagined a heaven, and has left entirely out of it the supremest of all his delights [...] sexual intercourse! [...] His heaven is like himself: strange, interesting, astonishing, grotesque. I give you my word, it has not a single feature in it that he actually values.

(Mark Twain, *Letters From the Earth*)

A Little Something *Fresh* from the Garden

Perhaps the Book of Mormon really deserves to be recognized as a special category of scripture. While almost anyone can appreciate its unexpected pleasures, perspectives presented are not as provincial as they first appear. *Lehi's Dream of the Tree of Life,* found near the beginning of the First Book of Nephi, demonstrates how *avant garde* it is, as well as showing off an extraordinary example of early American literary excellence.

For its inspiration, Joseph drew upon the Garden of Eden myth from the book of Genesis. Once, when earth's verdant resplendence provided them with a beautiful paradise for their exclusive domain, Adam and Eve were given some fairly simple instructions—namely, not to eat fruit from the tree of knowledge of good and evil. Every other species of vegetation was theirs for the taking, including fruit from the tree of life. Incidentally, we are told there was a river flowing through their garden.[1]

One immediate consequence of Eve and Adam's disobedience of sampling forbidden fruit was that both realized they were naked, and shouldn't have been.[2] More recently, popular speculation holds that partaking of that fruit symbolized awakening of a formerly suppressed sexuality in the young couple. Implicit in their act of disobedience is acknowledgement of mankind's first sensations of feeling uncomfortable and embarrassed when viewed in their natural state—in the buff. Soon thereafter, God expelled both of them from the garden to further prevent either from again enjoying fruit from the tree of life.[3] The very next verse relates that earth's first couple began producing offspring.[4]

Wasn't the world a lot simpler when you knew nothing more about sex than the old tale about Adam and Eve? No doubt today's seventh and eighth grade school children receive more factual information concerning sex and human reproduction than typical American adults knew during the early nineteenth century. That's one reason why Mormons tend to be severely astonished when they discover how graphic and clear the details were when Lehi passed along essential instruction to his children about the sexual facts of life, as reflected within his "Dream of the Tree of Life."[5]

Lehi's dream mentions neither Adam nor Eve. Neither does it recount the absurdness of their enticement, transgression and fall. Here the fruit is not a variety forbidden to man, for Lehi will actually invite us to consume our fill of it. There is, however, a suggestion that shame or embarrassment accompanies the partaking of this delicious fruit when viewed by a leering crowd, in public. Its allegory describing sexual intercourse, although merely suggestive, ought to be recognized easily enough by literate, *mature*, audiences.

Latter-day Saints are taught quite a different lesson about Lehi's vision when they study it in Sunday School, Seminary and even college level [LDS Institute] courses in Book of Mormon Studies. To them, Lehi's vision relates only simple truths about natural barriers to righteousness that any true believer might expect to encounter while following the strait and narrow path during life.[6] From it they are taught that they must expect to endure mocking ridicule and even suffer persecution from the world due to their steadfast faith and diligence in serving the Lord.[7] Keeping a sharp eye focused on their ultimate goal, the tree of eternal life, church members are encouraged to work hard, apply their hearts to the task of perfection and continue persevering even when it may necessitate parting with loved ones who neglect taking the gospel's message seriously enough.[8] Many snares and temptations will be set in their paths in order to test strength of one's beliefs, causing many to lose their way along "strange roads."[9] A typical Mormon infers little more than that stern, uncompromising warning when studying Lehi's vision.

After examining it from a different angle, readers will be able to recognize an alternate view of Lehi's dream and might even gather a distinctively enhanced message, for it is full of suggestive metaphors and subtly symbolic elements. If he had wanted to, Joseph could have told a much more erotic story, but held to a prudent line that shielded his work from receiving wide public exposure prematurely. Although some may prefer to accept the more restrained interpretation, one really ought to be able to recognize its greater potential as a classic tale of *double entendre*. What makes all of this so hilarious is the extreme polarity of its two interpretations, along with the fact that the vast bulk of its readers have been exclusively attuned to its more conservative rendering.

Try imagining Lehi as a sober, spiritually sensitive, puritanical father; timid about approaching his rapidly maturing children too directly with necessary information about sex—yet how he still might provide healthy instruction for them by describing a general representation of the process of sexual union and how babies are conceived. Lehi, like many a modern father, became too abashed about speaking with complete candor about such personal matters. Instead, his discourse takes the oblique route as he devised a superbly crafted parable, found in First Nephi, chapter eight.

In a Dark and Dreary Waste…

To provide a suitable frame of reference prior to slipping into Lehi's dream world, the reader must necessarily refresh his memory concerning an LDS teaching of man's pre-existence. They believe that we formerly existed as conscious spirit beings that, although co-eternal with God, were formed by Him from matter designated, with a wonderfully ironic touch, as "intelligences."[10] In that pre-existence, we [supposedly] knew one another and even engaged in a lively exchange of ideas by which some of us became favored by God due to our valiant support for His Plan of Salvation. Others rebelled, followed Satan and tragically lost their privilege of entering life and progressing towards eventual godhood.[11]

At the beginning of his vision Lehi returns to a primordial state before birth, greeted by "a man [...] dressed in a white robe."[12] The man beckoned Lehi to follow him and the hero remarked, "I beheld myself that I was in a dark and dreary waste."[13] If you read no further you might recognize a passing similarity to Dante's *Divine Comedy, The Inferno*, canto 1, as he met the poet Virgil in a *dark* wood. Here Lehi was not being led on a tour through the afterworld but into a pre-birth past. Could his "dark and dreary waste" possibly be describing the physical proximity in human anatomy from which life generates? After praying to the Lord for mercy, Lehi continued,

> 11. I beheld a large and spacious field [...] and I beheld a tree, whose fruit was desirable to make one happy [...] the fruit thereof was white, to exceed all the whiteness that I had ever seen.[14]

If with Lehi you can envision the female reproductive organs: a womb, ovaries carrying pure white ova, or eggs, and a large pair of fallopian tubes that appear to all the world as branches of a tree, you'll begin recognizing the underlying metaphors. Later in the novel that tree will receive clear identity as the "Tree of Life;"[15] Lehi was being only as graphic as prudent limits would permit. But then, just when you might begin getting the picture into focus, Lehi stepped forward to "*partake* of the fruit thereof." He found the fruit to be "sweet [...] white [...] and [...] it filled my soul with exceedingly great joy."[16] It makes no difference which construction is applied to his vision; it is metaphor in either case. Lehi doesn't really *eat* any fruit, but attempts to represent the sweetness and great joy he *anticipated* by entering life, or perhaps only in viewing this specific morsel or episode from life's grand banquet. The idea became immediately "delicious" to his mind, so much so that he wanted to invite his family to partake with him. Looking around to find them, Lehi,

> 13. [...] beheld a river of water [i.e., the flow of semen]; and it ran along, and it was near the tree of which I was partaking the fruit.
> 14. [When] I looked to behold from whence it came [...] I saw the head [*glans penis*] thereof a little way off [...].[17]

But again, just as the picture begins to register, Lehi interrupts with a short segment telling how he called out to members of his family to come along and join him in the fun.[18] All but Laman and Lemuel stepped forward. Continuing, after viewing "the head thereof a little way off," Lehi witnessed, as sure as night follows the day,

> 19. I beheld a rod of iron [i.e., big erection], and it extended along the bank of the river, and led to the tree by which I stood.
> 20. And I also beheld a strait and narrow path [i.e., vagina], which came along by the rod of iron, even to the tree by which I stood; and it also led by the head of the fountain, unto a large and spacious field, as if it had been a world.
> 21. And I saw numberless concourses of [sperm-sized] people, many of whom were pressing forward, that they might obtain the path which led unto the tree by which I stood.
> 22. And it came to pass that they did come forth, and commence in the path which led to the tree.
> 23. And it came to pass that there arose a mist of darkness; yea, even an exceedingly great mist of darkness, insomuch that they who had commenced in the path did lose their way, that they wandered off and were lost [i.e., from millions of sperm ejaculated, ordinarily, only one will fertilize the egg].[19]

Nevertheless, others continued forward, caught hold of the rod of iron, and,

> 24. [...] did press forward through the mist of darkness, clinging to the rod of iron, even until they did come forth and partake of the fruit of the tree [i.e., a fertilized egg attaches itself to the wall of the uterus where it receives nourishment].[20]

Wave to All the Nice People, Darling

Just at that moment of gratifying climax, Lehi's vision of the inner mechanics of sexual intercourse and conception terminated. Before closing out the entire episode, however, Lehi added a humorous sequel to his story by referring to a coincidental event that occurred as the lovers concluded their embrace: "And after they had partaken of the fruit of the tree they did cast their eyes about as if they were ashamed."[21] Here, the lovers were pictured somewhat poetically as having "partaken of the fruit of the tree" in the same sense any of us might experience fruition by engaging in the passions of an afternoon's tryst. The reason they were ashamed is because, across the river from the park where they had been making love, there was a

26. [...] great and spacious building [...] high above the earth.
27. And it was filled with people [...] and they were in the attitude of mocking and pointing their fingers towards those who had come at and were partaking of the fruit.
28. And after they had tasted of the fruit they were ashamed, because of those that were scoffing at them [...].[22]

A bit of an imagination is obviously needed for catching the meaning of Lehi's vision, but that is always true for allegorical constructions. Not all of the symbols seem to fit neatly into place, such as the perfectly white fruit. That's an important point. In the living, an ovary appears grayish-pink. Ova are almost microscopic, yellowish and opaque, but not purest white—usually.

What Lehi has patiently been describing is not sex engaged between two humans, but his vision of God making love to one of his wives. Another of those unique teachings of Mormonism is that during our pre-existence we became spirit children of God through the identical process by which we have more recently become fleshy, physical children of our earthly parents; Mormons believe we are literally spirit offspring of God.[23] Can a symbol so magnificent as a "rod of iron" ever refer to attributes so common as might be experienced during mortal intercourse? Because of the refined nature of that exalted spiritual fruit, we can understand why it did "exceed all the whiteness that I had ever seen," as Lehi has characterized it.[24] The fact that his allegory is directed from its perspective in a pre-mortal spiritual creation also explains why neither Laman nor Lemuel chose to accept Lehi's invitation to partake of the voyeur's escapade. Perhaps, unlike Lehi, they were not so anxious to peep in on the Holy Couple during a moment of such passionate intimacy.

By the way, scientific study of developing human ovum began early in the 1600s, by the Italian, Hieronymus Fabricius, founder of embryology, and later that same century by Regnier DeGraaf. Visual observation of human ova was achieved finally in 1827 by an Estonian, Karl Von Baer. In antiquity science designated male sperm as "seed," which was thought, following conception, to develop into the embryo.

Nephi's Confirmation, Another Witness of Jesus

Important substantiation for our special new explication of Lehi's Dream of the Tree of Life will be found as Nephi later prayed that he might also know the interpretation of his father's vision. He wanted to view the miracle for himself.[25] What follows carries the irreverent humor of Lehi's allegory another step further as the Spirit provided Nephi a glimpse of the same tree that Lehi saw, then tried supplementing it with enough context so that his young student would recognize future obligations when entering married life.

The Spirit assigned to guide Nephi in his quest really did his best to assist him in visualizing what Lehi had only suggested through a series of ambiguous symbols. Getting absolutely as visual as possible, the Spirit conjured up an expanded interpretation that Nephi proceeded to describe: "And [...] in the city of Nazareth I beheld a virgin, and she was exceedingly fair and white."[26] Then, "[...] an angel came down and stood before me; and he said unto me: Nephi, what beholdest thou?"[27] Nephi admitted he had seen "A virgin, most beautiful and fair above all other virgins."[28] Cautiously probing Nephi's understanding, the angel asked, "Knowest thou the condescension of God?" Father Lehi, of course, had already gained experience enough to comprehend God's condescension, for he had witnessed that act being performed from the most proximal vantage. Nephi, on the other hand, hesitated, seeming a bit uncertain while answering, "I know that he loveth his children; nevertheless, I do not know the meaning of all things."[29] Nephi's angel really couldn't draw the picture very much more explicitly, but he made another attempt, saying, "Behold, the virgin whom thou seest is the mother of the Son of God, after the manner of the flesh." Nephi's ignorance suddenly evaporated.

If you had previously read through this wonderful passage, you probably weren't aware that Mormon teachings are quite specific in denying the virgin birth of Jesus; many Mormons still aren't very certain how they should handle one of Christianity's most entrenched doctrines. A revered church president, nephew and namesake of the Prophet, gave the following instruction:

> The Christian denominations believe that Christ was begotten not of God but of the spirit that overshadowed his mother. This is nonsense. Why will not the world receive the truth? Why will they not believe the Father when he says that Jesus

Christ is His only begotten Son? Why will they try to explain this truth away and make a mystery of it?[30]

To LDS believers God Himself condescended when performing sex with a mortal woman, Mary, and that has to be what the angel is referring to while instructing Nephi. The union between God and Mary was successful, of course, for, says Nephi, "I looked and beheld the virgin again, bearing a child in her arms."[31] Having first satisfied Nephi's curiosity about whose tree of life had been cited for public edification, the angel then went on to explain a great many additional items of information unto his young pupil, none of which adds significantly to *our* understanding of Lehi's vision. Most of the remainder of Nephi's ramblings fall into the category of misdirection, inasmuch as those deeper mysteries of godliness are not intended for the eyes of children or unbelievers, indeed, "[...] it is not always wise to relate all the truth."[32]

Lehi's Corroboration—Practice Makes Perfect

A most significant event took place almost immediately after Nephi finished elaborating upon his father's vision. It will help confirm that Lehi was passing along sex education for the benefit of his children rather than offering stern warnings how they must resist worldly temptations. First, prior to Lehi's pious lecture to his children, his sons had returned to his tent after traveling back to Jerusalem one last time in order to secure an alliance with the entire household of Ishmael. Specifically, it was done so that "[...] his sons should take daughters to wife, that they might raise up seed unto the Lord in the land of promise."[33] Then, as soon as Nephi's curiosity had been satisfied concerning the mysteries of that tree of life, he and all his brothers "took of the daughters of Ishmael to wife."[34] Soon little children began appearing in the camp of Father Lehi.[35] Not only were Nephi and his brothers stimulated to partake, but Lehi, the old man, also accepted the joyous invitation. He helped produce two more sons in the wilderness: one named Jacob, the other, Joseph.[36]

Follow-Up: Adam's Desperation Prayer

It would be wonderful to discover at least one more example wherein Joseph left more of his special brand of humor in print. By combing through an assortment of his capricious wit we might more easily be able to confirm his intent and proficiency as a humorist. Surely, however, if he had laid it bare for the world to enjoy, he could never have been taken so seriously as a prophet of God. Joseph had appointed two serious tasks for himself and creating superb literature was only one vital phase. Change was his overall mission, and the revolution he envisioned demands somewhat more than a modicum of discretion. To satisfy the clamor for more of this genre, the best we can do is to review and reconstruct an episode that has recently been deleted from the LDS temple ritual. The entire ceremony is as completely misunderstood as the Book of Mormon, generally for the same reasons.

Although not directly related to Lehi's dream, Joseph Smith wrote parts for Adam and Eve into the LDS Temple drama that will help to further sustain a demonstration of Joseph's proclivity for mixing mischief with more solemn themes. He kept his mind both quick and fertile, and he more than willingly shared his humor with those who have the wit to catch on. This chronicle of events isn't found anywhere within the Book of Mormon. In fact the part examined here, once a true segment of the temple endowment ceremony, had to be removed from LDS ritual early in 1990. Only the most faithful Saints are ever allowed to participate in or even witness temple rites. The entire script for the ceremony was originally produced within Joseph's imagination, though it is known that he received inspiration from Masonic services in which he participated during 1842, while ascending to its highest degree. Not even a trivia genius would be expected to acknowledge him as one of early America's minor playwrights, though his work continues (usually in a motion picture version) with daily performances throughout the world.

The following anecdote from the temple presentation is being included as an extra bonus that will help confirm the depth and dryness of Joseph's humor, as well as his boldness in throwing a bit of sexist comedy right into his followers' faces without their ever catching on. If any of them recognized anything amiss, at least none seem to have protested. We must again repeat that these are things Gentiles will be wise not to brandish in front of their Mormon associates.

Attending the LDS temple ritual is both blessing and a highly sacred responsibility that is taken seriously by the Mormon people. They go to the temple, not to be entertained by watching its melodramatic theatric presentation, but to receive "endowments" that they believe might enable them to enter the kingdom of God and by which in some measure they expect to initiate their progress toward godhood. Mormons don't speak directly about those ceremonies anywhere outside temple walls, not even in church, not because they relish keeping secrets but because that experience has been characterized for them as ultra-sacred. They believe that if they were to speak publicly, or even privately, about things held in such holy regard, they could induce most regrettable consequences. Soon you'll know why.

After Mormons go to the temple to obtain their own endowments, they are encouraged to return there often in order to do "Work For the Dead," standing in during those same endowment ordinances as proxies for those who have died without hearing the Mormon gospel while in the flesh. Imagine, if you will, a solemn assembly of devout LDS men and women dressed in all white clothing, having pure white slippers, robes, sashes and bonnets. Official costume includes a short green apron made to represent the fig leaf clothing Adam and Eve sewed when they found themselves naked in the Garden of Eden. According to the temple's dramatization, after God discovered Adam and Eve's transgression, he mildly cursed and expelled them from the Garden of Eden, "lest Adam put forth his hand and partake of the tree of life and live forever in his sins." The next scene leaves the Genesis story far behind, for we discover that Adam built an altar of stones at which he and Eve said their daily prayers to God. Worthy observers often feel that a special segment of our first parents' lives has become dramatically reconstructed through God's grace by Joseph's revelation of this temple ritual.

Adam, of course, hadn't learned to speak perfectly well in English, but uttered a primitive language all his own, represented in LDS lore as "the pure Adamic tongue." Our temple-drama narrator continues: "When Adam was driven out of the Garden of Eden, he built an altar and offered prayer, and these are the words he uttered: 'O God, hear the words of my mouth!'" (Repeated three times). There follows approximately fifteen minutes of the temple drama material separating Adam's original prayer from the punch line. During the interim, temple patrons are led through various solemn ceremonial oaths, tokens and laws requiring secrecy, strict obedience and sacrifice. They change robes from one shoulder to the other, give and receive sacred "token" words, and distinctive handshakes intended to facilitate their course through celestial doorways in the afterlife. They consecrate themselves completely to the service of the Lord, and dedicate their time wholly at the church's disposal:

> [...] you do consecrate yourselves, your time, talents, and everything with which the Lord has blessed you, or with which He may bless you, to the Church of Jesus Christ of Latter-day Saints, for the building up of the Kingdom of God on earth and for the establishment of Zion. (pause) Each of you bow your head and say yes.[37]

For purposes of the LDS Church, that sacred personal oath of total commitment is obviously the most significant event of the entire ceremony, even though most attendees are doing work for someone who has long since died, leaving slim pickings should the church attempt garnishments under terms of those post-mortem covenants.

Finally the program moves on to what is known as the "Second Token of the Melchizedek Priesthood." There the "sign" is given by the entire audience, *en masse,* by "...raising both hands high above the head, and while lowering the hands, repeating aloud the prayer, in the Adamic tongue: "*PAY, LAY, ALE*" [repeated three times]. A character identified as Saint Peter explains: "When Adam was driven out of the Garden of Eden, he built an altar and offered prayer, and these are the words that he uttered, which interpreted are: 'Oh God, hear the words of my mouth,'" just as had been rehearsed fifteen minutes previously.

Since Joseph's humor buzzes right above everybody's head, don't feel bad that you just missed it, too. It was a private joke that only Joseph knew anything about—because the entire ceremony was produced in his imagination. Here, for the first time is the underlying story, imaginatively reconstituted, though *never, never* presented to those Mormon believers:

> Adam, having Eve in tow, who, although once a rather lovely and pleasing companion, due to some unknown and *mysterious* ailment began developing an enormous *bulge* where she used to maintain a trim waistline. That once-pleasant and delightful companion had, in equal proportion to her recent expansion, become increasingly *irritable.* None of this made much sense to Adam, for his woman refused to answer questions about her alarming increase in weight

and girth, but had been doing less and less to assist, as was earlier customary. Also, she began constantly sneaking snacks and craving more and more *food*, which Adam had so far felt obliged to provide.

Adam, burdened with a command to maintain this whole dry, corrupted and *godforsaken* planet, decided to appeal once more to the One Being he suspected might have been behind all his problems, for He had so cursed *him* above all other creatures. Adam had put up with plenty, had little to show for it, and understood *nada* about what was going on with Eve's mind and body; so he was about ready to throw in the towel, as you may well imagine.

Adam was caught in a bit of a bind, however. He couldn't address the Supreme Being openly without the woman also knowing what was up. If she were to catch on he might just find her in another one of her sullen *moods*. So, using only the simplest of words, he quickly fabricated rudimentary hand signals to let the Lord know what he *demanded* be brought *down* to him *immediately*.

Trusting in the Lord's quick wit to understand the [*unspoken*] part of his petition he began by raising both hands high above his head, then, lowering them first to his shoulders and down to his sides while repeating the following words aloud *three times*—

[*more*] **PAY!**
[*a better*] **LAY!**
[*and a keg of*] **ALE!**

CHAPTER 9

Troubles with Three Good Bad Guys

> Brother Joseph Smith, Jun., said it was not intended to tell the world all the particulars of the coming forth of the Book of Mormon; and also said that it was not expedient for him to relate these things.[1]

Somehow, against both simple reasoning and all that science has taught us to expect, succeeding generations of Lehi's family quite sharply divided themselves into good ambitious Nephites and evil lazy Lamanites, thus exposing a second generation genetic split that somehow defied typical patterns of distribution.[2] Laman, Nephi's chief antagonist, became a leader among the rebellious and wicked portion. His Lamanite descendants were categorized as hard-hearted because they resisted the Book of Mormon Lord's call for righteousness despite Nephi's magic, as well as visitations by angels threatening them should they continue their evil ways.[3]

Laman's group murmured all the way to the New World, driven and hounded forward by his very pious younger brother. The jealous venom of the older sons seems reminiscent of Cain, son of Adam and Eve, upon whom God placed a mark.[4] Lamanites earned a similar curse, blackness of skin, symbolic rejection of and by the Lord.[5] Nowhere else is Joseph's polarization of characters given such contrast; indeed, how might more distinctive symbols have been drawn? Although black of skin, Lamanites are not portraying black people, and certainly not American Indians. Their reputed blackness represents Nephi's moral judgment intended to prejudice readers' minds against them in a manner commonly encountered within America's race relations.

Soon those Lamanites began receding into the book's fabric, usually minding their business, yet incriminated for initiating the conflicts and many wars between those nations. A one-eyed view of history excludes their version of it, which the reader must intuit despite precious few clues helping to perceive critical Lamanite perspectives. The dark-skinned tribes reappear again and again, usually attacking the Nephites without sufficient moral cause. The Book of Mormon projects a provincial and unfounded notion that the virtuous are protected and supported by a just and omnipotent God. Therefore Lamanites were usually routed—but only as long as Nephites adhered to principles of righteousness.[6] Lamanites slowly but surely gained power as conflicts between the two families became more bloody, graphic, fierce and frequent. Once technology for war advanced, symptoms of Lamanite righteousness began blossoming as they and the Nephites gradually reversed their roles of decline and ascendancy. Those dark-skinned cousins even produced a prophet of their own, Samuel the Lamanite, just a few years before the birth of Jesus.[7]

Arrival of Jesus in the New World may find readers expecting the two families to reunite once again in peace and greater harmony, but we'll realize no such peaceful resolution as its pages draw to a close. After only a brief interlude wherein both clans became converted to Christianity, dwelling together prosperously, they inexplicably reverted to their petty rivalry by again engaging in a ferocious, genocidal war.

That new round of hostility found Nephite *descendants* failing to heed admonitions that the Lord had imposed earlier upon their Nephite *ancestors*. Therefore they diminished irreversibly under Lamanite domination, the latter group having been exempted from the Lord's wrath due to their *ignorance* of God's laws. While all that seems somehow reasonable, we'll need to again readjust focus. In a typical twist of underlying LDS theory, ignorance suffered by the heathen becomes a moral *windfall*, for "...they have not sinned against that great knowledge which ye have received...."[8] Today's Saint strives with his all to gather more and more coveted spiritual understanding, thus encountering a host of new principles, laws and obligations requiring obedience. In so doing he places himself into proportional jeopardy, because "...he who sins against the greater light shall receive the greater condemnation."[9] Failure to abide and magnify every one of those advanced covenants becomes a fatal blunder that renders further advancement a highly precarious proposition.[10] The teaching represents a snide and tragically cynical *paradox of ignorance and intelligence.*

Because Lamanites are so incompletely represented within the Book of Mormon it becomes difficult to generalize any definite moral truth. Rather, readers may elect to consider a possibility that both Lamanites and Nephites are being used to describe common elements of social conflict that have invariably served to retard human advancement. Among other possibilities, those two families represent the way diverse sectors of society split, often along lines pitting progress against irrational, embedded attitudes, often referred to in the text as "traditions of the fathers." By using a format of mythology Joseph may have (intentionally?) failed to convincingly portray human individuals, nevertheless, his work succeeded as fiction by sketching elements of our human nature. Just as we exist in a world that is both light and darkness, Lamanites and Nephites could represent good intentions in conflict with many not-so-good ambitions motivating the soul inside most of us, resulting in little headway for all of us. Those two diametrically opposing sides may refer to thoughts often at war with one another that, being unnaturally suppressed by a one-eyed, true believer's view of life, have been contrived behind a set of false premises. When thus inauthentic, our views will require extensive and invigorating re-definition.

Lamanites must see history from its opposite face, having suffered at the hands of all forms of genius offered by religion and politics. Moreover, they haven't become very successful because they lack the irresistible organizing strength that unifies them behind a single unyielding principle or objective. Enduring centuries of abuse, line upon line and layer upon layer, "Lamanite" plays upon the word *laminate,* which, in Joseph's day referred almost exclusively to thin sheets of metal, as in plates of gold, brass, copper, tin, etc.[11] In support of this interpretation, we find that Mormon had originally been instructed to withdraw the gold plates from a hill named Shim.[12] Significance of his metaphor may derive from the method used to manufacture metal laminates: a once formless shape is brought into use only after being constantly worked between heavy rolling mills until flattened (Picture Nephi, the blacksmith). That procedure must be followed by purification—pickling in acid—in order to remove a *black skin* that forms on the surface of the metal. If we were to think of his metaphor in terms of some spiritual value, one could concede that Joseph's theme may point out a necessarily humiliating event. Indeed, Lamanites have been literally humiliated within the story. Notice, too, that even as Joseph flattered his people with promises of future godhood, he likewise urged them to become more humble,

> When you commence, go in at the little end of the horn; for if you do not, but enter at the big end, you will either have to turn round and come out at the end you went in at, or go out at the small end, and be squeezed nigh unto death.[13]

The lowly laminate is a rigid material that, bound together with others of like thickness and shape, becomes a larger, stronger structure. Laminates have potential, when given suitable advantages in design, of achieving near-indestructibility. Joseph's Lamanite brethren, though excluded, suppressed and condemned by generalized innuendo and marked as outcasts, were destined to survive and flourish beyond his hopeful vision.

Not entirely surprising, laminates achieve further symbolic function when applied to the deeply stratified and hierarchical LDS society. Some feel that the church flexes moral muscle when promulgating parochial views of right and wrong, supposedly for the benefit of members, but which works to mold their utility through efforts to expand and glorify an underlying system. Members often feel beaten down by constant obligations of service under its ambitious, ostensibly voluntary programs. Mormonism operates through a priesthood composed of lay (non-professional) male members. It offers hundreds of service opportunities within the Church's multi-layered organizational structure, often extending several simultaneous service callings to members willing enough to put the rest of life on hold. There, all are occupied unceasingly in building mutual self-esteem in order to bond with one another and create their identities and sense of importance surrounding the core. With such an emphasis upon their lay ministry, Mormonism has become one of the most deeply embedded systems ever devised for obtaining salvation. Joseph may have framed his followers as Laymenites.

Laman: As a Humble Amateur, He Was a Much-Loved Brother

Investigating beyond the symbolism of Laman to discover autobiographical contexts is even more intriguing because it would seem to connect Laman's character with Alvin, Joseph's oldest brother. Although Alvin died in 1823, before the Book of Mormon project was fully underway, he spent his last couple of years assisting a master carpenter while building a home for Lucy and Joseph, Sr. Alvin continued lending support to the family even after entering his twenties, substantially mitigating the father's inability to provide. Although never rising to status as a journeyman in his trade, Alvin still gave worthy accounting of himself as a layman homebuilder.

Neither Lucy nor Joseph, Jr. left any doubt concerning the wholesomeness of Alvin's character; they each testified of his kindness, affection and piety.[14] In fact there isn't a mark in the family record suggesting anything near the degree of conflict between him and Joseph as there is in the Book of Mormon between Laman and Nephi. Therefore, finding no evidence for anything but a healthy relationship between Joseph and Alvin, we must infer that the wretched picture of Laman and Nephi describes something other than their sibling affiliation. Not only do we sense warm and affectionate ties between them, but Alvin happens to be one among the older Smith children whose hesitancy to associate with a church appears closest to Joseph's views; that is, neither seems to have inherited their mother's anxiety for membership in existing religious institutions. What, then, caused Joseph to represent such a sour relationship in his literature when no discord characterized the two during life? Did some difference between them only become apparent following Alvin's early death?

Although the fictional conflict between Laman and Nephi must not be portraying the two brothers standing on opposite sides of a heated theological debate, it may still highlight Alvin's reluctance to advance his views within the marketplace of public opinion. While both sons shared respect for each individual's natural right to exercise full free agency in matters of conscience, Alvin showed no evidence for persuading, directing, pontificating or attempting to influence the religious path necessary for anybody else. His spiritual inertia parallels Laman's reluctance to serve the Lord.

In contrast Joseph could scarcely occupy his mind with anything other than what more he might do to advance his ideals as far as humanly possible. Might that difference, amplified through a plotted course of fiction, suitably describe a subtle schism within the Smith family? That slight but distinctive separation in philosophy between two brothers is ultimately what reshaped America's religious landscape. Joseph determined that his cause carried such importance that he became totally committed to its promotion. He brought reasoning into service and used his intellectual gifts, deception, psychology, logic, propaganda, charm, his speaking and acting ability, appeals to patriotism and any other game he could invent for intervening effectively against the religious currents that seemed to sweep others downstream. The distance between Laman and Nephi doesn't represent animosities or typical sibling issues but how those two sons perceived their duty regarding the propagation of unpopular but pivotal truths.

Joseph's entry into Palmyra's debating society may have helped perpetuate one of Mormonism's most recognized hallmarks—its extravagant investments in world-wide proselytizing. Joseph's teachings assert that favored status during this current (mortal) stage of existence is due to one's valiant defense of God's plan of salvation during our pre-mortal state.[15] Joseph represented himself as Nephi embracing that posture of religious activism. His only criticism of Alvin would have been to point out how the defense of truth demands assertive offence strategy, active sponsorship and vigorous promotion in order to break down the barriers of traditional religion. To indulge the quest for truth merely for private edification or serene contemplations is hardly above cowardice, an abandonment of duty. Alvin's death proved to Joseph how necessary it is to advance one's own views closer to the mainstreams of thought.

In 1823, during his twenty-sixth year, Alvin died suddenly after taking medication from a quack physician who treated him improperly following an attack of gallstones ("bilious colic"). During Alvin's graveside services, the entire Smith family suffered intense grief exacerbated by an indignity perpetuated by a local preacher. Rather than offering words of consolation intended to comfort Alvin's family, the parson expressed an acrimonious view that, never having accepted the sacred ordinance of baptism, Alvin's spirit was doomed to suffer in hell throughout eternity. That minister's thoughtless cruelty may have planted the seed for Joseph's later teaching of ordinances for the dead, including temple baptisms. Regardless, Joseph noticed soon afterwards that his family began shifting into a higher religious gear as Hyrum, his remaining older brother, and Sophronia, his older sister, joined with their mother Lucy in requesting membership under the Presbyterian banner.[16] When his younger brother Samuel also joined, surely Joseph began feeling pressures to fall into line, and that may have animated his iconoclastic impulses enough to initiate his attack upon sectarian religion.

Lemuel: "A Man's Enemies are the Men of His Own House"[17]

Little distinction needs to be recognized between the two fictional figures, Laman and Lemuel, for the inner characters of both of Nephi's rebellious older brothers remain outside the reader's purview. If Laman represents Alvin, the oldest son, then Lemuel must logically symbolize Hyrum, almost six years Joseph's senior. Lemuel's symbol name in Hebrew means "dedicated (or belonging) to God," and since Hyrum followed his mother into Presbyterianism, Joseph may have viewed him among the carelessly credulous, or true believers. We could presume that Nephi's two older brothers represent Alvin and Hyrum simply due to corresponding sibling positions held within the Smith and Lehi families. In Hyrum's case, of course, significant ideological differences separated the two sons; he'd caved-in intellectually under psychological pressures to save his soul from hell. As soon as Joseph noticed his family starting their surrender, he must have decided that he was in jeopardy of becoming dominated by ecclesiasts; he felt threatened.

In real life, moreover, Joseph paid greatest honor and respect to both Alvin and Hyrum, so we must dismiss any assumptions that their fictional conflicts reflect bitter animosity. In the same way that Lemuel lends balance to Nephi's oppositionist sector, he helps depict the tipping of a fragile spiritual balance inside the Smith family. Their little clan had bonded earlier to conserve both economic and emotional support, but, until Joseph brought them together under his guidance, they never enjoyed unanimity in religious views. Joseph's experimental participation in folk magic and his interest with "glass looking" and treasure hunting placed him outside the pathways of an approved Christian walk. Being thus checked, rebuffed and rejected by orthodoxy and local ministers, Joseph soured entirely on typical religious experiences. Lucy recalled his admonishing her, "[…] you are mistaken in them [the Presbyterians]. You do not know the wickedness of their hearts."[18] There appears to be no good reason to suppose that Joseph hadn't determined long before his "first vision" that the religious world presented insufficient avenues for developing a sound philosophical position based on empirical evidence.

The suggestion that Nephi became a holy man is in opposition to the realistic view of exhibiting himself as such an overbearing stickler for perfection that he's transformed into a holy terror. Thus, his situation somewhat mirrors the one Joseph viewed as undesirable yet inescapable. He portrays his role as prophet through Nephi's obsession with the business of God, whereas in fact he suffered bitterly through conflicts within a society beset and distorted by ignorance and superstition compounded by delusions and deceit with regard to the fruits of faith. Effectiveness demanded that he begin living a double life. Hemmed in by society's presumptions, then suddenly finding himself outnumbered by his family's religious excitements, Joseph's best weapons were his arsenal of imaginative facades, symbols and masquerades and his discipline of never taking himself too seriously. Again we note how literature gives writers the world's best forum for airing and resolving grievances that cannot always be handled by simply dictating the truth to those nearest them. While Joseph always expressed high esteem for both Alvin and Hyrum, they, through Laman and Lemuel, symbolized the uncomfortable burdens of obtaining unfettered freedom from religious ignorance.

The one philosophical issue that might have forever divided Joseph's family represents a common predicament that likewise separates the family of man. At some point Joseph determined that quite a large population of individuals had been pressured to believe alike and might therefore be subject to a carefully engineered program of propaganda that would loosen or reverse their attachments to orthodoxy. How far could he promote the powers of discernment and reasoning before being unmasked by his own devices? Moreover, even though others must eventually burst that balloon, might its detonation catch the world's interest?

Laban, the Uncle Who Made All the Difference

Although the record acknowledges a family relationship that existed between Lehi and Laban, exact kinship is never specified.[19] Mormon scholars sometimes represent Laban as a "distant" relative, though we might think of him more familiarly, as was once suggested by a BYU professor, as Nephi's uncle.[20] Estimating by evidence from the text, Laban would likely have been well respected among Jerusalem's leaders prior to its destruction early in the sixth century, BCE. High public esteem notwithstanding, Nephi attacked him in the story as a member of Jerusalem's corrupt priesthood elite. Actually, Laban's fatal flaw lay merely in the fact that he held possession of a unique set of brass plates, a record of the Jews so ancient that it was supposedly inscribed with Egyptian characters.[21] Readers are led to assume Laban's brass record contained the original sourcebook to the Holy Scriptures. Had any such brass scrolls been kept they would certainly become the most sought after antiquity by modern Bible scholars. There is no wonder, then, that Lehi considered Laban's brass plates so necessary to his mission.

Initially Lehi ordered his four sons to return to Jerusalem with an assignment to secure Laban's plates and carry them along. Drawing lots, Laman, Lehi's oldest, was first to attempt securing those precious documents from his uncle. Laban rebuffed him sternly.[22] Subsequently, at Nephi's urging, all four sons gathered up their previously abandoned household wealth as a means to try purchasing Laban's valuable records. To anyone so conscientious about sacred accountability, such a foolish bribe would have been an insult, so Laban shooed them away in an even greater display of outrage.[23] He wasn't holding onto the brass plates for purely sentimental reasons, nor for profit, but took seriously his position atop the patriarchal heap.

Before the boys admitted total failure, the assignment of obtaining Laban's brass fell lastly upon Nephi's shoulders, forcing him to go solo. To succeed the young man called upon his reservoir of faith in God—but then resorted to rationalization, deception, treachery and, ultimately, murder in order to complete his task. One highly underrated incident during his ordeal reveals Nephi's correct nature—his claim of having heard the persuasive voice of "the Spirit," telling him, "It is better that one man [Laban] should perish than that a nation [i.e., future Nephites] should dwindle and perish in unbelief."[24] Of course the Ten Commandments found on those brass scriptures would have denounced as unholy and unlawful Nephi's resort to murder. Moreover, we must ask, why could not the "Spirit" whispering to Nephi also have exercised its holy, righteous influence to entice Laban to cough up the holy book and so avoid violence? What stands at the very pinnacle of irony is that those whisperings of that *unidentified* spirit to Nephi were paraphrasing words spoken by Caiaphas, the Jewish high priest in the New Testament: "Nor consider that it is expedient for us, that one man should die for the people, and that the whole nation perish not."²⁵ While speaking, Caiaphas was condemning the righteous Jesus to death.

Few readers understand this event as one of Joseph's earliest significant clues guiding them in choosing up sides. When Nephi returned later that evening to his uncle's home, alone, he found Laban passed out in front of his house from drinking too much wine. "Therefore," wrote Nephi, "I did obey the voice of the Spirit, and took Laban by the hair of the head, and I smote off his head with his own sword."²⁶ Laban, seemingly through Nephi's consideration for the greater good, suffered death without being permitted a fair defense, murdered in innocent blood despite his position as *lawful* custodian of the Jewish holy books. Laban, in Hebrew, means "white," an emblem chosen for its perfect representation of innocence, again supplying a clue readers must consider when separating good guys from the bad. Because Nephi portrays Laban as a drunkard, and Latter-day Saints scrupulously abstain from alcoholic beverages, they take sides against him in justifying Nephi.²⁷

Because Joseph created Nephi to symbolize himself, he seems to have been exposing a dark and uncomfortable side, regarding either his underlying psychology or personal ethics, both of which are represented repeatedly through his fiction. Would Joseph also be willing to adopt unconventional tactics, "any means necessary," to further his hidden ideology? In a work of good literature, writers are able to confess things they ordinarily couldn't, even murder, by couching intent in the riddle-master's language of metaphor.

Nephi's encounter with Laban suggests another actual event from Joseph's autobiography. The story relates an incident during Joseph's younger days while living with his father's older brother, once a favorite uncle, as well as a book of greatest importance that his uncle shared with Joseph's family. Represented near the saga's opening, Joseph may have placed his story there to suggest a literary acquisition that likewise initiated his enlightenment. The doomed relationship between Joseph and his uncle Jesse very likely inspired the dramatic report explaining how Nephi obtained Laban's brass plates.

CHAPTER 10

Painful Origins on Plates of Brass

*Great God, where is common sense and reason?
Is there none on the earth? (Joseph Smith)[1]*

A study of Christian religious history, although complex, rewards us with views of an evolving intellectual phenomenon, uncovering everything from similarities and parallel teachings, to minor contradictories, heresies and irreconcilable differences, when comparing later derivatives with earlier religious thought. Mormonism is rather unique, however, in that Joseph claimed that his revealed theology didn't descend from any established religious system, as did Lutheranism from Catholicism or Methodism from Anglican but that it came divinely presented as new revelation directly from the heavens. His remarkable assertion makes the attempt appear fruitless for anyone to trace his dogma from doctrines existing in the age immediately preceding his earliest spiritual quest. Yet, in reality, that's the exact place we need to begin looking.

Rather than limiting a search of Mormon evolution to descent through various forms of orthodox Christianity, those who investigate sources for Joseph's religious concept should prepare to expand their range of research to the fringes (at least) of contemporary religious environments. Early Mormonism's radical new ideology included a blending of applied conscious reasoning adjusted by appeals to deeper human needs. Joseph reached satisfying harmony by tapping into an eclectic synthesis of available ideas and popular myths, many of which can be traced to probable sources existing prior to Joseph's works.

One of the earliest insights within his book suggests a prophecy, in capsule form, of America's future discovery, its colonization and Revolutionary War. Nephi's vision also foretold how the Bible had become corrupted while in the hands of a "great and abominable church," but then projected a modern restitution of its lost truths for benefit of Jew and Gentile.[2] That forward-looking promise of Mr. Smith's future gospel restoration has never been too difficult for readers to apprehend and appreciate. Regrettably, of available newsworthy information Nephi might have chosen to project with respect to America's exciting future, his remarkably clear vision went blank before predicting any recognizable event of national importance subsequent to Joseph's introduction of the restored church. Accordingly, investigating the American scene prior to 1830 might suggest several influences on Mormonism's development.

More than any religious movement that established roots in the new nation, Mormonism follows the deist philosophy that spread from England and France into the American colonies during those few decades before and after the Revolution. In addition to finding solid deist influences in LDS doctrines, we'll note a conjunction linking Joseph Smith with the book written by popular deism's greatest spokesman, Thomas Paine. Thomas completed his book, *The Age of Reason*, in 1796, and a gift copy of it had been introduced into the Smith home just a couple of years prior to Joseph's birth. Joseph's grandfather, Asael Smith, seconded by his uncle Jesse, gave it an unqualified recommendation.[3]

The two Smith elders opposed organized religion and feared its influence upon Joseph, Sr. and Lucy, who had begun meeting with Methodists. The book became a best-seller, so whether it was that particular copy of Paine's book, or another one obtained from some other source, surely Joseph put his hands on it while young, read it and was strongly attracted by Mr. Paine's appeal to reason. Although Joseph's version of church history avoids all references to Paine's book, subsequent events suggest that it became one of his reading primers and a close companion during his studies of the Bible. *The Age of Reason* would become Joseph's inspiration for judging religion by the light of logic, for questioning of traditions and supposed priestly authority.

When writing his Book of Mormon, Joseph made report of a set of precious (but fictitious) brass plates that could symbolize equally *The Age of Reason*, or else the Old Testament gospel that Paine's book thrashed from end to end. Joseph's story tells how Nephi severed Laban's head to secure his uncle's copy of the sacred brass record before moving on to the New World.[4] His tale is only autobiographical when understood in its metaphorical sense. Nobody beheaded anybody. Rather, Nephi's violent act represented a change in the family tie Joseph shared with his uncle Jesse. Theirs was a relationship that Joseph recognized would sooner or later need severing.

Uncle Jesse, Salem, 1813

When seven years of age, Joseph contracted a severe bone disease, known today as osteomyelitis, inflammation of the bone marrow. Ultimately, surgeons had to cut into his left leg to remove sufficient infected bone so they could hopefully prevent amputation. Following the operation, mending would demand several months, and Joseph required a good deal of care. To encourage recovery his uncle Jesse offered to have him come stay awhile in the healthful climate near the seacoast by his home at Salem, Massachusetts.[5]

From the Smith farm in rural Lebanon, New Hampshire, Salem is about 130 miles south-east. Joseph's earliest ride through a larger, more metropolitan neighborhood had to register a marked impression upon the youngster. His character named Mormon told of being carried by his father into the land southward: "The whole face of the land had become covered with buildings, and the people were as numerous almost, as it were the sand of the sea."[6] Salem is a seaport village located to the north and just outside Boston's busy metropolis. Jesse's urban environment contrasted starkly with Joseph's backwoods upbringing. The two may have established a warm bond of friendship. Jesse's family included ten children, several of whom were old enough and able to help care for their convalescing cousin. During the stay with his uncle Joseph surely marked several differences in habits of worship and religious study within the two Smith households. At home in New Hampshire, Lucy had insisted on having family prayers morning and evening, as her mother had drilled into her during childhood. That more relaxed home atmosphere at Jesse's may have exposed Joseph to such a high magnitude of contrast that it actually became his first true revelation.

Throughout his months of recovery at Salem Joseph was never expected to attend church, not just because of his leg injury, but because Jesse adamantly opposed organized religion. We can only suppose how his curious young nephew, thirsty for information useful in forming sound judgments, inquired concerning Jesse's past explorations of Congregationalist, Universalist, and Deist views and that Jesse showed as much willingness to share his skepticism with Joseph as he had earlier with Joseph, Sr., and Lucy.

Jesse presented himself as stubbornly opinionated, very outspoken, and noticeably impatient with all the energy his brother's family expended in its religious pursuits. To help answer his many questions it would be perfectly understandable if Jesse simply referred his young nephew to Tom Paine's book, *The Age of Reason*. Joseph had ample time to investigate, read and reflect while off his feet. This period in his life may have provided Joseph with several prerequisites to accelerated learning—he had been blessed quite suddenly with abundant leisure, a highly stimulating environment, had cousins available to tutor him, and had all the intellectual motivation necessary to boost his educational opportunities. Even by age seven his character and discipline had begun showing the depth of their foundations, including an indomitable will.

When Jesse saw the receptive light of inquiry and reason shining in Joseph's youthful eyes, no doubt he would have anticipated having its great power shape the young lad's thinking. However, because religious outlook between these two families differed so radically, one would be greatly surprised if his wise uncle had neglected to caution him to hold his tongue concerning any budding religious skepticism, at least until he had matured more fully in his understanding, enough to defend his views intelligently.[7]

When, seventeen years later, in 1830, Joseph, Sr. visited his brother Jesse, bearing news of his son's wonderful visions, rising fame, the miracle of his important book and of his part in restoring the ancient gospel, Jesse was thoroughly taken aback.[8] Because those unforeseen recent developments demonstrated results completely opposite to his earlier expectations, Jesse was morally crushed, acting out in bitterness over such an odd turn of events. Jesse fumed against Mormonism and cursed it, refusing to read Joseph's book or ever hear it discussed in his presence.

Nothing else could have shattered the Smith family relationship so entirely. In the end, Jesse became the only member of the Smith family to express opposition so bitterly, while the remainder, including Grandfather Asael, seem to have approved or joined the new sect. The irony of it all is that, if Jesse had only reserved judgment and exercised the same open-minded inquiry that he had earlier encouraged within Joseph, he might have appreciated his nephew's interesting literary treatments, especially the way they paralleled Paine's deist tenets.

In an Age of Reason the Atonement Becomes Infinite

Although Paine's book had nothing in it that hadn't already been said, and has since been eclipsed by more thorough Bible critiques, *The Age of Reason* displayed a strong assertiveness while carrying sufficient intellectual fodder to ignite Joseph's fertile imagination. It may also have engaged his instincts for choosing a just cause worthy of great sacrifice. Paine's book must be read, digested and compared with Joseph's own creative thought in order to recognize the extent of inspiration the former had upon the latter. Ideas receiving only passing mention within *The Age of Reason* were enlarged and imaginatively developed by Joseph. Embryonic themes in the earlier work became the springboard Joseph used to launch his parody and critique of the Bible.

Thomas, as did Joseph, made manifest his firm disputation of belief in existing churches; he also expressed doubt, rather, an "absolute impossibility," of the virgin birth.[9] He suggested wholesale corruption of the Bible, doubted miracles,[10] posited man's eternal co-existence with God,[11] insisted on an unchangeable God[12] and strongly argued against the morality of an atonement that would cover a multitude of humanity's sins by requiring God to suffer for them.[13]

One of the more telling issues, central to both systems of thought, is how each looks forward to man's ultimate perfectibility. Christians view man's moral condition differently, for they speak of human nature tainted by depravity and insist that men are perverted creatures: "[…] every imagination…of his heart was only evil continually."[14] The Bible graphically portrays man's descent rather than ascent.[15] If men had a capacity for perfecting themselves, the whole purpose of a savior would seem superfluous or meaningless.

Both Deism and Mormonism refer to systems of underlying principles wherein universal *laws* govern men and bring order to the mechanics of heaven and earth. Further, both books adopted a relatively modern position that recommends a course of *experimentation* in order to support or reject evidence.[16] Many other themes overlap within the two systems, offering the key by which we'll recognize seeds that took root within Joseph's imagination and flourished throughout his subsequent teachings. One of many contentions broached by Thomas was his argument that "[...] moral justice cannot take the innocent [i.e., Jesus] for the guilty, even if the innocent would offer itself,"[17] referring to a perceived deficit of logic under-girding Christian atonement teachings. Following Paine's thinking, and in his bid to form a religion more accountable to reason, Joseph devised a doctrine within the Book of Mormon identified as the "infinite atonement," an amusing sidelight that helps trace Joseph's inspiration to its source.

Of course the idea of sin is already complex enough. Although analogous to bad behavior sin requires one to presume the existence of a God in order to give it meaning. A further level of abstraction is required to gather an appreciation for atonement theory (soteriology), the method by which sins had to be resolved before any of us could be found acceptable for presentation in the kingdom of heaven. In Christian gospel the atonement is thought to be a pre-arranged act that Jesus was ordained to perform on our behalf in order to allow remission of an individual's sins, thus establishing a state of grace that we, being sinful, could not earn by ourselves. However, should anyone characterize the atonement as infinite, it would represent something quite foreign to the biblical experience. Pursuing a rational ideal, Joseph took his Book of Mormon version of the atonement into entirely new territory. Like his mysterious teachings about Adam-as-God, modern polygamy and the process of eternal progression wherein the chosen might raise their status toward godhood, Joseph blunted the most direct, ostensible meaning behind his infinite atonement teaching, but with it created one of his most *deluxe* mysteries. When necessary referents and careful definition are omitted, an infinite atonement becomes so vague that it expresses an entirely subjective doctrine.

Today's Mormons read Joseph's words without comprehending them; his teaching of an infinite atonement is so out of accord with Christianity that Mormons couldn't preach it publicly once they fully recognized

Joseph's sardonic intent running through it. They presume that the word "infinite" must parallel a thought found in the book of Hebrews, "By the which will we are sanctified through the offering of the body of Jesus Christ once for all"[18] There, "once for all" doesn't necessarily refer to *all* sin, nor all sinners, but to the fact that, previously, animal sacrifice among the Jews had been prescribed as an atonement for the sins of the people once each year, year after year: "And he shall make an atonement [...] for the children of Israel for all their sins once a year."[19] The reference at Hebrews made blood sacrifice and other Jewish temple rituals obsolete by affirming that Jesus accomplished the required sacrifice once for all time, effectively terminating the practice of annual animal sacrifice.

Teachings of an infinite atonement from the Book of Mormon submitted a wholly different notion, actually proposing an inclusiveness that is absolute, meaning no less than this: *everyone must participate*, "[...] we would to God [...] that all men would believe in Christ, and view his death, and suffer his cross and bear the shame of the world [...]."[20] Of course they've never taught it that nakedly in Mormon Sunday School, but that doesn't mean that the teaching itself doesn't persist within Joseph's Nephite saga. His mysteries were never intended to be so explicit, but required delivery through latency and a vagueness of phraseology that takes advantage of reader confusion. Joseph understood that his gospel principles would normally receive filtering through impressions (a prerequisite *schema*) taken from orthodox Christianity. He determined to challenge and test his people's intelligence as well as their persistence in apprehending the boldness of his thought, despite the fact that he all but copied his idea from Thomas' work:

> 11. Now there is not any man that can sacrifice his own blood which will atone for the sins of another. Now, if a man murdereth, behold will our law, which is just, take the life of his brother? I say unto you, Nay.
> 12. But the law requireth the life of him who hath murdered; therefore there can be nothing which is short of an infinite atonement which will suffice for the sins of the world.[21]

Acknowledging that this bizarre teaching is not given adequate exposure anywhere in their proselytizing programs, we must continue by noting with all possible irony its complementary or "oppositional" doctrine. Current views disseminated throughout Mormonism concerning the atonement of Jesus display a thoroughly *finite* character that severely undercuts the atonement principle so prominently featured elsewhere in our Christian heritage. Forgiveness for Mormon sin is strictly conditional, based not only upon an individual's full repentance, but also demanding unending, untiring service within the church (as we've seen represented through LDS temple commitments). Salvation, recognized as a universal gift through God's grace, engenders one of Mormonism's greatest doctrinal conflicts with Christianity. First and foremost, Mormonism is a gospel of works that projects *premium exaltation* (Godhood) as man's ultimate destination—but one so sparingly administered that it can only be achieved "after all you can do."[22] Thus, Joseph distorted both the ends of salvation as well as the means.

For as much as readers need to be able to recognize how furiously contradictory his teachings are, none should condemn Joseph's thinking as simpleminded nonsense, nor too quickly criticize its anti-Christian spirit as a product of his ignorance or excess vanity. Rather than whimsy, he put shrewd reason and deep thought into the formation of his mystery of the infinite atonement. Fully comprehended, an *infinite*, all-inclusive atonement would eliminate much abstraction that clutters one of the most curious, if popular, mystery elements within Christian thought. Mormons thrive on a pragmatism that questions such staples of Christian doctrine as Original Sin and the nature of the Holy Trinity, two issues found paralleling Paine's objections.[23] To imagine that infinite suffering would actually be demanded of Jesus is a most troubling thought; perversely, it would require Christ's unbearable suffering throughout eternity (timeless, hence, infinite). The Bible never characterizes the atonement as infinite, but tells that Jesus proclaimed, "it is finished," was *removed* from his cross and later (painlessly) resurrected, making the atonement act *complete*, a terminal, *finite* event.[24] Theoretically, as Joseph designed it, universal participation became the only way to meet atonement obligations precisely as infinite and expansive as earth's mushrooming population. To advance the system's popularity, he recorded it as the preferred method among Zarahemla's brethren, "[...] and every man expressed a willingness to answer for his own sins."[25]

Subsequently, Joseph determined that the infinite atonement should likewise become the mode for his latter day believers:

> That every man may act in doctrine and principle pertaining to futurity, according to the moral agency which I have given unto him, that every man may be accountable for his own sins in the day of judgment.[26]

An atonement, payment for a world of sin, suffered once by Jesus, one time only, would require enormous (though hardly infinite) suffering, both physical and mental torture. On the other hand, requiring that each *individual* suffer for his or her own sins would not only ease the Master's agony, but shrink everybody's fair share of it to no more than a common headache and a nosebleed for each: Voila! Accounts could be kept precisely balanced without letting anybody get away with too much "on the house." Joseph perfected justice and equality while answering Tom Paine's objection against God having to atone unjustly for every unwise folly or sin man could devise. Mr. Paine would have been quite pleased to have known someone so attuned to common sense.

Bitter Pain, Exquisite Paine

As one possible acknowledgement to Thomas, his patriotic philosophical mentor, Joseph may have had his character Alma mention him while describing his earliest sudden moment of religious enlightenment. Alma, as we'll soon note, became the Book of Mormon's central figure in more ways than one. Alma's religious conversion took place following an astounding vision, described as a close parallel to Saint Paul's, but likewise resembling Joseph's own first vision of the Father and Son. After describing the anxiety and suffering he went through following realization of his carnal nature, Alma admitted, "[...] there could be nothing so exquisite and so bitter as were my pains."[27] The text describes Alma's fear, amazement and torment for past transgressions, and although sad memories can indeed seem painful, why would he persist in using the word "pain," primarily a physical response, to describe *emotional* distress or anguish? In two columns of print he repeats the word pain *five* times. Does his over-emphasis suggest another riddle? The pain-Paine association makes even more sense when we note that, previous to authoring his classic, *Common Sense*, Tom spelled his name Pain. While some instances of pain may, on rare occasion, be thought to exhibit a certain level of exquisiteness, Joseph's flash of intellectual stimulation from Paine was perhaps closer to the heart of his message. Viewing as we do the source of his enlightenment, we can readily recognize Joseph's willingness to acknowledge his mentor's promotion of more rational methods of thought.

Added to his employment of a playful pun, Joseph paid for his vacation to Salem by suffering excruciating pain. Once the operation upon his diseased leg became inevitable, Joseph insisted that the infected bone be cut away without aid of any anesthetic whatever.[28] Neither would he allow himself to be tied to his bed, perhaps only so that he might appreciate a once-in-a-lifetime event with infinite intensity, perhaps to perfect his sense of self-discipline—or, possibly, redemption. While watching his physician lay open his leg as routinely as any farmer might turn a furrow with his plowshare, there can be no doubt that he really experienced pain most exquisite. His harrowing experience purified him.

While his religious views hardly ever suggest close alignment with Christianity's most tangible teachings, they spotlight the richness of imaginative resources within Joseph's unique mind. He kept his creativity so active and unbridled that he may have traversed bounds of skepticism far beyond Tom's limited ability to reason. Compared with Mr. Paine's work, symbolized as brass, Joseph projected values for his own book as if written upon plates of pure gold.

To Voltaire, a Grateful Adieu

Although the popularity of Paine's view intensified throughout America, Deism's demise was both swift and foreordained. Among its faults, the fledgling philosophy bore no creed, claimed no organizational support and eschewed mystery and mythology. As a bare-boned ideology it depended almost entirely upon reason, so it suffered from an inability to take advantage of enormous powers delegated to churches from long-standing traditions. Deists seemed unable to perceive a reality that all of us want so much to believe: they had no saviors, no martyrs. Joseph would eventually resurrect, redirect and rename Paine's rational theology, but then correct deism's errors by adding in each missing element so necessary to its survival.

Joseph found Tom Paine's reasoned arguments and propagandizing inspirational, yet Paine's style lacked all the luster of literary genius, and could not have served to guide Joseph in the proper intellectual artillery needed to produce a work of such profound depth. Although Joseph's generous wit and scorching cynicism were innate, we'll need to look elsewhere to derive suggestions for planting his philosophical views alongside the parody and myth in his Book of Mormon. Inasmuch as we've already begun recognizing his incorporation of symbol names to orient readers, perhaps we can refer to them as we root out the inspiration of his more artistic accomplishments as author.

Joseph's probable resource and model was the most popular French satirist of the eighteenth century, Francois-Marie Arouet (1694-1778), who, during his stay at the Bastille, gained a new view of himself, adopted his colorful new name, Voltaire, and began forming ideas for persuading society to look more clearly at itself. Voltaire, by the way, shared Tom Paine's theological views: both were Deists.

Quite possibly, one of Joseph's early companions in Palmyra's debate society introduced him to Voltaire's witty novella, *Candide*, for it serves as a transparent model for his literary production. Like *Candide*, the Book of Mormon takes the form of a philosophical tale that enabled Joseph to say dangerous things from a safe distance. As did Voltaire, Joseph could trick his light-minded readers into thinking by polarizing and exaggerating both sides of a fictional conflict.

Both men unmercifully criticized current religious notions while promoting empiricism, the experimental method of determining truth. Unlike Voltaire, Joseph brought his book out as a factual, though ancient, historical account, partly to ply the experiment he hoped would eventually destroy the passivity that allows unreasoned thinking to develop an appearance of consensus. The two men held enough in common to suggest that Joseph admired Voltaire, perhaps using him as a role model:

- Both received their father's name.
- Each had a religious upbringing, beginning as believers, against which they later rebelled. Each expressed anti-ecclesiastical enmity.
- Each man suffered a mob-beating, prison and exile.
- Though each dabbled briefly at law, neither took legal practice seriously.[29]
- Both were accused of unscrupulous methods of money-making.
- Each has been perceived as a womanizer.
- Both men exhibited tireless energy.

- Both became harsh critics of excessive powers within the state and in society.
- They used scathing public sarcasm against opponents.
- Each chose a mysterious nickname for himself (Voltaire, Gazelem).
- Upon publication, each denied authorship of their most highly esteemed work of literature (*Candide*, *Book of Mormon*).
- Both men participated in the Freemasonry movement.
- Both defended the cause of others who had been oppressed by systems against which they felt they were at war.[30]
- Each of them utilized a theatrical format as well as prose to create dramatic, tragic works. Both men employed their wit to become noted controversialists in their respective ages.
- Each man, once dead and buried, was later exhumed.

Probably of even greater significance within our present study, Voltaire initiated Joseph's interest for powerfully visual character symbol names that assisted in orienting readers towards a correct understanding of his literature.

Voltaire's wit and use of symbol name provide key elements for linking the two skeptics. Further, note also how one may conceptually sketch Joseph's book and Voltaire's *Candide* alike, if only briefly and in general terms: A young believer (Candide/Nephi, each to an extent representing his author-creator)[31] murdered a local Jewish religious figure (Don Issachar/Laban), then fled the Old World for South America. From beginning to end we find melodramatic confrontations between various characters, religious wars and other absurd situations used in attempts to induce readers to question their closely held philosophical and religious notions, especially the naive yet prevalent assumption that the virtuous are preserved and prospered through heaven's favor. Each book's ending demonstrates a satisfactory solution—with Candide tending his garden and Lamanites gaining ascendancy over the misdirected, intolerant Nephite tribe.

Then, as he had done while recognizing Tom Paine's considerable contribution to his higher education, Joseph presented terse but distinctive kudos to Voltaire, the great French *philosophe*. He chose a pivotal character, Jacob, to close out his portion of the Book of Mormon with a most unexpected farewell to his readers: "Brethren, *adieu.*"[32] Mormon apologists have never been able to satisfactorily explain why Joseph had Jacob use the French salutation to sign off. Surely no better purpose will serve for his having so oddly translated supposed Reformed Egyptian into French, rather than the King James English he had been using throughout his book.

One possible reason why he, rather than Nephi, Alma or Mormon, became the one chosen to write "adieu" is that Jacob's name more closely represents the essential Voltaire, especially dissatisfactions he shared with Joseph against a whole world still in need of radical reform and drastic social redistributions. During the late 18th century, in Versailles, prior to the French Revolution, a society of political radicals formed; they were known as "Jacobins." By Joseph's day Jacobin (and Jacobinism) had come to be applied popularly to all promulgators of extreme political opinions.[33] Could Jacob have been one further affirmation Joseph presented to acknowledge *the* Frenchman who supplanted European complacency and who rightly deserves credit for igniting the French revolution? *Oui?*

CHAPTER 11

Samuel, Jacob and Joseph: How Team Players Engineered the Great Media Coup

"There's only way to eat an elephant…one bite at a time." (Proverb)

When viewing his book merely through a *single channel* mode, readers might easily note a sparse sense of humanity in Joseph's characterizations. As the author of a didactic fictional work, Joseph entertained specific objectives that weren't served by superfluous or tangential flourishes of florid prose, so players in his drama were pared down somewhat, almost like stick figures in a work of art. Consequently, the author's message lacks dimension, detail and intimacy: something's missing. A *dual channel* interpretation offers useful explanations of what all that emptiness accomplishes. His characters are primarily symbols rather than whole persons, and that's why description has been shorted. Its content becomes much more substantive when one encounters the hidden potential of its symbols. We've already seen this kind of economy in Joseph's treatment of Nephi, Lehi, Sariah, Laman, Lemuel and Laban.

The younger three of Nephi's brothers, Sam, Jacob and Joseph, obtained their roles as place holders because they don't function as characters in the story so much as for filling in three remaining slots necessary for registering the author's younger brothers—Samuel, William and Don Carlos. Having said that, and even while their silence is quite evident, one needn't necessarily imply that Joseph wasted any of their symbolic potential—he multiplied it by selecting three exquisite names for them. Joseph's objectives required building reservoirs of influence among readers. As example, Joseph gave Sam his position as one of Nephi's older but friendlier brothers, perhaps only to locate Nephi into [Joseph's] position as fourth child in Lehi and Sariah's family. The meaning of Sam's name adds little to assist our search for further substance. In Hebrew, Samuel signifies "heard of God." If any clue has been intended, no immediate organic connection with Joseph seems obvious.

Lucy's extensive genealogical record doesn't produce any striking probabilities, despite the fact that no other name achieved so great a prominence within the Smith family. Joseph had an uncle, a great-uncle, a great-grandfather and a great-great-grandfather—all named Samuel Smith. If he intended commemorating any of them, the likeliest candidate would have been his earliest American ancestor, born in Topsfield, Massachusetts in 1666. Joseph also had a younger brother, Samuel Harrison Smith, who became the church's third baptized member, then traveled hundreds of miles while distributing copies of the first edition Book of Mormon. Today he is often regarded as Mormonism's first missionary. As noteworthy as each of those Smith relatives might have been, Joseph couldn't promote *his* cause by memorializing any of them.

An entirely unrelated Samuel produced the strongest impression upon the young prophet. The biblical Samuel, son of Elkanah, an Ephraimite and native of Ramah, exemplified elements that Joseph may have chosen as his model.[1] Samuel is sometimes referred to as the "boy prophet." We might think of Joseph as another boy-prophet, for he claimed to have had his first vision of God prior to turning fifteen. Likewise, Joseph insisted on referring to himself as seer, a title borrowed from Samuel. Until the Greek term for prophets (*prophetes*) became accepted, Israelites had always referred to their oracles as "seers."[2] Joseph applied the caption to himself, thus adding some glitz to his credentials and lifting his credibility.

The biblical Samuel produced miracles, subdued Philistines, became a judge and ruler in Israel and an activist who helped bring order during his nation's formative years. Although these same ideals inspired Joseph his plan was to increase influence for himself and his new system of religion, and that's where Samuel contributed an opportunity for gaining advantage. Although the biblical Samuel became both a religious and political figure among the Jews, he committed a couple of prominent blunders by sharing power with his two sons, Joel and Abiah. When their corruption of bribe-taking and perverted judgment became intolerably pervasive, the Jewish elders demanded that Samuel reform the nation. Specifically, they had him terminate the rule of judges by installing a monarch to rule Israel.

While that move may have helped consolidate the desert tribes and merge them into a more modern state, it also made the new nation more closely resemble its heathen neighbors: "And the Lord said unto Samuel, Hearken unto the voice of the people in all that they say unto thee: for they have not rejected thee, but they have rejected me, that I should not reign over them."[3] So instructed, Samuel moved forward, anointing Saul. King David's kingdom followed Saul's, and his was followed by Solomon's. Nevertheless, the nation of Israel soon divided into two parts. The kingdom seemed doomed, lasting only 254 years. How would Joseph respond to that lesson of history?

Returning to the mid-1820s, Joseph enjoyed America's enlightened age of freedom. He reflected a current view of man's equality by ostensibly introducing it in a most rudimentary form among ancient Nephites. Showing typical American opposition to Great Britain's government, rule by kings, Joseph *revoked* the command wherein the Bible prophet Samuel introduced a monarchy. If it took no inspired seer to recognize recent advances in political science, at least Joseph should be given credit for perceiving the propaganda advantage he'd reap by lining up his Nephites behind the world's earliest successful experiment in *representative* democracy. To accomplish his move Joseph had his fictional character, King Mosiah, borrow a distinctive phrase from the Bible's Samuel. Rarer than any monarch you'll meet, Mosiah determined that he, too, needed to transform corruptible government into an enlightened system that would appeal to the people. In so doing he advised his subjects to no longer follow rule by kings. Thus he *reversed* Samuel's error:

> Therefore, choose you by the voice of this people, judges, that ye may be judged according to the laws which have been given you by our fathers [...] which were given them by the hand of the Lord.[4]

The "voice of the people" shows itself as a cameo pulled out of the First Book of Samuel, pointing directly to the earlier religio-political *snafu*, while at the same time proposing a style of government paralleling America's modern democracy. Among Nephites, their designated chief judge functioned simultaneously as governor and legislator, thereby *symbolizing* an entire gamut of America's governmental style. Today's Mormons view the American Constitution as having been inspired by God, so readers who are able to envision the book being composed during modern times will realize that Joseph expressly annulled Samuel's politics in order to amass a popular constituency by way of the enthusiastic nationalism being embraced by his American audience.

If ancient Nephite prophets could produce such wisdom prior to any civilization elsewhere, what other wonderful advancements might Joseph's scriptures suggest? He wanted to make his religion responsive to all the deepest impulses capable of driving believers closer to his way of thinking, and that may assist in explaining why today's Mormons are noted for their devotion to God, family and country—all are known essentials for helping to congeal and bind one's loyalties.

With a Name Like Joseph

Although Lehi's youngest son has an almost insignificant part in the Nephite saga, he's been allotted one of its more portentous names—Joseph. Its origins are Hebrew, meaning "increase," or "adding," easily suggesting the modern seer's ability to imaginatively fabricate scripture. More likely, might it describe his propensity for engaging in self-serving conflicts of interest by adding to his own stature throughout his book? Finding a name like Joseph at this still-formative stage of his story must necessarily throw the spotlight onto its author, and he soon parlayed the seeming coincidence into a media consultant's dream of self-promotion. Anyone bearing a biblical name of such prominence might easily understand how Joseph strongly identified with *Joseph*, the famously favored son of Jacob, the ancient patriarch whom God re-named Israel. With such a name as Joseph, any of us might be inclined to dream about possibilities of destiny on the rise (here, to reduce the confusion, italics will be used to designate *Joseph* of Egypt).

After *Joseph* of Egypt turned seventeen, his brothers, acting together, placed his life into grave danger. His conceit so angered them that they were ready to kill him until Reuben proposed to the others that they should toss him into a deep pit. Then Judah suggested selling him as a slave, conspiring with his brothers to deceive their father into thinking *Joseph* had been devoured by an animal. His brothers were piqued with jealousy over the favor Jacob had shown for *Joseph*—sewing him a gorgeous, regal tunic with many colors. Without much consideration for their feelings, young *Joseph* had rather foolishly boasted to them of his dream, interpreted to suggest he would someday become their superior.[5]

As is normal with any successful legend, *Joseph* triumphed in the end, helping to deliver his family from the severe famine that swept throughout all Egypt and Palestine. Finally, after reuniting with his twelve sons, Jacob bestowed blessings upon each of them, the two most promising being those pronounced for Judah and *Joseph*.[6] The kingdom of Judah, of course, outlasted that of Israel. From Judah's name we derive the generic words: Judaism, Jew, Jewish. But what ever happened to fulfill the fabulous blessing on *Joseph's* head?

From the Bible:

22. *Joseph* is a fruitful bough, even a fruitful bough by a well; whose branches run over the wall:

23. The archers have sorely grieved him, and shot at him, and hated him:

24. But his bow abode in strength, the arms of his hands were made strong by the hands of the mighty God of Jacob; (from thence is the shepherd, the stone of Israel:)

25. Even by the God of thy father, who shall help thee; by the Almighty, who shall bless thee with the blessings above, blessings of the deep that lieth under, blessings of the breasts, and of the womb:

26. The blessings of thy father have prevailed above the blessings of my progenitors unto the utmost bound of the everlasting hills: they shall be on the head of *Joseph*, and on the crown of the head of him that was separate from his brethren.[7]

Realize All Your Dreams, Line upon Line

It was not Judah, but *Joseph* and his two sons, Ephraim and Manasseh, who inherited the birthright among Israel's twelve sons.[8] Moses, too, promised much more abundantly to the descendants of *Joseph* than to Jacob's remaining boys.[9] But where is the record of *Joseph's* progeny, a flourishing multitude of mighty, durable *Josephites*? How did his "branches run over the wall [...] unto the utmost bound of the everlasting hills"?

Even in his youth our modern day Joseph had been grappling with the Bible so intently that he began uncovering quite a number of gaps in its story. Our world changed on the day he began engaging his imaginative mind to fill in some of those blank spaces. One of those glaring deficiencies impressed him as offering particularly rich potential—its neglect in showing fulfillment of Jacob's blessing to *Joseph's* posterity. Because the Bible record never conspicuously publicized the blessing's implementation, young Joseph seized the golden opportunity to *increase* his own reputation with it. While savvy enough to realize that he couldn't accomplish glorification through one great narcissistic leap, he demonstrated his genius for effective propaganda by taking smaller step-by-step maneuvers, thus gathering up the lost glory that *Joseph* never saw.

To effectively link his own myth with that of the Bible, Joseph chose to employ a roundabout, bit-by-bit, course for conveying a crucial point. While his major objective required that he land into a central spotlighted position, he understood that stealthy tactics would diminish liabilities from over-exposing himself. Joseph carried his rushing game forward in effective segments, using brief but constant bursts of energy. Try recalling Joseph's strange behavior, his manipulations and the strategic maneuvers he improvised during the Zion's Camp excursion. Good propaganda fiction can be similarly used to sway readers, so it will be essential to keep both eyes open and mind alert as we proceed.

Joseph quite openly identified his strategic ploy as the "line upon line" method, taking his cue from a passage in Isaiah. Quite seriously, however, Isaiah's original intent was to warn *against* the very tactic Joseph chose to engage:

From the Bible:

> But the word of the Lord was unto them [the unfaithful] precept upon precept [...] line upon line; here a little and there a little; that they might go, and fall backward, and be broken, and snared, and taken.[10]

Because Isaiah's words warn us to beware, Joseph had to recast them to infuse a less threatening, more seductive tone. He re-wrote it so—

> From the Book of Mormon:
> I will give unto the children of men line upon line, precept upon precept, here a little and there a little; and blessed are those who hearken unto my precepts [...].[11]

There. Now readers should feel less threatened as they continue. Except that, with defenses relaxed, many of them cannot anticipate how they'd be stepping into something of a psychological tournament. Joseph met Isaiah's artistic challenge by magnifying his stature one small segment at a time, then repeating the same strategy over and over to achieve a psychological coup. The following shows one example of how he engineered the process to give himself an advantage.

Step One: Joseph appointed Nephi to be his earliest *alter ego*. While introducing himself, Nephi simply referred to having learned "the language of the Egyptians," thus establishing a weak bond between himself and *Joseph* of Egypt.[12] Joseph could then join hands with the two of them by telling us that he, like Nephi, had been "born of goodly parents."[13] By 1835, supposedly, he also began translating hieroglyphics from ancient Egyptian papyri.

Step Two: Joseph made the bond between *Joseph* of Egypt and Nephi much stronger by introducing a cameo adapted from the Genesis account: "And inasmuch as thou shalt keep my commandments, thou shalt be made a ruler and a teacher over thy brethren."[14] As a newly proclaimed prophet, Joseph displayed enough of his personable skill and persuasive manners so that each of his seven siblings followed his religious lead; he literally became their ruler and teacher.

Joseph bolstered Nephi's parallel relationship with *Joseph of Egypt* by having him boast in the most conceited fashion concerning his authority, supernatural power and consecrated stature—causing Laman and Lemuel to became so wrathful that they conspired to dump him into the ocean.[15] By now readers may perceive Joseph's strategy materializing. For the time being, Nephi serves as Joseph's representative character. It is really he, not Nephi, who is being prepped to star in the big production. Joseph almost imperceptibly begins turning the spotlight towards himself.

Step Three: Nephi and his brothers had returned from Jerusalem, having murdered Laban in order to obtain their coveted prize—the brass plates. Shortly thereafter, among their contents, Lehi discovered his own family genealogy, "[...] wherefore he knew that he was a descendant of *Joseph*; yea, even that *Joseph* who was the son of Jacob, who was sold into Egypt."[16] Consequently, Nephites could lay claim to *Josephite* heritage.

Step Four: Joseph made an unanticipated allusion to the coveted blessing received by *Joseph*: "[…] his bow abode in strength […]." However, quite to the contrary, just when faced with another opportunity for marking Nephi's heroism, "[…] as I Nephi, went forth to slay food, behold, I did break my bow, which was made of fine steel […].[17] Because, most amazingly, Nephi's *steel* bow failed, could his reversal of fortune have called attention to some omission in Israel's promise? Did Nephi's broken bow signal God's failure to honor the great blessing given by old Jacob, the acknowledged patriarch of the Lord's chosen people? Was Nephi being used to emphasize something even more elemental—a flaw in our concept of God's omnipotence? His Omniscience? Possibly in God's existence?

Joseph must have designed Nephi's broken bow incident specifically as a reminder of how Jacob's blessing on *Joseph's* posterity failed the test of reasonable expectations. Could it also serve as his forewarning that this version of *Josephite* history would include a load of parody designed to decry, flaunt and disparage biblical ignorance and error?

Step Five: No single character could serve all of Joseph's literary needs without readily giving away his game, however, the fiction format offers as large a gallery of players as anybody might need. An entire dynasty of talented cast members can be used to express one's innermost ambitions and aspirations. Joseph finally began pushing in that direction as Lehi addressed his own last-born, whose name also just happened to be Joseph. His fictional namesake served no greater function than calling the reader's attention to his name, for the road to glory can hardly be won by proxies. Could even a giant Nephite fill the spotlight as graciously, as flamboyantly as a humble *little* Joseph? Lehi told him,

> 3. And now, Joseph, my last born, […].
> 4. I am a descendant of *Joseph* who was carried away captive into Egypt. And great were the covenants of the Lord which he made unto *Joseph*.
> 5. Wherefore, *Joseph* truly saw our day. And he obtained a promise of the Lord, that out of the fruit of his loins the Lord God would raise up a righteous branch unto the house of Israel; not the Messiah, but a branch which was to be broken off, nevertheless, to be remembered in the covenants of the Lord that the Messiah should be made manifest unto them in the latter days, in the spirit of power […].[18]

Without question Lehi has just made reference to the Bible blessing, never fulfilled, that Jacob pronounced upon the head of his favored son *Joseph*. But just as quickly, Lehi stepped off into a new direction, one that is completely unsubstantiated and unauthorized by anything found in the biblical account of *Joseph*. Where would he go with this new thread of thought? Is his reference to a latter-day Messiah speaking of Jesus? Can't be—Lehi said, "*not* the Messiah," but a *separate* branch.

Onward to Glory—with Help from Two Friends

Our task is to determine if Joseph safely moved his foot across the goal line into position as a *latter day* Messiah, which is where Lehi seems to be leading. No unkindness should be implied from noting the fact that Joseph would occasionally drop hints of his special position within the spiritual world. At an entry in church history for March, 1843, he simply inserted a brief cameo of words spoken by Jesus, "Virtue went out of me [...]."[19] Elsewhere he set himself up as the *de facto* savior of his people: "I will take you into heaven as my back load."[20] His boast far outdistanced any promise made by Jesus.

Within his book Joseph tried establishing himself as a chosen personage identified within ancient prophecy. That is one of the reasons his followers still reverence him so highly by maintaining hymns such as "Praise to the Man," sung in his memory. In his course of self-promotion he became so persistent and persuasive that a prominent LDS lecturer has recently begun suggesting how ancient traditions supported, not one, but *two* messianic figures, and Joseph qualified as one of them.[21] The popular speaker didn't gather his notions from reading tea leaves but only after accumulating an assortment of clues registering a remarkably close fit—all of them initiated by Joseph.

Step Six: To further that illusion of his sacred persona, Joseph arranged a way to have Moses testify of him using a proven modus—alteration of a biblical passage. The *original* declaration from Deuteronomy informs us, "The Lord thy God will raise up unto thee a prophet from the midst of thee, of thy brethren, like unto me; unto him ye shall hearken."[22] In the New Testament book of Acts those words are again quoted, but with an added assurance that Jesus fulfilled a role as the prophet foretold by Moses.[23]

Joseph, bringing that earlier passage from Deuteronomy into the Book of Mormon, still attributed to Moses, made changes to it that hardly seem substantial:

A prophet shall the Lord your God raise up unto you, like unto me; him shall ye hear in all things whatsoever he shall say unto you. And it shall come to pass that all those who will not hear that prophet shall be cut off from among the people."[24]

For a moment, Nephi the writer seemed to be conforming with Christian expectations by adding, "[...] this prophet of whom Moses spake was the Holy One of Israel; wherefore, he shall execute judgment in righteousness."[25] So far the only idea readers are given looks to all the world as if it were an honest, genuine prophetic testament of Jesus. Indeed, the identity of Jesus eventually received confirmation as that promised prophet.[26]

Step Seven: However, within three chapters following that messianic affirmation, Joseph accomplished a grand switcheroo by fabricating a *new* prediction that transposed the words of Moses to make them appear as if they came from the mouth of *Joseph* of Egypt. This time Mr. Smith had the passage testify of himself:

> 6. For *Joseph* truly testified, saying: A seer shall the Lord my God raise up, who shall be a choice seer unto the fruit of my loins.
> 9. [...] And he shall be great like unto Moses [...].
> 10. And Moses will I raise up to deliver thy people out of the land of Egypt.
> 11. But a seer will I raise up out of the fruit of thy loins; and unto him will I give power to bring forth my word [...].
> 15. And his name shall be called after me [*Joseph*]; and it shall be after the name of his father [i.e., Joseph Smith, Sr.]. And he shall be like unto me [*Joseph*]; for the thing, which the Lord shall bring forth by his hand, by the power of the Lord shall bring my people unto salvation.[27]

What good are one's friends if they can't insure one's glory? And while we're at it, let's not bypass the amusing fact that as soon as *Joseph* of Egypt was made to prophesy of Joseph, saying he would be "great like unto Moses," he promptly remembered to cover a very conspicuous void by amending his prophecy to foretell the future advent of Moses, born hundreds of years following *Joseph*. After creatively rearranging a famous Bible passage to get *Joseph* of Egypt to make reference to the latter day prophet, Joseph must have sensed how gauche it would have been to refer to himself too directly within his book, and therefore limited the prophecy to his *first* name only. Properly framed, riddles suggest the correct answer, but cannot give them away. Mormons accept the prophecy as valid.

Joseph's propaganda technique is recognized as a self-sell intended to underwrite the unwitting reader's investment in the intellectual process.[28] However, and despite such bold prompts, Joseph's awkward intrigue leaves *most* readers uninspired. The passage Joseph attributed to *Joseph* is usually among the signal objections religious investigators recognize; it becomes their cause for protest, leading many to resist all other attractive enticements of church membership. That prophetic text, the boldest Joseph ever made to glorify himself, arrives with sufficient glare demanding that it become the single entry the church had to include under his name in the index, despite what eventually becomes too obvious: the book is largely autobiographical and self-serving.

Jacob, the Stumblingblock

Nephi's two younger brothers, Jacob and Joseph, were born in the wilderness following Lehi's departure from Jerusalem. Forthright but just as subtle as his brothers, Jacob inserted a sly confession that his words weren't really true:

> 40. O, my beloved brethren, give ear to my words. Remember the greatness of the Holy One of Israel. Do not say that I have spoken hard things against you; for if ye do, ye will revile against the truth; for I have spoken the words of your Maker. I know that the words of truth are hard against all uncleanness; but the righteous fear them not, for they love the truth and are not shaken.[29]

Sound reasoning assures us that *if* the words of truth are hard, and Jacob pleads that he has *not* spoken hard things, it must be the case that he hasn't spoken truth. Could Jacob's double-talking warn us against something duplicitous regarding his contribution to the book?

An earlier reference to his name suggested one possible component of Jacob's symbolic role, the radical-revolutionary (Jacobinism) that we might presume introduced Joseph's ambition for change. Beyond that, the name Jacob is Hebrew, meaning "heel catcher" or "supplanter," in the sense of causing someone to trip and fall, and that appears to add a catalytic boost to the symbol's force; revolution and overthrow go hand in hand. Jacob's name draws its reference from the Bible's chief patriarch, whose name was changed to Israel. In the Bible, Jacob proposed a shady agreement for taking away the birthright from his older twin brother,

Esau, then practiced deceit while securing his blessing from their father Isaac—thus Jacob superseded (supplanted) Esau. Despite (or because of) those peccadilloes, Jacob retained sufficient favor to earn himself a role as the highly honored patriarch over a family of twelve memorable sons, including Judah and Joseph. But that's Bible history.

Within context of Book of Mormon literary symbols, concepts of tripping and supplanting have genuine significance. One single notoriously ambiguous verse in the book of Jacob, for instance, launched the most severe schism in modern LDS history. In it, Jacob condemned polygamy as an ungodly abomination—well, almost. Regardless, in 1843 Joseph produced a revelation that re-instituted the ancient perversion of marriage within a modern cosmopolitan setting along the American frontier. By doing so he not only instigated his own martyrdom, but also precipitated the historic LDS exodus from the eastern half of the American continent. His strategy, while appearing self-defeating, applied crucial elements in Joseph's revolutionary scheme for trapping followers, exactly as Jacob's name symbol suggests. My attempt at explaining what he was up to constitutes the final third of this book.

Speaking of Joseph's line-upon-line technique for promoting his cause, he also used Jacob's book to outline the program he planned to use to build his empire of believers. In order to transmit the strategic plan of his conquest, he had Jacob rescue a lost literary gem written by an old Jewish prophet bearing the unlikely name of Zenos. To explain why Zenos' book never made it into your modern Bible, the Book of Mormon tells us that the Holy Book suffered corruption in ancient times by wicked priests who clandestinely purged much that had once been considered precious and most delightful in the eyes of God—particularly when they foretold anything about Joseph's latter day restoration.[30]

As understood by the modern Mormon reader, Zenos had anciently written a wonderful allegory expressing the history of God's relationship with his chosen people throughout the world. That story, having been anciently dislodged from the heart of the *Old* Testament, needed resuscitation, and Nephi's brother Jacob fittingly took on the task. He located the lost allegory within Laban's brass plates, then painstakingly engraved the exact words of Zenos onto the gold plates. Joseph, inspired by hopes of success in winning his contest for souls, carried it over into the Book of Mormon. Once again in its complete form, it is referred to as the Allegory of the Tame and Wild Olive Vineyard.

CHAPTER 12

Zenos' Wild Allegory

"My wellbeloved hath a vineyard in a very fruitful hill."
(Isaiah 5:1)

Mormons relish a story from the Book of Jacob, despite its acknowledged complexity, which prophetically reveals the Lord's work of manifesting His gospel, first in ancient times, but again in His elaborate restoration of its fullness during the latter days. It is known simply as *The Allegory of Zenos,* or sometimes *The Allegory of the Tame and Wild Olive Tree.* Although it consumes but one chapter in the Book of Jacob (chapter 5), it is the longest single chapter of scripture to be found in either the Book of Mormon or the Bible. The fact that Zenos' fable has been preserved in the Book of Mormon ought to demonstrate God's deep concern, his wisdom and foresight on our behalf, although nowhere in it does the story condescend to flatter Him so. In order to discover another work of such cleverness, deception, truth, irreverence and piquant humor, you may search an entire lifetime.

Haven't We Met the Zenos Brothers Somewhere Else?

As with various elements within Joseph's book, introduction to Zenos is presented line upon line, first by Nephi, as if writing nonchalantly about any other well-known, genuine Old Testament prophet. The ancient works of Zenos had been carefully preserved, but only upon the sacred plates of brass that Nephi nabbed on the way out of Jerusalem in his bid to subdue a New World.[1] The many wise sayings and inspired stories Zenos wrote no longer grace the modern Bible, supposedly due to machinations of ancient priests who, while compiling and editing the Holy Scriptures, managed to corrupt it by stripping away nearly every prophetic reference to Joseph and his latter day restoration movement,

> [...] for behold, they have taken away from the gospel of the Lamb many parts which are plain and most precious [...]. And this have they done that they might pervert the right ways of the Lord, that they might blind the eyes and harden the hearts of the children of men.[2]

The name Zenos may sound vaguely familiar because of its popularity during ancient times, but in *Greece*, not Palestine. Both Zeno of Elea and Zeno of Citium were Greek philosophers whose works Joseph may have studied.[3] Zeno of Elea even lived during the fifth century, BCE, roughly parallel to the time period proposed as current with Jacob's record. His name is associated with complex philosophical paradoxes that typically question trust in our senses. Zeno is credited with inventing dialectic, or discourse reasoning. By coincidence, perhaps, the Book of Mormon abounds with examples of dialectics, the question-and-answer method of searching for truth.[4] Clearly, Zeno could have been an inspiration to Joseph Smith, for he would likewise have us question assumptions, truths and sure knowledge.

Another Zeno, of Citium, taught in Athens during the early third century, BCE. He is known as the founder of Stoicism, having taught principles of ethics, self-control and moral obligation. Either Zeno, or perhaps both, were being honored by Joseph in recognition for their enlightened reasoning and gifts for elevating the art of philosophical inquiry.

Initially the Book of Mormon Zenos shows up as a crude, self-centered rustic. Introducing himself, he writes, "Hearken, O ye house of Israel, and hear the words of me, a prophet of the Lord."[5] Perhaps such a light touch of humor requires a staged dramatization to visualize it—try imagining *Yosemite Sam* dressed in toga and olive wreath, acting the part of a circus sideshow barker. The Bible's Jeremiah can be used as a benchmark for modeling less arrogance: "Hear ye the word which the Lord speaketh unto you, O house of Israel"[6]

The 76 verse allegory of Zenos has cameos in it that imitate familiar segments from both Old and New Testaments, including Isaiah 5:1-7; Matthew 3:10; Luke 13:6-9 and Romans 11:16-27. All four Bible cameos, full length, placed end to end, wouldn't add up to a third the length of the allegory Joseph attributed to Zenos, allowing plenty of room for messages that may stray beyond biblical boundaries. With sufficient study it should become evident that Joseph crafted his allegory with immense attention to detail, for it is a perfect and clever work of art that omits nothing.

The allegory soon spirals into absurdness, and that is probably as much the intended point. Zenos' tale becomes just as cohesive and fitting if we accept his allegory as a three-act comedy loaded with satire that simultaneously critiques theology, insults God and draws an accurate blueprint of Joseph's plan of attack on the religious world. While today's Mormons are busily concerned about what is happening out beyond the "nethermost part of the vineyard," and of successes or failures of its tame and wild grafted olive branches, behind the scenes you'll want to keep track of subtle exchanges made between the Lord and his Servant.

Casting Call for Three: Vineyard, Servant, Master

The vineyard supposedly represents the world, so is spread far and near, with a "nethermost part" that is upstage, towards the rear, symbolizing the New World. Don't be thrown off track by an unexpected figure of an olive tree in a vineyard: both are authentic symbols depicting Old and New Testament themes. The Lord of the vineyard, its Master, presumably represents Jesus Christ but shows up even more appropriately if you begin thinking of him in his more ancient role as God the Father. Since his favored olive tree is growing quite old, we suspect that he, too, has been around a good while. He appears to have grown a bit sluggish in mental agility, occasionally tending to lose temper. This Master shows himself to be not as omniscient as we might have hoped, for he can never figure out what has been hampering the production of good fruit on his trees. Those trees are constantly resisting desired tameness by their wild nature, producing corrupted fruit. The Master's impetuous response to their evil tendencies is to order the trees cut down and cast into the fire,[7] rather like the Queen of Hearts might have done in *Alice In Wonderland*.

The Master's Servant suggests someone's identity as God's prophet, for he is generally out working in the vineyard. He seems more capable, in-control, less stressed, more understanding and even-tempered than the Lord. In fact he tries advising the Lord wisely on how to manage His affairs. When the Lord becomes flustered, it is his Servant who quickly places a finger on the root cause of the vineyard's problems. The servant's role unquestionably portrays Joseph, for that character reflects his own superior intellectual talents and leadership skill for managing the Lord's business.

The olive trees in the vineyard are of two kinds, tame and wild. The Lord, noting that his favorite tame olive tree (i.e., Judaism) began to age and decay, nourished it back to health long enough to produce young and tender branches (representing Nephites, Mulekites and other migrations of Israelites away from the land of Palestine). Those young (Nephite) branches were cut away and taken by the Lord for planting into the nethermost part of the vineyard (i.e., the New World), where they produced both tame and wild fruit (i.e., Nephites and Lamanites, respectively).[8] Although the Lord commanded his servant to pluck off and destroy all branches producing wild fruit, the wise servant suggested they try nourishing the tree a little longer.[9]

Meanwhile, decadent branches of the old tree (Judaism, Old World) had been slashed and thrown into the fire.[10] The Lord replaced those younger grafted branches with others that the Lord had his servant prune from a wild olive tree (i.e., Gentiles who were brought into the gospel via Christianity).[11] New branches were grafted into the old tree where they could take nourishment from its roots and in turn produce abundant, strong fruit.[12]

When the Master and Servant made their third visit through the vineyard, things were found in a state of total corruption. The young branches that had been grafted into the old tree had produced only inedible wild fruit, representing the apostate condition of Christianity—both Catholic and Protestant varieties.[13] Continuing their tour they visited the nethermost part of the vineyard only to find that everything there had also become corrupted; both Nephites and Lamanites had failed to produce righteousness.[14] Although the Lord gave up, now resolving to "hew down the trees of the vineyard," His wise Servant patiently cautioned Him to "spare it a little longer."[15] Thereupon the Lord devised a plan both wonderfully absurd and comical in portraying a scene of near chaos and utter confusion. He and his Servant created a religious madhouse by determining a strategy of grafting frenzy. They began exchanging branches from the nethermost part of the vineyard with branches from the original mother tree.

> 55. Wherefore, let us take of the branches of these which I have planted in the nethermost parts of my vineyard, and let us graft them into the tree from whence they came; and let us pluck from the tree those branches whose fruit is most bitter, and graft in the natural branches of the tree in the stead thereof [...].
> 56. And it came to pass that they took from the natural tree which had become wild, and grafted in unto the natural trees, which also had become wild. And they also took of the natural trees which had become wild, and grafted into their mother tree.[16]

Old Wine, New Bottle—New Wine, Old Bottle

What Zenos is describing (and what today's Mormons aren't going to comprehend very easily) is an essential element of Joseph's blueprint for the invention of modern Mormonism: the cross-grafting that takes place in the latter days is different from the earlier propagating done by the vineyard's Master. Initially, he propagated from the old mother tree by rooting its "young and tender branches" in the nethermost parts of the vineyard.[17] However, a new latter-day strategy was adopted to bolster that grafting-in process. In addition to bringing Gentiles into it (Mormonism), the Master's new tactic provided a blending of doctrinal structures that were intended to nourish them.

Conforming to the plan, modern Mormonism has extracted its version of Old Testament priesthoods (Aaronic and Melchizedek). It also features prophets who are said to reveal God's word, along with temples sporting a somewhat vapid adaptation of the ancient "holy of holies." Mormonism has developed its peculiar formula for abstinence that corresponds to Israel's old health laws (their Word of Wisdom: no coffee, tea, alcohol or tobacco) then adds to it regular days for fasting. A corrupted version of Israel's tithing law is enforced, and Mormon teachings also manage to have its members deny and reject their own natural roots as Gentiles, as if attempting outright displacement of Judaism. They've adopted "Zion" as the term best describing themselves, their religious kingdom and the ideal of the Latter-day Saint community. Mormonism likewise brought over Polygamy from the Old Testament. *Old wine, new bottle.*

Next, Mormonism supplements that Judaic mixture with a moderately eccentric form of Christianity: offices of apostles, bishops, teachers and deacons; weekly (Sunday) sacraments; zealous, world-wide missionary proselytizing; baptism, the laying on of hands, and a passion for perfectionism that would have been the very envy of John Calvin. To make our point even more evident, the Book of Mormon pushes far too many features of Christianity backwards into its "Old Testament" segment of time: Jesus Christ, the Virgin Mary, John the Baptist, faith with repentance, baptism and the Holy Ghost—all are too vividly described in the most ancient segment of history where they never legitimately fit. *New wine, old bottle.*

Getting Digged, Pruned and Dunged

Most impudent of all the allegory's images is that of the Master as he falters in his frustrated state of defeated confusion and weakness of mind. As the allegory reaches its climax, the Master asks, "But what could I have done more in my vineyard?" Then he's made to confess in a shrewd *double-entendre*: "I have digged about it, and I have pruned it, and I have dunged it [...]."[18] Getting "digged about" cannot suggest any genuine sense of welcome or comfort—very likely symbolizing the Mormon's persecution complex. Getting pruned must surely refer to feelings of being clipped by church tithes, budget, welfare, the building fund and other levies and offerings. Last, not least, being dunged became Joseph's relatively mild choice of terms used to describe the Master's output of revealed doctrine.

At his wit's end the Lord asked, "Who is it that has corrupted my vineyard?"[19] Readers may feel discomfited after watching God lose both His omniscience and omnipotence in one brief run of ill fortune. The astute Servant, of course, supplies a most insightful analysis of his Master's dilemma: "Is it not the loftiness of thy vineyard [...]?" What the Servant suggests has become one of Mormonism's most exotic—as well as one of its most criticized teachings—Joseph's great man-godmakingequalization scheme, "Have not the branches thereof overcome the roots which are good?"²⁰ His solution would be to make both branch (God) and root (mankind) *equal* in strength.

Two well-chosen symbol names, external to the Zenos allegory, Lehi (*le high* and mighty) and Limhi (limb-high), one a father figure, the other a king, tend to support the idea that Joseph viewed God as one whose stature was overrated and whose fall was overdue. By lopping down man's perceptions of God, Joseph determined that humanity, by maintaining earthbound roots, might begin taking their rightful position in the universe. Joseph tried teaching his people that they could eventually expect exaltation if they progressed inexorably on towards godhood. He would never have been so successful in his work by maintaining God in an awesome, elevated plane, far too distant and intangible, beyond man's common perception. That is why, when devising a new image of god for his people, Joseph enjoined an effective anthropomorphism, creating a being with human form, visible and of flesh and bone. Moreover, his god wasn't so heavily endowed with gray matter, either. Joseph hoped to make his people believe that they could hasten their rise to a higher step in the race between human evolution and man's extinction.

In Its Latter Days, a Fruitful Bough

Wonderfully, the Lord recognized his Servant's wisdom and undertook a positive transformation: "[...] we will trim up the branches thereof," he promised.[21]

> 61. Wherefore, go to, and call servants, that we may labor diligently with our might in the vineyard [...] that I may bring forth again the natural fruit.
> 62. [...] and this is for the last time [...]
> 64. Wherefore, dig about them and prune them, and dung them once more, for the last time [...].[22]

Wisely, Joseph designed remarkable restraint into the plan of his own latter-day task. No work that he accomplished could be expected to sweep away immediately all of the foolish traditions of the world but would require a careful balance throughout its entire course of development. The Master's instructions to the Servant were, therefore, cautious:

65. And as they begin to grow ye shall clear away the branches which bring forth bitter fruit, according to the strength of the good and the size thereof; and ye shall not clear away the bad thereof all at once, lest the roots thereof should be too strong for the graft, and the graft thereof shall perish, and I lose the trees of my vineyard.[23]

Mormonism's "bitter fruit" are those members who become disillusioned or worn down by many confusing teachings and the endless labor necessitated for "retaining a remission of your sins."[24] Joseph's religion was never meant to be any end in itself but a conduit by which the novice could move from point a to point b, *out of Mormonism*, which organization has historically attained one of the highest drop-out rates as well as induction records throughout all of religion. Wild branches were supposed to be cleared away by being dis-fellowshipped or excommunicated, although the Servant was cautioned to use all means to avoid tipping over the entire project too early, "For it grieveth me that I should lose the trees of my vineyard [...]."[25]

Joseph could forecast great success for his plan, for just as those hired servants went about laboring with their might,

72. [...] there began to be the natural fruit again in the vineyard; and [they] began to grow and thrive exceedingly [...]
73. [...] and they did keep the root and the top thereof equal, according to the strength thereof.[26]

Eventually the Lord was happily able to acknowledge how "[...] his vineyard was no more corrupt [...]."[27] Likewise at the conclusion of Joseph's larger allegory, the Book of Mormon, he developed an ending that has to be satisfactory, supplying a useful assist for confirming the symbolic intent of Zenos' allegory of the Wild Olive Vineyard. There, upper branches of zealously ignorant, overly religious, self-righteous, godly Nephites were gradually trimmed away until the vineyard was no more corrupted. It has to be the more honest, natural, down-to-earth and living-in-balance Lamanite brethren who provided the Master with "joy [...] because of the fruit of my vineyard."[28]

Almost at the parable's end the Lord affirmed his own wonderfully productive technique—"[...] for the last time have I nourished my vineyard, and pruned it, and dug about it, and dunged it [...]."[29] Perhaps a "chosen people," spoiled in their self-pride, will always require a little rough handling and chastening before they can fully enjoy the fruits of their labors, "[...] for if they never should have bitter they could not know the sweet."[30] This particular aspect of the teachings of Zenos, suggesting that wisdom comes following the discipline of adversity and affliction, dovetails perfectly with Voltaire's story of Candide. Notice, too, the resolution presented in Candide's search for a practical philosophy. Voltaire's hero and Joseph's Master of the vineyard each found harmony in reaping greater spiritual satisfactions from tending their gardens.

Although our present interpretation is only one way that Zenos' allegory may be rendered meaningful, it is at least as valid as theirs. Since it contains greater sense in identifying the plan of Mormonism in more explicit detail than interpretations maintained within their orthodoxy, I believe that Joseph must have wished it to be understood as represented here. If today's Saints argue how their contrasting view of the allegory has already been ratified by generations of LDS believers, try reminding them of how Mormonism earned its stripes in the beginning—by eschewing dubious traditions. The Book of Mormon comes to you with produce in either hand—you may accept the interpretation best suited to your taste.

CHAPTER 13

Omni: One for All, All in Fun

His book isn't just *about* Joseph as much it *is* Joseph—or at least the closest we may ever approach viewing his inner quality of spirit. However, while many true believers would give anything to acquire a scarf, trinket or artifact from his material possessions, the idea of reading his book in order to know him better escapes their imagination. Luckily its features often witness his "native cheery temperament" and humor.[1] He understood the value of adding some fun to learning and the process of inquiry.

He divided his epic into fifteen sections, or books, each named after one of its reputed writers, although it received a final definitive editing by Mormon. Then, of course, everything Mormon had neatly engraved with his Egyptian-like characters had later to become filtered and processed through Joseph's admittedly difficult, unlearned translation. That course guaranteed reader curiosity as to just how imperfectly Joseph may have transmitted ideas from antiquity and which of its supposed writers might be contributing, editing or abridging. Who owns responsibility if its translation should differ from the original writer's thought inscribed on the (entirely imaginary) gold plates, which, sadly, were taken back by the angel and are no longer available for responsible scholarly research?

Let's see: Lehi's works were abridged by Nephi. Both Lehi's and Jacob's words have been inserted in Second Nephi. Moroni devised the ending chapters for Mormon's chronicle but likewise spiked the Book of Ether with his extensive editorials. The Book of Ether covers a time period spanning numerous generations and an indeterminate number of authors. A couple of Mormon's letters and one of his speeches are found in the Book of Moroni. Helaman wrote Alma's final chapters, and so on. Truly, his book becomes a madhouse unless you first recognize that the author's intent was to take readers along for a great ride. His point might have been that the Bible has likewise undergone enough plastic surgery to turn Frankenstein into a pop star. Forewarned, almost anyone should be able to handle most of its confusion without excessive frustration.

Omni is the name given to one of four very short books (including Enos, Jarom and Words of Mormon), each but one single chapter in length, used as a point of transition between the books of Jacob and Mosiah. Entering this segment we'll note how Nephite history functions as a sort of time pump. So much compression occurs that confusion becomes inevitable as approximately 400 years of transitional history elapses during nine brief pages of text, and the whole suggests a blackout of the news media throughout a period of civil chaos. Readers must assume that Nephites underwent a period of ceaseless Lamanite wars, perhaps a cultural slump, or development so rapid that their historians couldn't keep pace. Its omissions force us into a spree of speculation.

As we proceed through this passage, what little meaning we obtain seems to pivot on the author's affinity for character symbol names as a major vehicle for presenting his novel's message. Throughout literature's long history, apprehending the meaning of symbol names has required readers first to presume an author's fictional mode and allegorical intent, then to attempt anticipating his aim based on reason consistent within the overall story.

While nothing will be lost to us if one or two of our present symbol interpretations should be found unreasonable, also be sure to note that a scant handful of well integrated name symbol specimens would normally suffice to sustain an argument that the Book of Mormon is indeed fiction, rather than historical. Throughout this study approximately four dozen of Joseph's name symbols will have been examined—quite possibly a record in known works of serious fiction. Joseph may have included a string of productive symbol names within Omni's book in order to provide a key or Rosetta Stone to assist readers in their interpretations and thus extract further insight from his work. As those names and their respective concepts assume greater complexity, Joseph's underlying philosophy will gradually rise to the surface, so deciphering these symbols is no incidental diversion. The list of contributors to Omni's relatively small, thirty-verse history includes Omni, Amaron, Chemish, Abinadom and Amaleki; all join together in fabricating its content. The word Omni is Latin for "all," as found in such familiar words as omniscience, omnipotence and omnipresence. Coming from Joseph, "Omni" represents something more than any individual's name: he spent the remainder of his life creating an intricate world that required him to participate as its newest god.

Chemish

The entire contribution Chemish added to sacred writ required no more than one averaged-sized verse to tell us nothing of even minor importance. Then he gave us the slip: "[…] And I make an end"—Poof! He vanished.[2]

Today the *chemise* describes a woman's undergarment, a slip. The word is French for "shirt," although the etymology shows an earlier root, "scort" meaning short.[3] Chemish, then, can be nick-named "Shorty," or "Mr. One-Verse." None of Omni's writers contributed less than Chemish.

Abinadom

Chemish handed the Nephite records over to his son, Abinadom, who nearly doubled the volume of his father's contribution to ancient wisdom literature. Within two verses included as his entire testament, Abinadom boasted, "I […] have taken the lives of many of the Lamanites."[4] His name should be sounded with deeply ominous portent, as "A bin o' doom." Mormons are taught to say it like "A bin a dum."

Amaleki

Amaleki, son of Abinadom, wrote the balance of Omni's diminutive book, nineteen verses, roughly two thirds of its content. Amaleki introduces the newly discovered people of Zarahemla, migrants from

Jerusalem to the New World, concurrent with, but separate from the Nephite hegira. With his report Amaleki also acquaints the reader with an entirely different, even more ancient civilization, the Jaredites—a people whose history will be included later in the Book of Ether.

Among all his introductions Amaleki includes Mosiah, a character who, without apparent benefit of lineage, became appointed as king over the land and people of Zarahemla.[5] Until learning of Mosiah's coronation, readers have been led to assume that the sacred records had always been handed down through the royal house of Nephi. In proposing one interpretive solution to the riddle, we find that Amaleki's symbol name has been composed from three words: A + Male + Ki. Ki is one of several accepted abbreviations for "king," as found in marginal notes referring to the Bible's Book of Kings.[6] Using that as our clue, Amaleki's symbol name hints the presence of an underlying political intrigue suggesting that, although Amaleki originally became heir to the throne (because he's been made keeper of the plates), he failed to ascend due to his youth. Mosiah proceeded to take control over the government, thus illegitimately displacing Amaleki's posterity as future royalty. Readers may sympathize with Amaleki's barely suppressed resentment as he confessed, "Behold, I, Amaleki, was born in the days of Mosiah; and I have *lived* to see his death [...]."[7] Can we view Amaleki as ambitious but frustrated and oozing with bitterness while trying to suggest, *sub rosa*, that Mosiah had usurped his rightful claims to the Nephite kingdom? The entire book tends continually to whisper messages about how men illegitimately assume worldly powers. Joseph's book has passed down a potent political manifesto that has never been given due recognition.

Benjamin

Amaleki continued by introducing Mosiah's son, King Benjamin, unto whom he transferred his cumulative Nephite records. Investigation into Benjamin's symbol meaning will help to demonstrate what a sharp mind Joseph had for penetrating Bible trivia. His reason for including Benjamin among the Book of Mormon genealogy would ordinarily slip by unnoticed, for, after thorough investigation, none of his accomplishments seem to suggest that his name registers pertinent meaning.

To discover what place Benjamin had, first recall that the name comes from one of the 12 ancient patriarchs whose descendants settled in the Holy Land following the Jewish Exodus from Egypt. Benjamin, youngest son of Jacob (Israel) and Rachel, became the only full brother of *Joseph* (of Egypt). At birth his mother named him *Ben-oni* (son of my sorrow), then she died. Jacob changed his son's name to Benjamin.[8]

To determine the simple relevance of Benjamin's place in the Book of Mormon, it is necessary to skip ahead a couple of generations to his grandson, Ammon, and ask one fairly innocuous question--

Q: Was Ammon (II) left or right-handed?

Clues: The Bible tells that at one time the tribe of Benjamin could boast of seven hundred *left-handed* sling throwers who became so expert that none would miss his target by a hair's breadth.[9] What makes that seem unusual is that the name Benjamin means literally, "son of the *right* hand." Joseph treasured such irony and snapped it up.

Later, in the account written by Mosiah, we'll read about Ammon who has been positioned as one of Mosiah's sons, therefore grandson of King Benjamin, making him another "Benjamite."[10] When he traveled on a mission to convert Lamanites, Ammon first volunteered his personal services to the opulently wealthy King Lamoni (i.e., "La money"). During his first day on the job, Ammon had to protect Lamoni's flocks, so he swiftly drew his sling and began flinging stones against a number of surprised Lamanite banditos. Following his brief scuffle, witnesses gave Ammon credit for killing six men with stones from his sling.[11] A world record, Ammon's feat has never come close to being duplicated.

A: Ammon was right-handed, no doubt. Joseph made biblical discrepancies, its contradictories and confusions his issue; his task was to overturn the Bible by employing humor and parody whenever possible. Symbolically, Joseph devised Ammon to compete with and out-gun the Bible's Benjamites as one of his hand-chosen seconds. Remember how it has been suggested that Joseph selected the name Ammon in honor of Amon, the Egyptian God? Joseph once made the staggering boast that, "[...] God is my right hand man."[12] It was a step above his characteristic arrogance, for he attempted peppering his story with riddles, then afterwards providing many essential clues intended to help latter-day readers solve the puzzle.

CHAPTER 14

Mosiah, the Prophet-Savior Combo

*"We don't call a man mad who believes that he eats God,
but we do the one who says he is Jesus Christ." (Helvetius)*

Mosiah (II), born into the upper crust of Nephite society, walked in the ways of his father, Benjamin, and thus, was proclaimed successor to his throne.[1] His name blends the two most lustrous personages within the Bible—one each from the Old and New Testaments: Moses and Messiah. Joseph's strategy was not to extend great honor to either biblical figure so much as to gain recognition as third member in a trio of sacred notables.

Because he's credited as the Nephite lawgiver, Mosiah's character refers to Moses' role in delivering the Ten Commandments.[2] However, conspicuously taking a cue from the Messiah, Mosiah began his reign as king at 30, reportedly the same age as Jesus entered his ministry.[3] Mosiah warned of grave destruction "[...] if [...] this people should fall into transgression."[4] So did Jesus: "It shall be more tolerable for the land of Sodom and Gomorrah in the day of judgment, than for that city."[5] As with Jesus, the Lord promised, through Mosiah, that believers would gain "eternal life."[6]

Joseph Smith developed Mosiah's prophetic aura as a self-portrait/caricature denoting a lawgiver-savior rolled into one. Adopting his "Moses role," Joseph also invented an extensive collection of religious laws. He recorded more than one hundred thirty revelations, now preserved in the church's book of code, *The Doctrine and Covenants*. Faithful Saints seeking to fulfill all righteousness, shunning the very appearance of evil, frequently consult his collection of regulations, as well as an abundance of his aphorisms and anecdotes preserved by numerous associates. To make more obvious his intentions, Joseph later developed a short, imaginative but manifestly spurious work, *Selections from the Book of Moses*. The volume resembles Genesis as little as possible while still suggesting parallel themes. It, too, has become part of the church's four Standard Works and has gained its status alongside the *Bible*, *Book of Mormon* and *Doctrine and Covenants*.

Recognizing Jesus (Messiah) as his success-model, Joseph determined that likelihood for bringing change to the world would improve if he were able to supply followers with evocative, familiar signals that would help perpetuate his memory as a martyr. The looming event became a beacon to him, and he never sincerely tried dodging the one fateful moment he'd scheduled onto his calendar. With fewer than ten days left to live, he told followers, "I do not regard my own life. I am ready to be offered as a sacrifice for this people [...] greater love hath no man than that he should lay down his life for his friends."[7]

His paraphrase of Jesus' words didn't indicate some merely casual relationship but, rather, emphasized mystical, more intimate ties. We find Joseph inventing new ways to press the point closer to his objective—the fixation he developed for enacting a modern atoning sacrifice. Only a month before martyrdom he bathed himself in the role of a savior: "I can go to the cross—I can lay down my life; but don't forsake me. I want the friendship of my brethren."[8] Again, before leaving town on his way to Carthage, he stopped in to say farewell to a number of associates. His parting words, recorded several times before leaving were, "I am going like a lamb to the slaughter." His allusion must be understood as one of the most recognizable messianic verses from Isaiah.[9]

So unusual within a supposed king's record, Mosiah writes a skimpy role in it for himself. Most of the action takes place outside his kingdom, and until its final couple of chapters he only participates as a distant monarch. Also curious for a king, but showing talent held common between himself and Joseph, Mosiah possessed mystical gifts for translating records from unknown, ancient tongues: he's another seer.[10] Even more unique, especially from the seat of *any* nation's government, we note Mosiah's desire to bring about revolutionary, *democratic* change.[11] Who cannot see that Joseph was trying to fingerprint himself to cast a bit more glow over his publicity campaign?

Abinadi, the *Other* Cantankerous Martyr

Appearing at the center of Mosiah's story is the figure of Abinadi, an annoying, nagging prophet who nevertheless succeeded in changing the course of Nephite history. Joseph's setting is critical, for he introduces Abinadi's preaching along lines of discourse more familiar around New England revivals from the early 1800s. Continuing an energetic oratorical style that also characterized Benjamin, Abinadi could be mistaken for one of old New England's hell-fire Protestant ministers.

Abinadi recited the Ten Commandments in full, but almost as soon as the last article of the Decalogue had been spoken, he commented, "[…] ye should keep the law of Moses as yet; but I say unto you that the time shall come when it shall no more be expedient to keep the law of Moses."[12] At this point in history it would have made no sense to attribute "prophetic utterance" to Abinadi's words. More likely, it may be seen as Joseph's recipe for placing "new wine into old bottles," his exaggeration or parody of so-called messianic Old Testament prophesies. Abinadi's audience, circa 148 BCE, might have walked away quite disturbed and confused, for Abinadi's projection of its termination makes those commandments seem the object of a subtle, subversive attack. Perhaps Joseph intended spotlighting a recognized contradictory between Old and New Testaments. Should a house divided stand without challenge?

Jesus supported the Law of Moses, saying,

> Think not that I am come to destroy the law […] I am not come to destroy but to fulfil […]. Till heaven and earth pass, one jot or one tittle shall in no wise pass from the law, till all be fulfilled."[13]

His personal endorsement gave the law his affirmation of inviolability…permanence. Accordingly, unless we somehow proclaim passage of heaven and earth, anyone honoring those particular words of Jesus must yet fall accountable under extensive provisions of the Pentateuch—*according to Jesus.*

Many years afterward, Paul, "the latecomer," traveled among the Jews preaching a distinct reversal in policy, for, "[…] ye also are become dead to the law by the body of Christ,"[14] and, "Christ hath redeemed us from the curse of the law."[15] Of course, while Paul may have encouraged abandoning ceremonial law, he certainly never undermined its ethical impulses or statutes. Abinadi's words omit essential context of the old dispute, and in doing so, casts a small shadow over values preserved within the Ten Commandments. The query isn't to determine whether we should or shouldn't honor the ancient Mosaic codes, or even the Ten Commandments, but only to note how Joseph took effective advantage of his literary pulpit to call to mind many unresolved disputes. He made his seer-service more indispensable by instigating a plethora of issues, begging question after question. Mystery and controversy characterized his entire life's work.

Parody from Head to Foot

Before the people finally made a martyr of him, Abinadi quoted to them an entire chapter (53) from the book of Isaiah, perhaps the most extensive and popular "Messianic" text from the Old Testament.[16] However, during the following chapter Abinadi turned Isaiah's words into a parody by misconstruing all the material that he had just plagiarized. The old goof somehow accomplished the enormous transition from pre-Christian messianic theory, once even too abstract for Jews to perceive it, into a radical obfuscation looking something like Catholic dogma, starting off with some heady confusion about the Father-and-Son:

> […] God himself shall come down among the children of men […] being the Father and the Son—The Father, because he was conceived by the power of God; and the Son, because of the flesh; thus becoming the Father and Son—And they are one God.[17]

To appreciate the absurdity, readers must try placing themselves anywhere in pre-Columbian America, but still within Joseph's chronology for the story, and centuries before Old World Christians permitted peasant beliefs (paganism) to slip into church liturgy as a purely cultural appeasement for early converts. No such Father-Son belief existed in Judaism, nor any of its Christian derivatives, until hundreds of years later, so Abinadi's mention of it would have had to arrive in such a refined form through osmosis.

Caricaturing Abinadi as if a prophet of the Old Testament period, Joseph found occasion for ridiculing expressions rendered obsolete over time. One opportunity for exploiting his Bible parody referred to a familiar passage that displayed exuberant exultation. As originally found in the book of Isaiah, the metaphor of "beautiful feet upon the mountain" seems made to offer distinct honor to those who proclaimed and published the sovereignty of God:

From the Bible:
How beautiful upon the mountain are the feet of him that bringeth good tidings, that publisheth peace; that bringeth good tidings of good, that publisheth salvation; that saith unto Zion, thy God reigneth![18]

Joseph applied the same metaphor within his Book of Mormon, but had Abinadi carry on about those beautiful feet far beyond what we might have expected from someone bearing words of righteous repentance. By the time Abinadi had repeated his fourth mention of beautiful feet, surely the courtesans at [Nephite] King Noah's palace were beginning to suspect him of that delicious pathological obsession, the *foot fetish*:

From the Book of Mormon:
14. And these are they who have published peace, who have brought good tidings of good, who have published salvation; and said unto Zion: Thy God reigneth!
15. And O how beautiful upon the mountains were their feet!
16. And again, how beautiful upon the mountains are the feet of those that are still publishing peace!
17. And again, how beautiful upon the mountains are the feet of those who shall hereafter publish peace, yea, from this time henceforth and forever!
18. And behold, I say unto you, this is not all. For O how beautiful upon the mountains are the feet of him that bringeth good tidings, that is the founder of peace, yea, even the Lord, who has redeemed his people; yea, him who has granted salvation unto his people.[19]

Abinadi: Fiery Prophet, Model Martyr

Of all criticisms leveled against the Book of Mormon, its monumental Bible parody has always been under-represented. One of its more unsettling parodies shows Abinadi, like Jonah, Elijah and other biblical personages, administering a stream of righteously indignant curses against an unrepentant nation.

> 15. [...] many shall suffer [...] the pains of death by fire [...]
> 16. [...] ye shall be afflicted with all manner of diseases because of your iniquities.
> 17. [...] ye shall be smitten on every hand [...] driven and scattered to and fro [...]
> 18. [. . .] ye shall be hunted [. . .] taken by the hand of your enemies[. . .].[20]

That string of stinging curses threaten enough severe physical retribution that it helps deliver meaning to Abinadi's character symbol name: *A bin o' die* [dying, death]. But that is Joseph's parody, too, not to be taken so seriously. Following Abinadi's lead, the Prophet frequently applied himself to the task of uttering curses against his foes and even his followers, when necessary. Among his more colorful maledictions, he recorded the following,

> And thus, with the sword and by bloodshed the inhabitants of the earth shall mourn; and with famine, and plague, and earthquake, and the thunder of heaven, and the fierce and vivid lightning also, shall the inhabitants of the earth be made to feel the wrath, and indignation, and chastening hand of an Almighty God, until the consumption decreed hath made a full end of all nations.[21]

Abinadi warned the people within Noah's corrupt Nephite kingdom of the wrath they would soon begin to suffer unless they turned to the Lord, but in so doing began upsetting the nation's prevailing status quo.[22] Much like Abinadi, Joseph, suffered imprisonment for little more than stirring up the citizenry.[23] Like Joseph, Abinadi could not be shut up by any legal means; a mob murdered him when they couldn't stand hearing him, nor about him, any longer. At one part of his testimony, Abinadi said, "But I finish my message; and then it matters not wither I go, if it so be that I am saved."[24] Showing an uncannily kindred spirit, Joseph testified,

> I see no faults in the church, and therefore let me be resurrected with the Saints, whether I ascend to heaven or descend to hell, or go to any other place. And if we go to hell, we will turn the devils out of doors and make a heaven of it. Where this people are there is good society. What do we care where we are, if the society be good?[25]

Joseph marked Abinadi as a type of bombastic, condemning prophet that the people couldn't silence without killing him, generally giving an impression of how neighboring Gentiles may have perceived the obnoxious, boastful Mormon chief, Abinadi's creator. Both prophets suffered death by mob activity said to be instigated by religious leaders.[26] If indeed he already suspected the manner by which he would more than likely face his own demise, Joseph couldn't have better represented it than through the distressing manner in which Abinadi suffered: "[...] he fell, having suffered death by fire; yea, having been put to death because he would not deny the commandments of God, having sealed the truth of his words by his death."[27]

Again the author has emphasized Abinadi's role as a figurative bin o' death, and in doing so comes closer to the prophetic act than anyone might have imagined. Since Nephites didn't survive long enough to realize the invention of firearms, death by fire had to suffice as the most basic representation Joseph could employ to foretell his own violent end. Joseph also fell by (gun) fire. He *fell* out from the window of the second floor of the jail at Carthage, Illinois when *fired* upon by the mob. Just like Abinadi, Joseph's followers said of him that he "[...] has sealed his mission and his works with his own blood [...]"[28]

As readers may discover suggested in subtle nuances throughout the book, recognize how Abinadi served as a prophetic figure previewing Joseph's *subsequent* life. Although admittedly this becomes difficult—how such wondrous parallels might achieve expression through random coincidence in the form of mere art—it becomes even more risky, or maddening, for those attempting to imagine an entire book exposing the intimate life, death and mind of the book's modern translator, but from its proposed perspective more than fourteen centuries ahead of events said to have taken place. Even the best of prophecies must acquiesce to reasonable limitations.

Cumulative evidence may tend to suggest that Joseph wrote a collection of sketches or blueprint scripts, using fictional characters, then improvised as real-life circumstances later indicated good opportunity. Acting as Mormon, Joseph became the writer who determined most of what went into his documented historical record. Steering toward his agenda with greater accuracy than any prophetic gift, Joseph continually honed his abilities to motivate and manage others in order to control surrounding environments, an easier task when the desired outcome is clearly pictured in one's mind. His Church diaries witness him cultivating psycho-manipulative skills even prior to Zion's Camp. Marked improvement in his efficiency came from taking further practice at every turn, each new introduction. Post-modern prophets are made, not born.

As a Relentless Political Paradigm, Amulon Grinds the Mill

In addition to Abinadi, the Book of Mosiah introduces several key characters such as Alma and Ammon. Here, though, we'll briefly consider one of its supporting role actors, dubbed Amulon, whose name marks him as a highly noteworthy fellow in Joseph's cast. Amulon suggests one of Joseph's more delightful symbol names, a beautiful example of how they ought to fit the character built around them.

For the Nephites' stubbornness in refusing to repent, and in partial fulfillment of righteous Abinadi's curses, the Lord overturned King Noah, an irredeemably wicked Nephite monarch. God sent a *flood* of fearsome and warlike Lamanites *pouring* across his borders (try visualizing them marching in *waves*), thus *inundating* Noah's empire. Those who were able, escaped, including Alma the elder, and Amulon, two former priests who had once served together in Noah's decadent palace.

Alma had been touched deeply by Abinadi's scathing curses and damning bombast. Therefore, inviting many others of like mind, they convened in the forests of Mormon long enough to cleanse and redeem themselves through the ordinance of baptism, then established their settlement in Helam, a land of a few days' journey from the land of Nephi. Alma's people thus became "proper" folks by setting up a "church of Christ" with all the trappings of an authorized priesthood, founded by Alma.[29]

From the opposite corner came Amulon and his unscrupulous cohorts, corrupted ex-priests of King Noah's court, who had taken a lower road while escaping from the invading Lamanite hordes. Along their route, those lusty fellows chanced upon a party of Lamanite maidens who had been out, as per custom, "to sing and to dance." Amulon's men kidnapped twenty-four of those lady Lamanites to serve as replacements for the Nephite wives they had earlier been forced to abandon as Noah's empire folded.[30] Then, as soon as they were discovered by Lamanite scouts, Amulon and his group pleaded for mercy, immediately turning traitors against the Nephites by teaming up with their former enemy.

(Incidentally, they were encouraged to keep their winsome young Lamanite consorts.)[31]

Polarities Joseph built into his characterizations of Alma and Amulon can hardly be ignored by the next time the two renewed their acquaintance. In the meantime Amulon gained so much favor in the government of the Lamanite king that, after his nation began expanding across Helam's borders, Amulon received a choice appointment as tributary monarch.[32] Their newly acquired land of Helam, originally a Nephite stronghold, had been founded and inhabited by Alma and his humble, righteous followers who had recently begun seeking religious asylum—similar to America's Pilgrims. Joseph couldn't have set the stage much better for recognizing Amulon's intentions for exercising unrighteous dominion over Alma, now his competitor for managing local power. Ideologically, Joseph caused their paths to cross in diametric fashion—Alma assuming moral high ground while Amulon dropped all religious pretensions in favor of solidifying his powerful position through secular politics.

To further polarize their characters Amulon and his brethren were assigned as teachers over all inhabitants dwelling in Lamanite-held territories. You can only imagine how humiliating that had to be for Alma because Amulonites taught nothing more than rudimentary skills of language arts and omitting even the most essential lessons in religious instruction.[33] Amulonites began laboring to neutralize the powers of church over state. Not only did Amulon exercise authority over Alma and his people but also taught Amulonite children to persecute the children of Alma's true-believer society. To vent his long-repressed spite Amulon loaded down Alma's Nephites with tasks, set taskmasters over them, and forbid them to pray aloud under penalty of death.[34]

Joseph makes it all too clear how Amulon liked grinding it in. His name derives from two words: A + Moulin. *Moulin* is French, meaning "mill." While Amulon's name gives testimony that this work was designed for achieving literary excellence, what should be of no less significance is the probability that Alma, Amulon and the community of Helam seem to be acting out an early episode of LDS history on which Joseph had the key role as scriptwriter and arranger. The brethren at Helem seem to foretell the exile suffered by the persecuted Saints that were forced to depart from Independence (Zion) Missouri, and for the same reason: a clash between religious and profane cultures. Zion's sufferings weren't as prophetic so much as they were pre-fabricated. Note again the possibility that Joseph had previewed a *subsequent* element of his plan.

Taking a closer look at what Amulon represented, we note that deeper down, Joseph may have imbibed just a touch of political anarchy. One of Joseph's most quotable, wise and thought-provoking musings from any available source condemns autocratic, oppressive authority. His insightful appraisal of men in authority has been preserved in one verse of his later work, the *Doctrine and Covenants*:

> We have learned by sad experience that it is the nature and disposition of almost all men, as soon as they get a little authority, as they suppose, they will immediately begin to exercise unrighteous dominion.[35]

His concise denouncement of the arrogance of power helps secure his true attitude toward authoritarian systems, sacred and secular—and incidentally, most unexpectedly, that of his own church. The disappointment comes from learning "by sad experience" just how close to home Joseph's words can hit. There is much irony and no accident in the fact that the very institution he conceived and organized is today commonly reported to be one of the most heavy-handed examples of people-power micro-management in the free world. Although Joseph, as mayor of the Saints' city of Nauvoo, invited others to reside there, he gave them fair warning, "The pagans, Roman Catholics, Methodists and Baptists shall have place in Nauvoo—only they must be ground in Joe Smith's mill. I have been in their mill."[36]

Having presented Amulon's cruel example of unrighteous dominion (one of the inevitable consequences of political ambition), perhaps now is a good time to try the other shoe on so that we may see how power gets distributed and handled by more righteous bearers of duly ordained authority, as practiced within the fair environs of Zarahemla, a brightly-illuminated town of two tales.

CHAPTER 15

Zarahemla—One City, Two Tales

No Book of Mormon symbol name is as difficult to decipher, nor as essential to one's orientation and understanding of the book, and of Joseph's philosophy, as Zarahemla. He couldn't have chosen a more appropriate community around which to sketch his critique of self-righteousness and presumed authority. Likewise, no location throughout Book of Mormon-land approaches Zarahemla's prominence, being mentioned 163 times in the text. Despite its distinction and renown an early search party sent to locate the town became lost and had to return.[1] Zarahemla's paradox stems from its isolation from the rest of the world, being surrounded by water or wilderness on every border.[2] Moreover, once having arrived, keeping up with the pace of its morally conservative city fathers must have provided an aura of tyranny made perfect. Today one may still encounter Zarahemla's spiritual heirs who consider themselves "*in* the world, but not *of* the world," implying that somehow they are able to transcend society's liberalizing drift by steadfastly adhering to platforms of conservative thought, even as they indulge an assortment of conveniences and simple pleasures that their fathers might well have considered decadent.

Encountered first in Omni's record, wandering Israelites established Zarahemla's city in proximity to an ancient, extinct regime—the Jaredites. The townsfolk were linked to the earlier civilization's fall by the welcome

Zarahemla—One City, Two Tales 123

they provided for Coriantumr, a lone survivor from the continent's earliest inhabitants. Once a king, the old man kept a room in Zarahemla until his end. As if bitten by a Jaredite bug of self-destructiveness, the Nephite kingdom imitated their long downward slide towards destruction. Thus, readers may have been fooled into feeling sadness due to its repute as a holy city. Supposedly the metropolis derived its name from a man named Zarahemla, its founding father, who became chief of a migrant population, likewise Israelites, who were oddly designated as "Mulekites." That name, in turn, evidently highlights their *stubbornness* (as well as suggesting *windy airs* of aristocratic superiority). As suggested by their symbol name, the hardy Mulekites had persevered through Jerusalem's destruction in 586 BCE, and had escaped to the New World in the company of a prince of royal lineage, a boy named Mulek, supposedly one of the sons of Judah's King Zedekiah.[3]

During their flight from the land of Nephi (c. 270-130 BCE), Mosiah and his followers accidentally stumbled onto the peaceful hamlet then soon began organizing local politics and taking charge. Once the two factions merged Mosiah's group promoted him as sole monarch.[4] King Benjamin, Mosiah's son, purified the town by driving away all of its Lamanites.[5] Soon Zarahemla became the only safe haven and home base for Nephites needing asylum. Ammon [the First] brought King Limhi's entire community to dwell there.[6] After suffering persecution from Amulonites, Alma (the elder) and his followers escaped from the city of Helam to encounter a welcome in Mosiah's burgeoning kingdom.[7] Somewhat as with America during the early 1800s, Zarahemla became a mecca for masses in search of sanctuary.[8]

Massive immigration halted, however, when Ammon [the Second] returned, bringing a large contingent of black-skinned Lamanite converts, the Ammonites. City fathers turned them out because of strict but unwritten (let's assume racial) policies. His Ammonites were directed to go away and build a city named Jershon, which bordered further off, nearer Lamanite territories.[9] The word Jershon (Hebrew, *Gershon*) means "refugee." Zarahemla soon became a highly centralized capital of both civil and religious affairs. Its governors, judges and high priests all maintained offices in the vicinity of its temple so they could help certify purity throughout its vast domain for as long as possible.

Eventually, despite (or perhaps, because of) its organization, size, firm authoritarian control and priestly structure, Zarahemla's defenses began crumbling. While at first the Lamanites wouldn't even dare attack it, ultimately they captured the town, if only for a brief moment.[10] Zarahemla's infrastructures began faltering as its people became more wicked, yet its total collapse was accompanied by a magnitude 10.0 earthquake, apparently made to resemble an awful day of judgment, a calamitous upheaval that announced the arrival of the recently resurrected Jesus.[11] The Lord readily admitted, "Behold, that great city Zarahemla have I burned with fire, and the inhabitants thereof." His words echo Revelation's day of reckoning: "Alas, alas, that great city Babylon, that mighty city! For in one hour is thy judgment come."[12]

Too soon after the savior's departure true believers rebuilt Zarahemla.[13] Following a period of peace and prosperity, and without sufficient explanation, the whole Nephite nation accelerated its slump into obscurity. Zarahemla received mention again after hundreds of years had passed, but only then as an old and worn place-name for the local battleground, seeming as if it had become a ghost town.[14] The people experienced gradual but irrevocable descent, a fate its author had distinctively foreshadowed since earliest Nephite times.[15] Undisputed analysis suggests that both Jaredite and Nephite civilizations folded due to a common fault—the people's lack of religious enthusiasm. Following his line of reasoning, we should easily conclude that the author means to imply that our own modern nation is likewise threatened should too many of us give in to relaxing of our nation's moral fiber. But can we be sure of his implication? Don't we worship and believe with sufficient zeal? Have we failed our tests of righteousness or provided insufficiently for the homeless refugee and poor of spirit?

Or could the truth be that Joseph intended something altogether different? Perhaps he really meant to suggest how irrational traditions and superstitions impose insurmountable obstacles upon humanity's greater potential. Useful new ideas that mankind might have nurtured to its own advantage tend to suffer poorer prospects when subjugated to scrutiny through a philosophical lens inherited from antiquity. This may be especially true whenever deep emotional contexts impose one generation's bad investments or unreasoned, unproductive theories onto the next generation—and the next. Conceptual changes typically meet with inordinate resistance even at the threshold of a new age; Zarahemla represented old school values in a narrow sense.

Behind lustrous postcard-like images, the idyllic image of Zarahemla evaporates. The community suggests vague, unidentified but illegitimate sources of power—its illusions may include such frauds as religious mythology, blind nationalism and a prevalent inability to distinguish celebrity worship from talented leadership. Whatever its subtle dangers, we are left with a distinct and uncomfortable sense of urgency lest we also become deplorable victims of the fate of those Nephites and Jaredites. A deeper appreciation of its symbolic values will help acquaint us with obstacles that Joseph felt hindered the future progress of mankind.

Coloring the Law

The name Zarahemla breaks down into three words: Zara + hem + la (law). In the Bible, one's garments, especially the hem, were considered symbolic indicators of moral qualities, virtues and/or guilt: "And besought him [Jesus] that they might only touch the hem of his garment; and as many as touched were made perfectly whole."[16] Conversely, on several occasions within the Book of Mormon, blood on one's garments signified guilt.[17]

One notable example comes from the book of Helaman. After Seezoram, Zarahemla's chief judge, had been found murdered, Nephi [the Second] instructed a local crime investigation team to check in with his corrupt brother, Seantum, to see if blood could be found "upon the skirts of his cloak," which we can assume would have indicated the lower hem of his robe.[18] What might normally be taken figuratively, as metaphor, the Book of Mormon turns literal. Assigning guilt prior to making a thorough evaluation of relevant evidence, or intuitively attributing a lesser value to any individual becomes a reasonable basis for addressing the Hem Law.

So, what's a *Zarah*-hem-law? The name's prefix derives from a biblical character, Zarah, sometimes spelled Zerah, second-born son of a set of twins given to Judah by his daughter-in-law, Tamar. During his birthing, Zarah reached his hand through the birth canal. Tamar's midwife tied a scarlet ribbon to his wrist just before he withdrew his hand, allowing Pherez (or Perez), his brother, first birth.[19] Pharez deserved his name because he came out breech-born, feet first; the name means "breech."

Indicated through the same context—specifically, the peculiarity of his birth—Zerah received his name. Since his name presents a choice of symbolic alternatives, let's simply review the exact unmodified authoritative quote from *The Interpreter's Dictionary of the Bible*: "**Zerah**: Scarlet (?), or dawning, or shining forth; perhaps a shortened form: 'He (God) has shown forth.'"[20] If the Interpreter's "scarlet" be allowed due to Zerah's scarlet ribbon, then Zarahemla's symbol name may be rendered as "the scarlet hem law," or more simply, City of Guilt. Nathaniel Hawthorne found the same colorful image appropriate for representing guilt when writing his now classic novel, *The Scarlet Letter*, first published in 1850. Scarlet refers to the symbolic blood [guilt] on one's garments, designating a sense of culpability that laws cannot always adjudicate. Zarahemla might well refer to one's bloodline, or station of birth.[21]

Perhaps Zarahemla doesn't signify present guilt any more than it does real blood, so much as referring to how we tend to sort and judge others while comprehending only superficial and isolated bits of their lives. Rumor, ignorance and fear are often the cause of devastating social injustice, and Joseph brought this aspect into focus by creating one of the world's most persecuted bodies of people, mostly through the instrumentality of philosophical distinctions that are hardly meaningful and impossible to prove.

Generations of practice have enabled our culture to advance its capacity for overcritical habits when viewing other men's manners, capacities and inclinations. Not uncommonly, prejudicial guilt derives from who you are, your parentage, the work you do, how you look or dress, your regional accent, or even the part of town where you grew up. Joseph used Zarahemla to spotlight a society sorted out by how convincingly one announced placement of their values, heart, mind and soul. Are you alike or different? Zarahemla-ism still exists wherever litmus tests are introduced as subtle prerequisites for advancing one's economic, social or political station within the neighborhood, community and society. Transgressors of the law, we must all admit ourselves *bona fide* inmates of Zarahemla whenever we permit issues of conscience to be mediated and settled by society's moralizers.

The most unwelcome and oppressed member of Zarahemla's commonwealth was a man named Korihor, a figure so distinctive in his independence of thought that he dared to question the people's set of common beliefs—but not shrewd enough to keep from speaking his mind in public. For the time being Korihor's objections to the community's accepted theology are irrelevant; each reader may argue the reasoning and merits of Korihor's objections, along with Alma's melodramatic responses—that isn't the point. Simply note the level of haughty disdain with which Korihor's dissenting opinions were treated: Alma labeled him as an anti-Christ, cursed him with dumbness, then notes that he was soon trampled to death as a beggar.[22] By holding that picture in mind, readers will catch some of the spirit of Zarahamla that Joseph secretly intended to criticize. As with Korihor, Joseph found it regrettable that honest, honorable dissent is poorly tolerated, especially within a manifestly pluralistic society, but even more so when people persists in imagining that an individual's status with heaven is reflected by such uncertain markers as social position or economic success. Why should it seem at all curious that in Joseph's book the anti-Christ Korihor doubles as a martyr to independent thought and freedom of expression?

It's No Place Like Home

Once able to recognize the underlying meaning of Zarahemla, we might naturally inquire to determine a basis for its origins in Joseph's world. His critical view, we can be sure, didn't materialize out of thin air, although Joseph seldom colored its landscapes in terms we would consider concrete. Why not? Possibly because behaviors deserving of such critical review usually hurt most painfully when hitting too close to home. Literary allusions can point readers toward an author's intentions without causing great pain to individuals he might be trying to protect, including one's family. Joseph came of age in Palmyra, New York, so we may safely assume that that particular "community of clean garment wearers," if representing aspects of Joseph's reality world, had to exist in western New York State, in and around Palmyra, during the years 1816-1830. Most of the social problems he observed or suffered were consequences of the day and age into which he was born and raised. Like the inmates of hell, Zarahemla may represent a society distressed by its past, not too certain about where it's going, but struggling, as most of us do, to somehow rise above our origins.

Palmyra—A Model for Zarahemla?

If a string of disappointing episodes throughout his youth ultimately set Joseph Smith onto his crusade to undermine the socio-religious establishment, he never detailed all of his specific issues and complaints in black and white. Here we are only able to suggest a reasoned sampling of the kinds of events that may have inspired him to take a swing at redistributing influences. Read carefully as you encounter Book of Mormon references to the city. One especially significant clue will guide you to its location as Joseph perceived it. The people who travel there are often said to go "down into the land of Zarahemla."[23] Conversely, those who leave it go "up out of the land of Zarahemla."[24] Joseph may have tried painting Zarahemla as his abstraction of hell-on-earth, perhaps a thumbnail sketch of his early life.

If true, he underscored those deep dissatisfactions when, during the latter half of 1832, he began keeping a record in his earliest journal. Joseph reverted to using a cryptic (riddle) mode of expression, writing, "I was born in the town of Charon in the State of Vermont, North America on the twenty third day of December AD 1805 of goodly parents who spared no pains to instructing me in the Christian religion."[25] If somebody had explained to his mother what was going on, she would have skinned him alive. The town of his birthplace, Sharon (not Charon), was hardly too complicated a word for Joseph, age 26, to have spelled incorrectly, especially when placing it on a document that he planned submitting into church records. Charon is the name of the boatman of Greek mythology whose duties included ferrying souls of the dead across the river Styx into Hades. Dante mentioned Charon within his *Divine Comedy, Hell*, Canto III.

Did Joseph imagine himself born into perdition? No single element or circumstance led to his unhappy attitude, but the Smith family became blighted by strong reverses year after year. Once it was a typhoid epidemic that led to Joseph's osteomyelitis. Next came economic disaster, freaky weather that ruined crops for several years running, then business fraud and even the threat of eviction from the home they had struggled to build. Their situation became so desperate that, while making the move to Palmyra, Lucy had to barter away the family's wool clothing in order to complete the 300-mile journey with her eight children. After arriving, the Smiths evaluated their situation so that they could agree on how they would unite in efforts to make ends meet. They tapped every resource and farmed out every working body to keep the family from scattering to the four winds. After nearly nine years they hadn't fully recovered and by 1825 it even became necessary for Lucy and Joseph, Sr. to indenture Samuel, Joseph's younger brother, in order to prevent being evicted from their farm after failing to meet a critical mortgage payment.[26] Child labor laws hadn't yet been written, and Samuel's term of servitude lasted only six months, however, it helps show the degree of sacrifice and, presumably, commitment that each family member joined into with the others. All can agree that the family's life was rigidly disciplined yet Lucy held it together by infinite faith and genuine motherly love. The Smith clan held united together through thick and thin, for life.

Not only did their poverty and necessity hinder the children's ability to finish their schooling but also for interacting within society. Consequently, citizens of Palmyra returned mixed reviews years later when attempting to recount their experiences with the Smith family. Town-dwellers may have expressed superiority over outlying farm families.[27] Attending church but rarely, the Smiths were regarded suspiciously when they did. Eventually three Smith family members were suspended from the Palmyra Presbyterian Church.[28]

Lucy's history tells of one representative chain of cruel events following the death of her oldest son, Alvin. The young man, age 25, had virtually been murdered by a quack "calomel doctor." Next, the minister officiating at the funeral began preaching about how Alvin would spend eternity in hell because he hadn't been baptized. Soon afterward, malicious local rumors persisted in affirming that her son's body had been illegally exhumed for medical research. Joseph, Sr. became so tormented by it that he had to dig up the body to prove it *hadn't* been disturbed.[29] Perhaps his anguish brings Zarahemla closer into focus.

In Palmyra all eleven-members of the Smith clan didn't live in a civilized, sawed-timber dwelling, but crowded into a tight 600 square-foot "rude log house."[30] They eked out their existence mainly as farmers, an occupation that has persistently transmitted the stigma of status among the lowest of professions. In the southern states at the time, gentlemen farmers continued working their fields by the sweat of black slaves. Joseph, during passage through his sensitive teen years, walked into town weekly, still suffering a noticeable limp from his leg surgery, to bring home his dad's newspaper. As with many growing boys, keeping Joseph in decent clothing became a chore in itself. One favorable writer explains,

"He was patched and badly shod even in winter [...]."[31] One of Palmyra's residents remembered, "I knew the Smiths [...] but they were too lowly to associate with."[32] Here, then, we may gain our clearest representation of Zarahemla, and something about it may even resemble communities that are familiar to us.

While writing Alma's record, Joseph interjected his impression of what being a member of the excluded caste was like:

> 2. And it came to pass that after much labor among them, they [Alma and Amulek] began to have success among the poor class of people; for behold, they were cast out of the synagogues because of the coarseness of their apparel—
> 3. Therefore they were not permitted to enter into their synagogues to worship God, being esteemed as filthiness; therefore they were poor, yea, they were esteemed by their brethren as dross; therefore they were poor as to things of the world; and also they were poor in heart.[33]

As literary symbol, Zarahemla becomes an ever-present embodiment of society. There, choices and achievements often become limited by appearances: one's dwelling, clothing, idiosyncrasies and speech; or one's ability to adapt to society's given norms, rather than appreciating one's reason, their passions, intellect and soul. Gossip alone has destroyed many a strong individual, and society has always suffered proportionally towards its own undoing.

How, then, can we describe Zarahemla's inhabitants more consistently with Joseph's thinking? Perhaps its people wander away from the *golden mean*: "moderation in all things"—not in following excesses, but, oppositely, by exercising abstinences according to other peoples' diminished interpretations of how everyone else ought to live. While the prophet frequently spoke on themes of individual rights, he never envisioned a world better than iconoclastic ideologues have desired in every age—a community less regimented and defined by its false gods, kings, potentates, priests, or any lesser lights in pursuit of social stature and political ambition. In Zarahemla, life's ultimate objective isn't about being honest with yourself so much as keeping in step with the current spiritual buzz inside your religious circle. Zarahemla City is Joseph's monument to self-righteousness, paternalism, authoritarianism, hypocrisy, exclusionary principles, of judgmental rejection and even condemnation of those outside religious, economic or cultural campgrounds.

CHAPTER 16

Alma, Part 1:
Portrait of a Mormon Soul

Alma's prominent location in the record proves helpful when searching for meaning. His segment of history assumes center stage, consumes nearly one third of its volume and offers a nearly unrestricted view of Joseph's mind. In it you'll find much of his essential, though irreverent, gospel; including many false gods, equivocation of the resurrection, insults to deity with plenty of levity and confusion galore.

If Not *the* Vision, at Least the *Ideal* Vision

Alma signifies the same in both Spanish and Italian—"soul," suggesting how one might introspectively discover those core essentials characteristic of Joseph's life, thought and message. One of the surest markers suggesting that Joseph reflected himself through Alma can be taken from his account of *The First Vision*, found in his primary autobiographical (church) history, as well as in *The Pearl of Great Price* but initially symbolized within the Book of Alma.

Alma's remarkable story of how the heavens first opened to him receives mention more than once during his record—with notable discrepancies.[1] Joseph, however, only began dictating details of his first vision in 1832 after successfully publishing his book and establishing his church. He supplemented that report in 1835, and again in 1839, with new, improved versions of the glorious visitation. Years between those editions of the vision allowed him sufficient time to test and gauge how much his followers were willing to accept.

In turn both visions, Alma's and Joseph's, show as adaptations of accounts given by St. Paul's recollections of events said to have occurred as he traveled towards Damascus while persecuting Christians. Both Paul and Joseph described a light in their vision as being "above the brightness of the sun."[2] Paul's story, recorded three times, has admitted variations, also,[3] yet Christians have never questioned his credibility so thoroughly as they have Joseph's. Those yearning deeply enough to affirm their faith in God willingly profess belief, choosing to suppress rational, wholesome skepticism. Might recognition of that propensity in human psychology have emboldened Joseph to proceed despite dissimilarities in his story? His book insists, "[…] if ye believe that [Bible] ye will believe this also."[4]

Although Alma's father, Alma the elder, had been a spiritual leader, Alma the younger developed reactionary attitudes in expressing his opposition to religion. As a young man, Alma traveled secretly with the sons of Mosiah to destroy the church that his father had founded.[5] One day, like St. Paul, Alma (i.e., Joseph) came to an extraordinary flash of insight. He realized how any open attack made against religion, be it ever so well reasoned, so thorough—even brilliant, would net him only hardened resistance from entrenched pious believers. The entire intellectual history of western civilization affirms how common sense reasoning becomes subordinated to superstitions, fears and obsessions. Some issues, religion chief among them, are governed by unyielding powers of passionate faith that cannot always be settled on a level playing field of resolute, reasoned discourse. Reaching for success in one's endeavors for redirecting the situation might logically allow for imaginative irrationality and bold exhibitionism.

"If Thou Wilt of Thyself Be Destroyed…"

Joseph's moment of enlightenment has been fictionalized for us. He ordained that his partner Alma deliver his confession by employing a luminous classic of grammatical sleight of hand. When, as an older man, Alma wrote to Helaman, his oldest son, to share the account of his initial conversion experience, he repeated the angel's words to him, but therein described the most unlikely message ever transmitted from heaven. Taken directly from the record, it says:

> 6. For I went about with the sons of Mosiah, seeking to destroy the church of God; but behold, God sent his holy angel to stop us by the way.
> 7. And behold, he spake unto us, as it were the voice of thunder […].
> 8. But behold, the voice said unto me: Arise […].
> 9. And he said unto me: If thou wilt of thyself be destroyed, seek no more to destroy the church of God.[6]

Because readers are expecting a message opposite to what has been written, their powerful subconscious corrects the angel's words (verse 9) as follows: "If thou wilt *not* be destroyed, seek no more to destroy the church of God." As written, the angel is threatening Alma that, should he *quit* his destructive endeavors against the church, he would risk being destroyed. The warning words form a magnificent conundrum in which Joseph omitted one essential negative component of the angel's command. It's a mental *trompe-l'oeil*, an illusion. Mormons never catch the error, demonstrating so perfectly how emotional needs easily steer our perceptions. What we find depends on what we're looking for.

Thomas Paine proposed arguing the case against religious superstition from grounds within the scriptures themselves.[7] Joseph, as illustrated through his tale of Alma, led the attack by working himself into the highest position attainable within society's dominant religion. From there he could turn it into a house of chaos and confusion and so intended breaking down its traditions from inside: "Alma thought it was expedient that they should try [test] the virtue of the word of God."[8] His new strategy would prove enormously appealing and quite effective.

Joseph simplified reasoning behind his theological experiment by drawing upon but three scriptural passages to demonstrate a true believer's most basic flaw of logic while viewing the New Testament: "[...] I learned in the scriptures that God was the same yesterday, to day, and forever. That he was no respecter of persons, for he was God."[9] Then, quoting James, "If any of you lack wisdom, let him ask of God, that giveth to all men liberally, and upbraideth not; and it shall be given him."[10] Sectarian ministers constantly challenged their listeners to "Take God at

His word," and that's just what Joseph proposed we do. Accordingly, if those scriptural precepts were trustworthy and true, not only would St. Paul, Alma *and* Joseph receive glorious liberal visions from God, but *every other person* who would apply. Paul held no special title suggesting how he might expect privilege as a unique special witness of Jesus, but neither could Alma, and certainly not Joseph—unless God indeed respected particular individuals.

By proclaiming the glorious story of his own first vision, though preposterous and totally untrue, Joseph presented an example and prompt for his readers, tacitly assuring a paramount spiritual experience for each and every one of them who might decide to participate in his simple experiment. Reason demands that *all* who ask shall be given a quite *liberal* vision, or else God *has* changed in that He selects but a few, choosing to regard mankind unequally. Thus, the (infallible) Bible's writers are caught misrepresenting facts, or God does not perform—at least not by adhering to specifications attributed to Him. Some readers may go so far as to observe that Joseph had determined a fair, logical, *empirical* method that could be used to *disprove* the existence of God.

Tainting the Experiment

Joseph, ever aware of the immense potential stored within his reasoning, decided to doctor-up the experiment so he could take advantage of prevailing anti-scientific attitudes. He had Alma instruct followers, "[…] behold, if ye will awake and arouse your faculties, even to an experiment upon my words, and exercise a particle of faith, yea, even if ye can no more than desire to believe […]."[11] Hopeful seekers of truth are thus led to disregard the most stringent rule of scientific experimentation. They dismiss objectivity when quartering an urgent desire to gather assurances that will bolster belief. Those who are sufficiently eager would never allow a blank vision to sour their hunger for an affirmative experience. As a third step, Joseph encouraged seekers to follow their dreams by whittling down their lofty, unrealistic expectations: "[…] behold […] you must study it out in your mind; then you must ask me if it be right, and if it is right I will cause that your bosom shall burn within you; therefore, you shall feel that it is right."[12] In thus reducing grandiose anticipations for receiving a glorious heavenly vision to nothing more than one's passively experiencing a *normal* range of body temperature (unmeasured, subjective), Joseph's promise eventually induced millions of participants to share in an even larger experiment. Through his imaginative enterprise he would be able to demonstrate with dramatic, even spectacular results, how desire to believe may also have misled virtually every religious seeker in history.

Continuing with the story, Joseph had to establish a clear motive for Alma's taking over the reins of a massive religious enterprise. Therefore, following Alma's successful bid for religious power, Joseph had the young prophet become a true pooh-bah: chief judge, high priest, governor over the land of Zarahemla and, when necessary, head officer in the military.[13] Likewise, by 1844, Joseph had consolidated leadership over the church, legal civil authority in his community, judicial power and military control, all within himself. Both Alma and Joseph served as the most significant chroniclers of events regarding their respective peoples—each acting as functioning historian within their respective religious empires.

With Korihor's Curse, One Saving Grace

Having for sake of his experiment staged all claims of priestly authority in order to achieve his own rise to power, Joseph's position lacked security as long as followers expected him to share it with a pair of *highly* regarded, well-established Competitors (i.e., Father and Son). A good work of literature should be able to handle such a simple dilemma, and the challenge spurred the young writer to fabricate an imaginative twist.

A decidedly melodramatic episode of Alma's story tells of Korihor, one of three characters designated as anti-Christs (the other two being Sherem and Nehor). Korihor fulfilled an awkward role as a preacher who, with comic absurdity, denied the *prophesied* arrival of Jesus long before there ever came any practical or reasonable possibility for doing so. Korihor exhibited eccentric foolhardiness while attempting to preach his weakly formulated anti-Christ doctrines in a land so thoroughly Christianized as Zarahemla. To further demonstrate the looseness of his grip on reality, Korihor demanded that Alma, the high priest, perform miracles as proof that he held God's power.[14] His meeting with Alma made Korihor look dumber yet.

Korihor began denying God and questioning the accepted teaching that Jesus would one day appear as foretold. His doubts wouldn't have seemed all that absurd if the year weren't supposedly 74 BCE when he and Alma met and in a spot on the other side of the globe from Palestine. If their meeting had taken place anywhere else on our planet, other than in Zarahemla, Korihor's denial about the future coming of Jesus Christ would have only seemed strange from the fact that never had anyone actually projected such distinctive and unmistakable assertions that Jesus was going to arrive on earth. When Korihor asked Alma to prove by a sign from heaven that he held God's power, Alma first tried putting him off. Only after insisting did Alma fulfill Korihor's request, granting him the most convincing evidence—but causing Korihor considerable disadvantage as a consequence:

> Now Alma said unto him: This will I give unto thee for a sign, that thou shalt be struck dumb, according to my words; and I say, that in the name of God, ye shall be struck dumb, that ye shall no more have utterance.[15]

If we assume that such a curse could validate Alma's powers, being struck dumb certainly provided no blessing for Korihor. It meant that he could no longer speak, deny God or question foolish dogma. For certain he could no longer annoy Alma. Zarahemla's chief Judge stood nearby and wanted to rub it in real good—to make Korihor confess how his stubbornness had led him to make a fool of himself. So the judge *wrote* Korihor a note asking, "Art thou convinced of the power of God? [...]. Behold, he has showed unto you a sign; and now will ye dispute more?"[16] The judge needn't have written to Korihor, for the stricken die-hard never lost his hearing. Dumbness doesn't indicate an auditory defect, but a handicap of speech. This perceptual error represents a brief but humorous incident witnessing Joseph's imaginative, but slightly wacky thinking.

What pushes his story right to the comic fringe, however, is Korihor's symbol name. Joseph composed it of two words: Kor (Cor), from *Coeur*, "heart," + hor, the sound-alike (homonym) word that is usually spelled "whore." Meet a most delightful personification of the whorish heart. Korihor takes his symbol name from the book of Ezekiel, where the nation of Israel was once characterized as having a "whorish heart" because they had been seduced by foreign idols.[17] Joseph had given Korihor the very same *Israelite* lineage Mormons always understood the Nephites brought with them from Jerusalem. However, we get a better sense of Joseph's intended irony by noting that Alma cursed Korihor with *dumbness*. It is both tempting and reasonable to imagine that Joseph mischievously formed this anti-Christ Korihor as a charade figure of Jesus himself. One of the more familiar (so called) Messianic prophecies from the book of Isaiah describes the Savior's refusal to speak in his own defense (i.e., during his trial before Pontius Pilate):

From the Bible:
> He was oppressed, and he was afflicted, yet he opened not his mouth: he is brought as a lamb to the slaughter, and as a sheep before her shearers is dumb, so he openeth not his mouth.[18]

Korihor continued enduring his humiliation in silence, begging for food, though finally suffering the horrifying indignity of being trampled to death by a crowd.[19] That final *coup de grace* may represent Joseph's concept of how modern Christians would perhaps respond could they learn the arcane heritage of ancient myths that had been integrated with earlier sacred literature to fabricate fantastic illusions of God-and-Son.

Alma's Confession

As with several other players in the story, Alma's confession of infidelity and hypocrisy had to be made quietly so as to not disturb readers' preconceptions about possible moral flaws harbored by acknowledged religious elites:

> And now it came to pass that when Alma had made these regulations [regarding church law and management] he departed from them, yea, from the church which was in the city of Zarahemla, and went over upon the east of the river Sidon, into the valley of Gideon [...].[20]

Any suspected ambiguity Joseph built into this verse could easily have been eliminated by writing, "And when Alma had finished regulating affairs in the city of Zarahemla, he departed for the valley of Gideon, across the river Sidon." Instead, he allowed a possibility that Alma departed from the very same regulations he had given to the church at Zarahemla as soon as he got out of sight.

Much later in the story Alma confessed again. Although normally declaring his teachings in tones of absolute certainty, Alma wavered in testimony concerning his own spiritual existence: "I would not that ye think that I know of myself—not of the temporal but of the spiritual, not of the carnal mind but of God."[21] How could anyone having convictions so slight and frail become a positive influence or inspire genuine faith?

As if such a hypocrite might require further mortification, Joseph developed an even more humiliating role for Alma—that of a typical father. No theme allows such a crushing of icons as a parent manifesting his most severe failings just when his children begin entering a stage as independent adults. As father, Alma never once mentioned his wife, though he does confess paternity for three young men: Helaman, Shiblon and Corianton. Alma's letters to his three sons provide a working guide to life among the Mormons.

CHAPTER 17

Alma, Part 2:
As Mormon As It Gets

At the time of his martyrdom in 1844, Joseph and Emma had but three sons (although she gave birth to another son five months afterward). Correspondingly, and by sheer coincidence, Alma listed only three sons in his account. He named them Helaman, Shiblon and Corianton.

Helaman, Firstborn of the Father

Although Helaman enjoyed status as Alma's oldest, one should be careful to note that he wasn't the "only begotten." Today's Saints commonly refer to Jesus as the firstborn son of God, recognizing that they, too, are the Father's begotten *spirit* offspring.[1] As eldest, Alma left Helaman in Zarahemla to maintain charge over all spiritual affairs of the church while Alma and his two younger sons performed a proselytizing mission among the Zoramites.[2] Their task wouldn't be all work and no play.

During his absence, Alma posted a nice letter to Helaman, comprising a goodly two chapters' worth of the Nephite chronicle in which Alma urged Helaman to "keep a record of this people, *according as I have done.*"[3]

His words seem to reflect on a saying of Jesus: "The son can do nothing of himself, but what he seeth the father do [...]."[4] As Jesus followed his Father, Helaman followed in Alma's footsteps by becoming the acknowledged high priest over the church.[5]

Helaman's name seems a bit irregular, not Hebrew, but even more certainly not resembling anything Mayan or Toltec. Joseph designed it to give an approximate sound of "healer-man." Helaman's role calls for him to mimic Jesus, but not too obviously. Subsequent to Alma's departure, Helaman re-established his father's church that had been running amuck with apostasy.[6] Readers might almost picture the newly appointed priesthood leader turning over tables at the porch of Zarahemla's temple.

Soon, however, he took over the lead in his family's trail of military conquest by leading a couple of thousand Lamanite youths into battle for their first encounter against a hardened Lamanite enemy ("Onward, *Christian* Soldiers"). Most significantly, miraculously, "to our great astonishment," Helaman brought every one of his young charges back without loss of a single soul.[7] Readers will be able to generalize the intended concept if they can recall a cameo of words spoken by Jesus, "[...] those that thou gavest me I have kept, and none of them is lost, but the son of perdition; that the scripture might be fulfilled."[8] Had Joseph woven another subtle parody into his story by allowing Alma's firstborn to one-up the Bible's healer-man?

Corianton and Isabel, Two Heavy-Hearted Lovers

While serving their Zoramite mission, Alma also wrote a letter to his third son, Corianton, but a much longer one than even Helaman's. Right away you'll get the idea that Alma wasn't at all pleased with Corianton, for his number three son had been out doing no good thing. In short Alma accused Corianton of committing fornication, then proceeded to thoroughly chasten him while marvelously depicting the wrath of God for Corianton, as well as for all readers who continue reading through this personal and, one might have supposed, intensely *private* missive.

Corianton, supposedly devoting his life to spreading the gospel, exercised his inspired prerogatives to visit the nearby land of Siron. You may recognize a notable parallel to the name *Siren*, deadly she-creatures of Homer's epic, *The Odyssey*, who tried luring Odysseus to his death. Today's

LDS youth can expect a similar, sobering warning about too easily falling prey to attractions of the opposite sex.

At Siron, quite innocently, Corianton wound up engaging a wonderful date with one of the lovely local Lamanite lasses. She had an irresistible, radiant smile, was full of wit, humor and charm, and carried stature as a princess among her people. These facts aren't made explicit in Alma's account, of course, but may be inferred, for the young lady's name, Isabel, is a Spanish derivative of Jezebel. In ironic contrast to Jezebel's bad-girl Bible reputation, her name in Hebrew literally means "chaste" and Joseph couldn't let such an opportunity pass without notice. Mirroring Jezebel's biblical status as the daughter of Sidon's King Ethbaal, Isabel is worthy of respect as the daughter of a Lamanite king.[9]

In his fiery letter to Corianton, Alma rudely called Isabel a harlot, for he harbored racist attitudes against Lamanites while demonstrating an intolerant, prudish posture towards premarital sex. He doubtlessly spread much worse dirt about Isabel at church meetings—Mormons are known to network their muddiest calumny and innuendo. Alma probably slandered her cruelly by insulting her people, her mother, father and all the animals in their village. When word reached the Lamanites at Siron, it incited the next great war between Nephites and Lamanites. Again, his text doesn't give complete details, but as soon as Alma finished writing Corianton's letter he immediately changed pace to report on the (surprise!) war that was at hand.[10] One must sift through what few clues he's given to discern a prophet's machinations, or too much of it falls beyond one's mental grasp.

To Corianton's further dismay, Alma began preaching all of the strange new doctrines that he had fitted-out with absurdity, logic traps and seeds of doubt. Alma suddenly lost his spiritual mooring and compass and wasn't able to affirm with certainty any plan for a resurrection: "No one knows [...] it mattereth not," he said.[11] "I do not say [...] behold, I give it as my opinion," he reported.[12] Today Alma would be expelled from his priesthood quorum for lack of convictions. Quite possibly, Alma was just trying to soften the blow for his wayward son so that he wouldn't expect salvation after carelessly making the major error of embracing the forbidden delights of woman-kind. In Mormon teachings, sexual sin is an abomination ranking "second only to [murder] in the category of personal crimes."[13] Word came later about how Corianton had cut from the main body of Nephites, the people he had once grown to love. Alma, his heartless, unforgiving father, had irremediably crushed Corianton's lifelong reputation into a shambles. The young man finally shipped out for parts north, in self-exile.[14] His name suggests an ingenious symbol combination: Cor from the French word *coeur*, meaning "heart," but with a "ton" attached to it. Have you ever met a guy more perfectly fated to haul his heavy heart around throughout life?

Alma's heartless attitude represents a trenchant element of modern LDS parenting. One revered nephew of the Prophet expressed deep anxieties should his children enter forbidden paths,

> I would rather take my boys and girls to the grave, while they are Innocent, than to see them entrapped in the wickedness, the unbelief and the spirit of apostasy so prevalent in the world, and be led away from the gospel of salvation.[15]

With Corianton's sad love story, another compelling parallel with the life of Joseph is highly probable. During 1826-27, Joseph and his father had traveled about 100 miles south of Palmyra on a mission to secure extra cash for their farm's annual mortgage payment. While working they boarded at the home of Isaac and Elizabeth Hale, where Joseph met and fell in love with their daughter, Emma. Compared to the Smiths, the Hale family had wealth and respect.[16] When Joseph, a poor money-digger and recently convicted "glass-looker," requested her hand in marriage, Isaac vigorously opposed the union, denounced Joseph as an imposter and drove him from the house. Joseph and Emma soon eloped. The two lovers waited seven months before returning to face Isaac's wrath and, incidentally, collect Emma's household furniture and livestock. Old Isaac tearfully rebuked his new son-in-law for *stealing* his daughter and said he "had much rather follow her to her grave" than marry Joseph, a deceiver.[17] For all the joy such a moment might have brought him, Isaac's sour attitude placed an unfair burden of onus upon Joseph. The heavy-hearted young couple returned *north*.

An Attaboy for Shiblon

What? Did you see that? Shiblon's letter from Alma flew by so quickly that you hardly had time to blink. Comprising merely 15 verses, it has been wedged between six pages of printed material for Helaman, and a huge chunk—eight pages—for Corianton, a transgressor of *scarlet* reputation. This segment of Alma's book ought to be a cinch to comprehend but isn't that easy. When you reach its intended conclusions, however, it becomes a totally truthful insight, especially if you've ever experienced a realization similar to the one Shiblon must have suffered when he was later able to compare letters with his two brothers.

As in his letter to Helaman, Alma began by telling Shiblon that he could expect to prosper if he kept the commandments. It is the oft-spoken, seldom-enjoyed Law of Rewards.[18] Alma's glowing promise of prosperity invites recollection of another "Shiblon," used earlier as a noun. From it Shiblon's name received an internal definition located nearer to the front of Alma's record. There the word shiblon identifies one of the Nephite silver "pieces" of exchange, or coins. "A shiblon is half of a senum; therefore, a shiblon for half a measure of barley."[19] You may think "small change." What did Shiblon do wrong to deserve that? How cheap! Not really, though. Sometimes we give our kids names such as Penny, Bill or Buck, so don't view it as the very worst—but close. In fact, Alma's letter to Shiblon tends to be upbeat, as well as ending quickly. Alma congratulated Shiblon on his "steadiness and faithfulness to God."[20] His dad encouraged him to continue. Shiblon had evidently suffered and endured much already and was given a pat on the back for his diligence and longsuffering.[21] Alma very briefly recounted his own conversion experience, which Shiblon had certainly heard many times already.[22] Again, Shiblon was advised to "continue to teach" while receiving a bit of good advice not to boast and to refrain from idleness.

Finally Alma applied some gentle guilt brokering on him, an admonition to "acknowledge your unworthiness before God at all times," then presto! He sealed the envelope.[23] Alma's correspondence ended nothing like, "Love Ya—Papa," but only, "Be sober. My son, farewell."[24] How much psychological manipulation does Alma's letter suggest? What do you imagine Shiblon ought to write in reply? How about, "Thanks for the letter, Pop. Uh, gotta go teach somebody"? While Shiblon must have appreciated hearing from his dad at all, comparing it with his older and younger brothers' longer letters may have caused him to drop his chin a notch.

One of the things happening with Alma's letters to his three sons throughout chapters 36-42 is a representation of what all adult Mormons experience at least once each year. It's called a bishop's interview conducted by the so-called "father of the ward." While visiting briefly during that face-to-face meeting, the bishop will review a standardized list of questions that continue probing for signs of righteousness and loyalty. He's mainly concerned with one's spiritual commitment, their habits at prayer; that followers are up to date on tithes and other offerings, and that they haven't cheated on their spouses, nor been lying. And he is bound to be generous in his praise for one's service to the church. Perhaps he'll offer some advice to improve one's spiritual life, but will always encourage members to continue in diligence, in temperate behavior and service to the Lord. But, once in awhile you may walk away feeling like you're a well used fifty-cent piece that just got buffed up because a little encouragement is usually all it takes to keep it rolling for another season. It all helps in maintaining smooth operations within the church, and members looking forward to their next annual visit—like being summoned to an IRS audit.

Alma's impersonal correspondence may have made Shiblon feel like just another one of the brethren, just another sibling. Oh, sorry, you didn't pronounce Shiblon quite correctly. It's one of Joseph's inside jokes. Mormons have a curious belief about their lineage, supposing they are descendants from the ancient tribe of Ephraim: "The great majority of those who have come into the Church are Ephraimites."[25] Anciently, members of the tribe of Ephraim were known to have had difficulty caused by their dialect when pronouncing the "sh" sound. Saying *shibboleth*, they would have dropped the first "h," pronouncing it "*sibboleth*."[26] Inheriting the same impediment of speech, Alma would have pronounced his son's name "Siblon," which we can imagine sounding very much like siblin', a contraction for sibling.

When Humor Runs in the Family

Although Joseph always kept his subtle sense of humor at the ready, he never let it bubble over nor exploited it as well as his potential suggests. Facing a terrific assortment of difficult situations and negotiations through life, he needed a store of irony and mirth within easy reach, or he surely would have gone irreversibly mad. If he sometimes had difficulty keeping a straight face, that may explain why friends described him translating the gold plates from behind a curtain, or with his face pressed into a white top hat.[27]

In the letter to Shiblon, his middle son, Alma includes a golden vein of low-level humor that runs nearly through it. Joseph's brand of wit might almost be thought of as a caprice, for Shiblon's ridicule in response to Alma, his stuffed-shirt father, doesn't develop more than a suggestion or spirit. In fact it only exists for readers capable of fitting themselves into Shiblon's shoes, and are able to see Alma feeding him one gag line after another, and can then imagine appropriate responses. The humor would be easier to recognize if scripted in the form of dialogue between father and son. (**Shiblon's**) part takes the form of reconstructed *thoughts* in response to the absurdities passed along by **Alma**, his overbearing, pompous father:

> **Alma**: For I know that thou wast in bonds; yea, and I also know that thou wast stoned for the word's sake [...] and now thou knowest that the Lord did deliver thee.[28]
> (**Shiblon**): Dad, you've got it all wrong. If God had *delivered* me, those stones would have missed my body. I could have died out there.
> **Alma**: I would that ye would be diligent and temperate in all things.[29]
> (**Shiblon**): Which is it, Dad, diligence or temperance? I can't very well be *temperate* if I'm going to concentrate on *diligence*.
> **Alma**: Use boldness, but not overbearance [...].[30]
> (**Shiblon**): Did I just hear you say that? Does overbearance still mean what it used to? Why, you're the most overbearing person I've ever met. Don't you remember how you cursed poor Korihor, and he soon died?[31]
> **Alma**: Bridle all your passions, that ye may be filled with love [...].[32]
> (**Shiblon**): You've got to be kidding, Dad. Doesn't *love* help *define* one's passion? How am I supposed to be *full* of love if I have to *bridle* all my passions? Uh, by the way, Dad, have you heard anything from Corianton lately?
> **Alma**: Do not say: 'O God, I thank thee that we are better than our brethren;' but rather say: 'O Lord, forgive my unworthiness, and remember my brethren in mercy—yea, acknowledge *your* unworthiness before God at all times.'[33]
> (**Shiblon**): Hmmm. 'O Lord [...] acknowledge *your* unworthiness before God?' I don't know, Dad; that might not be such a smart idea. Are you trying to get me into hot water, also?
> **Alma**: Be Sober. My son, farewell.[34]

(**Shiblon**): Darn it, Dad. What's with "be sober?" You haven't been spying on me, too, have you?

Gazelem

If a list were to be made of the ten best Book of Mormon references Joseph gave himself, Gazelem would be found near the top. In Alma it serves as a mystical code name revealing his true identity, but is also cross-referenced in the Doctrine and Covenants.

A couple of years following distribution of the Book of Mormon and the church's rapid growth, things began to heat up for Mormon followers. As might be expected of any burgeoning, assertive, maverick sect so disrespectful of Protestant orthodoxy, persecution dogged the early Saints. In 1832 and again in 1834 Joseph introduced revelations from God giving instructions to various brethren of the church. Supposedly to protect against such sensitive information becoming easily obtained by enemies, nicknames such as *Pelagoram, Zombre,* and *Baneemy* were substituted when those revelations received publication. Such zany nicknames no longer lend character to recent editions of the Doctrine and Covenants, though earlier printings maintain them in sections 78, 82, 103, 104 and 105.

In sections 82 and 104 Joseph referred to himself by the code name Gazelam (e.g., "And let my servant Mahemson [Martin Harris] devote his moneys for the proclaiming of my words, according as my servant Gazelam [Joseph Smith, Jun.] shall direct").[35] Bearing an inconsequential spelling change, his inclusion of Gazelem in the Book of Mormon should leave little doubt that Joseph intended to portray himself as the *servant:*

> And the Lord said: I will prepare unto my servant Gazelem [Joseph] a stone, which shall shine forth in darkness unto light, that I may discover unto them the works of their brethren, yea, their works of darkness, and their wickedness and abominations.[36]

Those having observed how light ordinarily shines into darkness, not "darkness unto light," will likely admit this could be another riddle clue left by Joseph, who wasn't bent merely on brightening up ancient Christianity so much as burning it down. When reading about Gazelem's shining stone, try recalling the two [seer?] stones Nephi used to get his blacksmith fire going. The word *Gazlen* is Yiddish (from a Hebrew root: *gazel*) meaning "robber," "criminal," "racketeer," or "murderer."[37] Taken together, definitions of the word Gazlen nearly match an 1839 Missouri warrant for Joseph's arrest on charges of "murder, treason, burglary, arson, larceny, theft and stealing."[38] Not only does Gazelem's symbol represent an image distinctly undesirable, but note the possibility that Joseph tried foreshadowing his extensive legal record, acquired *subsequent* to publication of his book.

Amalickiah, the King

In Alma's record Joseph drew another character especially well in order to identify that darker side of his soul; this man, Amalickiah, became another fiercely ambitious warrior. When introducing him, Joseph produced a highly visible clue that he intended to depict another facet of his personality, for Amalickiah "[...] was a large and a strong man," which has almost become a trademark or signature for Joseph.[39] But then, as if to throw believers off his track, Amalickiah was also counted as "one very wicked man."[40] Like Joseph, Amalickiah understood the powerful advantages offered through his use of flattery. Significantly, Alma accused Amalickiah of having led many believers *away* from the (orthodox?) church through his cunning and insincere praises, especially when promising that, "he would make them rulers over the people." Amalickiah's evil flattery applied almost the same wording Joseph would later attribute to God within his *Book of Abraham*: "God saw these souls that they were good, and he stood in the midst of them [presumably LDS believers], and he said: These I will make my rulers."[41] The cheap flattery in both cases stems from the very same source—Joseph knew he could win the affections of many followers by convincing them to imagine themselves persevering on an endless progression towards omnipotence.

Amalickiah was a political schemer who believed himself an admirable figure in a military outfit. He was after as much power and privilege as he could accumulate, "And Amalickiah was desirous to be a king."[42] In accordance with the script, during his last days in Nauvoo, Joseph established an autonomous secret society, the Council of Fifty, or "kingdom of God," with himself anointed as its king.[43] Surprisingly, of the many opportunities he had to engage in battles that would earn his desired glory, Amalickiah did not die during combat, but, like Joseph, became victim of an assassination.[44] The wound causing Amalickiah's death pierced him "*to* his heart." Among the four bullets taken from Joseph's body, one of them was "*under* the heart."[45] In this one instance, at least, coincidence surely played a part—life imitates art now and again.

An unusually complex combination of symbols has been enlisted for composing Amalickiah's four-part symbol name: *A* + *mal* (a Latin prefix meaning "bad") + *ick* (from the word *ichor*, a blood substitute said to flow in veins of the Greek gods of antiquity), + *iah*, the name-ending shared by five Jewish prophets, from Isaiah through Zechariah. The "Father in Heaven" of Mormon lore also has a body of flesh and bone, but with a more purified spirit substance coursing through His veins, rather than corruptible red human blood. One suggested interpretation for Amalickiah's symbol might be "a bad-blooded (or bastardized) god-prophet." In this instance, as with several other confessional clues, Joseph wasn't putting himself down, as may appear the case. His perspective and sense of opposition in all things allowed him to accurately cast himself in roles both good and evil. His firmness in stating the truth of the matter through fiction gave him the power to present himself essentially naked before the world, but without suffering the calamitous social consequences if he'd gone public with it.

In exposing his transparent self through literature Joseph may have exhibited much healthier psychology than heretofore assessed by highly qualified professionals. One may also safely assume that, having surrendered such intimacies from the depths of his soul, his monumental ego never seems to have spoiled him, corrupted his purpose nor distracted him from pursuing his original goal. Those revelations served him as the roadmap needed to help focus his highly disciplined mind towards their achievement.

CHAPTER 18

Alma, Part 3: Alma's Quasi-Chiasmi Find Their New Literary Heritage

> I told the brethren that the Book of Mormon was the most correct of any book on earth, and the keystone of our religion [...]. (Joseph Smith)[1]

Joseph's proud boast wasn't so totally facetious, for at least in its own genre not a book on earth can compare with it. Even errors cannot destroy its effect; too much correction would have ruined it entirely. Perhaps none of its underlying characteristics will certify to the Book of Mormon's pure perfection and intended designs as well as a set of three unrivaled *chiasmi* that Joseph devised to demonstrate his stratospheric acumen and mastery of literary skills.

Don't despair if the term seems unfamiliar. Chiasmi refers to an ancient form of classic poetry that develops poignancy or wit through a set of words or ideas observed twice during a couplet, but displaying the series in a reverse order during its repeat segment. One of the best known examples of this form of expression is the one from John Kennedy's inaugural address, "Ask not what your country can do for you, ask what you can do for your country."

It's called a chiasmus (ky-az-mus); plural, chiasmi, but is sometimes referred to as a contrapuntal phrase. The word comes from *chi*, the Greek letter X. This odd poetic structure seems to have achieved earliest popularity in *Greece* more than twenty-five centuries ago as great thinkers competed to see who could apply the best wit to their compositions. One of the earliest recorded chiasmi has been attributed to Bias (6th century BCE), one of the Seven Wise Men of ancient Greece: "Love as if you would one day hate, and hate as if you would one day love."

The Greeks were noted for their attempts at exploring for truth through the reasoning process. Composing Chiasmi became a favorite mental exercise because it helps develop lateral thinking skills and clarity when communicating ideas to others; working with its structure may assist in stimulating synthesis of new ideas. Its "X" characteristic comes into play when two halves of a statement are laid one above the other, with lines drawn between repeating elements, such as:

Better a witty fool

X

Than a foolish wit.

(Shakespeare, *Twelfth Night*)

This example demonstrates why sometimes the form is characterized as inverse parallelism. Not only did John Kennedy, Bias and Shakespeare compose examples of chiastic sayings but also Aeschylus, Aristotle, Francis Bacon, Winston Churchill, Diogenes, Albert Einstein, Thomas Jefferson, Abe Lincoln, Ovid, Thomas Paine,[2] Will Rogers, Seneca, Themistocles, Voltaire, Mae West and many others.[3]

There is good probability that Jewish writings didn't begin featuring chiasmi much earlier than Judah's return from Babalonian captivity, during the latter years of the 5th century, BCE, the period in which the Holy Scriptures began assuming their appearance as a collected work. Popularity for experimenting with the clever form began waning long before our modern age, that is, until LDS scholars suddenly began recognizing swarms of chiasmi in the Book of Mormon. Although discovery there surfaced relatively recently, the Saints have strained the limits of their media services in order to put forward the most attractive implications of their find.

Although basic rules for chiastic construction are almost too simple, aesthetic evaluation of more complex examples can test one's patience. For larger chiasmi the best way to preserve visual display of its **X** characteristic is to offset succeeding elements. Once center has been reached, word pairs then reverse. Each couplet or segment contains just one of the repeating word or phrase-elements.

We can view a beautiful example of a well-constructed biblical chiasmus found at Matthew 6:22.

    A   The **LIGHT**
      B   Of the **BODY**
        C Is the **EYE**:
        c If therefore thine **EYE** be single,
      b   Thy whole **BODY**
    a   Shall be full of **LIGHT**.

Ideally, key repeated elements should invoke greater meaning or power than words duplicated primarily for the sake of forcing completion to the form. Also, those paired segments are not limited to use of identical single words, such as joining *light* with *light*, so long as an equivalent root becomes part of the paired set. When appropriate, "moon-glow" or even "star-bright" could substitute acceptably when combined with light.

Another example, but more complex, is found at Matthew 7:16–20:

Matthew's Good Fruit Chiasmus

  A   **YE SHALL KNOW THEM**
    B   **BY THEIR FRUITS**. Do men gather
                      grapes of thorns, or figs of thistles?
      C   Even so every **GOOD**
        D   **TREE**
          E   Bringeth forth **GOOD FRUIT**;
            F   But a **CORRUPT TREE**
              G Bringeth forth **EVIL FRUIT**.
              g A good tree cannot bring forth **EVIL FRUIT**,
            f   Neither can a **CORRUPT TREE**
          e   Bring forth **GOOD FRUIT**.
        d   Every **TREE** that bringeth not forth
      c   **GOOD** fruit is hewn down, and cast into the fire.
    b   Wherefore **BY THEIR FRUIT**
  a   **YE SHALL KNOW THEM**.

Imagine the intensity of concentration demanded for composing such an extended chiasmus without bobbling syntax in order to achieve a beautiful x-shaped symmetry. Both of the above chiasmi from Matthew, along with several others, were imported into the Book of Mormon with its rewritten Sermon on the Mount given in the New World.[4]

It isn't necessary that repeating elements be precisely balanced—often there's ample accompanying word stock, sometimes none. Although an entire phrase or even a couple of lines may separate chiastic pairs, too much interposed verbiage tends toward obscuring of an otherwise meaningful specimen. Form alone is what keeps it together, rather than reliance upon rhyme or meter, as found in more conventional forms of English poetic expression. Technically, as long as his words continue repeating through the inverted structure, it will be difficult to disprove an artistic author's intent to construct his chiasmus.

Before reviewing three spectacular examples from the book of Alma, one must acknowledge that almost any collection Book of Mormon chiasmi will fall short of completion. The book is absolutely packed with them, both large and small, each presenting a new source of pride to the Saints. Readers should be able to locate a chiasmus by now; a slower reading pace helps when reviewing chiastic suspects. Although the chiasmus is easy to miss or ignore on an initial reading, it becomes an indicator that helps to accent an author's intent for creating a compelling literary message. The Book of Mormon must be considered as more than a merely historical or scriptural document. Indeed, neither its history nor scripture have proven themselves its most salutary features.

When Words Fail, Say It with an X

LDS scholars make their claim that chiasmi within the Book of Mormon confirm its "Hebraic literary heritage" brought by prophets who migrated to the New World from the land of Jerusalem in 600 BCE, long before the Old Testament had even been compiled. Those scholars have shortchanged us by withholding useful information about chiastic origins. They seem to ignore the subtle clue that chiasmus is not even a Hebrew word but Greek. Adding substantially to the puzzle, the Mormon record claims an entirely unrelated linguistic heritage—Egyptian.[5]

Since the poetic form registers as a literary X, the most symbolic character in the English alphabet, let's look a bit closer at its significance. What else can you do with an X besides cross days off your calendar?

- Anciently, X became the initial letter in the Greek spelling of Christ, (Χριστός), later adopted for representing his name, as in "Merry Xmas."
- As a signature mark, an X will satisfy legal requirements.
- It indicates a specific location on a map ("X marks the spot").
- At the bottom of a letter, it might signify a *kiss* (XOXO = "kisses and hugs").
- It serves as an algebraic symbol for any unknown quantity and for indicating the multiplication function.
- It provides a method for crossing out written errors to cover them over when they cannot be erased.
- In biology X represents a hybrid.
- In chemistry X indicates an acid radical.
- In politics X shows a voter's preference.
- In witchcraft the center of an X is where magic abounds. The floors of voodoo ceremonial temples are covered with Xs.
- The X is sometimes applied to designate a grade of refinement, as in XXX flour or *Dos Equis* beer (XX).
- The X may also be shown to symbolize a product's inferior quality (as in "Brand X").

Although other symbolic uses for the X exist, these seem most fitted to Joseph's purposes in producing the Book of Mormon, though the last item on the list (inferior quality) seems inconsistent with the magnitude of his accomplishment. In fact it isn't necessary that any chiasmus demonstrate added symbolic function. Joseph may have placed quantities of chiasmi into his book merely as an element of his literary style, charged by some critics as biblical imposture. Tom Paine suggested that the term "prophet" was originally meant to describe a poet.[6] Would this style of expression have appealed to Joseph in cultivating his prophetic stature?

The following three examples from the book of Alma are so exceptional that marking the elements of each of them in your own copy, if you have one, will be quite useful. Multiple chiasmi, set into a distinctive series, can actually be made to overlap one another. Using various colored highlighter markers may assist in subsequent analysis.

Alma's Great Geographical Chiasmus

Perhaps the most striking and easy to locate chiasmus lies in the geographical center of your recent edition of the Book of Mormon. Dividing the 531 pages of the latest Book of Mormon text by two (or multiplying it by one-half) yields page 265.5. To be precise, the reader is directed to the bottom of the first column of page 266 (one-half page beyond 265). At that exact spot, the book's center, Alma 22:29-34, there is an unusual chiasmus that really lies in the heart of its soul. Re-formatted, it registers the following appearance:

ALMA 22, THE GREAT GEOGRAPHICAL CHIASMUS

A   And thus the Nephites were nearly surrounded by **THE LAMANITES;**
B   Nevertheless **THE NEPHITES** had taken possession of all the northern parts of the land bordering on the wilderness, at the head of the river Sidon, from the east to the west, round about on the wilderness side; on the north,
C   Even until they came to **THE LAND** which they called Bountiful.
D   And it bordered upon the land which they called Desolation, it being so far **NORTHWARD**
E   That it came into **THE LAND** which had been peopled and been destroyed, of whose bones we have spoken, which was discovered by the people of Zarahemla,
F   It being the place of their first **LANDING**.
G   And they came from there up into the **SOUTH** wilderness.
H   Thus the land on the **NORTHWARD**
I   Was called **DESOLATION,**
J   And **THE LAND** on the southward was called Bountiful,
K   It being the **WILDERNESS** which is filled
k   With all manner of **WILD** animals of every kind,
j   A part of which had come from **THE LAND** northward for food.
i   And now, it was only the distance of a day and a half's journey for a Nephite, on the line Bountiful and the land **DESOLATION**, from the east to the west sea; and thus The land of Nephi and the land of Zarahemla were nearly surrounded by water, there being a neck of land between
h   The land **NORTHWARD**
g   And the land **SOUTHWARD**.
f   And it came to pass that the Nephites had inhabited **THE LAND** Bountiful,
e   Even from the sea east unto the west sea, and thus the Nephites in their wisdom, with their guards and their armies, had hemmed in the Lamanites on the south, that thereby they should have no more possession on the north, that they might not overrun **THE LAND NORTHWARD.**
d   Therefore the Lamanites could have no more possessions only in
c   **THE LAND** of Nephi, and the wilderness round about.
b   Now this was wisdom in **THE NEPHITES**—
a   As **THE LAMANITES** were an enemy to them […].

Speaking of brilliance! Not only is Joseph's chiasmus much larger than anything before it, but note how this extraordinary example even speaks of *land, wilderness, north* and *south* as if markers drawing attention toward the geographical center of the book ("X marks the spot" this time). Never before, not in any prose composition of comparable length, has such a complex feat been undertaken and concluded with such success. How expertly Joseph has manipulated mundane words! Anybody wishing to claim that the chiastic feature occurred purely by coincidence will be pushing credibility and probability beyond reason. The chiasmus stands consistent in its form, although quite in excess; here we see it beginning to take on greater lavishness, especially in how its reformatted diagram begins suggesting something visual (i.e., "Take aim at this spot"). Also note the excellent argument this allows for demonstrating that its author must have maintained a high degree of consciousness while composing his work. Do gems this grand assemble themselves following the mindless meanderings of someone engaging in the occult practice of channeling?

On the other hand could someone with an intuitive, incisive mind have analyzed earlier chiastic forms, perhaps because they're encountered frequently throughout the Bible, then engaged its style as part of a satire? Mormons would of course argue strenuously that credibility has already been stretched beyond reason by imagining such an ignorant rustic capable of sufficient intellectual attainment or sophistication. They have a very good point: try constructing one this magnificent in the first full-length book you write. Further, try locating any example one-half its size that *anyone* has constructed purely by accident.

Not intending to spoil anyone's pride in this rare poetic form from antiquity, we must yet try to understand how a collection of authors, separated by many years, determined how to place that very distinctive X into the exact center of their *combined* writings. Joseph was pointing out something quite significant and informative about himself. Alma's Great Geographical Chiasmus could serve as prudent evidence for the "single author theory," whether or not zealous believers or incredulous critics choose to subscribe to it. For all that dazzle, his centering of that symbolic X may discredit the sincerity of Joseph's lament when Martin Harris supposedly lost 116 pages of his book's manuscript.[7] He couldn't have demonstrated much cleverness when allowing such a loss to displace geographical center too far from its ideal location. Did that earliest copy contain defects that he already planned editing during his second go-around while working with a new scribe? Had Joseph previously recognized Harris' impulsive zeal, which he then used as a ruse to pick the old man clean for the funds needed to publish his book? Martin's guilt cost him at least $2000, a small fortune at the time.

One historical note that this chiasmus calls to mind as a symbolically centered X is its similarity with an early practice among Jewish scribes who copied old and worn Holy Scriptures. When completing a newly copied scroll, "They counted the words and verses and figured the *middle* verse of a book so as to prevent careless dropping of anything."[8]

Alma 36: The Triple Crucifixion Chiasmus

Without question it would be useless to go about trying to extract anything resembling chiastic structure in typical works of literature where none were originally intended. Likewise, some readers may discount particular chiasmi merely because they don't conform to someone's expectations of neatly balanced symmetry, or that they fail to signify wisdom or a lovely thought in the words of their elements. Those added characteristics may supplement chiastic form but don't necessarily define or qualify them. Besides, nobody's chiasmi are more meaningful than Joseph's. Therefore, when an entire chapter in the book of Alma begins and ends with the same phrase and follows every rule for chiasmus construction, one should not permit a slight excess of connecting verbiage to obscure one of literature's most starkly fascinating manifestations. This next chiasmus begs recognition as a familiar mental image, almost as if the author tried painting the scene with his words. The larger chiasmus "cross" spans an entire chapter, but with "my mind/my heart [...] Jesus Christ, thou Son of God" hung for display upon its crossbeam center.

What you're going to view in the Triple Crucifixion Chiasmus will appear a bit confusing at first, because, intertwining its structure are two minor symbolic crosses woven *through* the major cross, one before and one following Jesus Christ. It represents an even higher expression of the art than chiasmus experts have divulged previously. Because they haven't been expecting it, seeming reluctant to allow public acknowledgment, they sometimes tend to ignore the two minor crosses as anomalies without significant value.

Unfortunately, because my book's pages aren't poster-size, this feature-length chiasmus had to be re-formatted, giving it a lop-sided appearance. Readers must therefore supply an imaginative assist in viewing the big **X**. Those who are able to picture the structures taking shape may not know whether to be put off by the spectacle or awed by the uncanny ingenuity of its invention. When arriving at its minor crosses (crosses 2 and 3), beginning after element 1P, and again after element 1y, try reading beyond the offset caused by the diagramming method. Since reading its words will help in illuminating the image, you may continue following the original text, left to right, as usual, one line following another. The diagramming offsets are intended to aid in the visualizing process, and for confirming the symbolic (chiastic) representation of interwoven secondary crosses.

ALMA'S TRIPLE CRUCIFIXION CHIASMUS (Alma 36)

1A   My son, give ear to my words; for I swear unto you, that **INASMUCH AS YE SHALL KEEP THE COMMANDMENTS OF GOD YE SHALL PROSPER IN THE LAND.**
  1B   I would that ye should do **AS I HAVE DONE,**
    1C   **IN REMEMBERING**
     1D   The **CAPTIVITY**
      1E   Of our **FATHERS**;
       1F   For they were in **BONDAGE,**
        1G   And none could **DELIVER** them except it was the God of Abraham, and the God of Isaac, and the God of Jacob;
         1H   And he surely did **DELIVER** them in their afflictions. And now, O my son Helaman, thou art in thy youth, and therefore, I beseech of thee that thou wilt hear my words and learn of me;
          1I   For I do know that whosoever shall put their **TRUST IN GOD** shall be supported
           1J   In their **TRIALS, AND THEIR TROUBLES AND THEIR AFFLICTIONS,** and shall be lifted up at the last day.
            1K   And I would not that ye think that **I KNOW** of myself—not of the temporal but of the spiritual, not of the carnal mind but of God.
             1L   Now behold, I say unto you, if I had not **BEEN BORN OF GOD** I should not have known these things; but God has,
              1M   By the mouth of his **HOLY** angel, made these things known unto me, not of any worthiness of myself; For I went about with the sons of Mosiah, seeking to destroy the church of God;
               1N   But behold, **GOD** sent his holy angel to stop us by the way.
               1O   And behold, he **SPAKE UNTO** us, as it were the voice of thunder, and the whole earth did tremble beneath our feet; and we all fell to the earth, for the fear of the of the Lord came upon us.
                1P   But behold, the voice said unto me: arise. And I arose and **STOOD UP**, and beheld the angel. And he said unto me: If thou wilt of thyself be destroyed, seek no more to destroy the church of God.

THE MAKE-BELIEVE MARTYR

2A   And it came to pass that I fell to the earth; and it was for the space of **THREE DAYS AND THREE NIGHTS** that I could not open my mouth,

    1Q   Neither had I the use of **MY LIMBS**.

    1R   And the **ANGEL** spake more things unto me, which were heard by my brethren, but I did not hear them; for when I heard the words—

        1S   If thou wilt be destroyed of thyself, seek no more to destroy the church of **GOD**—

2B   I was struck with such great fear and amazement lest perhaps I should be **DESTROYED**, I fell to the earth and I did hear

    1T   **NO MORE**.

    2C   But I was racked with eternal **TORMENT**, for my soul was harrowed up to the greatest degree and

        2D   Racked with **ALL MY SINS**.

        2d   Yea, I did remember **ALL MY SINS** and iniquities,

        2c   For which I was **TORMENTED**

        1U   With the **PAINS** of hell; Yea, I saw that I had rebelled against my God, and that I had not kept his holy commandments. Yea, and I had murdered many of his children,

2b   Or, rather led them away unto **DESTRUCTION**;

    1V   Yea, and in fine so great had been my iniquities, that the very thought of coming into the presence of my God did rack my soul with inexpressible horror. O, thought I, that I could be banished and **BECOME EXTINCT**

    1W   Both soul and body, that I might not be brought to stand in the presence of M**Y GOD**, to be judged of my deeds.

2 a   And now, **FOR THREE DAYS AND THREE NIGHTS** was I racked,

    1X   Even with the **PAINS** of a damned soul.

    1Y   And it came to pas that as I was thus racked with torment, while **I WAS HARROWED UP BY THE MEMORY OF MY MANY SINS**, behold , I remembered also to have heard my father prophesy unto the people concerning the coming of one

    1Z   **JESUS CHRIST, A SON OF GOD**, to atone for the sins of the world.

    1AA   Now, as **MY MIND** caught hold upon this thought,

    1aa   I cried within **MY HEART**:

    1z   **O JESUS, THOU SON OF GOD**, have mercy on me, who am in the gall of bitterness, and am encircled about by the everlasting chains of death. And now, behold, when I thought this, I could remember my pains no more;

    1y   Yea, **I WAS HARROWED UP BY THE MEMORY OF MY SINS** no more.

Alma's Quasi-Chiasmi

3A   And oh, what joy, and what marvelous light **I**
   3B   **DID**
    3C   **BEHOLD**;
     3D   Yea, **MY SOUL** was filled
      3E With **JOY** as exceeding
                             1x   As was my **PAIN**!
                                1w   Yea, I say unto you, **MY SON**, that there could
                          1v   **BE NOTHING**
    3F   **SO EXQUISITE** and so bitter as were
                        1u   My **PAINS**.
                1t   Yea, and again I say unto you, my son, that
                       on the other hand , there can be **NOTHING**
   3f   **SO EXQUISITE** and sweet
  3e   As was my **JOY**.
              1s   Yea, methought I saw, even as our father
                  Lehi saw, **GOD** sitting upon his throne,
                  1r   Surrounded with numberless concourses of **ANGELS**,
                      in the attitude of singing and praising their God;
  3d   Yea, and **MY SOUL** did long to be there.
  3c   But **BEHOLD**,
             1q   **MY LIMBS**
 3b   **DID** receive their strength again,
3a   And **I**
            1p   **STOOD UPON MY FEET**,
           1o   And **DID MANIFEST** unto the people
         1n   That I had been born of **GOD**. Yea, and from that time until now, I
                   have labored without ceasing, that I might bring souls unto
                   repentance; that I might bring them to taste of the exceeding joy of
                   which I did taste; that they might also be born of God,
        1m   And be filled with the **HOLY** Ghost. Yea, and now, behold, O my son,
                  the Lord doth give me exceeding great joy in the fruit of my labors;
       1l   For because of the word which he has imparted unto me, behold, many
                 have **BEEN BORN OF GOD**, and have tasted as I have tasted,
                 and have seen eye to eye as I have seen;
       1k   Therefore they do know of these things of which I have spoken,
                as **I DO KNOW,** and the knowledge which I have is of God.
      1j   And I have been supported under **TRIALS AND TROUBLES OF EVERY**
              KIND, YEA, AND IN ALL MANNER OF AFFLICTIONS; yea, God has
              delivered me from prison, and from bonds, and from death;
     1i   Yea, and I do put **MY TRUST IN HIM,**
     1h   And he will still **DELIVER** me. And I know that he will raise me up at
            the last day, to dwell with him in glory; yea, and I will praise him forever, for
            he has brought our fathers out of Egypt, and he has swallowed up the Egyptians
            in the Red Sea; he led them by his power into the promised land;
    1g   Yea, and he has **DELIVERED** them out of
   1f   **BONDAGE** and captivity from time to time.
   1e   Yea, and he has also brought our **FATHERS** out of the land of Jerusalem;
          and he has also, by his everlasting power, delivered them
   1d   Out of bondage and **CAPTIVITY**, from time to time even down to the present day;
 1c   And I have always retained in **REMEMBRANCE** their
        captivity; yea, and ye also ought to retain in remembrance,
1b   **AS I HAVE DONE,** their captivity. But behold, my son, this is not all;
1a   For ye ought to know as I do know, that **INASMUCH AS YE SHALL KEEP**
      THE COMMANDMENTS OF GOD YE SHALL PROSPER IN THE LAND;
      and ye ought to know also, that inasmuch as ye will not keep the commandments
      of God ye shall be cut off from his presence. Now this is according to his word.

Flaunting the world's most magnificent chiastic portrait before the world without being caught shouldn't have been made to seem so simple. Where have all those cute two-and-four liners hidden themselves? The critical aspect isn't so much that Joseph created a lengthy, stupendous chiasmus here, but reasonably appraising its symbolic value makes the visual aspect of the message seem too obvious. By placing Jesus Christ squarely at its center, and with a smaller cross on either side,[9] he portrayed the crucifixion of Jesus in a unique, mind-boggling literary rendition that has never before received adequate acknowledgment. While Mormon pride accompanies other Book of Mormon chiastic structures, for this one they've chosen to suppress recognition and media attention. The most logical reason for silence seems to be that Mormon teachings have always spurned the use of crosses, the most universal symbols of Christian belief. They don't place them atop their chapels nor display them within—that is, in any crucifix form seen in almost every other church, Catholic or Protestant. Properly informed Mormons don't accept the cross as suitable for jewelry but even more especially not as an aid to worship.

Reluctance to embrace the symbol should be awarded due merit; the crucifix represents a form of cruel torture and a death so inhumane it has legally been banned throughout the civilized world. Other Christians may consider the unbearable suffering it represents as one of its important virtues or have simply preferred displaying the cosmic symbolism of *Ichthys*, the fish. Incidentally, during Roman times there were several forms of cross construction, one of which, the *crux decussata*, or St. Andrew's cross, was set up in the form of the letter X. It is only by tradition that we've come to recognize the Latin cross (*crux immissa*, the T shape) as the form upon which Jesus died.[10]

So, what's the big deal? Might we not suppose that Joseph tried drawing attention to Jesus' act of atonement by placing him into the *center* of our lives and worship? Those who believe it so may have made the error of reading false graciousness into Mormon text. To see this better, let's try contrasting Christ's parable of the Prodigal Son (Luke 15:11-32) with Alma's hard-nosed attitude towards Corianton, his likewise wandering son (Alma 39-42). Who's the forgiver? Which son can we expect will refuse to return home? The intensity and single-minded craftsmanship that Joseph put into his prize chiasmus requires a bit more honesty and depth in viewing both image and its context. This particular chapter, Alma 36, is not merely describing Alma's conversion—so similar to St. Paul's—but represents a family letter that Alma (name symbol: "the soul," i.e., God) wrote to his son Helaman (name symbol: "healer-man," i.e., Jesus Christ). Throughout the passage Alma described himself as having done the suffering, "I fell to the earth [...] I could not open my mouth, neither had I the use of my limbs."[11] The angel threatened Alma with destruction.[12] He began feeling "[...] harrowed up by the memory of [his] many sins."[13] Alma lapsed into a coma for three days and three nights during which his soul was "racked, even with the pains of a damned soul."[14]

The underlying experience Alma described seems to show him taking upon himself the sins of the world by suffering those *infinite atonement* pains. Christians often view their Savior's sacrifice with some perplexity as to whether it was God suffering through his Son, or a man-Savior whose Godly nature either allowed or inflicted agonies upon himself. It helps annotate one of several mysteries of godliness resulting from the corruption sown throughout the early Christian church when it began assimilating well-established polytheistic pagan cults that worshipped a divine Father, Mother and Son.

Alma's Six-Chain-Linked Chiasmus (Alma 42)

For sheer mental achievement Joseph's Chain-Linked Chiasmus of Alma 42 will run circles around any other in existence. To keep pace with its patterns, it should be copied, trimmed and pasted into a single scroll, for these six distinctive chiasmi span one entire chapter but actually overlap one another *just enough* to make a unified but very bold statement. It ought to prove a couple of points, one being that they were singularly conscious constructions, not accidental. Possibly even more evident is the fact that their poetic artist was fooling everyone who would buy in on the story that God had only enough time to spare for one private interview with modern mankind and, thus, He hit upon the idea of selecting an ignorant backwoodsman to represent Him in carrying a latter-day gospel throughout the world.

As symbolic fare, these six Xs will do something that is beyond most readers' credence. In fact Mormons must be forgiven for sniggering in their doubt of what they would wish weren't true. Alma 42 is one of the most important chapters in the whole Book of Mormon, primarily because it identifies more Christian doctrine than any other chapter in the book. However, this segment constitutes part of Alma's long, sad letter to his wayward son, Corianton (Symbol name: "heavy heart" i.e., the guilt-ridden sinner). If you can picture a large X covering each full-length chiasmus you will have rubbed out the entire chapter, just as when using a manual typewriter after making a typographical error too long to erase. The X-ed out material contains ten doctrines most central to Christian thought; including: the fall of man, repentance, man's probationary estate, spiritual death, the resurrection, the plan of redemption, the atonement, mercy, justice and law. In Roman numerals X represents 10. Did Joseph score himself a perfect round?

While checking format against the book's text, appreciate how none of its verses escape the span of chiasmi. Once again our offset diagram is only offered as a necessary illustration convenient in confirming qualifying forms. Those choosing to read the entire text may follow each line in turn.

ALMA 42, THE SIX-CHAIN-LINKED CHIASMUS

1A   And now my son, I perceive there is somewhat more which doth worry your mind, which ye cannot understand---which is concerning the justice of God in the punishment of the sinner; for ye do try to suppose that it is injustice hat the sinner should be consigned to a **STATE** of misery.

   1B   **NOW BEHOLD,** my son, I will explain this thing unto thee.

     1C   For behold, after the Lord God sent our **FIRST PARENTS** forth from the garden of Eden, to till the ground, from whence they were taken—yea, he drew out the man, and he placed at the east end of the garden of Eden, cherubim, and a flaming sword which turned every way,

       1D   To keep **THE TREE OF LIFE**.

         1E   Now, we see that the **MAN** had become as

           1F **GOD**, knowing good and evil; and lest he should put forth his hand,

             1G And take also of **THE TREE OF LIFE**, and eat and live forever, the Lord God placed cherubim and a flaming sword,

               1H That he should not **PARTAKE** of the fruit—

                 1I And thus we see, that there was **A TIME** ranted unto man to repent,

                1i Yea, a probationary time, **A TIME** to repent and serve God. For behold,

               1h If Adam had put forth his hand immediately, and **PARTAKEN** of

             1g **THE TREE OF LIFE**, he would have lived forever, according to the word of God,

            1f Having no space for repentance; yea, and also the word of **GOD** would have been void, and the great plan of salvation would have been frustrated.

          1e But behold, it was appointed unto **MAN** to die— therefore, as they were cut off from

        1d **THE TREE OFLIFE** they should be cut off from the face of the earth—and man became lost forever, yea,

Alma's Quasi-Chiasmi

1c   2A   They became **FALLEN MAN**.
And now, ye see by this that our **FIRST PARENTS** were cut off both temporally and spiritually from the presence of the Lord; and thus we see they became subjects to follow after their own will.

1b   **NOW BEHOLD,**

2B   It was not expedient that **MAN**

2C   Should be **RECLAIMED** from this temporal death, for that would destroy the great plan of happiness. Therefore, as the soul could never die, and the fall had brought upon all mankind a spiritual death as well as a temporal, that is,

2D   They were **CUT OFF FROM THE PRESENCE OF THE LORD,** it was expedient that mankind should

2E   Be reclaimed from this spiritual **DEATH**.

1a   Therefore, as they had become carnal, sensual, and devilish, by nature, this probationary **STATE**

2F   Became a **STATE** for them

2G   To **PREPARE**;

2g   It became a **PREPARATORY**

2f   **STATE**. And now remember, my son,

2e   If it were not for the plan of redemption, (laying it aside) as soon as they were **DEAD** their souls were miserable, being

2d   **CUT OFF FROM THE PRESENCE OF THE LORD.**

2c   And now, there was no means to **RECLAIM**

3A   **MEN** from this fallen state,

2b   Which **MAN** had brought upon himself because of his own disobedience; Therefore, according to justice, the plan of redemption could not be brought about,

3B   Only on conditions of **REPENTENCE** of men in this probationary state, yea, this preparatory state; for except it were for these conditions, mercy could not take effect except it should destroy the work of justice. Now the work of justice could not be destroyed; if so,

3C   **GOD** would cease to be God.

2a   And thus we see that all **MANKIND WERE FALLEN,**

3D   And they were in the grasp of **JUSTICE**;

3E   Yea, the **JUSTICE** of God, which consigned them forever to be cut off from his presence.

3F   And now, **THE PLAN OF MERCY** could not be brought about

3G   Except an **ATONEMENT** should be made;

3g   Therefore God himself **ATONETH** for the sins of the world, to bring about

3f   **THE PLAN OF MERCY,**

3e   To appease the demands of **JUSTICE,**

3d   That God might be a perfect, **JUST**

3c   **GOD**

4A   And a merciful **GOD** also.

3b   Now, **REPENTANCE**

3a   Could not come unto **MEN**

4B   Except there were a **PUNISHMENT**, which also was eternal as the life of the sould should be, affixed opposite to the plan of happiness, which was as eternal also as the life of the soul. Now, how could a man repent except he should sin?

4C   How could he sin if there was no **LAW**?

4D   How could there be a **LAW** save there was

4E   **A PUNISHMENT?** Now, there was a punishment affixed,

4F   And a just **LAW GIVEN**, which brought remorse of conscience unto man.

4G   Now, if there was **NO LAW GIVEN**—if a man murdered he should die—

  4H Would he be **AFRAID** he would die
  4I **IF** he should murder?
  4i And also, **IF** there was no law given against sin
  4h Men would not be **AFRAID** to sin.
  4g And if there was **NO LAW GIVEN**, if men sinned what could justice do, or mercy either, for they would have no claim upon the creature?
  4f   But there is a **LAW GIVEN**,
  4e   And **A PUNISHMENT** affixed, and a repentance granted; which repentance, mercy claimeth; otherwise, justice
  4d   Claimeth the creature and executeth the **LAW**,
  4c   And the **LAW** inflicteth
  4b   The **PUNISHMENT**, if not so, the works of justice would be destroyed,
5A   And **GOD**
  4a   Would cease to be **GOD**.
 5B   But God ceaseth not to be God, and **MERCY** claimeth the penitent,
  5C And **MERCY** cometh because of the atonement; and the atonement bringeth to pass the resurrection of the dead; and the resurrection of the dead bringeth back men
   5D **INTO THE PRESENCE OF GOD**; and thus they are restored
   5d **INTO HIS PRESENCE**, to be judged according to their works, according to the law and justice.
  5c For behold, justice exerciseth all his demands, and also **MERCY** claimeth all which is her own; and thus, none but the truly penitent are saved.
 5b   What, do ye suppose that **MERCY** can rob justice?
6A   I say **UNTO YOU** Nay; not one whit. If so, God would cease to be God.
 5a   And thus **GOD** bringeth about
  6B His **GREAT** and eternal purposes, which were prepared from the foundation of the world. And thus cometh about the salvation and the redemption of men, and also their destruction and misery.
  6C Therefore, **O MY SON**, whosoever will come may come and partake of the waters of life freely; and whosoever will not come the same is not compelled to come; but in the last day it shall be restored unto him according to his deeds. If he has desired to do evil, and has not repented in his days, behold, evil shall be done unto him,
   6D According to the restoration of **GOD**. And now, my son, I desire that ye should let these things trouble you no more,
    6E And only let your **SINS**
    6F **TROUBLE** you, with that
    6f **TROUBLE** which shall bring you down unto repentance. O my son, I desire ye should deny the justice of God no more. Do not endeavor to excuse yourself in the least point
    6e Because of your **SINS**,
   6d By denying the justice of **GOD**; but do you let the justice of God, and his mercy, and his long-suffering have full sway in your heart; and let it bring you down to the dust in humility.
   6c And now, **O MY SON**, ye are called of God to preach the word unto this people. And now, my son, go thy way, declare the word with truth and soberness, that thou mayest bring souls unto repentance,
  6b   That the **GREAT** plan of mercy may have claim upon them.
 6a   And may *God* grant **UNTO YOU** even according to my words. Amen.

One will be hard pressed at this point to deny that an artistic genius was moved to generate extreme creativity, that he demonstrated wholly unanticipated gifts by his imaginative skills and that some quite significant ideology must have inspired such unparalleled compositions. One must likewise reason that during Joseph's generation a prudent author would want to deliver *these* messages on the sly. By now his reason for stealth has to be plain enough: his crossword commentary outrageously abused the Christianity from which he expected to obtain the great majority of followers—followers whom Joseph desperately needed.

One must begin to perceive, especially in this final chiastic vision, an attitude of vehement denial and rejection of orthodox Christian teachings. Those able to comprehend that side of the message, combined as it is with previously undisclosed pictorial images, may glean the gist of something akin to a warning label on a bottle of poison. One might even visualize a series of skulls-and-crossbones, six of them. Alternately, can we say that religious issues marked for nominal consideration within the text have now been given an overlay of Xs that seems to suggest, subliminally, perhaps, that access will be denied? Is it a rejection, or perhaps confession? Does it signify Joseph's supremely passionate but private rage against wholesale confusions that necessitated a creative vent? We must carefully continue studying both positive and negative potentials in his book in order to extract the message from it that is most consistent.

To grant him due credit, Joseph's chiasmi are distinctive innovations, for they tower above all previous examples. They accomplish more: he not only expanded the form but did it with panache. These delicate visual models interweave to fabricate symbolic images and statements of ideological purpose that, had they been presented more candidly and forthrightly, would certainly have assaulted the sensitivities of most nineteenth century readers. Even today one's allowing himself to be publicly labeled as *the* anti-Christ remains a most damning accusation, so that deliberately subduing his attack, in 1830, had to be a most prudent move.

Joseph's intent may simply have been to suggest that those enthralled readers ought to begin examining their thoughts more closely, to question earlier assumptions. To doubt and weigh one's formative training is perhaps the greatest task [and risk] that any of us must face during life. Joseph surely understood that dealing too directly with other human beings, especially when championing an unpopular or radical social cause, frequently leads to failure in dialogue. Therefore, the propagandizing methods he chose to employ demonstrate highly insightful techniques and have been consummately effective, as history has shown. The social change that he envisioned simply cannot occur while sitting at a corner table of some coffee house but must be engaged on a larger scale.

His intent seems to have been to sift through society, conscripting a large enough segment of it, forcing them (or their descendants) to listen to what he had to say, eventually, even if he couldn't be there at that future date to meet with them eye to eye. Considering his ample inventiveness, who could turn away from a work of unquestioned allure and of brilliance in its concept? Perhaps only those most intimately immersed in its illusions will have power to resist its more dynamic proportions. The prophet's new poetic form has given a chill to LDS intellectuals who previously took pride on the richness of chiastic examples found in their keystone scripture. Recently, elite Mormon apologetics teams have begun to back off by defining more carefully what constitutes a chiasmus, possibly to imply denial of undesirable elements in those that are shockingly spectacular, more animated and *so* full of meaning.[15] A Mormon's major claim for the existence of Book of Mormon chiasmi is that they greatly reduce the possibility that unaided earthly genius would have been able to create such noble works. We can easily credit Joseph with having much more intelligence than an LDS image usually admits, but that doesn't explain the unexpected appearance of ancient literary forms that have been transformed through sophisticated treatments not previously encountered anywhere else.

Further, his book begins to look less like the product of a 19th century mind, not by conceding authentic native antiquity shown through those creations, but by demonstrating a genius far too advanced. Mormons, I'm sure, will press the question of how an ignorant nineteenth century farm boy could possibly have created such works. The brilliance, of course, speaks volumes, and with enough timelessness deserving everyone's attention and even some applause; amazement wouldn't seem inappropriate. Following that well-reasoned inquiry of the LDS just one step further, who might be so bold as to take even greater intellectual risk by attributing such gifted creativity as a quite fabulous anomaly from pre-Columbian culture in America? Has any Mayan or Mesoamerican archaeological site yielded comparable length, complexity or analogous visual symbolism?[15] Who ever accused the Aztecs of being such clever seducers and swindlers?

Since more than a hundred chiastic structures have been logged within his "Golden Bible," hopefully the world will not hesitate too much longer in awarding Joseph appropriate recognition for his genius. These amazingly complex chiastic examples should add immeasurably to the book's stature as an immortal literary classic; they serve to confirm the fact that Joseph was indeed its sole author. While taking innovation well beyond the simple imitation of previous models, he prodigiously comprehended and took command over the form's impressionistic potential. Regardless of where his intellect first sprouted its wings, he *over-amped* the poetic form beyond anything previous—either Hebrew or Greek (or Egyptian) and imparted elaborate, novel interpretive twists. As he had elsewhere created a satire of the Bible throughout his book, these chiasmi magnify his talents "above the brightness of the sun," one might imagine. His souped-up, blown-out invention registers as a spectacular, jazzy new pictorial-literary form: *quasi-chiasmi*. Neither wholly Greek nor Hebrew, it's all-American.

CHAPTER 19

A Hostile but Faithful Witness, Part 1: The Descent of Jesus Christ

"The test of a first-rate intelligence is the ability to hold two opposed ideas in the mind at the same time, and still retain the ability to function."(F. Scott Fitzgerald, *The Crack-up*)

    Its most publicized attraction, an anticipated highlight and main reason many readers persevere through three quarters of the Book of Mormon's bulk, is to experience Jesus' visit in the New World so they may compare it with what they've previously received by way of the Bible. The book's recently appointed subtitle reflects the church's efforts to generate focus toward that sublime prospect; their media campaigns promote it as "Another Testament of Jesus Christ." Supposedly, Mormon abridged the current version of Christ's visit, now compressed into twenty chapters of Third Nephi, originally written by an eyewitness with the familiar name [and spotless credentials] of Nephi [the third].
    Good reason suggests that, if Jesus were truly a savior for all mankind, he needs somehow to provide his saving gospel to many multitudes throughout the world who would otherwise have remained ignorant and unbelieving, thus losing their best chance at salvation, for "God is no respecter of persons." After discovering that reasoned criticism of Christianity's limited scope generated through Tom Paine's writings, Joseph developed his speculative tale regarding Christ's post-resurrection

venture to the western hemisphere.[1] Which other author of our modern age ever assigned himself a proposition of such magnitude, invested with such impressive possibilities?

Having conceived such a sublime occasion for unlocking his creative urge Joseph knew he would at least capture reader curiosity. While taking such influence into his hands, how would he direct those powers? If he had wanted to promote Jesus or enjoin Christian living the matter would have quickly become self-evident through the Savior's words and actions. Instead, as he had been doing since page one, Joseph continued borrowing basic elements from the Bible in order to yield high recognition factors, then massaged and reduced those lively features with utmost subtlety and parody until they resembled the most juvenile of stage props. Posing only as the book's translator, Joseph risked losing nothing of his reputation, meanwhile standing to gain a great boost for his position against sectarian religious fallacies.

Normally for readers getting so far into it, they've come prepared by thinking of Jesus as an unassailable hero while reading about him in the New Testament. They uniformly anticipate getting a view that is recognizable, familiar but unique, wise and triumphant, with a few memorable words to enlarge and energize faith. They desire and expect more of a sequel than what the Book of Mormon delivers. Instead, they get bombarded, first by Christ's wild, nerve-pinching introduction, then by its stale, uninspired remake of his Sermon on the Mount, followed by a gradual and boring descent into a syrupy, maudlin finish. Joseph's resulting image of Jesus doesn't appear so promotional as expected, but seems aimed at diluting or undermining traditional views. Parts of Third Nephi's record do bear a general resemblance to recognized events from the New Testament, including: Christ's calling of twelve ministers, his Sermon on the Mount and the administration of bread and wine in remembrance of his atoning sacrifice. If nothing in the account reflected recognized vistas, curious inquirers wouldn't have wasted so much of their time pouring over its complex, slightly skewed scenarios. Consequently, records of Christ's visit appear familiar—perhaps too familiar. To some, its re-run redundancy becomes a disappointment and annoyance.

Joseph obviously cribbed much of the material from the most available source, his copy of a King James edition of the Bible. Hence, charges of plagiarism are among the oldest of all Book of Mormon criticisms; early detractors dubbed it the "Golden Bible" hoping to cut short its successes. However, underestimations by those unfriendly critics were no less far off the mark than the acclaim generated by Joseph's converts. During his New World introduction, Jesus wasn't entirely the same gentle teacher as we've learned about from the New Testament but is transformed into a fearsome adaptation distorted mainly from *The Gospel According to St. Matthew*. Greatly exaggerating the already fabulous New Testament account of an earthquake that occurred precisely simultaneous with the Savior's death,[2] Joseph's new version shows Him arriving resurrected in the New World accompanied by earthquake, destruction and deadly mayhem throughout the entire continent. Sixteen great cities were destroyed from the violence and fire, "And many great and notable cities were sunk, and many were burned, and many were shaken till the buildings thereof had fallen to the earth, and the inhabitants thereof were slain, and the places were left desolate."[3] If not satire, what?

To survivors of that apocalyptic event, the entire vista became thick, dense and pitch black for three whole *days* before Jesus could locate his audience.[4] The embellished account derives from Matthew's record of only three *hours* of darkness following Jesus' death.[5] With intent that we must hope represents Joseph's mischievousness, this savior spoke to those horror-stricken souls from out of the blackness, claiming full credit for having brought about the weeping, wailing, death and colossal terror.[6] Expectant but dumbfounded readers hesitate to conclude that the world of good and evil, light and darkness had been tragically turned upside down. Most Book of Mormon critics have been gospel students much too shrewd to fall for the counterfeit goods but not quite on their toes enough to identify full dimensions of an artifice in search of people with awe to spare. They may have understood plagiarism, prophecy and parable only too well, but have somehow failed to absorb their lessons of profound literature. Joseph's work cannot be fully appreciated without ascribing his gifts as a master at parody.

The Mother Hen Parody

Introducing Jesus through such a deformity of character didn't impose sufficient abuse, so Joseph continued by drawing his pejorative portrait along a different plane. He selected a simple poetic metaphor from Jesus' words in Matthew, then expanded it:

From the Bible:
O Jerusalem, Jerusalem, thou that killest the prophets, and stonest them which are sent unto thee, how often would I have gathered thy children together, even as a hen gathereth her chickens under her wings, and ye would not.[7]

Here, a rather picturesque figure of speech would seem entirely adequate; no significant clarification should be expected by expanding its simple theme. Perhaps intrigued by the odd depiction assigned to Jesus in a role obviously maternal, feminine, Joseph needled his readers with its key phrase several times.

From the Book of Mormon:
4. O ye people of these great cities which have fallen, who are descendants of Jacob, yea, who are of the house of Israel, how oft have I gathered you as a hen gathereth Her chickens under her wings, and have nourished you.
5. And again, how oft would I have gathered you as a hen gathereth her chickens under her wings, yea, O ye people of the house of Israel, who have fallen; yea, O ye people of the house of Israel, ye that dwell at Jerusalem, as ye that have fallen, yea, how oft would I have gathered you as a hen gathereth her chickens, and ye would not.
6. O ye house of Israel whom I have spared, how oft will I gather you as a hen gathereth her chickens under her wings, if ye will repent and return unto me with full purpose of heart.[8]

As the same thought becomes recycled a second, third and *fourth* time, the reader must begin to sense the author's intent for roasting Jesus with parody. Note Joseph's effective use of irony: the hidden personality behind the voice had just entered from offstage performing more like a fox in the chicken yard than as its mother hen.

Old Things Done Away

Destruction on land and darkness of sky becomes apt introduction to the bashing taken by a popular gospel message Jesus had once preached on mountains surrounding Palestine. Try imagining a more damning obloquy than that suffered by two of Christ's most memorable verses from his Sermon on the Mount. Joseph obliterated them.

From the Bible:
45. [...] he maketh the sun to rise on the evil and on the good, and sendeth rain on the just and on the unjust.
46. For if ye love them which love you, what reward have ye? Do not even the publicans the same?
47. And if ye salute your brethren only, what do ye more than others? Do not the publicans also?
48. Be ye therefore perfect [i.e., in likewise loving others unconditionally], even as your father which is in heaven is perfect.[9]

From the Book of Mormon:
47. Old things are done away, and all things have become new.
48. Therefore I would that ye should be perfect even as I, or your Father who is in heaven is perfect.[10]

Joseph simply blew off the original verses 45, 46 and 47, demonstrating, as *newly* written, how "old things *are* done away." Most Christians had become quite fond of that teaching of unconditional love. Slave or free, black, white, rich, poor—God's love was so perfect that it didn't matter how ugly, cute or even how righteous or evil you were. Christians encourage each other to emulate that specific instance of perfect love, "even as your Father in heaven is perfect." To Mormons, however, the highly popular biblical ideal has now been purged, suspect of having been tampered with anciently by apostate priests rife with corruption. The new message given to the Saints says you must become perfect, almost exactly opposite in value to the meaning Christ intended, as most understand it. Joseph may have been echoing the late deist, Tom Paine, a noted critic of the notion of unconditional love: "[...] and to say that we can love voluntarily, and without a motive, is morally and physically impossible."[11]

(Due caution must temper appraisals of the LDS by non-members. Would-be critics are wise in exercising restraint lest they judge behaviors relative to perceived sub-standard values generated within Mormon scripture. For example, no analysis concerning this segment of Third Nephi should suggest a conclusion that Saints are transformed by their beliefs to neglect love of humanity. They generally perform their parts about as well as any Christian, Muslim or Jew. Joseph probably wasn't trying to remove love from the world—were such a thing possible—so much as to demonstrate how the human condition is powerfully transformed through language functions, propaganda and peer pressure).

Miracles (and Parody) on a Budget

Using the logic of "believe that, believe this," Joseph sometimes expanded miracles just a step beyond those of the Bible. He recognized that such hyperbole was not more than his followers were able to assimilate but instead viewed limits of human credulity approaching the infinite when encroachments are effected line by line. Whereas St. Matthew bears witness of a generous miracle when Jesus provided a meal for a multitude from only a few loaves and fishes, the Book of Mormon has him repeat his magic, supplying bread and wine for aboriginal North Americans—but from thin air. Believe that? Believe this one.

From the Bible:
And he commanded the multitude to sit down on the grass, and took the five loaves, and the two fishes, and looking up to heaven, he blessed, and brake, and gave the loaves to his disciples, and the disciples to the multitude.[12]

From the Book of Mormon:
3. And it came to pass that he brake bread again and blessed it, and gave it to the disciples to eat.
5. And when they had given unto the multitude he also gave them wine to drink, and commanded them that they should give unto the multitude.
6. Now, there had been no bread, neither wine brought by the disciples, neither by the multitude.
7. But he truly gave unto them bread to eat, and also wine to drink.[13]

Now I Know Where Bad Comes from

Throughout the reconstructed record, Jesus' reputation takes it on the chin. His arrival in the New World was an anti-climactic event because everything about him and his teachings had already been discussed and settled upon public thoroughfares throughout Zarahemla. Already long since, Nephites knew his first and last names and his mother's name. They had heard about John the Baptist. Speaking in tongues had been around hundreds of years prior to his birth, since the early days of First Nephi.[14] Truthfully, his gospel had actually begun wearing thin by the time Jesus introduced himself by means of earthquake, smoke and darkness.

Any readers anticipating restoration of a lost gospel principle or two will feel shortchanged when realizing how much of the visit constituted repeat material, or worse, how much more had actually been altered or deleted rather than restored. No new parables, not a wise insight do we find. On the other hand, the advanced doctrine of baptism had been both preached and widely practiced for many decades.[15] Readers might suppose how some mysterious agent may have come through far ahead of schedule, preparing a better audience in the New World than Jesus met in Judea. Conversely, was Joseph attempting to take the early lead in order to redirect the Lord's character slowly, inch by inch? Had he tantalized his readers in order to steal a bit of thunder? To a writer inspired by hopes of massive change, strategic advantages posed few obstacles that couldn't be overcome by a deft imagination. Several of his supposed authors have already disclosed a remarkably frank, if unpublicized, custom of confession. In that manner, just as with those other surreptitious admissions, Joseph had Jesus reveal himself as more than an unusually mischievous fellow. In Mosiah's testament, when Alma (the elder) prayed asking the Lord to instruct him concerning judgment against un-repentant sinners, word from the Lord pinpointed sin's origins: "For it is I [Jesus] that taketh upon me the sins of the world; for it is I that created them; and it is I that granteth unto him that believeth unto the end a place at my right hand."[16]

Faithful apologists usually approach such ambiguity within that confession of the Lord by begging reader's indulgence, as if the misunderstanding resulted from Joseph's imperfect schooling in the arts of grammar. The same Lord also admitted, "I give unto men weakness that they may be humble."[17] Years later, realizing that hardened followers would tend to mentally mitigate those unexpected, otherwise unacceptable views, Joseph delivered his acerbic opinions with even greater bluntness: "No one lives without fault. Do you think that even Jesus, if he were here, would be without fault in your eyes?"[18]

Bringing About the Bowels of Mercy

By adopting a sham version of King James English while writing his book, Joseph sketched embarrassing bloopers within sermons delivered by the most sober and honorable of Nephite preachers. For example, scripting a role prepared for his character named Amulek, Alma's quite fortunate missionary companion (the word is *Amulet*, but spoken in an overdone New Englander's dialect),[19] Joseph wrote:

> And thus he shall bring salvation to all those who shall believe on his name; this being the intent of this last sacrifice, to bring about the bowels of mercy, which overpowereth justice, and bringeth about means unto men that they may have faith unto repentance.[20]

As blessed at first sight as mercy must appear within this typically austere volume, to "bring about the bowels" suggests a mild vulgarity. We might imagine the phrase being an earlier expression made obliquely to signify *moving* of the bowels—defecation. When using it to refer to God's mercy, Joseph created a crude insult. To Mormons it is understandably unthinkable: Joseph's inference suggests that mercy is a heap of dung. Amulek's double meaning could have been avoided by expressing it differently, simply, "[...] to bring about God's mercy [...]."

In his analysis of the Christian gospel, Tom Paine expressed himself more directly, though not so rude, saying, "[...] in truth, there is no such thing as redemption."[21] Paine's sentiment may easily have inspired Joseph to show no mercy.

Taking a Narrow Path Less Traveled

Another insult, milder still, was devised to remind us of a side of godhood that constantly puzzles rational minds. Joseph's symbolic gesture makes the Lord appear caught in two contradictory poses as he putters interminably through a load of concerns and a myriad of trivial issues. If the subtle caricature seems all too brief, it registers as a parallel to that of the "Master" in his Allegory of the Wild Olive Vineyard by describing a rather myopic Lord.

Joseph's minor affront occurs during Alma's feature-length letter to Helaman. Alma writes of God, "[...] for he doth counsel in wisdom over all his works, and his paths are straight, and his course is one eternal round."[22] Make it visual: straight path...round course? While the images oppose each other they don't necessarily indicate that God is the target of vicious animosity. This kind of humor was irresistible to Joseph, and his imagery of an Omnipotent Father may have been borrowed from a popular riddle of antiquity:

> I go around in circles
> But always straight ahead,
> Never complain
> No matter where I am led.
>
> Answer: The [Big] Wheel.

Joseph's insults never dominate the saga, so poking fun at deity was no more than incidental to his primary objective. In order to prove his point more effective, he needed to deliver his religious critique above (or below) a certain intellectual level of detection, and that's why he sheltered much of it with riddles that have never been well appreciated. Attacks are brief and camouflaged when accompanied by familiar scriptural sounds, yet the parody can hardly be denied. Such barbs (and there are many others) cannot be charged as grammatical accidents, yet these examples certainly could not have sprung from the mind of some ancient bard from Tenochtitlan, Mexico. In order to project such cynicism without permitting his position to become too evident—the real man walking that straight and narrow path—Joseph, no doubt.

CHAPTER 20

A Hostile but Faithful Witness, Part 2: Spotting A Host of Dubious Gods

> "Why be so certain that you comprehend the things of God, when all things with you are so uncertain?" (Joseph Smith)[1]

During its later colonial period, as Americans further separated themselves from the world Europe had become, they began discovering new ways of thinking and ever-increasing powers for self-determination. Crossing the ocean gave immigrants the opportunity to leave behind encumbering prejudices, injustices and ignorance; to some, that promise held greater attraction than any gold rush. Such a liberal political configuration impressed many with possibilities for asserting their position in the world, of redesigning their potentials for success and self-fulfillment—and, for some, to begin redefining what they had been taught about God. What once presented the blessing of freedom of conscience has produced a comparative surfeit of divergent sects—a house while, if not divided, isn't united. Looking backwards at the set-up history began to wedge into one of religion's great transformations—it all seems so inevitable.

The student's willingness to merge their investigation of LDS mythology with that age of political, moral and intellectual upheaval will enable them to more fully appreciate the Book of Mormon. No insight became more essential to Joseph than his realization that meaningful social changes were subordinate to, and dependent upon, preliminary recalculations in man's perceptions of deity. While a review of his accomplishments will further demonstrate the young prophet's mastery of subtle satire, it will also show how thoroughly and systematically he engineered his attack upon contemporary theology.

Examination into this aspect of LDS doctrine is not being engaged with the purpose of pleading for religious loyalties, nor to encourage anyone to abandon any variety of faith. Emotions engaged by such an appeal would surely cause reason to falter, yet it becomes impossible to make our connection with Joseph while attempting to sidestep the very core of his teachings—thus orientation to his teachings is entirely germane to any attempt to understand Joseph. Our goal is to identify in his works a set of tools being implemented to advance his propaganda. Correctly interpreting the contents of his message will help show that, concurrent with promoting himself as a prophet of God within a community of believers, he used his book to establish an ideology aimed at religion's downfall.

In its writing he constantly devised new ways for exploiting the variety of common conceptions and evident misconceptions people have of who or what God is, of His visual or physical appearance, and of man's relationship and duties towards Him. Re-setting values, definitions, and especially limitations, upon God became one of his primary strategies. Occasionally we'll meet a sort of self-absorbed, slow-witted Lord, as in his Allegory of the Wild Olive Vineyard (Jacob 5); but there are also views of God as a source of magic; a protector of the virtuous and valiant; there's a God of prosperity, and one who punishes mercilessly whenever men forget how much he loves them. Joseph tried articulating several aspects of the creator's personality—mainly His moodiness, truculence, imperiousness and wrath. Sometimes Joseph's God directs His people to behave quite foolishly, even with fatal consequences.

We too, perhaps with increasing frequency, may discover that God is quite out of touch with our personal lives, that He doesn't consistently hear or acknowledge our prayers, or is too busy to look after our special and immediate needs—concerned as He is with zillions of other worlds, jillions of evolving creatures. That is where Joseph performed masterfully: he succeeded at the difficult task of challenging readers to inquire within themselves what their actual beliefs about God are. What does experience, made much broader in a modern world, tell us? Try meeting him on his own ground as he attempts persuading readers to search inwardly, swaying them with many rather difficult views of God that seem intended to crush obsolete perceptions one by one.

An Accountable, Unchangeable, Semi-supreme Being

People have always wondered about God or the gods, so it isn't any secret that theology itself has constantly evolved over thousands of years, and everywhere throughout the world. In developing his views Joseph used an exploratory, experimental method to enlighten. His intention was to define the Almighty in ways that actually tend to whittle down the possibilities of His existence and supreme power. The Book of Mormon is the only holy book making such limitations upon God. What other religious document entertains the amazing speculation that "God would cease to be God"? Within Mormon thinking, inexorable law, rather than God, can be seen as an irresistible supreme force. For instance God cannot invoke His mercy at the expense of justice: "What, do ye suppose that mercy can rob justice? I say unto you, Nay; not one whit. If so, God would cease to be God."[2]

Alma's words intended confusion by creating an outlandish contradictory, for we find at least one instance wherein God slighted justice by exercising his mercy, thus breaking Alma's inflexible rule. Earlier in the story, Ammon, the powerful missionary, had effectually cancelled absolute preeminence of justice above mercy by saying, "Behold, he [God] did not exercise his justice upon us, but in his great mercy hath brought us over that everlasting gulf of death and misery, even to the salvation of our souls."[3] Try imagining how utterly meaningless the entire book would seem if such expressions were merely uncoordinated opinions that differed among its set of stooge authors. At the very same time, however, let's acknowledge the boost that Joseph enjoyed from his book: shortly after its publication he entered center stage wielding enormous, even destructive, power. Ascribing to him a larger caliber of intellect, one may easily discern his purposes for promoting such mental conflict—when people oriented towards faith become bewildered by cognitive dissonance, they'll often attach themselves tenaciously to the nearest guru who's handing out the cleverest answers. Who hasn't been a sucker for a platitude now and again?

Joseph established many views of God, often in opposition, to give readers a wide enough assortment to toss around in their minds. If a believer doesn't like one God in particular, and has enough courage to set aside or reject Him, sooner or later he's liable to question the rest of those Gods as part of a confusing, ridiculous whole.[4]

A God of Miracles…Don't Hold Your Breath

A rule, supposedly quite firm, is that God is constant: The Mormon God is unable to change or, again, "God would cease to be God." As evidence of constancy, He must continue manifesting His power today among mankind with a display of miraculous acts, just as He has been reported doing for ancient believers:

> And if there were miracles wrought then, why has God ceased to be a God of miracles and yet be an unchangeable being? And behold, I say unto you he changeth not; if so he would cease to be God; and he ceaseth not to be God, and is a God of miracles.[5]

Moroni's words have just encumbered followers with a necessity of standing perpetually vigilant for genuine signs of His miracles and wonders in order to certify God's unchangeable nature. However, when Sherem came looking for a sign of Jacob, and Korihor a sign of Alma, each was smitten with a crippling curse and speedy death for expressing that urge to put his private doubts to rest.[6] We, therefore, find present day Mormons feeling stymied—understandably reluctant in the endeavor to procure honest answers to their questions—yet seeking miracles fitted to genuine needs. Reports of miracles in today's Mormon Church are very sparse, anecdotal and so poorly documented that the few of them that have been reported display earmarks of urban myth. Accordingly, today's Saints suffer from double minds concerning signs and miracles. A typical view registers the *miracle denial* expressed by one of its early presidents:

It is a wicked and adulterous generation that seeketh after a sign. Show me Latter-day Saints who have to feed upon miracles, signs and visions in order to keep them steadfast in the Church, and I will show you members of the Church who are not in good standing before God, and who are walking in slippery paths.[7]

A God Meaner Than the Junkyard Dog

Serious believers recognize how important a comprehensive knowledge of God is. More precisely, "It is the first principle of the gospel to know for a certainty the character of God,"[8] for believers are expected to adopt His virtues, thoughts, and every other trait so they can eventually assume habitation in the celestial kingdom. Of all Godlike attributes, members are often most loathe to adopt His petulant anger:

> And we see that except the Lord doth chasten his people with many afflictions, yea except he doth visit them with death and with terror, and with famine and with all manner of pestilence, they will not remember him.[9]

Perhaps here, at least, Joseph carried cynicism close enough to the edge so as to give himself away. The view shown requires no strenuous argument or further clarification to reveal an image made intentionally repugnant. Can anyone derive faith or peace while worshipping that God of death and terror? Perhaps no other caricature of deity provides a better view of Joseph's use of propaganda to eliminate deceitful, doubtful or unwarranted gods. After a few such encounters, nearly anyone might experience disturbing pangs of doubt.

A Genie in Your Lamp

- We can see that the Lord in his great infinite goodness doth bless and prosper those who put their trust in him.[10]
- And thus they did prosper and become far more wealthy than those who did not belong to the church.[11]
- I the Lord am bound when ye do what I say[...].[12]

This generous and affluent helper-God seems to counteract most effects of the Junkyard Dog. We should be able to achieve a great advantage in all we do if able to keep Him happy. That sounds promising, but is He a keeper? Yes, but only for those who gamble their personal destiny to the unseen God who subjects them to simple, predictable laws—and only when Divine Providence consistently favors those who pursue righteousness.

What can we say, though, when we've been doing *all* that can be expected, and more—only to witness one desired blessing after another fall through our hands? Conversely, if we are blessed, haven't those blessings been regularly equaled or bettered among many non-believers and even a host of successful scribes, hypocrites, Protestants and Catholics? A god whose rules promise reward to the righteous tends to lose credibility whenever an untimely sickness threatens, an investment fails, or when disappointments occur in our career or family life, but especially when wicked neighbors obtain the bounties of His succor. This particular God seems designed to invite loss of credibility from those who check empirical evidence against explicit covenants and promises.

Moreover, even should you win, you'll lose. A further complication needs to be factored in for the fortunate few who achieve prosperity in the course of their persistent gospel observances. After experiencing windfall profits, house rules prescribe the unlikelihood that you'll live long enough to relax and enjoy them, because,

> [...] he doth require that ye should do as he hath commanded you; for which if ye do, he doth immediately bless you; and therefore he hath paid you. And ye are still indebted unto him, and are, and will be, forever and ever [...]."[13]

Perhaps honest hard work, then, is the sensible course for all who see themselves as less than perfect. Today's Saints are counseled to refrain from indebtedness.

The God Who Should Have Known Better

If anyone should ever be so blessed as to receive specific directions from the Lord telling what he must do, we might expect him to follow that prudent advice. What happens, though, if those instructions lead us into a needlessly perilous, even life-threatening, situation? Ammon, true believer and servant of God, demonstrated how genuine wisdom might reside in a more skeptical view.

> 2. And the voice of the Lord came to Ammon, saying: Thou shalt not go up to the land of Nephi, for behold, the king will seek thy life; but thou shalt go to the land of Middoni [...].
> 8. [...] as Ammon and Lamoni were journeying thither [to Middoni, *as directed*], they met the father of Lamoni, who was king over all the land.
> 20. [...] And he [the king] stretched forth his hand to slay Ammon.[14]

For a God who's best insights are so pathetic, so faulty and nearly fatal to heroic chosen servants, might there be some hesitation from those who haven't yet experienced perfection or complete synchronicity with heavenly wisdom in seeking counsel? In more modern times Joseph and his God-who-should-have-known-better developed a close relationship at the most unpropitious moment—just as he took lead over his new church. For example, it was by God's command through Joseph that many thousands of Saints flocked into Missouri to settle Zion, there to await the second coming of Jesus. His God seemed to have been entirely oblivious to the reality that it would cost dozens of lives and the bulk of Mormon property before being altogether banished from the state.

A Trinity, Plus or Minus One

Among Hebrews, today as anciently, only one single Almighty God is acknowledged. Christians, subsequent to the great Council of Nicaea (325 CE), advanced the theory of God's true nature by hypothesizing a Trinity composed of Father, Son and Holy Ghost—*separate* manifestations of a *single* essence. "It was not a logical or intellectual formulation but an imaginative paradigm that confounded reason."[15] Pure assertion, anciently, of such a baffling metaphysical view has tended to effectively circumvent rational discussion about God's nature and existence. Still, due to the necessity it represents, the Trinity-Unity approach has accommodated the needs of many millions of believers, proving how much more determined we must become before attaining the clarity of reason that has been weakened due to centuries of man's exposure to domesticating processes.

One bright aspect of this popular search for truth is that attempts to reconcile such non-knowables have offered mankind an inexhaustible supply of two irreplaceable intangibles: optimism and imagination. Joseph excelled at both. His LDS doctrine stretches Christian Trinity rhetoric a step beyond traditional views by its teaching of *Godhead:* "The Father has a body of flesh and bones as tangible as man's; the Son also; but the Holy Ghost has not a body of flesh and bones, but is a [separate] personage of Spirit."[16] While his view helped complete the transition to a plurality of gods by proclaiming three distinct, *separate* beings, Joseph's view excelled by minimizing nebulous abstractions endured by Jews and Christians. Encouraged by the gratitude showered upon him by followers, Joseph pushed them hard to become perfect in preparation for joining the throng as gods themselves. Not even the Greeks were so egalitarian, and no one had ever proposed higher aspirations for the general run of mankind.

Then, recognizing that the corporeal nature of God precluded His omnipresence, Joseph supplemented his Godhead theory with a separate facet—likely a whole new entity. He added to those former *three* beings a mysterious spirit substance that fills the immensity of space, but functions as a conscience for each human. The new substance is variously known as the Spirit of the Lord, Light of Christ, the Light of Truth or the *Spirit of Christ*. "For behold, the Spirit of Christ is given to every man, that he may know good from evil."[17] This god-like spirit is separate and distinct from the Holy Ghost. We have to suspect that the Spirit of Christ must be an eternal substance, yet, how it came to be particularly designated "of Christ" would lead us to consider this element as an emanation from the Son rather than of the Father or Holy Ghost. While the ultimate status of the Spirit of Christ cannot be thought of as Godhead, it (He?) appears to have special functions requiring powers beyond anything either mortal or angelic. Serving as a conscience throughout the entire human race, it would have to maintain an extraordinary ability for entering your brain to impress its holy influence upon you. In order to instruct man properly and wisely, the Spirit of Christ must be *omniscient*. It is manifestly omnipresent, the *sole* deific essence within LDS theology made to fit that universally acknowledged feature. It seems as though Joseph, if he had cared to institute such a platform, might have used this invention of spirit *alone* to restore the earlier solitary God of Judaism, but he didn't because his focus was aimed into the future—away from past experience.

Mormons have not yet been instructed of what relationship the Spirit of Christ might have with the spiritual component presently inhabiting Jesus' physical body. By now readers may likely recognize that

Mormonism represents views of God that aren't well thought out, nor clarified, and are made no more cohesive than either set of beliefs, Catholic or Protestant, both of which have always been snobbishly rejected as apostate by the very basis of LDS restorationist gospel. Or were Joseph's mystery teachings a plot to sprinkle eternal truths with enough "spherical reasoning" that they'd be too difficult to reduce to finite, debatable formulae? Could Joseph have actually been trying to squeeze a fourth element into the LDS godhead?

One ever-present probability suggests that Joseph was attempting to restructure our foundational references concerning God by removing certain functions from the Father's domain. For instance, he seems to have been able to bring the office of godhood down to a more human (attainable) level simply by creating a supreme being who wasn't personally omnipresent—he'd delegated that characteristic to the Spirit of Christ. Thereafter, man-Godmaking has become recognized as Joseph's most progressive violation against the entire Judeo-Christian heritage. However, by newly defining God with limitations of space and function and by giving Him a corporal presence he may have re-positioned the Lord optimally to allow mankind a fresh run at seeking their own exciting opportunities for dominion upon this minute speck of space matter.

Fatherandson

Mormon theology does more to displace God the Father than it does to supply any satisfactory concept of who or what God is, or even what He does. Who created the earth? Jehovah. To a Mormon, Jehovah is the designation applied to the pre-mortal Jesus, actually earth's creator, along with Adam and others who had proven themselves valiant in the pre-existence.[18] Then...who created man? Again it was Jesus:

> Behold, I am he who was prepared from the foundation of the world to redeem my people. Behold, I am Jesus Christ. I am the Father and the Son [...] all men were created in the beginning after mine own image. Behold, this body, which ye now behold, is the body of my spirit; and man have I created after the body of my spirit [...][19]

Joseph F. Smith, sixth Mormon president, Joseph's nephew, became confused while reading the above passage, commenting, "It is the Father who is speaking." A subordinate editor had to correct his error.[20] Admittedly, it is difficult to conceive that the Father really has such an insignificant role regarding planet earth. What do we make of God's appearances to Abraham or Moses? Apparently, those, too, were visitations made by the pre-Mortal Lord, Jesus-Jehovah. Finding out what happened to the LDS God (the Father) isn't going to be so easy, simply because Joseph all but wrote Him out of the picture. Implicit in Joseph's teachings is an idea that man's final judgment will become a task of *self-evaluation*: "A man is his own tormentor and his own condemner."[21] In fact, although we dare not abandon ourselves entirely to the earthiness of Joseph's mysteries, the single burden remaining to be attributed to the Father, as you might only remotely imagine, is to assist continually His many wives in begetting new spirits to fill His many creations,

> For we saw him [Jesus], even on the right hand of God; and we heard the voice bearing record that he is the Only Begotten of the Father—That by him, and through him, and of him, the worlds are and were created, and the inhabitants thereof are begotten sons and daughters of God.[22]

LDS mortals who *eventually* assume the immortal mantle of exaltation are to be likewise granted "eternal lives," meaning, primarily, they will attain rejuvenated powers for procreating an endless spirit progeny.[23]

The Shadow God

From the Bible:
Thus saith the Lord, cursed be the man that trusteth in man, and maketh flesh his arm, and whose heart departeth from the Lord.[24]

From the Book of Mormon:
And it came to pass that when the brother of Jared had said these words, behold, the Lord stretched forth his hand and touched the stones one by one with his finger. And the veil was taken from off the eyes of the brother of Jared, and he saw the finger of the Lord; and it was as the finger of a man, like unto flesh and blood [...].[25]

Smith's Mormon God of passions—sensual, physical, intellectual, and appearing in a body "like unto flesh and blood"—as with his invention of a "Spirit of Christ," challenges other, equally theoretical, equally mysterious concepts. In his novel construct, mankind would now be given a view of itself and the unseen Creative Force in a relationship that eliminated imagined disparities separating them. Think how great an advancement it would urge upon humankind.

With plans for his martyrdom already maturing and fewer than three months remaining, Joseph perceived that a ripeness of time had arrived for placing his ultimate teaching (to some, his ultimate blasphemy) on the boards, minus any mincing of words and mystery of intent:

> Here, then, is eternal life—to know the only wise and true God; and you have got to learn how to be gods yourselves, and to be kings and priests to God, the same as all gods have done before you, namely by going from one small degree to another, and from a small capacity to a great one; from grace to grace, from exaltation to exaltation […].[26]

Charles Darwin didn't publish his acclaimed theory until long after Joseph's martyrdom and then viewed only evidence of man's distant past. Joseph was looking into man's evolution with perspectives projected beyond time's horizons, yet he has never been credited with such illumination equal to, perhaps even more significant than, one of the most celebrated minds of the nineteenth century. Acting more as a prophet than some will find worthy for consideration, Joseph encouraged us to think far in advance of our fleeting, temporal existence.

Among its Christian detractors, Mormon views of man's perfectibility are pejoratively referred to as Godmaking. However, they've completely neglected acknowledgment of the flip side of their cognitive nightmare wherein Joseph cut deity back to an eminently manageable *shadow-god*.

The Adam-God Doctrine

To its biblically literate public, back when our nation represented a new frontier to all her sons and daughters, the Garden of Eden fell into place as its most ready-made metaphor describing America's immense, expansive, unexplored magnificence. Independence from European roots received extensive nurturing through a generalized perception formed by our men and women as though beginning afresh in this untamed, untainted new land as *Adams and Eves* in paradise reborn.[27]

That awareness of expanding opportunity has been credited with inspiring far-reaching effects upon America's literature and its history as well. Utilizing themes of evil, sin, innocence and tradition, younger authors induced fresh initiatives to separate our country from stale European history, habits and Old World perceptions: "[...] the literal use of the story of Adam and the [fortunate] Fall of Man—as a model for narrative—occurred in the final works of American novelists[...],"[28] including James Fenimore Cooper, Nathaniel Hawthorne, Herman Melville, Henry James and Walt Whitman, among many.

Likewise at the core of Joseph's strategy stands his resolve for empowering men to restructure entirely their views of the world. In addition to casting God into a new mold, before he could shape men after his greatly expanded image, he had to return to earth's most remote beginnings in order to re-create Adam. The first man became his representative personification endowed with infinitely higher nobility of character and much broader powers than were ascribed within the Genesis account. Thus, "Adam's fall," LDS theorists affirm, "was upward."

Now Mormons submit to a logic-driven, non-biblical doctrine that causes other Christians to shudder, known as the Adam-God Doctrine. It is a teaching that goes hand-in-hand with the belief in a finite God of flesh and bone. Many Saints suppose that the doctrine originated from Brigham Young following the Saints' arrival in Utah territory:

> Now hear it, O inhabitants of the earth, Jew and Gentile, Saint and sinner! When our father Adam came into the garden of Eden, he came into it with a celestial body, and brought Eve, one of his wives with him. He helped to make and organize this world. He is Michael, the Archangel, the Ancient of Days! About whom holy men have written and spoken—He is our Father and our God, and the only God with whom we have to do.[29]

To frame the perspective appropriately, realize that Brigham never scaled such intellectual peaks unaided during his term as church president. His words merely reiterated a belief that Joseph produced earlier when fashioning a cameo from the book of Genesis: "Now we see that the man had become as God, knowing good and evil [...]."[30] A few months after publishing his first book the Prophet encased the Adam-God teaching within Mormon doctrine by inscribing the following revelation:

> Listen to the voice of Jesus Christ, your Lord, your God, and your Redeemer [...] for the hour cometh that I will drink of the fruit of the vine with you on the earth [...] And also with Michael, or Adam, father of all, the prince of all, the ancient of days [...].[31]

No Bible student worth his salt would have had difficulty identifying the "Ancient of days" as God the Father because, aside from Joseph's peculiar new usage, that term had never been applied to any being other than God. Joseph's words pointed to a cameo taken from the Bible's book of Daniel: "Until the ancient of days came, and judgment was given to the saints of the most high [...]."[32] While adapting Daniel to his revisionist campaign, Joseph began acting in the part he had scripted for the "Servant" in Zenos' allegory—trimming an overgrowth of lofty limbs and branches to promote balance between root and top. His view seems to infer that mankind will slowly discover its role advancing nearer to that of the gods.

Throughout all sects of Christendom no other vital element of theology has been challenged more directly by such strategic attacks. Joseph labored meticulously to break down every previous image about God. He may have modified more theological concepts more thoroughly than anyone at any equivalent fourteen year period in history. His malice wasn't to hurt or insult God, as if a madman who actually *believed,* but harbored hatred against Him, or even that he felt some petty jealousy. Joseph's only true malice was against the body of hide-bound superstitions persevering throughout the one and only known advanced civilization within the entire universe—as if a dated relic reaching backwards into history's adolescence.

CHAPTER 21

A Stratospheric Genealogy—Capped by Ether

> Eurus is monarch of the lands of dawn…
> Warm Auster governs in the misty southland,
> And over them all presides the weightless ether,
> Pure without taint of earth. (Ovid, *Metamorphosis*)

Having earlier raised reader expectations that they would soon learn something inspirational or of interest about the rise and fall of America's most ancient civilization, the Jaredites, embarking upon Joseph's account must elicit a clear note of discord. How ought one make good sense of a book attributed to an improbable prophet carrying such an inflated cognomen as Ether?[1]

Its modest 31 pages supply all available information concerning a fragmented dynasty spanning 30 generations, one that finally collapsed under an orgy of bloody war. Its climactic battle covers nearly two chapters while profiling its last pair of titans, Shiz and Coriantumr, contestants to the finish in their manifestation of lunatic, suicidal rage. Following Jaredites through centuries of turmoil, you'll view one conflict after another as kings and kinsmen undermine one another, holding each other captive for life while they jockey to obtain power over their fellow men, sometimes by cunning, often by massive military exhibitionism. It's all so entirely, even deliriously, senseless. The pun is Joseph's, alone; but that's to be expected following exposure to ether, a brew used as an anesthetic even prior to the Civil War but known since the Middle Ages as *sweet vitriol*.

Ether's story is so filled with symbolic possibilities that it requires ardent dedication to reconstruct the message that Joseph intended with it. Take for instance the dominant name symbols at its beginning and ending—Jared and Ether, respectively. The name Jaredite has been chosen to characterize America's earliest inhabitants. That once proud nation relentlessly crumbled due to political chaos that cascaded downward under the weight of civil wars. The name has been borrowed from Hebrew, *Yered*— literally, "descent."

Ether, as Ovid's poem helps explain, has about as far opposite a meaning as possible. The word, of Greek origin, refers to the *upper* regions of sky beyond the clouds. It would be a good guess that the symbols, Jared and Ether, are encouraging us to "stretch as high as the utmost heavens, and search into and contemplate the darkest abyss." What other hidden truth or general idea might have been suggested by bracketing the book of Ether within those two symbols so starkly counterpoised in opposition? Assuming a representation of heaven and hell, perfection opposed by corruption or cognition silenced by nihilism, how do you fit them into Joseph's ideological priorities? Has a multiplicity of current events caused us to lose track of issues less than two centuries old?

Near the book's beginning Jared and his brother (addressed only as "the brother of Jared") share a story setting that may very well point the way. Before obtaining dominion over the New World, Jared and his brother came "[…] from the great tower, at the time the Lord confounded the language of the people […]." We imagine a myriad of unfamiliar languages streaming from the tower of Babel. And so it was during the early 1800s: America's greatest import at the time seems to have been immigrants from every nation. About 60 per cent English, the remainder included African slaves, but also Dutchmen, Spaniards and "heavy infusions of Swiss, Welsh, French, Scotch-Irish and German."[2] Palmyra itself became a representation of that aggregation of nationalities as soon as work began on the Erie Canal around 1817, the year just after the Smiths arrived. Soon thereafter people began carrying their cargo across the state of New York on *barges*. How did Jaredites transport themselves to the New World? Not by sail but—of all ironies—by constructing barges.[3] Was Joseph painting a pair of scenic postcards for describing two connected elements of his early Palmyra environment?

The brother of Jared is described as "a large and mighty man, and a man favored of the Lord."[4] Joseph wouldn't have characterized himself differently. Prior to settling down in the New World the brother of Jared endured "many years" in the wilderness;[5] likewise, the Smith family. From 1800 through 1816, before they settled in Palmyra, the Smiths had moved at least half a dozen times to somewhere within an eleven-mile radius, for them an economic *wilderness* bridging Vermont with New Hampshire. When carrying his petition before the Lord, the brother of Jared first acknowledged mankind's sinful state, prayed asking forgiveness for his sins, and was suddenly blessed by a face-to-face interview with a glorious personage claiming to be "the Father and the Son." That personage gave the brother of Jared a promise of redemption.[6]

Joseph's earliest record of his visionary experience presented all the same essentials and in similar sequence:

> [...] I pondered [...] the darkness which pervaded the minds of mankind. My mind become exceedingly distressed for I become convicted of my sins [...] Therefore I cried unto the Lord for mercy [...] the Lord opened the heavens upon me and I saw the Lord. He spake unto me saying, "Joseph my son thy sins are forgiven thee.[7]

During the fourteen years subsequent to publishing his book, Joseph applied himself to gathering an extensive following. He rose to become a recognized leader among them then dragged his people through brutal religious persecution in Missouri. His people were crushed and banished from the state by a governor's order of extermination. Newspapers condemned him; politicians branded him. Enemies robbed, mobbed and imprisoned him and, later, impatient creditors would force him to declare bankruptcy. He escaped his guards while en route to a change of venue, resettled and reigned supreme in Illinois. Rise—fall—fighting one battle and one foe after another. He stirred up then ducked organized persecutions and attempts to extradite him back into Missouri. His life became a contentious struggle from one end of it to the other.

Those familiar with the Book of Ether might imagine that I've just summarized the bulk of its contents, for it is likewise full of opposition and overthrown kingdoms. Joseph provoked then fought opposition high and low in order to play out his Ethereal fantasies to the absolute hilt, and if any other author had produced two such similar works, you can bet that his biographers would have picked over those events with minutest attention to detail. However, today both friend and foe consider him one of America's most *mysterious*, enigmatic characters. Why?

Let's not abandon hope for understanding Joseph's reasons for engaging his charade. While one may without great difficulty gather a gist of his meaning, particulars revealed in his fiction are so scant and scarce that readers will always be forced to indulge in speculation about what caused him to oppose religion while simultaneously nurturing a culture of pseudo-Christianity. If he didn't choose to tell all, he still seems willing to permit open access to his views for anyone willing to massage his symbol-clues for greater understanding. The Book of Ether may carry us back just far enough to obtain a few precious slivers of evidence pointing to the genesis of its author's inspiration. Gone are the comic characters that make us smile or question our gods; we've arrived at the business end of the Book of Mormon.

Escape from a Tower of Babel

Upon observing his claim, "No man knows my history. I cannot tell it: I shall never undertake it," even his most critical biographers seem entirely too willing to accept him at his word. Those are often the highly regarded historians asserting that his martyrdom was a "chance event;"[8] without exception they've underestimated his great fictional work. Joseph didn't misrepresent its value when he told followers, "The Book of Mormon is the keystone of our religion [...]."[9] Critics often dismiss those words as hype because the book conspicuously omits such LDS essentials as temple endowments, baptisms for the dead and the mortal sins of alcohol and tobacco, while supposedly condemning the practice of polygamy as an abomination in the sight of God. The most suitable way to perceive the Book of Mormon as a keystone is by using it to connect Joseph's autobiographical segments when otherwise one might view him imperfectly.

Although only a few readers completely ignore every instance in it where Joseph included brief references to himself, several glitches cause many searchers to abandon their quest for full disclosure. They often experience frustration before realizing that there is definite purpose and design in all that causes their confusion; they've been stymied whenever attempting to integrate adjunct puzzle parts—author, saga and philosophical position—into an historically contiguous panorama.

Something as crucial as knowing where to begin will help salvage what appears to be a very busy but near-meaningless episode. While most library books are formatted so readers can open to page one, Joseph's has his genesis located where none expect, in Ether, just ahead of its ending. Jaredite history opens with an extended roster of Ether's family tree:

> He that wrote this record was Ether, and he was a descendant of Coriantor. Coriantor was the son of Moron…the son of Ethem…the son of Ahah… Seth…Shiblon…Com…Coriantum…Amnigaddah…Aaron…Heth… Hearthom…Lib…Kish…Corom…Levi…Kim…Morianton…Riplakish… Shez…Heth…Com…Coriantum…Emer…Omer…Shule…Kib…Orihah… Who was the son of Jared.
> Which Jared came forth with his brother and their families, with some others and their families, from the great tower, at the time the Lord confounded the language of the people, and swore in his wrath that they should be scattered upon all the face of the earth.[10]

While appearing to satirize the Bible's detailed but pointless genealogies it contains a most engaging "keystone" possibility. This list of names begins with Ether, then runs backwards to Jared and his brother, the New World's earliest colonists.

Though not mentioned by name, neither here nor in the Bible, reference is to the Tower of Babel, a near-universal synonym for confusion.[11] Joseph designed that time-backwards genealogical clue to indicate his own heritage from colonial America. How so? Ether's list of names runs *in reverse* through thirty generations, including himself and Jared, but points to only *one* generation previous to Joseph. If thirty *years* be subtracted from 1805, his birth year, then the date would be 1775. That was the birth year for Lucy Mack, Joseph's mother, but a babe during America's colonial era.[12] His clue, as slim and tenuous as it might seem, could point to the genesis of his split with religion. What is certain, though, is that he didn't name the book Ether without good reason. We can't expect the whole story to stand out as if it were some float in the Rose Parade: part of the magic has to be found by solving its riddles.

Offering a second clue early in Ether's second chapter, Joseph tried to further invoke that concept of America's colonial period. Using the method he'd mastered, he invented a unique code word, "*deseret*, which by interpretation, is a honey bee."[13] It appears that Jaredite *colonists* brought with them to the shores of America the world's sweetest symbol for *colonialism*. Today, Deseret remains a ubiquitous term throughout Mormon country; it's even the state name the early Mormon legislature requested prior to Utah, that is, until Washington bureaucrats figured out that they might have been abetting the nation's only sectarian monopoly.[14]

America had almost been waiting for Joseph Smith, or someone like him, to come along for quite some time. Things of this nature never occur in a vacuum, and effects are always preceded by their causes. This great new land first became colonized by those with a strong desire for a more liberating experience than the one provided for them in the Old World. Essential to the souls of many colonists was the freedom obtained here to worship according to personal choice. Fortunately, America's several colonial settlements were ventures engaged too broadly and diversely for any single agency to succeed in capturing religious hegemony. As a consequence, these shores soon attracted: Pilgrims, Unitarians, Dutch Reformers, Anglicans, Quakers, Mennonites, Moravians, Dunkers, Lutherans, Catholics, Jews, Episcopalians, Baptists, Anabaptists, Seekers, Deists, Congregationalists, Presbyterians, Methodists, Pentecostals, Universalists and a number of less formal religious societies.

As religion began taking on an appearance akin to a smorgasbord it must have dawned on ministers of each new sect that winning the war of saving souls requires ever-strenuous justifications of one's ideology. Learned professors felt pressures to justify religious footings upon supporting Bible passages, never too clear or concise, and, as evidenced by such varieties of religious expression, confusing and often wrought with contradictory data. At times such conditions began appearing somewhat contentious as orthodoxy within American Christian faith began loosening its grip. Hard line Puritanism fell by the wayside as revivalism became a norm along the American frontier. Try visualizing a scrambled mass of confusion similar to the ancient Tower of Babel—each one going his own way, using terms and language too difficult to render any universal, unifying set of beliefs. Joseph's reference to the Tower, an episode in Genesis, was surely meant as a marker along his own spiritual evolution. Ether's thirty generation-years pointed to his mother, not his father, perhaps due to the way Joseph perceived the power structure within his family circle. Let's add to that the possibility that his mother may not have been very discrete about the way she tried stuffing religion down his throat.

Joseph and Lucy Revisited

Both of Joseph's parents, Joseph, Sr. and Lucy Mack, were born during the reign of England's King George III, becoming heir to that mass of early religious diffusion; each of them, however, responded differently to its stimulus. Neither of their families became firmly anchored to any competing sect, yet each admitted loyalty and reverence to Christian values. Surveying the story within Joseph's own immediate ancestry will lend necessary perspective helpful in pointing out good reason for the strategy of mystery throughout his term as Prophet.

Following her marriage to Joseph, Sr. at age nineteen, Lucy prodded her husband to attend Methodist meetings, though he never shared her religious enthusiasms.[15] At one time Joseph professed faith as a Universalist, in doctrine a step above deism. He registered his preference, perhaps, based upon a legal loophole allowing members of certain religious sects to decline payment of annoying taxes otherwise imposed throughout New England in support of local ministers.[16] Similar to Asael, his father, Joseph was considered "avowedly Christian but basically irreligious."[17] Having endured Lucy's melancholy brooding because they hadn't yet found a church to join, Joseph began confiding to her the contents of several visions and dreams he'd had. However his interpretations for those dreams affirmed his earlier reluctance to affiliate with any particular religious group. As Lucy recalled,

> From this time forward, my husband seemed more confirmed than ever in the opinion that there was no order or class of religionists that knew any more concerning the kingdom of God that [...] such as made no profession of religion whatever.[18]

Her husband's elaborate visions replenished Lucy's reservoirs of pious pride and helped assuage her longing for Christian spirituality in the home.[19] She never saw it as his ingenious ploy to counter her intense longings in order to place organized religion on the family's back burner.

Lucy, on the other hand, served up religion for breakfast, lunch and dinner. More than anyone else, Lucy Mack Smith became the major influence in shaping young Joseph's life. What may not be quite as apparent is how our lives are often most markedly molded by subtle dynamics existing between positive and negative forces in opposition. Piety, for all our willingness to salute its good, can and often does stir up reactions of rebellion within the child who feels confined by performances and attitudes expected inside a pious home environment. As most any member of a large and strictly religious household might testify, rare is the family that has enjoyed full exemption from fissures resulting naturally from pressures to conform. The Smiths weren't above any in this regard: Lucy's intimate home atmosphere didn't merely encourage Christian living but established it as a norm, more likely the prerequisite. Their home became highly regimented in patterns of worship.

> The children were required to sing hymns together on their knees and to listen to prayer morning and night in which their parents poured out their souls to God, as the donor of all blessings, and prayed, apparently at some length, that their children might be saved from sin.[20]

Two well-meaning parents were trying to raise nine children as best they knew how. Joseph never thought to blame his mom for indulging such anxiousness and overbearing influence in the home environment, for she couldn't un-believe everything she'd already accepted all her life. It wasn't her fault. Older folks often cling to behaviors they can't easily change, and Lucy might well have won the gold medal for an obstinacy that had benefited the family by keeping it united. Any parent who has tried getting a *certain* child to eat all of his or her vegetables will recognize that parent-child wars can become a no-win enterprise. Here again we've discovered a source of *family* conflict that may have been intentionally reflected within Ether's contentious dynasty wars.[21]

Good strategy for any child might have suggested that such conflicts are best entertained and given some form of expression by means of fantasies common to youth. To come out openly in rebellion against his mother would have gained Joseph nothing except bad feelings, family feud and diminished influence. If Joseph were going to make war, then he would do so against the prevailing religious myth, not the mom, and he would have to learn how to manipulate his tactical moves by engendering the discipline of a Jesuit. Does Ether's story replay Joseph's early childhood tensions between himself and Lucy, along with her dominance and perhaps harsh techniques for *encouraging* his participation in the Christian walk? The young prophet supplied but a veiled glimpse of how he perceived his mother's tyranny: "I was born […] of goodly parents who spared no pains to instructing me in the Christian religion."[22]

How did Lucy become so enamored to her unyielding passion for *some* religion? Within a decade of Joseph's death, she wrote her son's first complete biography. In it she provided a perspective that has earned her respect for its great candor yet reveals as much about her as of her son. While sharing the story of her life's journey, Lucy presented herself as a strong-minded, proud woman, very anxiously and thoroughly attached to the Christianity that she in turn inherited largely from her mother. Lucy, last-born of eight children, outlived everyone else in her family. Of equal significance, she obtained her upbringing in a rural and extremely limited cultural environment at Gilsum, New Hampshire. How limited? We might imagine her being raised to adulthood close to civilization's most remote outpost, as a cloistered nun.

Her father, Solomon Mack, was illiterate for most of his life and absent from home during most of Lucy's. As much as any other occupation, he could be described as a soldier of fortune, spending many years in the military during the Seven Years' (French and Indian) War and throughout the American Revolution. During his later years he became an eccentric convert to Christianity following an accident that inflicted severe head injuries.[23] While he slowly recovered, his wife taught him to read and write, after which he authored, published (1811) and distributed his flamboyant testimony of the Savior's redemption. Having left indelible impressions on his family, he died in 1820 at age eighty-eight.[24] Joseph hadn't yet turned fifteen.

Lucy's mother Lydia not only educated all her children but also continually exhorted them to fear God and walk uprightly before Him. She called them to daily prayer morning and evening and certainly became the key figure in Solomon's conversion.[25] He described her character as "pious and devotional,"[26] and, doubtless, no other legacy could have endowed their children and grandchildren with more enduring nor substantial consequences. From reading her book we note that Lucy obviously adored her oldest brother, Jason, a man thoroughly disposed to religious enquiry and who later became a minister of the gospel—a Seeker, recognizing no true church.[27] His strong, sincere religious views affected Lucy most deeply, and she, rather than young Joseph, became first in the family to express persistent anxiety over which church was right for her.[28]

Lovisa, her oldest sister, once suffered a deathly illness that lasted several years before she experienced a miraculous, sudden cure. She attributed recovery to her faith in Jesus.[29] Shortly before Lovisa's recovery, Lucy had been given responsibility, beginning at age sixteen, for constant care over another older sister, Lovina, who lingered with consumption (tuberculosis) for three years. Held captive upon her deathbed, Lovina presented a heart-rending figure of drama and melancholy as she prepared to meet her God. She used her last moments on earth to inspire Lucy's unflagging faith in Jesus.[30]

Impressed so constantly and deeply with the things of God, Lucy carried ardent piety upon her sleeve and a religious chip on her shoulder throughout life. From those emotion-laden experiences marking her upbringing, Lucy's faith in God's providence became one of the most conspicuous manifestations of her personality. She brought all of those childhood experiences *lovingly* to bear upon her own children. Late in life she could boast of her success at child-rearing, telling how she had "raised them in the fear and love of God, and never was there a more obedient family."[31] There was nothing in his heritage for Joseph to resent; he became devoted to his mother, and that helped give the Smiths their appearance as a model family. For her, Mormon piety became a natural showcase for the basis of one's pride; moral perfectionism and longsuffering service has since become one of the church's established hallmarks. From there God's grace becomes subordinated to works intended to secure one's exaltation over and above salvation. Lucy's obsession with family history also helped point the way toward today's LDS reputation as expert genealogists. Looking back into Ether, Joseph may well have selected his mother's known penchant for family history as the perfect way to position her within the first chapter of his Jaredite saga.

To be both fair and honest, one should recognize that Joseph likely continued his family's pattern of rigorous religious observance throughout his entire married life—but that doesn't mean that he bought into it with all his heart. A skilled propagandist may use prayer as an effective means for spreading an otherwise difficult message. Forms of worship and acts simulating religious authority have been used since time immemorial for bringing followers into alignment with all kinds of teachings. Reverence in one's bearing proves no man a God-fearing son, while piety has habitually served to advance the ambitions of astute politicians. Since Joseph detested family discord he avoided fights with his mother by exercising reservoirs of his self-discipline and imagination. It is entirely possible, knowing all that we do about Smith family dynamics, that Lucy may have provided her son with his earliest model as a make-believe martyr.

In addition to suggesting earliest Smith family history at its beginning, Ether's ending becomes the one nobody could have seen coming. It tells of an apocalyptic, dramatic action-fantasy pitting two warriors in a hateful, mortal obsession to gain ascendancy over the (seemingly unconquerable) opponent, even at the cost of reducing an entire civilization to shards and bones. The reader will find Ether's conclusion appropriately symbolizing Joseph's "big sleep," the martyrdom he absolutely knew had been created as his destiny.

CHAPTER 22

Martyr's Journal, Part 1:
A Pause for Breath…Then Immortality

In truth…I tell you a grain of wheat remains a solitary grain unless it falls into the ground and dies; but if it dies, it bears a rich harvest. (John 12:24)

Nauvoo, western Illinois
Sunday, June 23, 1844. Shortly after midnight

Even though his book had been produced and widely distributed throughout the preceding fourteen years, only Joseph understood its pointed relevance while leading into his final dilemma: "For it must needs be, that there is an opposition in all things […]." Clearly, weakness of scale in opposition gave him pause to consider, for his subsequent encounter with enemy rabble, if insufficiently aroused and focused on their task, would annul his considerable labors calculated to generate a stirring performance. The next mob he met wasn't going to augment his understanding of hatred, for experience had already taught him the fine art of gauging adversaries. Indeed, few individuals have ever matched his gift for inciting sustained persecution throughout such an extended period of time. Joseph had, during an assortment of violent incidents, been torn from his home by a mob, had been beaten, covered with hot tar, falsely imprisoned, and had even survived a governor's orders of extermination for himself and his people. Dozens of vexatious lawsuits had forced him to study enough law that he qualified as a municipal court justice in his hometown, one of Illinois' two largest cities. Opponents had run him and a multitude of his followers out of Ohio, then Missouri; now his Saints were again being threatened with expulsion or annihilation. Opposition? Compared to sufferings and struggles endured by the Mormon prophet, few can expect to experience conflict at such a constant pitch.

If he'd placed higher value on life he could have easily saved his skin by fleeing to the Rocky Mountains or perhaps Texas—presently an independent nation—however, preservation of his people had become his single most urgent concern. All the longhorn cattle in Ft. Worth wouldn't have tempted him to abandon the kingdom he had built from scratch. Although firmly convinced of his everlasting destiny, the opposition he needed momentarily would have to rise too intense for anyone to squeeze through it alive. Timing and effect had always been crucial; now they meant everything. If Joseph couldn't even think of turning tail, neither could he surrender just yet. Time would work its little miracles if he were only able to find a temporary place of refuge until opposition forces developed a sense of organization tight enough for them to choreograph an effective course of action.

Early death had become one essential component of a plan to unify and perpetuate his people, who, in turn would preserve his works for future ages to decipher and thereby establish his legacy. As with every other key venture he undertook, acceptance of an early grave followed complex lines of reasoning and ethics blended through Joseph's unique character. Should such a man be described as obstinate or persistent? Some have characterized him as a trickster and charlatan, while millions more consider his teachings essential to their salvation. So few men have mastered as well his ability to position themselves with such distinctive polarities—opposition through and through.

Moreover, visionary heroes almost never live to enjoy the full fruits of their labors in shifting society's paradigms—the final test essentially rides upon that man's ability to put genius and experience to work for the good of mankind. Those daring enough to undermine established institutions must believe so wholly in what they're doing, so, perhaps we can safely assume that faith in his cause and hope for mankind encouraged Joseph to overcome an instinctive fear of death. He could hardly have been oblivious to the values his exit could elicit if packaged as a vividly memorable, emotionally evocative experience—as a martyring. For more than 50 million souls who die ignominiously and are remembered so briefly, only one ideal martyr can rise and fall. Exceptional ones may live on in immortality by having their wise words studied, discussed and debated for many generations. Such grandiose visions kept Joseph focused while guiding his mission to its successful conclusion.

The great bulk of humanity tend to resign themselves to life's limited terms and to death's inevitability when it arrives. How absurd, he must have thought, that so many imagine it as a curse brought on by Adam's simple sin—just an apple to satisfy his appetite. Except for himself who else had ever learned to cheat the great equalizer by directing his appointed end to serve a noble cause? Regardless of how he fantasized it, Joseph's last breath would cut off every future opportunity he might have had for influencing the direction and destiny his Saints would take. His first, last and most genuine concern had always been to perpetuate their existence: "I care not what sacrifice I am called to make for such a kingdom. If it be friends, wealth, or even life, at the purchase of such a kingdom, it is cheap."[1]

The Mental Side of Martyrdom

For constructing a moving, memorable event, Joseph's end demanded staging wherein opposing forces clashed with sufficient heat to produce fusion. Such a moment was not to be softened up or dulled by sloppy workmanship. If left to chance critical decisions might easily become appropriated by careless and unstructured elements among his many foes. We can imagine men such as Socrates, Caesar and Jesus, men whose deaths are dramatized and recalled even centuries later. Those memorable icons are assigned much meaning through the nature of the event, as much as from the individual who suffered during those last moments of life. If carried out impulsively with insufficient pathos, fury or injustice, the resulting incident might leave little more than a dead brother, a fallen leader. Bury him; share mutual grief among friends. Then change one's clothing and catch up on afternoon chores. Schism was too common an element under such circumstances not to recognize how easily it could vitiate the kingdom that Joseph had to relinquish for its own good.

Done well, his people would be able to carry his courageous martyrdom seared in their hearts, accompanied by provocative images capable of attaching them more permanently to his cause. He needed full assurance that his final moments would be, decisively, both an explosive and riveting event. To make that happen, mob forces needed time to settle in and think their way through a fairly simple process. They'd need time to convene, endorse the objective, define tasks, decoy the Governor, arrange attack strategy, appoint look-outs, map routes for get-away and decide how running contingencies, should any occur, were to be managed. If able to coordinate a quick, foolproof coup, they would mobilize what little courage they had to make good their strike. Joseph realized that, although a small handful of assassins would suffice for the main event, a larger crew of rowdy agitators would be quite helpful in whipping those few into rage sufficient to kill in cold blood despite fears of later reprisal or prosecution. Unless they could ignite sufficient malice to make hatred boil over, how memorable an event could his death become? Heaven forbid his end should arrive through the whimsy of one single doughhead operating alone.

After fourteen years of his leading a double life as god to more than 25,000 believers, his martyrdom's success required Joseph choose a temporary place of absolutely safe retreat—outside Nauvoo. In order to replenish his resolve so as to follow through with his end of the deal, he also needed to suck in one last lungful of fresh air before taking his final step into the land of eternal silence. However, feigning as though he intended to flee justice, Joseph wrote Governor Ford expressing a polite but firm refusal to turn himself in, lest "some bloodthirsty villain [...] find his opportunity to shoot us. We dare not come [...]."[2] Then, about 2 A.M. on Sunday, June twenty-third, after gathering Hyrum, his older brother, to accompany him, as well as Willard Richards, an apostle of the church and Porter Rockwell, his personal bodyguard and trusted friend, Joseph pushed off in Aaron Johnson's leaky skiff from Nauvoo's wharf. Porter did all the rowing. The other three used their boots to bail water from the boat as fast as they could until reaching the Iowa shore. They arrived after an exhausting row following sunrise early Sunday morning.[3] Landing opposite Nauvoo, in Iowa, near Montrose, they located a brother who sheltered them at his cabin for a few hours' rest.

After midday Joseph again tried convincing Hyrum to take a steamer down the Mississippi, then up the Ohio to Cincinnati and, thus, at least save himself. Cowardice had always been severely eschewed among the Smiths, so Hyrum simply refused to budge from his brother's side until this recent unjust attack had reached an appropriate resolution. To the very end Hyrum expected the Lord to take charge over their affairs and obtain Joseph's release.[4] To his certain recollection they hadn't once let up in performing faithful service and always as Joseph gave instruction. Recent glorious prosperity and wild growth throughout the Lord's restored kingdom testified how they had earned both His gratitude and benevolent protection.

The Die is Cast

Turning to his loyal friend Porter, Joseph asked, "Porter, what shall I do?" Porter's rowing the boat had been sufficient, but, like most everyone else at Nauvoo, he had been taken aback by all the craziness occurring these past two weeks. Their frail house of cards toppled after the city marshal and a detachment of the Nauvoo Legion marched against the *Expositor* press, destroying it and burning all remaining printed sheets. "You are oldest, and ought to know best," said Porter, offering his undying loyalty and support, but caught flat-footed at being asked his opinion in matters of such gravity.[5]

Joseph turned to his brother, "Hyrum, *you* are the oldest; what shall we do?" Joseph already knew how Hyrum would respond, for his brother had always been a simple, trusting, honest man, pure in heart…and so easy to predict—one good reason why Joseph had brought him in as assistant church president. During the past couple of years Joseph had arranged their lives so sweetly that Hyrum wanted for nothing. He desperately wished to salvage a part of that good life. Though Joseph, as mayor, carried out city council orders, Hyrum, anticipating his brother's outrage, promoted a resolution for smashing the *Expositor* press.[6] Caught in a moment of frustration and desperation, he suggested the extreme action during an emergency session of the city council without pondering consequences very thoroughly. Hyrum felt an immense weight of embarrassment and guilt for having acted so rashly at a pivotal crisis. His stomach churned when Joseph asked what they must do, for he knew how poorly he had played his part getting them into this mess. Until now

Joseph had always called the shots, so Hyrum had to be wondering, "What kind of advice would God have me give my brother?"

"Let's go back and give ourselves up," he answered, again without thinking it through very completely. His super-discretion would cost both him and Joseph their lives, but Joseph was already certain of that: "We shall be butchered," he offered tentatively, giving Hyrum one last chance for an out. Since nearly four years the mantle of family patriarch had rested upon Hyrum; ultimately, then, at his insistence the brothers re-crossed the Mississippi back to Nauvoo.

Previous to that moment Joseph had never voluntarily submitted his person to capture. Rather, as fugitive from extradition demands issued by three governors, he had made himself invisible while shuttling himself among the homes of highly trusted followers.[7] This incident marked a radical change in his strategy, for the fullness of time had finally arrived; the church was destined to lose its head. The following Monday, June 24th, Joseph, together with Hyrum and more than a dozen members of the Nauvoo city council, traveled to Carthage on horseback to submit themselves to legal proceedings. After his brief withdrawal from excited crowds that had either been cheering him on or conspiring to destroy his power, Joseph yielded his fate to the two-edged sword of Illinois civil justice.

The Mormon Prophet's life would end three days later in a brief gun battle in which the Smith brothers were numerically overwhelmed by a coterie of armed Anti-Mormons that had swollen to as many as two hundred.[8] Hyrum was murdered first by shots from several of the men who rushed their upstairs jail-room, its door too warped to latch. The raiders were members of an unofficial *ad hoc* unit composed mostly from state militia charged with keeping the prisoners in protective custody, and who had banded together to perform only one task. Joseph aimed his smuggled-in six-shooter back towards the stairs and emptied it. Then, glancing out from the jail's open second story window, he saw the huge mob gathered below, beckoning to him. While attempting to leap into their midst he received assist from two bullets directed from the stairwell behind him. Screaming "O Lord, my God!" he expended his last ounce of energy drawing himself across the sill, then fell. Several shots from below ended his life as the entire population of Carthage quickly began vanishing in anticipation of probable Mormon vengeance. The raid on its little jail had been so well coordinated that fewer than three minutes were consumed.

In a way that most men never can, Joseph had known for a long time that his final battle would be there waiting for him on time with all of the action, spectacle and innocent blood that anyone could have desired. His shrewd guessing or an uncanny gift for estimating probable outcomes was *not* what gave him the inside edge but, rather, a more remarkable ability, one that isn't easy to fathom. Joseph's insights came from a keen faculty for visualizing, planning and directing his own destiny, just as he envisioned it, rather than leaving anything to chance, other fallible men—and certainly not to God. His considerable genius at taking such control can be confirmed by noting the exquisite detail with which he was able to record events of his life, even pre-figuring much of the drama surrounding his martyrdom, not in his extensive collection of historic journals but hidden in that same great fictional work that he had authored and published those fourteen years previously.

CHAPTER 23

Martyr's Journal, Part 2: Winning Position in a War of Words

I am not like other men. (Joseph Smith)[1]

While never achieving outward polish from having completed formal schooling, Joseph's fine intellect and thirst for knowledge were deep and constant. If his people's ultimate destination were going to include godhood, they, too, would need to make attaining education their proverb, for "the glory of God is intelligence."[2]

As a young teen he realized how society seemed quite divided by the world of ideas, becoming seriously engrossed in understanding popular thought and reasoning. Joseph had special interest for knowing why many people expressed deep anxieties concerning the respective positions of man and God in the universe. In his journal he referred to that tumult of opinions as a "war of words."[3] As he investigated religion more thoroughly he became less sympathetic due to its lack of sound reason and practical instruction. Earliest recollections of his youth witness his despair over "the darkness which pervaded the minds of mankind."[4] Later he would experiment with and exploit popular mystical beliefs, associating himself with astrology, ritual magic, divining rod and amulet and those charming, enchanted seer stones [5]

At about the time he married Emma Joseph's active interest in occult treasure hunting faded, but that's when he embarked upon his even more mystical career as translator of the gold plates. His plan to save the world had been brewing for several years before he finally decided that writing a book could help. Perhaps as early as his middle-teen years he had determined that a clever new strategy might bring everyone else up to par: followers would find his modern ideas much more palatable if he placed them alongside a format that was nominally Christian but energized by rational thoughts that trimmed away superstitions he judged especially fallacious, and about which most people had already developed some skepticism. After his ideas took hold he could begin introducing more and more practical reasoning to his doctrine while gradually peeling away its more infectious false traditions.

A couple of stiff problems gave grief to Joseph, one being the impossibility of contending openly against the familiar Christian faith favored throughout America. Most evidently, if outspoken about such matters, he would become permanently marked as an anti-Christ infidel, one that an influential segment of society would have shunned.[6] Throughout his boyhood Joseph cherished no illusions about splitting from religious views held by his mother and other family members. They would have made him an outcast following any attempts to breach their circle of belief. How many of us could have handled being thought a faithless blackguard of the family, or a cancer requiring excision?

Joseph's second problem followed from the first. In order to be effective in his plans for gradually changing the world he would have to go about his program in a plotting, deceptive manner, full of mystery and scheming. Nobody could know what he was up to, especially not his family, so he necessarily began leading a double life. That mode of constant duplicity became one of his most closely guarded secrets. To expose himself as a fraud while still alive, after having once claimed such elaborate heavenly visions, would have brought about greatest outrage and scorn from all. Further complicating his mission was the absolutely essential task of devising some method for revealing his experiment, plan and strategy, but only to a future generation yet unborn. Leaving no evidence of his intentions would make no sense whatever; his labors would have become a meaningless, futile exercise of wit. Without leaving a set of clues to guide them, followers wouldn't have had any way to understand the point that he wished to make. In the world's most literal of miracles, Joseph accomplished both his deception and its revelation in a single work of genius, the Book of Mormon.

Can we say Joseph was hypocritical and two-faced? Does it make him a scoundrel? Perhaps so, but let's not judge too rashly. Many of the Bible's most revered characters—Abraham, Jacob, Moses, Peter—were no better. The greatest of them were liars, murderers, swindlers, even blasphemers. Who can deny it? When you are one lone voice fighting to redefine the public's perceptions of such essential principles as truth and human freedom, strict ethics must be carefully weighed against the likelihood of their effect and ultimate success. "That which is wrong under one circumstance, may be, and often is, right under another," said the prophet.[7] Besides, he would explain all essential details within his Book of Mormon using the language of parable, symbol and metaphor. Story-telling has always been acceptable, even when requiring a good bit of dressing to convey the message. When intended to project an essential moral point, no story should automatically be considered unethical. If so, he reasoned, perhaps the entire Bible becomes suspect. Joseph, therefore, painstakingly illuminated the nature of his predicament through a character named Shiz.

Meeting Shiz Half-way

Near the end of his book, just ahead of Moroni's epilogue or postscript segment, Joseph projected one of several representations of his own death into a mythical story concerning Coriantumr and Shiz, the very last pair of Jaredite warriors to meet in combat:

> 29. And it came to pass that when they had all fallen by the sword, save it were Coriantumr and Shiz, behold Shiz had fainted with the loss of blood.
> 30. And it came to pass that when Coriantumr had leaned upon his sword, that he rested a little, he smote off the head of Shiz.
> 31. And it came to pass that after he had smitten off the head of Shiz, that Shiz raised up on his hands and fell; and after that he had struggled for breath, he died.
> 32. And it came to pass that Coriantumr fell to the earth, as if he had no life.[8]

If the quite incredible death of Shiz could have been expressed in the form of a riddle, Joseph might have asked: When does a head that has been severed from its body take a breather? His answer: When you're Joe Smith, the Mormon Prophet, preparing to make a grand exit that everyone would long remember. His Book of Mormon is filled with curiosities, ironies, non-sequiturs, conundrums and riddles made to shield meaning from readers expecting to understand the tale merely through passive encounters. That's the main reason it has always been so difficult to comprehend. Joseph selected the name Shiz to represent himself at the end of his career as tactician and vigorous campaigner in the universal war of words.

The absurdity of describing Shiz taking a gasp for air following his fall shows much greater potential as a powerful literary token than by illustrating ghastly realities experienced on ancient battlefields. Might a brief breather serve to flag that moment of hiatus and introspection that Joseph bought on the western shore of the Mississippi, and which he used to build resolve prior to final submission? Could it represent the delay that he intended utilizing to parlay a sure but ignominious death into the saintly image of martyrdom? The word Shiz comes from the Greek, *schizo*, meaning to cleave, cut, split or divide. The word choice seems so ironic because in Ether's account we find Shiz intensely focused, steadfast and persistent, so unwilling to compromise or slack off in his pursuits for destroying Coriantumr.[9] Therefore, it appears that, rather than portraying a psychological weakness, Joseph presented this useful figure to exemplify his double life.

As expected for a man with his descriptive name, Shiz develops more complexity by the minute, surely too much to comprehend at one's initial encounter. Although Joseph never exhibited double-mindedness, he certainly had to wonder about the ultimate effectiveness of his plan. At issue wasn't so much whether he had done the right thing, but whether or not he had done the thing just right. Could he count on others to submit to his will without their ever knowing what he hoped to accomplish? If Joseph's religious teachings were usually thoughtful and provocative and sometimes presented logical insights by which to perceive theology, nothing characterized his newborn kingdom better than subtle perception encircled by a myriad of darkest mysteries: "And now I show unto you a mystery, a thing which is had in secret chambers, to bring to pass even your destruction in process of time, and ye knew it not."[10] As certainly as his day as a martyr would arrive, he knew that his people could likewise resign themselves to a radical new view of the universe once they'd discovered the hidden set of truths underlying his flagrant gospel of satire and religious criticism. Few conscientious persons pass through all of life's difficulties without struggling over second thoughts or discovering oppositional elements capable of inducing them to question and occasionally reconfigure their schema. He had to hope that followers would come to terms by seeking a rational response.

Ether, Gilead, Lib and Coriantumr

In Joseph's myth of ancient America, Coriantumr became a warrior and leader among the Jaredites, coming into power just as his civilization began entering their final period of self-annihilation. King over a mighty people, Coriantumr had long equivocated in his policy of repentance, always resisting the righteous counsels of the prophet Ether until too late.[11] Joseph encouraged readers to become more involved intellectually when seeking to understand his mysteries.[12] Those who do will imagine Ether representing a powerful (religious) spirit and, consequently, perceive much more of Joseph's meaning. Those only able to visualize Ether as a robed seer calling his nation to repent of idolatry and wickedness will also find Joseph's message coherent but a bit narrow by comparison. As an anesthetic, ether overwhelms the consciousness; as a chemical, it's extremely flammable. What more could one ask of their literary symbols?

Prior to dispatching Shiz, Coriantumr had conquered Gilead, another Jaredite opponent. Joseph borrowed Gilead's name from a well-known district of Palestine, east of Samaria, where it still receives recognition as a barren "hard rocky region."[13] Could Gilead have helped Joseph describe the rugged terrain before him—his difficult task of confronting the harsh landscape of persecution, denial and rejection? Alternatively, perhaps we might recognize Gilead's symbol as depicting the impenetrable exteriors of a (Palmyra?) society that would try shutting Joseph out.

Following victory over Gilead, Coriantumr slew a persistent and powerful warrior who had "obtained unto himself the kingdom [...] a man of great stature," named Lib.[14] What a powerful concept Lib must represent as monarch over a kingdom. Surely he could signify a noble political ideal. Liberty seems obvious enough—but with a critical deformity. Perhaps Lib had his name shortened to help readers visualize liberties cut back to the stump. Joseph's Sunday sermons frequently included issues associated with liberty, or lack thereof.

Ether, Gilead and Lib may represent a combination of three pervasive forces—religious, social and political—that Joseph felt diminished potential for experiencing fullness of living, individually, as well as collective humankind's reduced capacity for maximizing its progression. His work can be perceived as an attack upon the sterile conventions of a society being crushed under the weight of its own institutions. For Joseph, one's lifelong dwelling on sectarian religious theory made for a wasteland of spirit because it generally tended to erode freedom to think independent from debilitating traditions we've inherited. Society's more successful figureheads of authority, assisted by public religionists, tended to smother open dissent, the free flowering of spiritual identity and expression. Joseph may have interpreted omni-present structures in society as a method of domesticating and subjugating people that nature had created free. He once explained to English converts arriving from Liverpool that, "There are several objects in your coming here. One object has been to bring you from sectarian bondage."[15] He frequently railed against the creeds of men but eventually noted a weakening in forces opposing his programs of religious and social dissent, "It feels so good not to be trammeled."[16]

Evidently quite conscientious throughout his youth, he determined that he should dedicate his life to creating a movement that he hoped would eventually defeat enduring religious traditions, thus protecting future generations from its spell of ignorance and mystery. Only America had such a singular potential for redefining society, having previously abandoned such universal European norms as monarchy and aristocracy and by demanding the legal separation of church from state in its advanced secular Constitution. Regardless, spiritual views were still widely perceived in Joseph's day as some of the funding necessary to our existence and well-being. To learn about God, gain faith and obtain eternal salvation were thought to be among man's most important purposes in life. At that very moment in history, of course, Joseph's attack upon such core principles of Christian thinking would have been considered a strike against the spiritual heart of man's immortal soul. His war of words opposed little more than a force of opinion, a common consciousness that he frequently referred to in his book as "traditions of the fathers." Good or bad, those worldviews have become deeply internalized throughout society. No better than aristocracies, opinions may perpetuate themselves without rational means of support, thereby retarding individual development and even impeding human progress. Such ideas, even though espoused by a fragile minority, if well established, unopposed, cooperatively financed and assertive, cannot so easily be beaten, passed over or brushed aside. Consequently, unless Joseph carved his own vision from within the most popular religious medium of the day, essential changes might drag on throughout eternity. He chose to accept the responsibility for questioning western civilization's most prominent foundation.

Because he set his mind in diametric opposition against all that had so widely been assumed innately good and that had been supported by powerfully structured institutions guarding sacred traditions, he devised another brilliant symbol name to help characterize himself in his fiction. It was a clue he hoped would someday guide future readers towards properly evaluating his satire of American society, politics and religion. The name Coriantumr combines two words, *Coeur* (French, "heart"), + *Tumor*, or "cancer." Joseph's adopted nickname suggests a "Heart of Consuming Corruption." He arranged that name in his book knowing that, had he been more straightforward in conducting his campaign, readers would have seen him as a blight against the Christian soul's upward reach, a parasite or cancer that would have to be dissected and removed from polite society to prevent his corruptions from infecting future generations.

Anyone might observe how earlier free thinking intellectuals had been too honest and forthright with their iconoclastic reasoning and, consequently, had been defeated simply by the limited intellectual capacity within humanity's masses. Revolution and war, not democracy, are often viewed as the most efficient forum for propelling change throughout much of the world. Such a message as Joseph carried within his bosom, if spoken plainly, was unthinkable to a large segment of Americans living in his day. Few could be expected to pay attention to any unlearned youngster who hadn't paid his dues into strong, tested, longstanding instruments of society (established family, wealth, orthodox religious background, advanced education, politically connected) usually considered essential in civilization's forward march. Joseph had none of that; not some—not any.

His quick, reflective mind stumbled into the idea of how a clever media subterfuge might serve more efficiently as an agent for change in the long run, even when it avoided established rules of persuasion. Stealthy methods of argument, such as subtle parody, metaphor and double entendre provide a better means of reaching many people who lack the unerring ability to discern correctly that an argument is being presented before their minds become stretched and challenged by deeper realities and fresher outlooks. Hence Coriantumr (i.e., Joseph) seems to have been quite a forward-thinking and subversive element in the skeptical enlightenment movement of early American history. Is his theme of "opposition in all things" still so difficult to perceive? Would all his ceaseless labors amount to nothing because his own highly evolved mind was so complex that his Saints would never discover the sources giving inspiration to his mysteries? "I have the whole plan of the kingdom before me, and no one else has," was the most he ever admitted to them about it.[17] Would he be convincing? Could he hide his duplicity, even from family, his wife and all his trusted brethren? "I can keep a secret until doomsday," he had boasted, never once faltering in his iron resolve.[18]

His decision to obscure intentions under a cloak of mystery obligates researchers to work out and weigh their own inferences. As long as they would limit their speculations to the platform he supplied within his works and words, bolstered by reason, none would be locked out from access to Joseph's mind. Not only have we now been invited to share many details of his psyche, but are also able to enjoy all of the silly and melodramatic methods that he invented for depicting a subtle psychosis that continues affecting our species.

Would he have the courage to follow through with his plan, even when he faced that anxious moment just before taking the fatal bullet? His optimistic view that humanity is destined to progress gave him confidence in its future, and, even though Shiz had to be sacrificed, he also represents that one last chance wherein Joseph faced the temptation to flee for dear life rather than yield. Without submitting to the test, one can only duck, not conquer the fear that blocks achievement of a lifelong ambition.

Joseph had begun acquiring the skills of self-mastery quite young in life, at age seven—under a surgeon's knife, after refusing the alcohol that would have numbed his exquisite pain, or the leather straps that would have restrained his freedom of movement. Because Shiz suffered his death at the hands of Coriantumr—*both* warriors representing Joseph—one may more reasonably view him as being in charge of the entire final furious battle and its apparent tragic outcome. Within himself Joseph created that heart of consuming corruption so essential to infiltrating and co-opting his share from society's ineffective, counterproductive, often lethargic, though always influential minority. Joseph founded Mormonism to sprout an activist, highly structured American cult, realizing that no matter how useful or advanced his political and social ideals were they would never amount to a hill of beans without securing accompaniment and essential backing of a popular movement.

How long, though, would he be able to edge his plans forward in total darkness? How many years should be required for someone with Joseph's intelligence, wit and charming manners to fabricate new scripture, devise corresponding doctrines, attract many converts and organize them into a vital system of ranks and priesthoods? How much time should be necessary in order to form a thriving, fruitful body before submitting to the martyrdom that would launch it far enough into the future that he could disappear assured that it would survive and continue flourishing? Joseph calculated all of his variables with utmost attention to detail. He began to envision his future struggle until it became more and more clear, as tangible as if it were memory. He concluded with great confidence that he would be able to accomplish everything by the time he had aged nine moons.

CHAPTER 24

Martyr's Journal, Part 3: Such A Short Lifetime, Only Nine Moons

I shall not be sacrificed until my time comes; then I shall be offered freely. (Joseph Smith, 1843)[1]

As he gained valuable experience and thousands of new followers, Joseph became ever more convinced of his plan's chances for success. He visualized his end so well that he began intimating its approach, even suggesting a structure for its timing, thereby allowing followers their opportunity to anticipate the event. None of his prophecies received more repetition and reinforcement than the fact that he would eventually become sacrificed to mob anger.

Early January, 1838, as persecution raged through Kirtland and he knew he must soon flee from Ohio, Joseph tried assuring associates that they need not fear immediate danger to his life,

> Well brethren, one thing more. I do not want you to be concerned about me, for I shall see you again, let what will happen, for I have a lease of my life for five years anyway, and they will not kill me till after that time is expired.[2]

He made certain that leading church members had sufficient occasion to recognize his approaching demise: "Elder Wight said that Joseph told him, while in Liberty Jail, Missouri, in 1839, he would not live to see forty years, but he was not to reveal it till he was dead."[3] Joseph persisted in spreading his predictions, as Brigham recalled, "I heard Joseph say many a time, 'I shall not live until I am forty years of age.'"[4] He scattered those ill omens regarding his death among so many associates, sisters as well as brethren, not so much because he fell subject to morose foreboding about it, but as likely due to its being the one ever-present event in his expansive storehouse of future-visions.

Wouldn't such a prophet, curious and forward looking, ever think to reason out why his early death could possibly be of strategic advantage to the noble cause he spearheaded? Might we reasonably deduce that a man of known intelligence and imagination, one with some foreknowledge concerning his fate, would likewise have had enough judiciousness to reach ahead in order to conceive some likely instance, some especially inflammatory issue that would render his violent death inevitable?

For sake of his followers, good reason might well have suggested that God pursue an opposite course, for man's gifts in producing the Lord's revelations had lain dormant for centuries. Moreover, when, after its brief restoration, Joseph's death left the church in disarray, his dynamic "mouthpiece for God" revelation process fell utterly defunct. Ever since that day the church has been run by administrative fiat, reduced in doctrinal terms to modest claims of "inspiration"—never direct—and hardly to be distinguished from matters common to any other business. Most recent attempts at expanding doctrinal canons have only proven his successors' comparative impotence, their failures in following through with or even comprehending Joseph's spiritual pathway.

Speaking of doctrine, none seems more in contradiction with the prophet's philosophy than his pre-appointed destiny with assassins. When did he [or God] change? Had some unknown condition in a fickle cosmos overturned immutable laws, scuttling eternal truth by *dictating* his end? Church members of the day were all caught off guard because their beliefs rejected predestination, or an all-powerful, disembodied rule of fate. Mormons teach the law of free agency—they exercise choice; supposedly, men are "agents unto themselves."[5] Do so-called laws somehow dissipate whenever expediency demands that another martyr be sacrificed?

One must weigh Joseph's record before rendering such a judgment. He had never demonstrated the personality of a chump who would allow himself to become victimized by chance circumstances; rather, his mental quickness allowed *him* to take advantage of circumstances time and again. Joseph was a contender, a wrestler, the courtroom scofflaw, a fugitive from justice. When terrorized, being torn from his home by violent mobbers; during endless harassment, hounded by fiendishly vile jailers; and again, while staring down the barrel of a cocked pistol, he had always resisted, kicked back, confronted and boldly rebuked his oppressors. He was not the one to yield.

Repeatedly throughout his life Joseph increased his charm factors in order to perform as well as any of his starring characters. Note some of the prominent roles that he scripted for himself among his mirror heroes:

- Nephi (the bully)
- Ammon (once mistaken for the "great spirit")
- The conniving, overbearing Alma
- Helaman (the Christ figure, general-in-command)
- Mormon, a courageous, pure descendant of Nephi who had assumed full command of the Nephite army at the remarkably tender age of sixteen.[6]

Why would he rearrange his whole psychological make-up, his entire persona, just so he could turn a blind eye or meekly accommodate this one fatal instance? Nothing seems so entirely absurd. Conversely, the clairvoyant's skill is either to know enough concerning a particular outcome or to plan for it carefully enough in advance that he can refine audience focus to recognize a predicted event once it has taken place. His method for baffling the crowd reinforces his own credibility. More than any other reason, Joseph seems to have been so persistent in sharing all of his death predictions because doing so would later become one certain method to validate his claims of having been a true prophet. Our question now becomes, "What are the chances that doleful event could be offered as an instance of self-fulfilling prophecy?" Did he fully orchestrate the final act in his dream-drama as a self-made "'Bin o' Die"?

Within his Book of Mormon he created a useful reference, a time line pointing towards his death; with it he established the most refined estimation imaginable. Even before beginning his book he had carefully engaged his uncompromising discipline and immense powers of mind to lay out exactly how much time he would need to accomplish a complex, very delicate plan. Then, as author, he proposed a very simple but accurate symbolic approximation for the total length of his life, adapting recognized terms from a biblical prophecy. His clue has been set into the Book of Mormon as if it were just another careless *non sequitur* within the story. One reason this red flag has never been understood is that he had so precisely gauged the pretentiousness of his book's vernacular that readers automatically underestimated his ability to manipulate words.

Today's Mormon believers, by the way, view the fictional tale as literal, rather than figurative, so are totally unaware of this new alternate analysis. Here is how he developed a background for his calculation: following his last headless gasp, Shiz gave up the ghost. Corinatumr, however, survived, even though becoming "as if he had no life" following the conquest.[7] Joseph could afford to say this of himself in a work of literature, for it would actually be his deeply embedded philosophy that he aimed to preserve *dormant* for another age to revive in consciousness.

After some unspecified length of time the people of Zarahemla discovered Coriantumr, hardly by chance the identical solitary survivor that had been placed on ice at the conclusion of Ether's saga. The figure of Coriantumr helps bridge the gap between two civilizations in somewhat the same manner Joseph may have pictured himself standing between two spiritual worlds: primitive-pagan-Christian and an incipient rational-modern-futurist.

If Coriantumr represents Joseph in his struggle to shift intellectual tides within mankind, then newer, more sophisticated forms of battlefield artillery would need to be employed. Although psychology and propaganda may provide a more effective means for eradicating tenacious past traditions before reason takes hold, that process would easily consume generations, more time than Joseph could project for himself even during an extended span of years. Thus, Coriantumr had to become "as if he had no life." Joseph surely had enough wisdom to understand that he could never expect to realize the full effect of his labors no matter how thoroughly he exhausted himself. And if he had tried to come clean during his lifetime, though his logic be flawless, his credibility and effectiveness would have been obscured under mountains of scorn.

According to the story, then, the Jaredite nation had experienced brutal wars of mutual self-destruction; their numbers had dwindled until only Coriantumr remained. When discovered by Zarahemla's people, Coriantumr couldn't have been too young, for, "he dwelt with them for the space of nine moons."[8] The unlikely expression appears to be a piece of jargon Joseph borrowed to make his book sound more authentic. Within the Book of Mormon those nine moons don't indicate a cheap cliché but express an uncanny prediction Joseph made showing the length of his own life, using Coriantumr as his alter ego and a prophetic time period adapted from the Biblical prophecies of Daniel. Daniel enrolled an incongruous manner for signifying an extended period of time by expressing it as *one-week-per-year*:

From the Bible:
2. In the first year of his reign I Daniel understood by books the number of the years, whereof the word of the Lord came to Jeremiah the prophet, that he would accomplish seventy years in the desolations of Jerusalem [...].
24. Seventy weeks are determined upon thy people and upon thy holy city, to finish the transgression, and to make an end of sins, and to make reconciliation for iniquity, and to bring in everlasting righteousness, and to seal up the vision and prophecy, and to anoint the most Holy.[9]

To enable them to infer something suitable with regard to Daniel's application of seventy weeks could take many weeks for a class of Bible students to debate. Some think it one way, some another. The following is a typical (though not universally endorsed) interpreted synopsis of the Bible passage:

In [the Bible, Book of Daniel] chapter 9, the vision of the Seventy Weeks deals with the time of the exile and punishment of Judah for her sin and disobedience. Jeremiah said that it would be seventy years—that is, from the fourth year of Jehoiakim's reign (605 BC) to Cyrus' conquest of Babylon (538 BC).[10]

Regardless of the fact that the math lacks precision (showing only 67 years), and would likewise be incorrect for alternate interpretations, the symbol of having each week represent one year stuck in Joseph's mind. By accepting his use of Daniel's symbolic yardstick, we'll find that Joseph's calculation skills weren't so abysmal. Sufficient documentation exists to show that he steeped himself in popular folklore, including astrological charts and the magic of amulets, so creating a forecast of this nature was nothing foreign to his temperament.[11] A moon or lunar month equals 29 days, 12 hours and 44 minutes, conventionally rounded off at 30 days. Nine moons, then, would be equivalent to 270 *prophetic* days. Converting those prophetic days into Daniel's week-years, 270 must be divided by 7, the number of days in one actual week. The answer (quotient) is 38, plus a remainder of four-sevenths of a week-year.

Figuring the remainder; if one-seventh of a year (365 divided by 7) represents just over 52 actual days, the four-sevenths of a year left over (4 x 52.14) would then comprise 209 actual days as a maximum Joseph could live beyond his 38th birthday while still enjoying a lifespan of nine-moons. He lived 38 years, plus 187 days. That built-in leeway period of 52 actual days, his final one-seventh of a year, provides the greatest accuracy this prophetic method allows for correlating moon-year time with our modern annual calendar.

In summary, Joseph was born on December 23, 1805, turning 38 on December 23, 1843. He entered the fourth-seventh of his final year (remainder) on May 29, 1844, being assassinated 29 days later, on June 27, 1844. The leeway seventh he gave himself (death's 52-day window of opportunity) didn't expire until July 19th, 1844, so he met his end near the very center of the target period he assigned. His arithmetic achieved far greater accuracy than what some Bible scholars have calculated for fulfillment of Daniel's prophecy.

How on earth, though, did he do it? How can any man think that way? Anybody capable of exercising such control over events and over the behaviors of the masses of people throughout his community is powerful, sobering, astonishing—and I'm certain to some, all too, *too* incredible. However, one must stop long enough to realize that this occurrence didn't just happen *one day* in 1844 nor within any ordinary community along the Mississippi, nor are we conducting a discussion about your average commonplace religious philosophy. Finally, it is certain that we haven't randomly selected just any bright young charismatic *member* of that community. Alternately, one may be inclined to attribute Coriantumr's nine-moons and Joseph's lifespan to nothing more than a freakish, fortuitous coincidence or even to a clumsy and bizarre mathematical trick. Even then, probabilities can still support a proposition that he used it as one of his clues, consciously designed, scrupulously calculated and purposely inserted for giving witness to an emotional event that would galvanize and perpetuate the faith of contemporary believers. His martyrdom so traumatized his followers that they lost all chance of analyzing the incident as fulfillment of his literary promise.

To flag the clue, Joseph, while designing his temple at Nauvoo, instructed the architect to decorate each of its side views with nine moons. Two months prior to martyrdom Joseph told his Saints, "I calculate to be one of the instruments of setting up the kingdom of Daniel by the word of the Lord, and I intend to lay a foundation that will revolutionize the whole world."[12] One can infer that Joseph determined to invoke important changes in society and that the seriousness and calculating methods he used for attacking the problem eliminates accounting him as any mere pretender simply intent upon fooling his followers and feeding his ego. He became immovably wed to his philosophy, believing in the good he, alone, could bring about.

If, as manifest through all he's revealed about himself, his teachings have been miscalculated by popular successors, what unspoken object or effect, undeclared in any of his public writings and speeches, did Joseph originally have in mind for which Mormonism needed to be invented? If, as he once confessed, "I am not so much a Christian as many people suppose,"[13] what true beliefs *did* he hold within his bosom until his appointed doomsday? What philosophical formula *couldn't* he reveal while planning on becoming its first *glorified* martyr? If, as our analysis of Coriantumr's symbol name suggests, the Book of Mormon actually holds a work of fiction, not a saga depicting ancient pre-Columbian history, surely Joseph would have placed much more abundant and recognizable literary evidence into it with which to give accurate interpretations of his life, his method and philosophical views. Perhaps, as Coriantumr's dark symbol name suggests, Joseph wasn't really preparing his followers to become the purified Christians so many of them are struggling to emulate today, so distant from his time and place in the world of ideas. The implications of what we're able to discover seem quite enormous, for any event moved forward by such a detailed plan arrives screaming that some greater purpose stands behind it.

With so many complex questions left to consider it may yet take years to ascertain all of the issues Joseph addressed with regard to a fragmented world. For now, let's return to following the thread of our investigation, next to fill in the picture by examining one of the most essential ingredients needed for setting his plan into effect—The Polygamy Plot.

CHAPTER 25

The Polygamy Plot, Part 1: The Essentials

From the Bible:
And he [Solomon] had seven hundred wives, princesses, and three hundred concubines: and his wives turned away his heart.[1]

From the Book of Mormon:
24. Behold, David and Solomon truly had many wives and concubines, which thing was abominable before me, saith the Lord.
27. [...] Wherefore my brethren, hear me, and hearken to the word of the Lord: For there shall not any man among you have save it be one wife; and concubines he shall have none.
30. [...] For if I will, saith the Lord of Hosts, raise up seed unto me, I will command my people; otherwise they shall hearken unto these things.[2]

    The LDS custom of taking multiple wives in marriage by male members embraced within its teachings a seldom-recognized feature that exceeded biblical origins. Though indeed practiced by Hebrew kings and patriarchs, their ancient biblical form of polygamy never achieved the expression of faith upon which eternal salvation depended. Submitting themselves to second-hand commandments of a modern prophet, latter-day believers tend to relinquish their essential volition, by which device Joseph Smith became first ever to make polygamy the imperative condition among followers serious enough to expect eternal communion among the gods.³ What on earth led him to fiddle with the relatively stable dynamics of monogamy? Like his Adam-God doctrine, polygamy became another of Joseph's teachings for which Brigham Young received too much credit, even among church members who ought to have known better. It is one of the consequences they've suffered through Joseph's practice of doctrinal secrecy—"the mysteries."

During the 1850s, long after his death and a large majority of Mormons had moved to Utah, many of those who stayed behind in Illinois, Ohio and Missouri, but who still believed in Joseph's restoration idea, began rebuilding eastern Mormonism under the title of the Reorganized Church of Jesus Christ of Latter Day Saints (RLDS Church). The most contested principles dividing those two major groups were rules for recognizing succession in church presidency (they pitted Joseph's lineal descendants against the quorum of apostles) and whether or not the practice of polygamy belonged among his authentic teachings. RLDS leaders claimed that Joseph never taught nor practiced polygamy. Their view is that the passage from Jacob, shown above, strongly condemned the odious custom. Brigham (they charged) introduced plural marriage after moving the Saints westward. He strengthened his new position over the Utah faction by rewarding its more successful leading men with recognition and domestic privilege.

In sharing their sympathies with Emma, Joseph's widow, the RLDS have overlooked simple realities. Emma bitterly, steadfastly refused to acknowledge Joseph's revelation, eyewitnesses to implementation of its provisos, as well as documentation of his marriages engaged with dozens of women. Emma may have stood by her denials due to deeply emotional, very private issues. Even though their 17-year marriage suffered much rough water, Emma submerged herself within Joseph's theology and devoted herself to his support; she had done nothing to warrant his disloyalty. Nevertheless, plans for perpetuating his kingdom depended on polygamy. Working around his wife's resistance, Joseph nurtured the principle along, step by step, as the ace card he used to set up his own martyrdom.

Reviewing the other side of the issue, according to the subsequent official LDS (Utah) version of church history, Joseph's interest in polygamy centered among the *earliest* of his concerns: "There is indisputable evidence that the revelation making known this marriage law was given to the Prophet as early as 1831."[4] In thus *delaying* the timing of his inquiry, the Utah branch likewise deserves criticism for stubbornly sidestepping a couple of almost obvious facts. The truth is this: polygamy was part of Joseph's plan *from the beginning*. It was irrevocably being pressed into Mormon doctrine and eventual practice as early as 1829, even while writing of it as an abomination within his Book of Mormon. The ambiguous verse upon which that puzzling doctrine turns is the last one quoted above: "For if I will, saith the Lord of Hosts, raise up seed unto me, I will command my people; otherwise they shall hearken unto these things." Hinging God's will upon that big "if," Joseph formulated a very glaring and distinctive easy-out: why have so many of his critics allowed him a strategic convenience by overlooking such an elementary ploy? The only thing that Joseph needed to do was to profess that, in spite of all his pleadings and protests, God had insisted polygamy be established within the new order, to "raise up seed" unto Him.

Soon after dictating the full revelation on plural marriage, Emma received word of it and begged Joseph to let her destroy the document. He permitted her to have her way mainly because a second copy, word-for-word, had already been prepared for posterity but also because he had no intention of allowing the revelation to be published during his lifetime. Had he straightforwardly taken the church apostles into his confidence, boldly published his intentions, supported both the spiritual and practical advantages of his teachings under God's command, he might have been able to legally introduce and defend his doctrine by appealing to the Constitution's Bill of Rights' first article grant of religious tolerance. In today's world, that is how the church would have to proceed. It should be quite evident that Joseph wasn't trying to negotiate the widest possible acceptance for his new principle.

For a teaching having such far-reaching effects upon civil life in his community, Joseph's method for privately introducing it became a tactical blunder that only a simpleton wouldn't have been able to understand. Instead, his surreptitious program ignited fears, suspicions, doubts and fantasies, thus producing definite deterioration in levels of his credibility and markedly inferior results than a more prudent course would have netted. He chose the clandestine route because he realized that, of itself, Christian scripture offered no support for his teaching. More significantly, his objective wasn't to present God's will to the people but to carefully inculcate critical responses among his followers in a manner allowing him perfect control under the guise of a highly volatile issue.

Nephi's brother Jacob gave polygamy its earliest *entrée*, not rejection, for that became the essential scriptural text allowing Joseph to argue its justification. Only subsequent to distribution of his Book of Mormon did he begin to appear, using whatever semblance, wrought up in curiosity over the Lord's permissiveness for the practice anciently. What piqued his curiosity? Didn't Joseph have tons of *other* concerns with establishing righteousness on earth? Consider a few of his responsibilities—

- Priesthood restorations and setting up church organization
- Preparation for the expected Millennium
- Training and disbursing missionaries throughout the world
- Apostasy that occasionally ran rampant
- Building the Nauvoo Temple
- Dodging legal proceedings during some 40 vexatious lawsuits
- Construction of his private mansion, the Nauvoo House
- A flood of Saints migrating from Europe
- Profitably selling those migrants extensive tracts of land surrounding Nauvoo
- Directing the Nauvoo Legion
- Fighting frequent ridicule from a vicious, unsympathetic press
- Sitting as Mayor and judge on the Nauvoo municipal bench
- Running for the U.S. presidency

Did he *practice* polygamy? Where on earth did Joseph find the time to dream it up? It isn't any wonder that Emma refused to give rumors serious concern. Again, why would Joseph have even thought to question the principle when, as plainly shown within the New Testament text, priesthood offices (from bishop to deacon, essentially every male in any position of church authority) had already been clearly established as callings reserved for *monogamous* brethren?[5] Polygamy could never have blossomed out of Joseph's earliest Christian upbringing. The answer seems to be evident chiefly from hindsight: Joseph made his inquiry part of a detailed promotional plan of which only he remained cognizant. His reasons for introducing the peculiar new marriage commandment may have been entirely different from those commonly supposed.

Of course one of its acknowledged purposes in modern times would have been to propagate plenty of rock-solid Mormons in an exponential explosion designed to outnumber the entire state of Illinois if allowed to continue unchecked for only four generations. Even more immediately, though, because everyone considered it a sufficiently exotic practice, polygamy carried inflammatory potential for inciting scandal. In his day Joseph became America's leading, most assertive and fearless proponent of controversy. Carefully leaking knowledge about it among his own church members, simultaneously maintaining public secrecy regarding his personal experiments with its practices, Joseph kept awesome powers on a short leash.[6] With that much control he could easily have formed and controlled his own destiny as a religious martyr. Nobody's will could have dominated Joseph's, and it gave his prophetic reputation a huge boost while heading towards Carthage to announce, "I am going like a lamb to the slaughter [...]," knowing, not guessing, that he would never return.[7] Given such foreboding circumstances, any of us could have prophesied the dire events about to break.

A few simple righteous issues such as tobacco smoking, alcohol drinking, priesthood authority, tithe paying or even his wacky new scriptures couldn't marshal sufficient potential to incite any mob to gather in murderous opposition. Necessity, then, required Joseph find some highly emotional, scandalous bone of contention powerful enough to incite narrow-minded sectarians to resort to lynch law, thus advancing his induction as the religious martyr demanded within his dynamic career projection for, as Tertullian observed during Christianity's earliest membership drive, "The blood of martyrs is seed of the church"

Joseph had previously established a nine-moon lifetime for himself, creating a covenant that he charted with great detail and set into motion without ever being inspired, persuaded or compelled by external force. Polygamy became his powder keg, one that he fine-tuned ever so intricately from its beginning, one that he absolutely knew couldn't fail. Setting its fuse was not at all that critical, being little more than a matter of proper timing, accompanied by his immutable self-discipline—and of course his gifts for directing local affairs as if leading the Boston Pops Orchestra.

For Joseph polygamy wasn't as much an issue of living righteously before God, nor even of lusty sex, as it was his method. With it he could control power—power that could build and bind a large society of pariahs together—exactly as history has confirmed it. He set no limits upon his determination to see Mormonism survive, and he was ready to do anything to assure that it would prosper long after he disappeared from the scene. Among all the mysterious beliefs he set up, polygamy helped expose fissures in hardened ways of thinking. He used the exotic practice as a good-morning slap in the face at conventional, so-called puritanical concepts of righteous conduct, but using the Protestants' own Bible for his paddy-whack. His already eccentric religious views attracted non-conforming Christian believers like an electro-magnet and, having gradually brought them further and further along, finally forced believers to question, "All this and polygamy, too…well, why not?"

The sixty-six verse document he dictated, purportedly a revelation from God, was dated July, 1843, less than one year prior to his timed assassination, yet he continued concealing his doctrine from the public eye, and, while denying everything, spread it around ever so selectively. He was cautiously waiting for the scurrilous facts to be published by embittered local apostates, former members from within the church's *highest* councils. Those men were his hand-picked Judases. Joseph's circle of intimates supplied him with enviable intelligence-gathering services, so, after detecting a few prospective traitors by discreet observations and his highly assertive testing methods, he devised a clever tactic to excite fear within the men. He planted vague but quite unsettling rumors into circulation, beginning with the city's police force. Joseph informed his peace officers in meeting that, among "some of my most confidential friends," a Brutus or Judas was planning to overthrow him and destroy the church.[8]

William Law, a counselor in the church presidency, and William Marks, the Nauvoo Stake President, suspected Joseph tried implicating them. Both started behaving as if they had targets pinned to their backs. Accusations and denials were argued in city council where Joseph was able to spot and identify opposition sympathizers, thus expanding his list of slandered adversaries.[9] Those bouts of outrage began intensifying starting in January through June, 1844, as Joseph slowly worked up the animosities of his select crew by picking fights with them, name-calling and assessing arbitrary fines, publishing innuendo against their names, threatening to expose and arrest them, mercilessly backing them into the corner. His tirades built towards a boiling point as he bullied them, publicly denouncing them until they felt they had to play his game his way.

Who were those abused brethren? Were they the most wicked and depraved among men, or apostate traitors seduced by Satan? What kind of characters did they exhibit before and after Joseph's push towards martyrdom? Conversely, did the Prophet demonstrate unusual attitudes or employ special techniques when dealing with them, different than in his relationships with other followers?

CHAPTER 26

The Polygamy Plot, Part 2: Opposition from a Chosen Few

Our city is infested with a set of blacklegs, counterfeiters and debauchers....[1]

Joseph recognized that every system harbors rudimentary weaknesses peculiar to its culture so gave himself an early strategic advantage by selecting polygamy, an issue so emotional, so visceral, that questions about any actual wrongs involved with it would never need become subject of rational debate. America's Christian community could only view the practice with abhorrence, a throwback to the barbarism of antiquity. Therefore, our founding fathers had scorned to establish any federal laws limiting its practice. Mormons, too, became blind-sided when "spiritual wifery" arrived at their doorstep, and since Joseph introduced the revelation without publicity or fanfare, members didn't know how to respond. As word began filtering down, his Saints were stung by the rumors because Joseph's earlier public denials had been communicated with convincing nonchalance: "Set our women to work, and stop their spinning street yarns and talking about spiritual wives."[2] Such dissimulation is most unsettling, for when tongues wag, one's ratings can only plummet.

Still, the list of conspiracy members trying to curtail Joseph's influence grew slowly in proportion to the speed with which his marriage mystery circulated. The most vociferous of his local opponents justly feared that his exotic religious excesses might never cease, and, whereas Joseph tried projecting how *their* minds had been darkened, the record suggests that there's more to the story. Following composition of his final revelation Joseph's moods swung more noticeably while he concurrently documented in church publications his suspicions of a local conspiracy. A sense of rising paranoia becomes perceptible in his behavior as he caught members flinching while introducing them to his multiple marriage novelty.

Despite any turmoil induced by whispers of polygamy, that alone hadn't sufficient odium to accomplish Joseph's purposes. Without stretching the truth, one may doubt that any overthrow conspiracy would actually have taken hold prior to a reign of tyranny that Joseph introduced into Nauvoo and after harshly cutting asunder relationships that could have strengthened him. Joseph seems definitely to have worn two quite contrasting masks by which he addressed loyal followers and a relatively small number of disillusioned former Saints. Public opposition to Joseph was limited to such a minority that examining only a few of its most prominent leaders will help set the story straight. The six men at the focus of this chapter formed the nucleus of a partnership that set up a scandalous local newspaper, the *Nauvoo Expositor*. Its avowed purpose aimed at extinguishing Joseph's power, polygamy and Nauvoo's emerging status as a city-state, approximately in that order.

William and Wilson Law

The Law family emigrated from Northern Ireland to America. After moving to Ontario, Canada, brothers William and Wilson became church converts, then moved to Nauvoo in 1839, the year it started sprouting Mormons and became a real settlement. William, three years younger than Joseph, brought wealth with him, becoming a substantial investor in Nauvoo's commercial progress. He owned a steam-operated grain and sawmill; he and his brother became joint proprietors of a general store.

A man of civic affairs, Wilson rose quickly to become member of the first city council, elected in 1841 after Nauvoo received its charter from the state legislature. Wilson also progressed from brigadier general to the exalted rank of major general in the Nauvoo Legion, and as such, became one of Joseph's bodyguards and trusted confidants. William took a position as captain while receiving an appointment in his church calling as second counselor in Joseph's presidency. In 1842 William served a two-month mission in the eastern states with none other than Hyrum Smith. The following year, after a posse from Missouri illegally abducted Joseph, both Law brothers helped form the party assigned to ride out in attempts to rescue their spiritual head from certain death beyond the Mississippi.

The first sign of a rift came as William opposed Joseph's control over Nauvoo real estate, as might have been expected, for he competed against the Law brothers in a lucrative market. Joseph had purchased or taken agency over the sale of great tracts of nearby land, then established a seller's market among the European convert immigrants he'd urged to gather to Zion's rich soil. In 1842 Joseph complimented his position as Nauvoo's most successful realtor by getting himself appointed as the city's Registrar of Deeds. William suspected that Joseph had been taking church donations in order to finance his land speculations, but the last straw fell when he suspected the prophet of making advances to his wife, Jane (even though they'd been married ten years and had eight children). Joseph dropped William as counselor in April of 1844 as the new opposition party began noticing its constituents suffering ex-communication on the barely sufficient charge of "unchristian-like conduct." Bringing his city nearer to anarchy, Joseph likewise cut Wilson from his position as a brigadier general in the Nauvoo Legion. So far, the Prophet's actions don't seem gauged to short-circuit any trouble, but to add more juice to the voltage.

As soon as the Smiths were martyred, William disappeared into Iowa. By 1870, he had moved to Wisconsin and entered the practice of medicine. He died there in 1892, age 83.

Robert and Charles Foster

Robert Foster, an Englishman born in 1811, joined the church prior to 1831. Educated and influential, he accompanied Joseph to Washington in 1839 to assist in pleading the Mormon cause before President Van Buren, yet his relationship with the Prophet was not without a few ripples.

Robert became a licensed physician, likewise serving as a Hancock county magistrate. In 1841, age thirty, he became a trustee of the University of the City of Nauvoo and in 1843 received election as a local school commissioner. Later that same year Robert stood in as chairman of the dinner party organized for celebrating the grand opening of Joseph's Nauvoo mansion.

Maintaining financial interests in Nauvoo land, Robert entered into a partnership with William Law. They purchased lumber for building out the city, mainly for constructing homes and commercial property, but failed to observe implications of Joseph's undeclared monopoly. Once the Prophet found himself in competition he used unfair influence to try persuading workmen, church brethren, to boycott the Law-Foster partnership.[3] There's hardly any way of glossing over the fact that, despite absence of regulations restricting such business irregularities, Joseph engaged in unethical practices aimed at dominating Nauvoo's real estate market.

Joseph and Robert also found themselves in competition over Brother Foster's wife, Sarah. Once, when Robert had to leave town on business matters, Joseph took dinner with Mrs. Foster, using the private opportunity to discuss with her his new teaching of plural wives. Robert came home, observed the two together, afterwards demanding from his wife to know if her conversation with Joseph included the hottest topic around town—*celestial marriage*. To get at the truth, Robert finally had to place a gun to Sarah's head to get her to confess, yes, Joseph had begun expounding his latest innovation in doctrine.[4]

Robert's brother Charles became another dissident leader after perceiving widespread dissatisfactions resulting from all the abnormalities of Nauvoo city management. However, instead of fighting against the injustices locally, face to face, he wrote of his discontents in an article that he mailed to the *New York Tribune*.[5] Among his complaints, he felt that money supposedly appropriated for building the temple had been used by Joseph for secular purposes—private profits. Work on the temple dragged behind more lucrative building projects. Although his deduction concerning fiscal matters may have been most astute, Charles had punched a dent into Joseph's famous ego while everyone else had been turning a blind eye to the obvious.

Early in March, Joseph lambasted Charles in a public meeting for submitting his column to the Tribune, although he avoided initially naming the article's author. Such public castigation brought Foster to attention, for Joseph had included a real threat to his safety should it become necessary to take matters further: "I despise the man who will betray you with a kiss; and I am determined to use up [i.e., have them killed] these men, if they will not stop their operations."[6] Suddenly, Charles Foster stood up and asked, "Is it me?" After some wrangling, Joseph admitted, "You said it." When Charles made protest, Joseph *fined* him ten dollars. When his brother Robert tried backing him up, Joseph threatened to fine him also. Curiously, but a month prior to martyrdom, both Robert and Charles attempted warning the Prophet of a conspiracy that had been formed to take his life.[7] Aside from Joseph's antics for inciting bitter animosity, one might have perceived the Foster brothers as the most loyal among his friends.

Francis and Chauncey Higbee

Francis and Chauncey were the two oldest sons of the Honorable Judge Elias Higbee's eight children. The judge, a church member since 1832, had been honored as one of several Nauvoo bishops, but had died of cholera one year prior to the Expositor affair. Judge Higbee once served as a historian for the church and had, along with Robert Foster, accompanied Joseph to Washington in 1839. The men presented a petition to President Martin Van Buren requesting redress against the state of Missouri for killing several Mormons, driving out all remaining members and confiscating their vacated property. Mr. Van Buren judiciously declined taking action, fearing war would erupt between the states.

Both Francis and Chauncey followed their father into the legal profession; both served as officers in the Nauvoo Legion—Francis rising from a second lieutenant to Captain, then Colonel. Their community perspective and gifts for discernment led the two young Higbees to became especially vocal against Joseph, suspicious and resentful of his legal maneuvers, evasions of ethical precautions and outright abuses of power. During one early courtroom examination, Francis swore so adamantly in trying to convince a Carthage judge that Joseph had received stolen property that his testimony had to be rejected. Anyone examining the first half of 1844 in church history might well note the sense of deep frustration experienced by Francis as he and Joseph fought tooth and nail against one another in courtrooms at Nauvoo and Carthage.

When William Law organized an opposition church, Francis (along with Robert Foster) became his apostles. On the darker side, while conducting secret opposition meetings, Francis, still empowered as a local justice of the peace, administered a solemn oath of membership to each sympathizer:

> You solemnly swear, before God and all holy angels, and these your brethren by whom you are surrounded that you will give your life, your liberty, your influence, your all, for the destruction of Joseph Smith and his party, so help you God![8]

Joseph couldn't successfully rattle anyone so visibly as he could Francis, who has also been quoted expressing the sentiment, "By God, all I want to live for is to see this city sunk down to the lowest hell, and by God it shall!"[9]

Chauncey, the younger Higbee, earned repute as a good lawyer and public notary. He went on to become a respected judge and eventually entered the Illinois state legislature as a representative. However, late in May of 1844 he was caught by surprise and understandably upset when Joseph blackened his name to inaugurate a smear campaign by re-hashing a juicy tidbit of innuendo—and in the local press, the *Nauvoo Neighbor*. During 1842 four women had filed a complaint subscribing testimony that Chauncey had "[...] brought about their ruin by deceit in representing that Joseph Smith taught that promiscuous sexual relations were not sinful when kept secret."[10] Truth of the matter isn't easy to discover because Joseph had been baiting his people with just such teachings that suggested the relative nature of morality. Further, Joseph's own published version of history acknowledges ample deceit of his own in making public denials of his plural marriage doctrine.[11] By founding his religion upon conundrums and mysteries he had helped set up and promote his own undoing.

Just for the sake of argument let's imagine true what the innuendo suggested—that Chauncey had taken his pleasure by tricking four virgins into having sex. None of the four women he'd "ruined" charged Chauncey with violence or force, and from examining their complaint, we don't perceive that he tried convincing any of them that promiscuous sexual relations were necessary, only that they weren't sinful. Were those women not capable of discerning for themselves the rights and dangers of sexual liberation, other than to accept second-hand information? What a powerful influence mere mention of the Prophet's name carried abroad. We have to inquire if there wasn't some associated fad or fashion that might have prompted young Chauncey to plunge into a hobby of such depravity using a not too clever line, meanwhile finding splendid success throughout a city of supposedly chaste LDS women?

Chauncey, only 23 at the time, had recently lost his father, was an impressionable lad, and, though perhaps impulsive in his *affaires d'amour*, was also one of Joseph's faithful followers. He couldn't have been extremely seasoned or wary as to the ways of the world nor of the church's leading brethren, his presumed role models. Also recognize that Nauvoo exhibited itself as a bit of a whirling ride at the time; new doctrines and exotic rumors constantly whizzed by the city's youth. If today's LDS Church has placed all evidence for being a cult behind it, that couldn't have been the case in 1844 when one might commonly expect to note eastern Gentiles rolling their eyes at mere mention of the word Mormon. The reality is not that Chauncey didn't have his way with all four of the plaintiffs, or even a dozen more too shy to confess for that matter, but he may have unknowingly been setup by Joseph, an adept expert in situational ethics, and who was quite capable of sleazy manipulations. It wasn't the first or most scurrilous affair that had taken place under the early church's umbrella.

Stirring the Opposition

Serious students of early Mormon history must honestly and patiently assess the LDS movement, reserving judgment and especially resisting any emotional tugging that would sway opinion due to natural sympathy favoring a group of persecuted underdog believers. Historically the great majority of Mormonism's problems can be traced directly to Mr. Smith's tenure as prophet during its first fourteen years of existence. To imagine otherwise pits contemporary views common throughout the entire nation against Joseph's relatively small band of zealots, for we know quite well that they couldn't locate any permanent dwelling space inside national borders and were finally forced to abandon the states in order to work out new social codes while molding their eccentric version of civilization. The church has diligently engaged itself during the 150 years since he died to remedy an early bad reputation and to establish itself as a respectable system capable of producing some of the most clean-cut, best-educated, articulate, conservative, and law-abiding citizens in the world. Their image and accomplishments, especially since mid-twentieth century, have earned our genuine respect and anticipations for recovery.

Early Mormons earned a less-than-stellar reputation the hard way, not primarily resulting from persecution initiated primarily by intolerant competing religious sects. Joseph contrived the foundations for that tumultuous early period: hardly any of it resulted from happenstance of time and conditions ordained solely by a rough, raw society on the American frontier. It was all part of a plan, his psychology of propaganda. To Joseph agitation of oppositional views became one of the elementals, a necessary, primary adjunct of his philosophy, having underwritten it through prescriptions in his Book of Mormon.

Developing their keen sense of how to roil the establishment must become basic to would-be revolutionaries, for that is the way many significant changes in the world are introduced. It is also natural that those firmly ensconced within the system tend to conserve values favoring their living style, rather than to promote innovations that could infringe upon their comfort zone. The "law of opposition" wasn't just Joseph's invitation for everyone to begin persecuting his church, but played an absolutely integral role for describing his attitude towards good and evil. To him the very concept of bad behavior, sin, even evil, became wholesomely relative: "That which is wrong under one circumstance, may be, and often is, right under another."[12] "What many people call sin is not sin."[13] Acknowledging his teachings of opposition, some have mistakenly understood Joseph's relativism as his benign attempt at introducing *yin* and *yang* into a western school of philosophy.

He framed his opposition teaching somewhat more urgently while using Alma to state his case: "Now, how could a man repent except he should sin?"[14] Following Alma's logic, Mormons tend towards elevating their perceptions of disobedience; for them, evil has been necessary from the beginning. For instance, unless Adam and Eve had made that pivotal transgression (sin by common definition, except among Mormons), all of us would still be anxiously waiting as spirits without bodies, clamoring for mortality but unable to make that essential step of progress. Lehi had once lamented, "[…] they [Adam and Eve] would have had no children […] doing no good, for they knew no sin." Continuing, the old prophet produced his thoughtful meditation on life's deeper meaning, "Adam fell that men might be; and men are, that they might have joy."[15] Such sayings had become part of Chauncey's catechism, and he justly suffered confusion by everything they implied. However, he evidenced no difficulties in recognizing where he needed to begin searching for that highly esteemed joy—again and again.

Civil laws established for the common good of society held fewer constraints for Joseph because, "I am above the kingdoms of the world, for I have no laws."[16] That side of the latter-day prophet has been severely down-played by every church historian as well as by each and every one of Mormonism's leaders, even though it helps define his very essence. More recently the church has fervently begun supporting layers of professional apologetics teams employed specifically for defusing a myriad of unpleasant facts and inventing lopsided deniability when confronting its earliest historical truths.

Joseph's quite extensive core teaching of opposition is not one to be dismissed or glossed over. Simplistic explanations asserting how Joseph meant *only* to suggest how we all must cultivate discipline in overcoming bad habits and wicked thoughts don't sufficiently cover the practical advantages of opposition. Taken as a whole, his teachings encouraged followers to plunge into ways and thoughts that had been rigidly taboo in ages past: "I want the liberty of thinking and believing as I please. It feels so good not to be trammeled."[17] If other leaders have commonly failed to achieve such consistency within their creed, they do so only because they neglect acknowledging how elastic ideology can be. Joseph set creeds aside because they tend to restrict one's options and circumscribe the mind with limitations.[18]

Little Foxes Spoil the Vines

During its first few years the infant church developed within precarious economic circumstances. Moving from place to place brings people who are already poor to the very doorstep of desperation. There is some question if its body, first known as the Church of Christ and, until 1838 as the Church of the Latter-day Saints, could have continued flourishing without Joseph's creative revelations that eased members' consciences about necessary guerilla survival techniques. Due to a superior attitude supported within Mormon teachings ("the only true church on earth; God's chosen people; a royal priesthood"), many non-member neighbors had shunned them entirely, thus making economic co-existence difficult for dependent members within the LDS community. To assure that all would be supplied with essentials, Joseph took a radically dangerous misstep while formulating doctrine. In September of 1831, at Kirtland, Ohio, he directed his people through his sure and encouraging word of the Lord,

> 27. Behold, it is said in my laws, or forbidden, to get in debt to thine enemies;
> 28. But behold, it is not said at any time that the Lord should not take when he please, and pay as seemeth him good.
> 29. Wherefore, as ye are agents, ye are on the Lord's errand; and whatever ye do according to the will of the Lord is the Lord's business.
> 30. And he hath set you to provide for his saints in these last days, that they may obtain an inheritance in the land of Zion.[19]

Today's church education manuals avoid sharing the complete historical background for those four verses. However in 1831 the brethren had little doubt about their obligations. Their mission included getting the Saints through lean times, even if they had to steal and plunder, but only against non-member Gentiles, "the world." Consequently, Mormons quickly gained the worst reputation as unwelcome neighbors throughout many communities. Some of the severest persecutions ever suffered by the Saints followed that key revelation.

Quite regrettably, as always happens, some few of the brethren became too eager, got caught up in the adventure and overindulged their calling. Often we see how a few immature enthusiasts can ruin it for the rest, or, as Joseph once put it, "The little foxes spoil the vines."[20] When names of some of the brethren were brought up in council for giving the church an unwholesome reputation, they were brusquely excommunicated from membership, but that didn't happen until 1843. Joseph brushed them right off, rebuking them severely, publicly: "I despise a thief," he said.[21] Today that identical revelation is reverently preserved, unchanged, unchallenged as part of the LDS way of life.

Such severity in his reaction to those wayward brethren deserves further consideration. What signal did Joseph just give to all his church members? By finally cautioning them that little foxes spoiled vines, wasn't he promoting the virtue of moderation—against earlier habits of plundering Gentile neighbors? In just over a decade, had Nauvoo's prosperity improved the Saints' fortunes so greatly that they could afford to turn away from contemptible ways formerly countenanced, or rather, sanctified through accepted revelations?

One can hardly dispute the fact that he unscrupulously committed affronts to the peace, security and moral welfare within the various communities hosting his people, but there's no libel in saying so because we've been able to learn most of this pertinent information from Joseph's accounts. He wasn't trying to hide his evils nearly as much as today's believers seem to be, as he once admitted, "If I have sinned, I have sinned outwardly."[22] Again, if you hadn't already noticed, we're not investigating a coven of Caribbean pirates or a gang of six-gun toting bank bandits but the lead honcho of a religion that has lately begun laboring 24 hours every day to establish itself as the champion of moral righteousness throughout the world.

Moreover, this was not the last instance when Joseph gave moral relativism a major organizational boost in his gospel dispensation. Nearer the end of his tenure as prophet he developed the most unconventional wrinkle imaginable for any religious tenet, one that might just as well have inclined many good people to disregard commonly accepted strictures on all civil behaviors. Joseph delivered his last revelation to his loyal followers, perhaps in part as their reward for all they had endured by suffering his confusing, mysterious and contradictory plan of salvation. It told them, in some of Joseph's plainest English, that whatever they did would not be condemned by God, that even blasphemy would not prohibit their taking a place of glory in the Celestial kingdom—where eventually they would become processed into gods. In it in fact for his most faithful true believers, behavior had only the least of common restraints, chiefly in opposing murder of innocent persons, presumably fellow Saints. His daring revelation is the same one that officially introduced his people to, and made *mandatory*, the practice of Celestial Marriage (i.e., polygamy).

> Verily, verily, I say unto you, if a man marry a wife according to my word, and they are sealed by the Holy Spirit of promise, according to mine appointment, and he or she shall commit any sin or transgression of the new and everlasting covenant whatever, and all manner of blasphemies, and if they commit no murder wherein they shed innocent blood, yet they shall come forth in the first resurrection, and

enter into their exaltation; but they shall be destroyed in the flesh, and shall be delivered unto the buffetings of Satan unto the day of redemption, saith the Lord God.[23]

After experiencing a life full of sorrows and woe, who might suppose all of Satan's buffetings too stiff a price for eventually enjoying full privileges and every pleasure of godhood? When Nephi asserted that he had "[...] spoken plainly that ye cannot err,"[24] he meant exactly that: extreme opposition placed moral perfectionism right into bed with libertinism. Joseph commingled those two principles in creating Mormonism, thereby establishing the very essence of contradiction.

All of this banter and counterpoint may seem quite baffling to those who are experiencing their first encounter with Mormonism, but such psychological effects are very powerful tools that can be efficiently utilized when herding members of religious cults—as demonstrated in the case of Chauncey Higbee and his four tattle-tale girlfriends. If, on the one hand, I can cause you guilt anxiety about whether you wear a beard, communicate with former members who have been ousted from church because they might possibly challenge the strength of your religious convictions; or drink a coke or have coffee with a friend; or even, on the first ("fast") Sunday of the month, take a drink of water before noon—or perform any number of otherwise normal behaviors—and on the other hand can convincingly offer you assurance that your energetic loyalty and service to the church, your "heart, might, mind and strength," will absolve you from condemnation for most any sin, without a doubt I could also convince you to do many things that you would never have imagined without my inspiration.[25]

For someone to hope that Mormons would be incapable of synthesizing, transposing, generalizing, and rationalizing the inspired instructions their Prophet gave to them is to make oneself blind to human nature. Likewise, it discounts the actual intent Joseph built into the marvelous piece of machinery he'd set into motion. Chauncey Higbee became one of many converts who had been brought in before becoming fully aware. His passion for learning truth set him up as a victim. Any of us might have done likewise, for we still live in an age that hasn't yet succeeded in gaining consensus on our views of the unseen world—enough to deal honestly and rationally with our visible, real world.

Dissidents Coalesce

Three important points to consider regarding Nauvoo's dissidents will help place events into clearer perspective. One feature shared in common—their civic prominence—set these six men apart within the community; they came from Nauvoo's most prominent families (while several other prominent leaders also transformed themselves into active dissidents). Less prominent citizens might have been too easily humiliated or too intimidated to fight back, so Joseph didn't need to bother kicking around the local small fry. The prophet was anticipating a voluble response, so he raised his hand against those with economic backing, legal firepower and enough self-esteem to express their outrage. He had to go head to head against the chosen few.

When publicly scorned by Joseph, each of the dissidents suddenly discovered how the façade they had accepted in good faith no longer supported their roles within a tightly knit society. Shunned as outcasts among the pariah Mormons, they became virtual *zeros*. Blind-sided by such sudden opprobrium probably felt something like falling through a gallows trap door, for these men, the ones bold enough to resist Joseph's abominable teaching of polygamy, were simply not the guilty ones.

Secondly, they were all spiritually attached by actively associating with Joseph and the Saints; they were not listed among inactive members, new converts, Jack Mormons, its brief or part time hangers-on. They didn't perceive Mormonism as a social gathering only, but rather, thoroughly believed in Joseph's restoration movement. The Prophet, they reasoned, had temporarily lapsed in his spiritual focus, had suffered strain, a falling out with God. Perhaps unendurable tensions had unstrung him, causing him to overreact by sating underlying avarice and fleshy lusts. They hoped that they could cure his sickness by shaming him, yet saving the church.

A third point is that none of them opposed Mormonism, *per se*, but Joseph's doctrine of polygamy [and his economic hegemony]. His teaching of plural marriage was what united them in such strong opposition. At the end of April the ex-communicants and dissenters actually formed a new church group that competed locally with Joseph's. They appointed William Law their new president while electing to maintain faith in the Book of Mormon. They attempted acting responsibly in preserving their community's moral fiber. As the new church got underway, modeled after Joseph's organization, they set up a committee to visit Mormon families in attempting conversions.

One may reasonably expect that the Fosters, Higbees and Laws all sensed reluctance throughout the LDS community to condone Joseph's polygamy teaching, a practice that never accrued popular participation among the Saints, even after moving to Utah. There, polygamy became a burden as well as a badge of accelerated faith among only a minority of members, invitations being extended to worthy (usually, the more financially secure) LDS males. Utah church leadership finally had to exert its religious muscle in order to get members to *indulge* the practice. Its early members' reluctance in embracing polygamy taught the church that they would need to develop increased rigidity in doctrinal compliance lest they forfeit control altogether.

Back then, of course, Nauvoo's young usurpers had to recognize how a ready-made town with 20,000 inhabitants awaited their taking control over it; the city may have showed signs of becoming divided against itself. Men with a sense of public awareness, with fingers firmly on the city's pulse, had to recognize how its citizens demonstrated reluctance, becoming nearly paralyzed with indecision as they waited to see which way the community might lean—only because acknowledged leaders had been keeping such a tight a lid on what was expected of them. For a full nine years following its introduction, Joseph's revelation about celestial marriage became a suppressed doctrine, never receiving public acknowledgement until 1852, after Brigham figured the Saints had safely migrated out of social and legal jurisdiction. A successful coup at Nauvoo would have netted the young conspiracy movement great power, along with the potential for making huge fortunes among its leaders. Indeed, their greedy investment would have paid off handsomely—they simply miscalculated Joseph's market value and completely misread his underlying agenda. Without a doubt Joseph knew that many of those he worked with had been suffering from deep-seated instabilities—some radical, some fanatical, but all of them subject to manipulation. He pushed; he pulled; he rattled their cages until a few capitulated.

Once they had coalesced, the apostate faction imported a press of their own and printed up the first and only edition of the *Nauvoo Expositor* on June 7. The fledgling issue promised to expose the gamut of corruption, including lurid suggestions of seductions stemming from the peculiar policy Joseph had been both denying and quietly introducing throughout the city. As soon as that first issue hit the street, Joseph jumped into the driver's seat so he could steer his own course to its finish. As Mayor of the city he called the town council into special session to declare the libelous sheet a threat to the city's continued peace, therefore a nuisance requiring abatement. Behind closed doors the language became excessive, the arguments emotional and heated. Don't let that fool you—Joseph kept his steady hand at the controls.

In published proceedings of that city council meeting, held Monday, June 10, under Mayor Smith's direction, the council subscribed to a city ordinance "Concerning Libels and for Other Purposes." While the document specifically prohibited any interference with "liberty of the press, according to the most liberal meaning of the Constitution," it still presumed a privilege of prosecuting those who published material judged inflammatory.[26] Then, having purchased the slightest color of legal position, they proceeded, *ex post facto*, to exceed even the narrow but highly illegal provisions they had garnished for themselves. During the extended meeting, both Joseph and his brother Hyrum mercilessly slandered opposition leaders. Hyrum expressed himself in favor of declaring the *Expositor* a nuisance, thus falling under their new mandate against libels. A few minutes later he stated that he believed the best way would be "to smash the press and pi [scatter] the type."

One by one of the remaining councilmen began concurring that the paper indeed presented itself as a nuisance, but they were prompted by Joseph's intense anger, now a formidable force outside of reason. The source of his influence rested partly on the fact that every Mormon in that council chamber had received his public office, community respect, and likewise anticipated achieving his eternal salvation based largely upon Joseph's will and pleasure. And don't we all tend to appease such powerful persons when they express their deepest emotions while expecting our immediate, cooperative response?

When councilman Warrington, a non-Mormon, cautiously deferred, Joseph tried, unsuccessfully, to railroad him into siding with the majority.[27] Finally, by resolution of the city council, Joseph ordered the *Expositor* shop turned upside down—in sharp disregard of the U.S. Constitution, not to mention Joseph's own 12th LDS Article of Faith.[28] Anywhere else in America, that act would have set off loud alarms, for patriot's blood had purchased a guarantee of its citizens' freedom of the press and their natural right of dissent. Conversely, Nauvoo affairs were not being managed as elsewhere in America. For anyone else, such disregard for law would have been cause for a sound thrashing. However, for Joseph, who had already been mobbed, tarred and feathered and had a vial of acid forced between his teeth, who had been driven from two states and legally or illegally imprisoned but had dodged court proceedings more than three dozen times, yet continued steadily rising in fame and popularity and who had recently threatened to become the next U.S. President, no whipping on earth would have silenced the arrogance, continued annoyances and threats to local political and social stability.

After a contingent of Joseph's Nauvoo Legionnaires destroyed the *Expositor*, all of Hancock county rose into an uproar. Armed men began to assemble and cross into Illinois by thousands, causing Mayor Smith to declare martial law on Tuesday, the 18th of June.[29] Three days later the Illinois governor, Thomas Ford, traveled in person from Springfield to Carthage, Hancock county's seat of government, to demand that Joseph be taken into the anti-Mormon environs outside of Nauvoo for a severe, entirely lawful chastisement that would teach him proper respect for Constitutional rights and legal procedures. Naturally, when Ford's posse showed up during Sunday morning of the 23rd, they expected to encounter the prophet poised to deliver his weekly sermon—and how they'd have loved making his arrest sorely humiliating. Except that Joseph didn't need any Holy Spirit to outguess them; that was the day that he had ducked out of town in order to catch his final breath of freedom across the Mississippi. He took real meaning from Shiz's character symbol: not only did he leave the church headless but had split the scene.

Exasperated with a situation rapidly perceived as slipping beyond his control, Governor Ford pledged the faith of the state to guarantee Joseph's safety, while hoping to entice him into custody. Frankly, Mr. Ford caught himself in a bind when making that promise, for not even angels could have protected Joseph from the hostility, the simmering agitation and sheer hatred of the Carthage Grays, whipped up by one Thomas Sharp.

Tom, an attorney who lived in Warsaw, Illinois, south of Nauvoo, had recently become editor of the *Warsaw Signal*. He had taken up the popular cause in opposition to Mormonism, seeming to suffer particular issues against Joseph for perpetually hogging local center stage. In turn, the secular Mormon paper of Nauvoo, the *Wasp*, zeroed in on Tom, a contender for the job as poster-boy among Joseph's opponents. One biting editorial referred to him as "Tom-ASS," which only exacerbated the rivalry, creating a blood-feud.[30]

Tom Sharp joined hands with Charles Higbee to prosecute as Joseph's final case approached trial, entering "treason" on their warrant for arrest.[31] They deemed it a necessity because Joseph previously had his case (the earlier writ listed "riot") dismissed at his own Nauvoo municipal court. The Prophet had learned how to take advantage of invoking the *habeas corpus* privilege extended by the Illinois state legislature, a feature they had originally intended to simplify the adjudication of municipal ordinances, not so that Joseph could scotch the law. Esquires Sharp and Higbee feared a slippery and courtroom-savvy Joseph would have invoked a double jeopardy plea if arrested a second time on the original charges.

By then the seal on Joseph's fate had already been affixed, not only by upsetting the Constitution's first amendment, but also by mercilessly antagonizing his opponents so thoroughly during his sermon on the last Sunday in May:

> The Lord has constituted me so curiously that I glory in persecution […] If they want a beardless boy to whip all the world, I will get on the top of a mountain and crow like a rooster: I shall always beat them [...] I will hold on and fly over them. [...] Come on! ye persecutors! Ye false swearers! All hell, boil over! Ye burning mountains, roll down your lava! [...] I will come out on the top at last.[32]

Joseph had seldom acted out his rage more eloquently, nor performed with purer arrogance and contempt. Some might also discern a hint of downright lunacy, though in the long run he did come out on top. By 1844 Joseph had become the ultimate plotter of outcomes, the marionette-master of both friend and foe alike. His enemies had completely underestimated him, and not one of them had any idea how they had been so expertly manipulated by his hand. While they were unable to see beyond Joseph waving his red cape in a display of masculine bravado, he deftly stepped aside in order to assure a more permanent future for his beloved, beleaguered kingdom.

His revelation on celestial marriage carried on for 66 verses, yet only the first four are necessary for demonstrating that members were accountable to its terms and were not being offered any option for casually rejecting this essential principle.

1. Verily, thus saith the Lord unto you my servant Joseph, that inasmuch as you have inquired of my hand to know and understand wherein I, the Lord, justified my servants Abraham, Isaac, and Jacob, also Moses, David and Solomon, my servants, as touching the principle and doctrine of their having many wives and concubines—
2. Behold and lo, I am the Lord thy God, and will answer thee as touching this matter.
3. Therefore, prepare thy heart to receive and obey the instructions which I am about to give unto you; for all those who have this law revealed unto them must obey the same.
4. For behold, I reveal unto you a new and an everlasting covenant; and if ye abide not that covenant, are ye damned; for no one can reject this covenant and be permitted to enter into my glory.[33]

Here his fabrication of dogmatic binds thwarting free agency demonstrates a tactic so characteristic that his revelation shows itself undeniably authentic—vintage Joseph. He used that power to control followers, to alienate opponents and, last of all, for achieving the one objective he started out with—that his unlikely fictional account of ancient American civilization, the Book of Mormon, would be preserved throughout several generations of controversy. His scheme received its propulsion through the most unlikely of strategies—that of becoming managing director of his own opposition.

We'll conclude our exposition of Joseph's polygamy plot by investigating his innovative methods for assuring that his kingdom would be shouldered and borne off by trustworthy, hand-picked successors. Also, we'll see how he eliminated a prominent pair of losers from taking over power once the Carthage Grays had completed their lawless acts of committee vigilance.

CHAPTER 27

The Polygamy Plot, Part 3: Testing Games

> [...] the Lord seeth fit to chasten his people;
> yea, he trieth their patience and their faith. [1]

Faith of his followers offered a boon to Joseph that would have been sinful to waste. Faith, however, as with dormant yeast, requires stimulation to arouse and boost it until transformed to its full potential. When simple faith becomes exercised skillfully in order to promote the maturing process, it begins to assume powers that quicken one's imaginative and creative energies. Exceeding faith, the next step towards perfection, doesn't come from reading or hearing only but usually takes root following a structured refinement process. Building one's faith upon acts of excess obedience may help intensify the surrender of followers who have previously committed themselves. Challenging and testing helps gauge faith's qualities, thus enabling a leader to extract maximum service from his pool of subordinates.

Joseph inaugurated a principle known as the *law of sacrifice*, non-standard throughout Christianity, by which followers are [amicably] urged to pledge unreservedly everything they possess, or whatever they may yet obtain, for promoting the church. One of the benefits of making such commitments is that, when properly concluded the individual's conscience becomes an ever-watchful collection agency. Hadn't God tested father Abraham's faith in requiring sacrifice of Isaac, his only son? Today's Mormons recognize such highly refined expressions of belief as superfaith.[2] Members who habitually express their superfaith may, with no apparent disrespect, be referred to as true believers.[3]

Part of Joseph's genius consisted of the versatility and inventiveness employed while conducting his testing program. Although the principle is as old as Adam, one of the likeliest probabilities for his introduction to the art may have come from Geoffrey Chaucer. "The Cleric" in his *Canterbury Tales* preserves one of the world's favorite examples of how a monarch tested the fidelity and patience of his longsuffering wife. According to Chaucer's fable, of several humiliating demands ordered by Griselds's insecure husband, not one of them could persuade the woman to balk at devotion and obedience, not even when he announced that he had decided to replace her with a *new wife* of great beauty and higher nobility. Perhaps Joseph's wife Emma prayed that her husband's taunts of polygamy were likewise intended merely to test her faithfulness.

Try recalling Joseph's earlier efforts, as during his Zion's Camp expedition—the variety of highly effective strategies he constantly engaged throughout his tenure as prophet. Several revelations presented to the church were little more than marketing research to discover the limits of his believers' credulity and loyalty. Some of those tests would have surely driven persons like you and me back into a simpler world that takes a light view of fantasy, pious suppositions and comic mythology. Likewise, thousands of early Saints left the church, embittered and suspicious, but never quite certain of how the con functioned.

Edwin's Test

Testing one prosperous Saint, Edwin D. Wooley, the Prophet demanded that all merchandise be delivered from his Nauvoo dry goods store, which he promised were going to be placed into service in the kingdom of God. Edwin submitted, boxing everything from his shelves, excepting that which had been placed in his store on commission, but then offered that as well—his personal contribution. Joseph took Edwin's willingness to sacrifice as satisfaction for the test, instructing him to return all goods to their shelves.[4]

On another occasion the industrious disciple furnished Joseph with five hundred dollars to pay lawyer fees. On his final journey to Carthage, Edwin's home was one of several stops where Joseph uttered the oft-quoted words, "I am going like a lamb to the slaughter." Two years later Edwin began an exodus march to Utah with two of his three wives and six out of seven children. He would go on to become a respected bishop in Salt Lake City where his solid devotion to the church continued until his death in 1881.

Though Joseph's testing method became a widespread phenomenon throughout the early church, his program doesn't appear to have been engaged for needless ego satisfactions, as might be judged evidence of a tyrant's paranoia. More significantly, we'll note how he established his procedures as a means for separating jackrabbits from the turtles within his flock and how he used that knowledge to advantage when rolling his plan for a grand *finale* into motion. By creating specific tests, then administering them to various members of his inner circle of superfaithful true believers, he enabled himself to more objectively calculate all available resources. Then, having determined the extent of his powers, he could plan ahead with all the confidence of a seasoned commodities trader.

Heber's Test

To Heber C. Kimball Joseph actually demanded, in the name of the Lord, that he give up his wife, Vilate, to become one of Joseph's own plural wives. Such a test might have stunned anyone. Although most men would have surely considered Joseph beyond redemption for even thinking it, Heber passed the test (or failed miserably, depending on one's perspective) by placing his wife at the Prophet's disposal. Joseph only meant to determine Heber's willingness to submit.[5] In the end, Heber became the most married man in the church, eventually taking 43 blushing brides.

As a young man Heber learned the potter's trade. He and Brigham Young were born the same year, 1801. Like Joseph, both were Vermont natives. Not only had they joined the church together, but, early in 1835, both men enjoyed being inducted into the church's first quorum of apostles. They maintained their fast friendship, creating a powerful pair of leaders who worked well shoulder-to-shoulder. Heber would later succeed as first counselor during Brigham Young's church presidency, becoming his useful right hand. Before Utah even became a territory, while it was briefly an unsecured property designated as the [provisional] State of Deseret, Heber found himself elected its Chief Justice and Lieutenant-Governor, under Brigham.

Brigham's Test

By 1839 Brigham Young had become the church's lead apostle. Joseph once singled him out as one of only two of the church's leading brethren who had conducted themselves with unswerving loyalty. The other was Heber Kimball.[6] Brigham's submission to Joseph's will became established as fact following rigorous testing. Likewise, his considerable administrative abilities became evident following several years of Joseph's continued close observation and conscientious mentoring.

Brigham doesn't appear to have been the most literate among the earliest twelve apostles; certainly he had not half of Joseph's charm nor humor, but along with unshakable faith brought valuable aptitudes for leadership. While his no-nonsense administrative control flowed partly from a childhood spent in rigorous labor and harsh discipline, most of his leadership savvy resulted from how well he concentrated on patterning himself on Joseph's authoritarian model. His subordination to the Prophet became so deeply embedded that, following the martyrdom, Brigham experienced great difficulty in taking upon himself succession as prophet over the Mormons. First, a handful of potential leaders laid claim as Joseph's ordained successors. Because no definitive policy existed, church authorities later devised a simple procedure to determine succession in the LDS presidency: rather than anyone's pretending to heaven's guidance, the apostle with longest tenure is appointed to lead.

Prior to becoming christened "Lion of the Lord," Brigham cautiously had to poll his quorum members among the twelve apostles as to how or *if* they should ever try re-establishing the church's top office, the first presidency.[7] Perceiving none of them liable to object or interfere with his ambitions, Brigham cautiously proceeded in presenting himself, initially as church president, although it took several years to complete the move.[8] Challenged by the mechanics of how best to complete his transition to a new administration, Brigham once attempted reversing Joseph's order of the priesthood by subordinating the office of prophet: "[…] the keys and power of the Apostleship are greater than that of the Prophets."[9]

Both revelation and true prophetic succession ended with Joseph, even though the title of prophet is maintained as an honorary (perhaps hopeful) gratuity that has been all too casually applied to subsequent office-holders. Modern church leadership has attained superiority mainly through the arts of business and finance, property management, church administration and their iron-clad control of a captive media.

> After his death, no less than during his life-time, President Young continued to uphold and sustain Joseph, his prophetic and moral character, as the valiant servant of God, and the honored instrument chosen of Him to open up a glorious dispensation of the Gospel to the children of men; the keys of which, President Young always represented the Prophet as still holding, though laboring, for the time being, in another sphere:
> "You may say Joseph was a devil, if you like, but he is at home, and still holds the keys of the kingdom, which were committed to him by heavenly messengers, *and always will*[…]"[10]

Joseph needed dependable yes-men in his circle, so he continued testing Brigham in order to verify his capabilities, inclinations and limitations. Once, in a meeting of mostly priesthood brethren, Joseph had Brigham stand before the congregation. Then he proceeded to severely chastise him verbally for something he might have neglected doing—but Joseph carried his reproach beyond what would have been expected or appropriate for two leading brethren standing in a gathering of Saints.

Brigham, once a working man—carpenter-glazier-painter, had always struggled to comprehend the things of God. He appeared physically well-conditioned and self-confident, but Mormon gospel doesn't allow such a fierce and embarrassing rebuke as Joseph began dishing him in full view of the membership.[11] Both men knew it, and Joseph should have been ashamed of himself. Brigham could have thrown Joseph's own words back at him, but didn't. Naturally, every eye was on the two men to see how Brigham would respond after Joseph's harangue. When it became Brigham's turn to respond, he humbly asked, "Joseph, what do you want me to do?" And the Prophet burst into tears, came down off the stand and said, "Brigham, you've passed."[12]

Brigham thought he had achieved the pinnacle of faith but which we might recognize as massive common stubbornness and what could be termed a fatal investment in his own pride. Religious cult groups, becoming more familiar since the second half of the twentieth century, generally follow the same pattern: low-level obedience is followed by increasingly irreversible commitments that invariably escalate far beyond agreements made earlier with a faith so earnest, innocent and simple.[13]

Once, Joseph, while speaking to a group of followers, admitted, "Brethren, if I were to tell you all I know of the kingdom of God, I do know that you would rise up and kill me." Brigham quickly stood up to object, "Don't tell me anything that I can't bear, for I don't want to apostatize."[14] Brigham had descended across the line bisecting discipleship into the exalted realm of true believers but brought along useful aptitudes that helped him mature into a resolute, recognized leader, one whom Joseph wisely nurtured and kept chief among his leaders.

In 1844 that depth of commitment became the commodity Joseph prized most highly. He soon intended reaching the climax of his career in spectacular fashion, not as much for his own benefit so much as for the confused kingdom he had created out of the expanding complexities that underlie religious theory. Now that his vision had become a living, prospering reality, he couldn't allow it to vanish.

He hoped that he could keep it from being wiped out by the mob that would murder him, so he desperately needed a strong leader to succeed him in piloting the great movement to its subsequent destiny. Brigham had pledged his support early in the church's development, had achieved distinction among the first twelve apostles, served energetically, showed humility, subordination and total commitment to Joseph's projections for the kingdom. Most admirably, Brigham showed rare talent for taking command when assuming charge of those below himself in the corporate structure. He passed every test that Joseph had devised. Joseph chose Brigham.

Sidney's Test

What did Joseph do next? He ran for President of the United States. How sincerely did he desire the nation's highest political office? Not one bit; he wasn't that vainglorious, "[...] my feelings revolt at the idea of having anything to do with politics."[15] He didn't select Brigham to become his vice presidential running mate, but James Arlington Bennett, an influential nonmember friend of the Mormons, but who, being an Irishman, wouldn't have qualified.

Sidney Rigdon, next chosen as Joseph's political sidekick, was over fifty years of age, but still a highly respected figure within LDS congregations. Sidney had jumped onto the LDS band-wagon at the very beginning, having previously served as a licensed Baptist minister. Before that he had helped Alexander Campbell found the church now formally recognized as the Church of Christ. By 1830, before coming into contact with the Mormons, Sidney had opened a communal society around Kirtland, Ohio. When Parley Pratt converted him to Mormonism, Sidney brought his entire congregation into the new movement. Even before Joseph could adequately appraise the depth of Sidney's faith he quickly took the enthusiastic minister aboard as his first counselor.

Although quite knowledgeable of religious theory and usually more animated and outspoken than even Brigham, Sidney demonstrated his zealous fanaticism with so much pretentiousness and oratorical bombast that he managed initiating conflicts between the Saints and their Gentile neighbors.[16] He appears to have had a broad streak of vanity, never achieved highest marks for constancy, nor did he demonstrate unflagging loyalty to Joseph. Along with several church leaders, Sidney became openly doubtful about Joseph's introduction into the church, in 1843, of the Celestial Marriage teaching, but by then his reputation among Mormons had begun to wane.[17] Joseph suspected him of mounting an opposition to his one crucially excessive doctrine. As a test he hoped would throw Sidney further into that opposition camp, Joseph openly accused him of being a member of the anti-polygamy conspiracy that had been forming, then dropped him from acting as counselor in the first presidency.[18] Sidney, stunned and bewildered, professed his undying loyalty to Joseph; the Prophet, however, was unmoved.

Now, in 1844, he was accepting Sidney as running mate in the biggest push for legitimate power he would ever make? The matter wasn't all that relevant because Joseph had no desire for the oval office. Instead, his strategy seems to have been to select an inspiring ruse of sufficient importance for getting Brigham and nine more apostles sent far outside Nauvoo. Joseph called them to the eastern states as spokesmen for his presidential campaign—and, simultaneously, to prevent them from screwing up plans for his martyrdom.

While they were gone stumping for him to become America's eleventh president, Joseph concluded his plan, recognizing that after a brief moment of disorganization and instability, his flagship would courageously sail on with return of the twelve. He didn't want the quorum together, too near, on the possibility that they might have prevented the conflicts he planned setting into motion from ever achieving the appropriate level of radioactivity. By church statute the quorum of apostles stands "equal in authority and power" to the first presidency.[19] Theoretically, had they been present, they could have banded together, interceding to mitigate damages before things turned so ugly late in spring.

Conversely, if present, had they not intercepted breakup of the *Expositor* office, they might easily have assembled a ready-made legion of 5,000 armed soldiers and marched them to Joseph's rescue at Carthage. Lastly, had his twelve apostles reacted precipitously to the stinging alarm that they all would have experienced immediately following Joseph and Hyrum's death, they could have endangered themselves individually or even have led half of Nauvoo into slaughter. Joseph avoided risking consequences that might threaten his kingdom. He had arranged his passage into Carthage as a one-way trip and wanted to prevent any safety net that might abort the wild ride ahead.

Hyrum's Test

Somewhere along the way Joseph learned something very smart about presenting an effective disguise; "Halo Effect" is the term psychologists use. He gathered nearest to himself all of the finest, most strictly virtuous men he could find, making unlikely that any outsider, even when suspecting a Gazelem or Amalickiah, would connect all the other dots. With perfect contrast his relatively stable, supportive and upright family helped complete a picture-perfect view of solidarity.

His brother Hyrum, almost six years his elder, became a respected church pillar, first as one of only a handful of eyewitnesses to the golden plates, then as an indefatigable missionary. Hyrum later inherited the office as Patriarch over the church, finally becoming Joseph's closest confidant and the church's Assistant President. Nobody pushed harder to promote Joseph's religious ambitions. In civic affairs, Hyrum became one of Nauvoo's most active city councilmen.

Hardly anyone disagrees with the fact that Hyrum had been Joseph's first choice to succeed him as prophet. He had taken him into his highest circle of leadership because Hyrum demonstrated reliable dedication while maintaining an inside position as patriarchal head of the Smith family. An elder brother, when not one of the nabobs in the rat pack you're leading, can become a bit of a competitor, an attention-getter or maverick. Joseph always regarded family division with potentially disastrous consequences and thus resisted exposing any hint of his true plans to any of them. They were raised as naïve believers following their mother's religious regimen, so they would have been extremely hostile in exposing him, were they ever to suspect the other side of Joseph's identity.

Hyrum became every bit as much a lackey as Brigham had been, sensing Joseph's needs and catering to them; the two may have competed for the prophet's approvals. When Joseph finally decided to introduce his revelation concerning polygamy, Hyrum nominated himself as the one most able to convince Emma of the Lord's hand in it. Instead of persuading her, Hyrum reported receiving the tongue-lashing of his life. Joseph had warned Hyrum of the certainty that he would fail the task.[20] Again, as soon as the *Expositor* newspaper began publication, Hyrum perceived Joseph's intense outrage, then supported him by urging the city council that it be declared a nuisance, and abated. He had become carelessly overconfident when gauging and implementing the power of his position and habitually failed to think things through as thoroughly as he should have.

Hyrum also suffered from having limited finesse in his leadership skills. He enjoyed his status over the church, as well as their present prosperity. He had no relish for another Saints' exodus, or of accepting the pioneering struggles demanded in a barren, unsettled Rocky Mountain desert. He basked in glories reflected by Joseph and the fact that Hyrum wouldn't fit in as the leader Joseph needed to carry the kingdom forward seems, in retrospect, altogether plain. Once the brothers had crossed the Mississippi, in Iowa, half way to freedom, perhaps to a new start, Hyrum didn't have enough guile in him to suggest to Joseph that they could make a run to Texas or Oregon, as Joseph had hinted. "Let's go back and turn ourselves in," he said, not valuing his life as much as honor. How could such a straight, clean guy like that ever become successful at leading the congregation exposed to Joseph for so long? A form of dictatorship was called for, and Hyrum hadn't been gifted with the Machiavellian arrogance of executive office.

As the elder sibling, Hyrum could easily have exercised much more discernment in extracting them from their scrape—had he not had his head somewhere above the clouds. One week following the *Expositor's* destruction, as Gentile wrath heated up surrounding Nauvoo, Hyrum decided it was time to write Brigham Young (presently stumping through the eastern states for Joseph's Presidential candidacy) in order to advise him immediately to gather home the twelve apostles. Joseph quietly instructed Hyrum to put a hold on that recall note. The Prophet dispatched a letter of his own only after events assured him that the havoc and martyrdom would have concluded before word could be delivered.[21]

Again, but a few minutes before the raid on Carthage Jail, Joseph handed Hyrum a loaded single-barreled pistol so that he could defend himself. Hyrum almost recoiled, "I hate to use such things or to see them used," he said.[22] The mob killed him before he could return fire. One might almost suppose that Hyrum had the heart of a dandy.

Regardless, long before that fateful moment, Joseph's test for Hyrum's worthiness had already been concluded. Hyrum flunked it. Worse, he never even recognized that the test had been administered. He felt flattered that his brother had offered him an immense raise within the organization. What was the test? Instead of asking Hyrum to throw himself down from the temple spire or some other absurd command that he knew Hyrum would accept and knock himself out trying to accomplish it, Joseph tested the Saints' reaction to having Hyrum step in as their new prophet. It took place on a Sunday, nearly a year in advance of the martyrdom when Joseph told the assembly of Saints that he would not prophesy any more but proposed that Hyrum would become prophet to the church.[23] By the following Monday morning the clamor had become so great that Joseph had to terminate his experiment. Some of the brethren told Joseph outright how they "could hardly consent to receive Hyrum as a prophet." Joseph replied, "I only said it to try your faith."[24] The test had proven conclusively what Joseph already suspected.

Regrettably, although Hyrum was everyone else's sentimental favorite to succeed his brother, he simply didn't have the right amount of arrogance, guile, administrative wiles, nor long-distance vision. He couldn't produce enough Amalickiah from inside. Consequently he was not the man Joseph would have been able to count upon in the dire and unstable circumstances the church was soon to find itself.

But no matter, for Joseph kept a useful slot picked out for Hyrum among his endless assortment of church offices. Though not equipped with Brigham's administrative strengths while coordinating high-level negotiations, Hyrum held principal value as a very popular co-martyr. Having two slain brother-prophets would do nothing but add shock to the horror among Nauvoo's Saints. That grief would transfix their humanity with enough common sorrows to unify them like a well-mortared masonry wall. It looks as though Joseph thought of everything.

Some may have felt wonder how any follower might have been led to volunteer such willingness to relinquish so much of himself through these rather bizarre testing techniques without also questioning whether the entire restoration movement, particularly his Book of Mormon, weren't likewise fables or games concocted to develop, test and validate faithfulness. Among other things, Joseph's tests were designed to help demonstrate with force of practical example and for the benefit of every nation, kindred, tongue and people, Saint, Jew and Gentile, what precarious dangers were in store for those who felt adventurous enough to enter headlong into the mysterious and uncertain world of religion.

CHAPTER 28

Moroni, Last of the Mormons

> The palefaces are masters of the earth, and the time of the Red Men has not yet come again. My day has been too long. In the morning I saw the sons of Unamis happy and strong; and yet, before the night has come, have I lived to see the last warrior of the wise race of the Mohicans. (James Fenimore Cooper, *The Last of the Mohicans,* 1826)

Entering the segment attributed to Moroni, at long last we've arrived at the ending of Joseph's Nephite tale. Their battles have been fought and lost, and circa 421, CE, holiness has withdrawn its austere countenance unto more ethereal realms. Civilization, despite the temporary detour in its decline towards a more primitive culture, has at last produced a climate of comparative mildness and personal freedom. One entire millennium of relative social stability may be expected throughout the land before hordes of Europeans would begin tramping across great expanses of its unspoiled beauties, meanwhile befuddling indigenous natives with disease, genocide, spiritual, cultural, moral and social disarray.

Because his writings follow behind that titanic, climactic battle between Shiz and Coriantumr, Moroni's concluding composition serves quite appropriately as a peroration to Joseph's masterwork, for it quite shamelessly solicits added glory for the author. Inclusion of epilogues in literary works became common sometime during the early seventeenth century, following Shakespeare (cf. *A Midsummer Night's Dream*), but popularized by Ben Jonson (cf. *Volpone; Cynthia's Revels*).

Moroni I

As with Nephi, Mosiah, Ammon, Alma, Mormon and some forty others, scale of Moroni's character has been given a boost by having his name attached to more than one member of the book's cast. The first Moroni, a commander-in-chief of all Nephite armies, must have thought himself an awful demon, for his confession of it has been concealed in what is intended to resemble a diplomatic dispatch to Ammoron, his battlefield opponent. The newly commissioned captain cast aside all semblance of tact when addressing Ammoron, reputedly a wicked Lamanite leader that Moroni regarded with haughty contempt. His letter reveals the young officer's inexperience as a student of suave diplomacy.

> 7. I would tell you concerning that awful hell that awaits to receive such murderers as thou and thy brother have been [...]
> 9. And now behold, we are prepared to receive you [...].[1]

After bravely cashing in his lone intellectual sparklet, Moroni proved his want of military savvy by so miscalculating his own defensive operations that he allowed Lamanites to capture a whole city after he thoughtlessly abandoned it:

> And now as Moroni had supposed that there should be [other] men sent to the city of Nephihah, to the assistance of the people to maintain that city [...] therefore he retained all his force to maintain those places which he had [earlier] recovered.[2]

Thus, enemy Lamanites, given free access, quickly stormed Nephihah, slaughtering many thousands of Moroni's unfortunate countrymen.[3]

To cap his failures of military protocol, Moroni refused to admit any culpability for the huge loss but began blaming his disappointments upon others—his people's ever-increasing tendency to wickedness and to the fact that the nation's leaders neglected catering to the capacious needs of his army.[4] In a letter home to Zarahemla's civil government, he presented an abysmal attitude that seems to have infected him with impatience compounded by a most disgraceful weakness of character, as indicated by his unabated carping and sniveling. Moroni spread the onus for his army's collapse here, there, and everywhere else but where it rightly belonged—with himself:

> 1. [...] to Pahoran, in the city of Zarahemla, who is the chief judge and the governor over the land, and also to all those who have been chosen by this people to govern and manage the affairs of this war.
> 2. For behold, I have somewhat to say unto them by the way of condemnation [...].[5]

In condemning "all those who [...] govern and manage" the nation's defenses, Moroni exposed himself to the unkindest cut, for we've previously read that, "the [new] chief captain took command of all the armies of the Nephites—and his name was Moroni."[6] Shouldn't such strategic misfeasance suggest a reduction in Moroni's rank and pay, dismissal for incompetence or possibly being court-martialed for gross insubordination and neglecting command assignments? Were the most elementary precautions against barbaric pillage and plunder too complex for Moroni to comprehend in 74 BCE?

Not the true-action hero many first time readers imagine, but rather, Joseph designed Moroni as one of several swell headed fops who carried the Nephite nation down to its wobbly last legs. Moroni can be seen as a too-young and inexperienced, conceited, high-born military brat who had received his commission at the precocious age of twenty-five, had gotten elevated to higher rank too rapidly, without sufficient training or crucial field experience of action in battle. He achieved his position through patronage by chief judges at home, who then proceeded to secure public assent to their bureaucratic bungling through a rubber-stamp version of democracy.

Moroni II

Several hundred years later, nearing the end of the record, Mormon, keeper, compiler and editor of his nation's records, chronicled the battles leading inevitably to extermination of his Nephite brethren. In the end, none survived to whom he could pass his records except his son, Moroni (the second), last of his nation and tribe, final record-keeper, last of the

Nephites: "[…] and I even remain alone to write the sad tale of the destruction of my people."[7]

Now that's almost too good a clue for pointing to one probable origin of the book's conception. That moment as Moroni realized that his tribe was doomed to be completely and eternally extinguished may offer insight to Joseph's inspiration. His work followed close behind James Fenimore Cooper's *The Last of the Mohicans*, published in 1826. Although the two volumes share only a few interesting [but significant] internal similarities,[8] Cooper's, by far the literary inferior, received a much warmer reception at the box office.

Because nobody remained after Moroni to carry on the gold plate traditions, he became saddled with the angelic task of guarding them during the next fourteen centuries before passing them on to Joseph for translation, publication and distribution. One quite interesting fact is that, by the time those plates were delivered, Moroni had mastered conversational English sufficiently well to instruct Joseph fluently in all his responsibilities concerning the records. Alas, though, whatever else he had been doing for well over a millennium, Moroni never thought to produce the book's English version himself—a task that would have earned him not only Joseph's esteem but quite certainly the undying gratitude of every last one of its comatose modern-day readers.

Throughout the world today there are more than 100 architecturally inspiring LDS temples, most of them (e.g., Salt Lake; Los Angeles; Washington, D.C.; Orlando and Campianas, Brazil) exhibiting a larger-than-life-size statue of Moroni upon its tallest spire. Passers-by make an understandable error of interpreting its gold-leafed figure as an idol to honor pagan deities. Those Moroni monuments are actually intended as a reminder of the humble service rendered by the sentinel and guardian of Mormon's golden plates. Moroni is easily recognized by the trumpet he's holding to his lips, possibly suggesting one of the angel's few pastimes engaged throughout his unique but endlessly boring vigil.[9] The trumpet, no more than a dramatic and fanciful accent, certainly bears no ostensible relationship to Moroni's activities described anywhere in the Nephite text.

While still in the flesh, poor Moroni experienced insurmountable difficulties in absorbing any message of why an entire civilization was collapsing around him. He could not decipher nor correctly articulate the reasons that had caused it to experience such awful throes of disintegration throughout hundreds of years. Thus he went about doing the same as every Nephite leader since First Nephi's arrival—by creating one last book with which to assure future readers' intense discomfort, his book of Moroni. He couldn't see that people had had enough of prophets speaking the second-hand word of God, enough of the Nephite's self-righteous egotism, male chauvinism, their blustery arrogance, paternalism, and especially their annoying mind games while brokering guilt among all of their less righteous comrades.

Of messages featured in Moroni's book, one is so pious and distinctive so as to top the list—his doctrine of *Think-Wrong, Go-To-Hell*: "[...] wherefore, should he be cut off while in the thought, he must go down to hell."[10] *Which* contraband thought Moroni might have been referring to is of little genuine consequence (dare we risk *thinking* it?), yet Moroni's harsh attitude is what deserves our careful inquiry and perhaps much wholesome soul-searching.

For sheer judgmental audacity, Moroni has everyone else beaten. He's another stuffed shirt windbag who can't relinquish a bad idea but must try tormenting it just a bit further to see if he can get it to fly, when in the past it hasn't blessed a single soul with a moment's solace. Some guys simply can't discern the purest simplicity of nature's beautiful plan but seek to extend their narrow-minded opinions and social influence far beyond appropriate boundaries. Moroni hangs right in there by playing his part as a gate-keeper who won't let you finish his book without first inflicting one last batch of onus upon you through his spastic invective and knee-jerk attempts at assisting every sinking soul in sight.

His name consists of two words: More + oni, an improper plural form of *onus*.[11] Although correct form would have rendered his name *More-onuses*, Joseph adopted an ending more aesthetic and appropriate for related plural subjects, such as *cactus* (cacti), *bacillus* (bacilli) and *fungus* (fungi); hence, Moroni. This opinion isn't offered merely as a flippant and cheap diagnosis. We can be relatively certain that "More oni" was the symbol intended by Joseph because Moroni's harangue against wickedness didn't begin in the book with his name on it, but 17 chapters *earlier* when he took over the Nephite chronicles from his father Mormon. His final book was truly a continuation—by adding more onuses.[12]

Moroni's First Corinthians Cameos

While drawing down the curtain, and in addition to exercising his gifts for imputing guilt, Moroni performed an almost anticipated prophetic feat by referring to several specific spiritual gifts that were evidently intended to suggest their application to his multi-talented creator, our omnipresent Mr. Smith. In theory, those readers who have already been convinced enough to have accepted the author's earlier bait—too-explicit pre-Christian prophecies of Jesus—will be the ones emotionally primed to be overawed by that same remarkable effect as Moroni foretells Joseph's advent. The book's final chapter (Moroni 10) presents a resume of spiritual gifts that are helpful in recognizing Joseph's considerable talents. To add a glint of authenticity to its appearance he borrowed a highly recognizable selection from First Corinthians as his cameo or donor passage. To that he added one extra special spiritual gift in his description, one that quite definitely clinches identification of the book's author:

From the Book of Mormon:
9. For behold, to one is given by the Spirit of God, that he may teach the word of wisdom [...].
10. And to another [...] the word of knowledge [...].
11. And to another, exceedingly great faith [...].
12. And to another, that he may work mighty miracles [...].
13. And to another, that he may prophesy [...].
14. And again, to another, the beholding of angels [...].
15. And again, to another, all kinds of tongues [...].
16. And again, to another, the interpretation of languages and of divers kinds of tongues.[13]

Of teachings left by Joseph, his stringent LDS health law (no alcohol, tobacco, tea or coffee) has become one of the church's standard, most visible features. The reason why he associated his health guidelines with the "Word of *Wisdom,*" rather than calling it something like *Advice for Better Health,* was that he strived to implant as many signals as possible for followers so they would make the mental connection between himself and Moroni's list of First Corinthian virtues. The word of wisdom supplied a conspicuous marker.[14]

That he claimed to be a *prophet* is indisputable;[15] that he claimed to *behold angels* is most essential to his testimony[16] (though here Moroni wedged it illegitimately into his passage—it didn't make its appearance as part of First Corinthians, chapter twelve). To assert that Joseph worked miracles with language and diverse tongues may seem a rather controversial attribute for anybody to substantiate, but seeing how he has mustered more than twelve million followers by using little more than the *poorest* quality of English gives convincing weight to his argument. Is that further reason for his studying such diverse languages as Hebrew, German and Egyptian? In order to further associate his name with a facility for tongues, we note that among Joseph's lifetime literary productions was his original interpretation, *the Inspired Version of the Holy Scriptures*, now printed privately by an LDS splinter sect.

While no one can claim that Joseph spent his years in idle pursuits, isn't his a testimony to the efficacy of establishing goals in one's youth? In short, every gift of the spirit that Moroni specified in his cameo seems to a reasonable degree intended to apply particularly to Joseph, perhaps for no greater purpose than assisting him in obtaining status as an immortal among his followers. For a man to set all that down into print, then go about living his life so that every clue would eventually be positioned correctly denotes a monumental accomplishment of self discipline and Spartan dedication to principle.

—In Conclusion—

Introducing the Seventh Literary Wonder of the World

> You can declare at the very start that it's impossible to write a novel nowadays, but then, behind your back, so to speak, give birth to a whopper, a novel to end all novels.
> (Gunther Grass, *The Tin Drum*)

So it seems, Gunther. Millions have at one time or another actually held a copy of America's earliest example of literary genius in their hands. Quite evidently, very few have been very well able to appreciate enough of its richness and wonder. During the late 1800s, Sir Richard Burton thought it "thoroughly dull and heavy." Mark Twain likewise assigned it lowest marks for being "insipid…chloroform in print." Lesser critics haven't been so charitable.

My primary objective in writing this book has not been to lampoon or diminish a work that is still considered by several millions of believers to contain the word of God, but to legitimately redirect its perspectives for the benefit of everyone else who might yet be enriched by it, and thus to magnify the stature of a delightfully impressive, even highly significant work of American Literature. Joseph infused it with so much that is genuinely pertinent that I believe it deserves a second look from many of those who have previously scorned it lest they become seduced by its heterodox (or heretical?) versions of history and Christianity.

Admittedly, the Book of Mormon contains numerous technical weaknesses, including one of its most notable errors, that of suggesting a Jerusalem-Israelite ancestry for American aborigines.[1] But if the reputation it carries as an uninspired religious fraud has been its greatest obstacle to fame, that is likewise what prevented early critics from detecting its stunning artistic triumphs. Joseph could not have achieved full effect by doing it any differently. If we cannot expect the Book of Mormon to rise above its lowly position in the eyes of a discriminating (or jaded?) public, still, there probably isn't any book to be found containing such a wealth of multi-level impressions that are so subject to each reader's point of view. A good many other works featuring highly complex character-and-plot structures have enriched our canons of literature, so that shouldn't necessarily limit this work's chances for achieving greatness.

Reviewing several of its innovations may help suggest a better position for it with respect to other works: Joseph brought a net rise to the intellectual level of world literature by his creative accomplishments in at least three separate areas. One has been noted in our study of his incredibly bright, visual poetry, the *Quasi-Chiasmi*. Another point has been scored through the perfection he achieved in creating *literary overlay*, the duality of opposing messages traveling side by side along the same words, same page, same book. His third literary wrinkle is, in my opinion, almost too uncanny—his ability to fabricate living literature by projecting a biographical preview. Fourteen years prior to his arrival at Carthage jail he published the outcome of that event in a format that would have dumbfounded his believers regarding those future plans to obtain martyrdom even had they comprehended his work as fiction. Who else has demonstrated such inventiveness while so enriching our literary heritage?

At least two human factors explain why the Book of Mormon has never been acknowledged as great literature, but each of those have something more to say with regard to *our* span of attention and of the tenacity of one's pre-judgments. Whenever a jury returns a verdict, either "guilty" or "not guilty," we usually esteem that opinion, but are less enthusiastic when the jury is hung. For the same reason, and because of its protean complexity, most Book of Mormon readers have followed critics who have supplied them with succinct and facile analyses—either *pro* or *con*. I suspect that, in Joseph's one famously unloved book, those two extreme positions deliver verdicts more indicative of a pair of passionate agendas that don't truly reflect the book's substance. When the polarity of reader's opinions is capable of being manipulated by a schema that is pre-disposed and emotionally driven, the results obtained cannot deliver as much useful information as when they embark on their journey of discovery impartially, as if without some particular view to defend or decry. In other words, you cannot absorb as much from it by taking the book where you choose to go, but must learn to follow Joseph's lead. By combining a healthy skeptical view with a welcome acceptance of its complexity, advanced symbolic imagery and the underlying realities that its author tried depicting, the book will suddenly begin to rise several levels in its appeal to one's aesthetic sense. Such widely disparate perceptions of his book's messages have forced it into a unique limbo in the catalogue of American Literature. To some, the humor, skepticism and parody may one day locate its position as an ageless classic on a par with any, yet it will need a fair re-appraisal by factoring in additional literary analyses as they become available. Joseph can be humorous, irreverent, intelligent, obscene, melodramatic and wise, sometimes all on the same page. Or he is sober, solemn, pious and contemptuous of a perverse generation deeply in need of humiliation and repentance. Intelligence became his yardstick for godhood, joy his purpose in life; neither of those ideals can be righteously faulted.

Although we've searched it for cohesive messages, we're forced to admit the existence of its highly integrated duality. That isn't merely unique, but, done to the nines, may be the feature that preserved it into the twenty-first century. Part of its author's camouflage secret reveals his understanding of how most readers tend to blindly carry their own iconography into its reading, whereas non-conforming artists like Joseph normally attempt interrupting or breaking down those conventions. He used his understanding of this aspect of human psychology in a highly creative manner, quite possibly intending it as a hard lesson that each of us needs to reckon with.

After Samuel Pepys, the most celebrated of all diarists, completed writing his memoirs in a form of shorthand, his work couldn't be deciphered for another century and a half. Joseph ensconced his life and ideology within a system of subtle metaphors and allegories that have remained largely obscure for 175 years. The point is that, like Pepys, he preserved for our generation a pertinent time-capsule view from the first decades of 19th century America. That treasure, fresh and hardly touched, now beckons to those who will mine it for new and rewarding insights, for Joseph's ancient vision says much about who we are, what's ailing us and how this nation has managed to arrive at its current political condition. Too much speculation need not be entertained on whether his book is authentic or fictional, so much as pursuing specifics relating to which, why and how earliest traditions—social, political and religious—continue exerting dominance over the lives of autonomous individuals.

"Immediately after the Revolution, American critics, editors, and authors clamored for the immediate creation of a native, indigenous, original American art."[2] Many held genuine hope of discovering somewhere among our young country's talents an exponent of literature that would bowl the world over with exceptional works of fiction, while perhaps the very book they sought lay wasting on the shelves of unsophisticated but hard working pioneers. Quite possibly, if it weren't for well-founded sentiments favoring the likes of Homer, Sophocles, Dante and Shakespeare, Joseph's work would compete at any level among *all* of the world's classics. If we consider only American literature, the contest isn't even close. Joseph published the Book of Mormon five years ahead of Mark Twain's birth but a good twenty years ahead of the most renowned works of Hawthorne and Melville. If Washington Irving and James Fenimore Cooper beat him to the print shop, and indeed, both men gave a wholesome boost to America's literary stature, Joseph's work contains enough substance to outscore either of them. What a notable writer he'll be acknowledged once critics catch on! The commanding lead assumed by eccentric geniuses has often provided the criterion to confirm them among history's prophetic figures.

Could fate have posed more extreme ironies for any piece of fiction? Note the delightful paradox poised by Joseph: as long as Mormon followers took his book at face value, his religion would rise, making him an immortal among true believers. *After* the truth of his book be discovered, though his religious successors might scoff or turn pale, it would allow his literary work to fill up the void in his reputation. He's earned a solid position for himself as the earliest genuine, unequivocal immortal among American men of letters. Our exploration of Joseph's life and work has necessarily been too-brief, limited to culling some of its choicest excerpts in hopes of encouraging everyone in finding something, if not duly elegant, at least enjoyable and more intelligent than earlier expectations. It is a work to bring both bemused delight and deeper thought to a wider reading public. Joseph not only deserves his place in American literature, but among those greats of world literature as well. He once calculated that his book had a good chance,

> Now let us take the Book of Mormon, which a man took and hid in his field, securing it by his faith, to spring up in the last days, or in due time; let us behold it coming forth out of the ground, which is indeed accounted the least of all seeds, but behold it branching forth, yea, even towering, with lofty branches, and God-like majesty, until it, like the mustard seed, becomes the greatest of all herbs.[3]

Speaking for myself, and I acknowledge that a certain degree of subjectivity is always going to be evident, fulfillment has come following an arduous course engaged for discovering hidden roots of Joseph's meaning while unearthing his refreshing approaches to questions that may cause anyone to pause in solemn contemplation. In the process of becoming an advocate of his literature, I've been forced to examine and reevaluate earlier opinions and values. Clarified, his philosophical position earns an acknowledgement and commendation, and, for a fresh, younger audience, an even greater voice. It is most gratifying to discover someone with enough heart, wit and foresight to deeply impress future generations with a view from early America's skeptical underground when it was just too incendiary for his day to accept. His infinite subtlety of method not only witnesses a man of wisdom but a message that deserves all the discourse it may amass hereafter.

Not only does Joseph impress with his art but we can also perceive him picturing a more hopeful future for mankind. As an optimist and forward-thinking humanist he qualifies abundantly in all essential criteria as a prophetic figure—larger, better than most. Minus clouds of mysteriousness he becomes immensely personable. The common man will find no more sympathetic advocate than Joseph.[4] Alas, many may revolt at the method he used in conducting his deception; some may fume and reject his atheism. Nevertheless, as an artist capable of producing a work powerful enough to urge his perspective *eventually* into a broader arena of public awareness he approaches the proportions of a mega-personality, an ideologue-hero—and, by the way, one that we have yet to come to terms with. Perhaps a sneering and unimpressed audience will continue to maintain that he appears heroically, tragically psychotic. While that may express honest reactions, shouldn't we also ask when and where a more grandiose example of craze-against-the-system has succeeded so well at insinuating itself into such a highly visible niche in contemporary society? Engaging an extraordinary or arduous path doesn't make any man a fool, and his strategy of becoming a martyr wasn't particularly stupid, either. At any point in history what military strategist wouldn't have been more than willing to lose one marginal battle if it might be turned to advantage in pushing forward a noble agenda? One can only proceed during a limited span of years, while the battle to free men's souls will continue without end. "True victory lies in your role in the conflict, not in coming through safely."[5] Any way we look at him, how can we not pronounce this New Englander an American national treasure? Only because he's always been so incredibly misrepresented through previous interpretations?

Must his Christian critics judge the Prophet unstable on grounds that he introduced new concepts of the gods, himself acting as the greatest of them? If so they may be ignoring noble roots. Let's not forget the accusation once brought against one of the most highly esteemed philosophers of antiquity— "[...] Socrates is a doer of evil, who corrupts the youth; and who does not believe in the gods of the state, but has other new divinities of his own. Such is the charge."[6] Because Joseph became so absolutely convinced about the justness of his cause, he settled on an ethic of using any means necessary, never having to deviate from the militant maxim that he subsequently distilled from his tactical blueprint: "...I say it is expedient when you strike at an enemy to strike the most deadly blow possible."[7] Where else do we find such intensity, such passion in rebelling against dubious, sinuous, traditions? Or of an individual's demanding the right to control his destiny through stellar intellectual forces?

Of course not every great work of literature is modeled alike for pleasing the ear, having soothing, kindly thoughts, clever plots, clear diction and flowing grammatical configurations. The Book of Mormon received its façade of awkwardness solely to help Joseph achieve his masquerade as a sincere but unlearned youth. If his tactic accomplished its intent, doesn't that become a bright token of his success in the craft of literature? Mark Twain, Herman Melville, F. Scott Fitzgerald, Ernest Hemingway and James Clavel, for example, all produced good fictional works, but you don't ordinarily go to sleep and wake up with them in your head for ten, twenty or forty years of your life—as with true believers. Does even Shakespeare have a following of 12 million that actually consider him second only to Jesus? What more outward, more dramatic signs of lifetime achievement can we project for a man born into abject poverty and brought into manhood along the frontiers of a new nation?

If the Book of Mormon may be reviled as propaganda fiction, it also contains a premium quality of literature in its own right. It has highly sophisticated poetry, humor and blasphemous twists that border on being riotous. If people are perpetually stuck or confused by its dogma, unable to connect with its plot/subplots, they may still be able to admit that its essence has been deepened and bolstered by underlying ironies, masterfully subtle parody, and characters that, as literary, non-historical figures, actually stand up well above the page because they've enabled its author to demonstrate to us something true about human nature.

His book has mystery and symbol, or as noted in his temple drama, "signs and tokens" that are intended to help readers achieve self-understanding, which he thought to stylize as an attractive celestial kingdom. Excuse my enthusiasm, but isn't this the best of what literature once was and what it ought to be? It appears that the Book of Mormon may need to carry its appeal over to an audience of intellectuals with more sophisticated, modern tastes. Hopefully, though, before anyone else dives headlong under its spell by becoming another convert they'll become the newest true believers in the powers of intensive mental cultivation and the dynamic forces of high amperage literature. Given sufficient orientation, there should be little danger in approaching such a book, and I can absolutely assure anyone willing to make a reasonable effort that they will yet discover many new and significant, highly rewarding delights upon its pages. Surely that has to be why Joseph characterized it in the beginning as a buried golden treasure. Make no mistake; the message it brings has much greater depth than we can possibly examine through this introductory exploration. Though some may think I'm suffering from hallucinations, the euphoria of having risen beyond the bishop's reach, I still have little doubt that the Book of Mormon is truly the seventh literary wonder of the world.

NOTES

Chapter 1—p. 1-8
An Unlikely Martyr

1. Smith, Joseph. *History of the Church of Jesus Christ of Latter-Day Saints*, Brigham H. Roberts, ed. 4:574. This indispensable, six-volume set is generally referred to as the Documentary History of the Church, [hereafter, DHC].
2. *Pearl of Great Price, Joseph Smith-History*, 1:33, [hereafter PGP, JS-H].
3. Truman G. Madsen, *Joseph Smith the Prophet*, p. 106.
4. Wilford Woodruff, General Conference Address, April 6, 1890.
5. *Doctrine and Covenants* 132:57. Joseph's revelations for guiding the church are collected in the Doctrine and Covenants, [hereafter D&C].
6. See John Henry Evans, *Joseph Smith, an American Prophet*, p.10-15. The characterization quoted is found in a review of Evans' book by Ronald Walker, et al., *Mormon History,* U. of Illinois Press. 2001, p. 122-123. See also Scott Faulring, ed., *An American Prophet's Record, the Diaries and Journals of Joseph Smith,* Introduction, p. xii.
7. DHC 6:317.
8. Whitney, Orson F., *The Life of Heber C. Kimball*, p. 322.
9. DHC 6:317.
10. Jan Shipps, from *The Prophet Puzzle*.
11. DHC 6:78.

Chapter 2—p. 9-15
Zion's Camp: Launching the Apotheosis

1. D&C 57:3.
2. DHC 1:395.
3. The Zion settlement of Independence, Missouri had been in part conceived as a gathering spot for poor church members, and money donated by members to purchase lands there had been billed as the Lord's method for insuring a sense of equality among the brethren. E.g, see D&C 42:30-32; 78:1-3; 82:12; DHC 2:514. On at least one occasion church members were brought up on charges of "A want of benevolence to the poor." (DHC 2:445)
4. D&C 63:29.
5. A claim that Joseph's call to settle at Independence was merely an unfortunate choice of location isn't justified; he'd earlier inspected the environs and well understood the temper of its people. Recent Mormon writers have also begun to notice, "Even the most cursory examination of the Mormon experience in Missouri reveals wide differences between the Mormon and non-Mormon forms of social organization in the 1830s. An intensive investigation reveals that the two societies were in opposition, and that conflict between the two was *virtually inevitable*.…" (Marvin Hill, *Quest for Refuge: The Mormon Flight from American Pluralism*, p. xi.). While in Missouri, Joseph received the word of the Lord that Zion's sufferings were "…expedient in me [God], that they should be brought thus far for a trial of their faith" (D&C 105:19).
6. See DHC 1:395-399 for a Missourian article detailing the mob's rationale for action.

7. Ibid. 1:394
8. Ibid. 1:419.
9. Ibid. 1:423-424.
10. Ibid. 1:437.
11. Ibid. 2:63: "…having provided…firearms, and all sorts of munitions of war of the most portable kind…."
12. Ibid. 2:39.
13. D&C 103:20
14. DHC 2:66-67.
15. Ibid. 2:70.
16. Ibid. 2:79-80.
17. Ibid. 2:80.
18. Ibid. 2:95, 101, 106, 114.
19. Ibid. 2:107.
20. Ibid. 2:71-72.
21. D&C 1:29; 47:1-3; 85:1.
22. DHC 5:335.
23. Ibid. 5:401
24. 2 Nephi 2:13

Chapter 3—p. 16-24
Coming to Grips with a Tale Twice Told

1. Joseph Conrad, *Nigger of the Narcissus*, Preface.
2. Book of Mormon, title page.
3. Hugh Nibley, *Teachings of the Book of Mormon*, Semester 1, p.435.
4. DHC 5:399
5. Respectively, at Mosiah 27:9; Alma 18:13; 32:28, 30; 33:21-22; 36:22; 40:5; 42:15.
6. 2 Nephi 25:20. See also Alma 5:43, 13:23.
7. Mormon 9:31.
8. DHC 6:185.
9. DHC 6:608
10. 1 Nephi 16:10.
11. 2 Nephi 2:11.
12. Ibid.
13. 2 Nephi 2:16.
14. DHC 3:295.
15. "Much preliminary work remains to be done on the Book of Mormon Onomasticon [list of names]." Paul Hoskisson, "Book of Mormon Names." Ed. Daniel H. Ludlow, *Encyclopedia of Mormonism*, Vol. 1. (1992). Previously Mr. Hoskisson completed a brief study, "An Introduction to the Relevance and Methodology for a Study of the Proper Names of the Book of Mormon." J. Lundquist and S. Ricks, ed., *By Study and Also by Faith*, Vol. 2, pp. 126-135. (1990).

Chapter 4—p. 25-30
Capturing the Scene with a Mormon

1. 3 Nephi 5:9.
2. Mormon 1:5.
3. 1 Nephi 2:16, 4:31; Mormon 2:1; Parley P. Pratt, *A Voice of Warning*, p. 88.
4. Mormon 1:2.
5. Scott Faulring, ed. *The Diaries and Journals of Joseph Smith*, p. 4. Word spelling and punctuation are Joseph's, showing minimal corrections.
6. O. Turner, *History of the Pioneer Settlement of Phelps and Gorham's Purchase*, (1851), p. 213-215. See also Evans, p. 32.
7. Fawn Brodie, *No Man Knows My History*, p. 169; Pomeroy Tucker, *The Origin, Rise and Progress of Mormonism*, p. 17.
8. Thomas Paine, *The Age of Reason*, Gramercy Books, 1993, p. 46. Benjamin Franklin, *Autobiography*, Penguin Books, 1986, p. 9.
9. Scot Facer Proctor and Maurine Jensen Proctor, eds., *The Revised and Enhanced History of Joseph Smith by His Mother*, p. 111; [Hereafter, Proctor and Proctor].
10. Ibid. p. 62.
11. 1 Nephi 1:1.
12. E.g., DHC 5: 265; 6: 307. Joseph's work required him to study Greek, Hebrew and German.
13. D&C 93:36. Joseph inserted another excellent confession of his memory skill: Moroni, his final alter ego, testified, "And now I, Moroni, have written the words which were commanded me, according to my memory [...]." (Ether 5:1).
14. DHC 5, Introduction, p. xxxii.
15. 2 Corinthians 10:18.
16. Proctor and Proctor, p. 121.
17. Mormon 1:2.
18. Pomeroy Tucker, *The Origin, Rise and Progress of Mormonism* (1881), p. 16-17. Others also remembered hearing members of Joseph's family referring to him as the family genius. See Mrs. Horace Eaton, "The Origin of Mormonism" (1881), which in turn has been quoted in Clark Braden, *The Braden-Kelley Debates: Public Discussion of the Issues Between the Reorganized Church of Jesus Christ of Latter Day Saints and the Church of Christ (Disciples) held in Kirtland, Ohio beginning February 12 and closing March 8, 1884* (1884), p. 46, 348.
19. Proverbs 22:1.
20. Mormon 1:3.
21. Mormon 1:5.
22. 3 Nephi 5:12.
23. Mosiah 18:30.
24. PGP, JS-H 1:3.
25. See Ether 11:14-18

NOTES

Chapter 5—p. 31-36
Nephi, Part 1: A Journey Too Far for St. Paul

1. E.g., 1 Corinthians 16:21; Galatians 6:11; 2 Thessalonians 3:17; Philemon 1:19.
2. 1 Corinthians 4:1.
3. 1 Nephi 1:1-3.
4. Mosiah 27:8-11; Alma 36:6-10.
5. PGP-Abr.1:23.
6. Alma 18:2-3.
7. 1 Nephi 1:8-9.
8. 1 Nephi 1:10.
9. D&C 76:69-70.
10. D&C 76:71.
11. D&C 76:81, 84.
12. PGP, JS-H 1:28.
13. 2 Nephi 27:19; B.H. Roberts, *Defense of the Faith and of the Saints*, 2:396; DHC 6:308.

Chapter 6—p. 37-42
Nephi, Part 2: The Two-Story Myth of Nephi

1. E.g., KJV, Genesis 6:4 says, "There were giants in the earth in those days [...]," while the NIV reads "The Nephilim were on the earth in those days [...]."
2. See 1 Nephi 17:48-54. Joseph's history documented his famous temper, e.g., "Josiah Butterfield came to my house and insulted me so outrageously that I kicked him out of the house, across the yard, and into the street." (DHC 5:316; see also 5:524).
3. Nephi resolved a dispute with his elder brothers by touching them to produce an electric shock. (1 Nephi 17:53-54). During Joseph's day, mischievous youth were known to do this very thing. The Leyden jar capacitor had recently (c. 1745) become a popular entertainment and an occasionally noisome pastime. In the south, men would startle plantation servants from behind by discharging the static spark against any exposed part of the body. (See Henry F. May, *The Enlightenment of America*, p.136, 375 n6).
4. See J. Strong, *Strong's Complete Dictionary of Bible Words* (Strong's numbers 5303, 5307).
5. Jacob 2:23-32; Mosiah 11:2; Alma 10:11.
6. 1 Nephi 2:16, 4:31; Mormon 2:1.
7. E.g., DHC 5:302.
8. 1 Nephi 2:5, 18:7; PGP, JS-H 1:4.
9. 1 Nephi 2:22; Genesis 37:7.
10. 1 Nephi 17:11, 16; see also 1 Nephi 16:23.
11. PGP, JS-H 1:35; see also D. Michael Quinn, *Early Mormonism and the Magic World View*, p. 37, ff.
12. Madsen, p. 105.
13. 1 Nephi 13:20-28. Joseph found several ways to take advantage of Isaiah's text, importing more than 20 complete chapters (see Book of Mormon index under "Isaiah").
14. 3 Nephi 22:15-17. Italics indicate word changes from Isaiah 54:15-17.
15. 3 Nephi 23:1.

16. 1 Nephi 1:4.
17. 1 Nephi 17:4.
18. 3 Nephi 8:5.

Chapter 7—p. 42-50
Lehi and Sariah as Joseph and Lucy

1. 1 Nephi 1:17.
2. 1 Nephi 16:20.
3. Marquardt and Walters, *Inventing Mormonism*, p. 63,ff.; see also PGP, JS-H 1:56; DHC 3:29.
4. Statement of C.M. Stafford (1885) in *Naked Truths About Mormonism*, 1:1. Original publication in the Yale University Library (see Marquardt and Walters, p. 118; 139 n. 8). While giving his son Hyrum a Patriarchal blessing on December 9, 1834, Joseph, Sr. admitted, "Though he [the father] has been out of the way through wine, thou [Hyrum] hast never forsaken him nor laughed him to scorn." (See Richard L. Bushman, *Joseph Smith and the Beginnings of Mormonism*, p. 208,n 56).
5. 1 Nephi, chapters 3, 7.
6. See *Smith's Bible Dictionary*, "Lehi."
7. Genesis 17:15.
8. See Strong, Op.Cit. "Sarah," "Sarai." (Strong's numbers 8287, 8293)
9. Proctor and Proctor, p. 91, n4.
10. Ibid. p. 84.
11. Alma 32:4.
12. 1 Nephi 5:3.
13. Proctor and Proctor, p. 63-66; 88-90; 94.
14. E.g., Proctor and Proctor, p. 51-53, 81.
15. Ibid. p. 88, 126-134.
16. Ibid. p.58-59.
17. Ibid. p. 64-66; 67, n10.
18. Ibid, p.112.

Chapter 8—p. 51-62
Lehi's Dream of the Tree of Life

1. Genesis 2:9-10.
2. Genesis 3:7.
3. Genesis 3:22-24.
4. Genesis 4:1.
5. 1 Nephi 8.
6. 1 Nephi 8:20.
7. 1 Nephi 8:26-27.
8. 1 Nephi 8:17-18.
9. 1 Nephi 8:32.
10. PGP, Abr.3:22.

11. PGP, Abr. 3:28.
12. 1 Nephi 8:5.
13. Ibid. v. 7.
14. Ibid. v. 9-11.
15. 1 Nephi 15:21-22.
16. 1 Nephi 8:11-12.
17. Ibid. v. 13-14.
18. Ibid. v. 14-18.
19. Ibid. v. 19-23.
20. Ibid. v. 24.
21. Ibid. v. 25.
22. Ibid. v. 26-28.
23. D&C 76:24.
24. 1 Nephi 8:11.
25. 1 Nephi 11:1-3.
26. 1 Nephi 11:13.
27. Ibid. v. 14.
28. Ibid. v. 15.
29. Ibid. v. 17.
30. Joseph F. Smith, *Box Elder News*, Jan 28, 1915.
31. 1 Nephi 11:22.
32. DHC 6:608.
33. 1 Nephi 7:1.
34. 1 Nephi 16:7.
35. 1 Nephi 17:1-2.
36. 1 Nephi 18:7.
37. Bob Whitte and Gordon H. Fraser, *What's Going On In Here, An Exposing of the Secret Mormon Temple Rituals*, p. 31. All quotations given from the LDS temple ceremony have been taken from this very accurate resource. Comparison between this and other temple expose sources show insignificant variations. Another good verbatim text is contained in Chuck Sackett, *What's Going on in There?*

Chapter 9—p. 63-72
Troubles with Three Good Bad Guys

1. DHC 1:220.
2. The split between Nephites and Lamanites, including the Lamanite curse of black skin, is described in 2 Nephi 5. See also Mos. 9:12; Jarom 1:5-8.
3. Nephi's brothers couldn't restrain him by bonds. (1 Nephi 7:16-18) He shocked them in order to secure their cooperation. (1 Nephi 17:53-55; See also 1 Nephi 3:28-29; 18:12-22.
4. Genesis 4:15.
5. 2 Nephi 5:21.
6. Jarom 1:10; see also 3 Nephi 10:12, more righteous people are spared destruction.
7. Helaman 13-15.

8. "…where there is no law given there is no punishment; and where there is no punishment there is no condemnation…." (2 Nephi 9:25; see also Helaman 7:23-24; Alma 9:19). A study of Joseph's epistemology shows it to be thoroughly original, hopelessly circuitous and complex. One is given to understand that, without knowledge, one's salvation is utterly assured. Increasing one's knowledge, while imperative, demands increasing one's commitments, yielding higher risks of failure—but also promising infinite rewards. In another instance, Satan is considered an incredibly intelligent being, Lucifer ("light" his descriptive name), but who is destined to rule in outer darkness.
9. D&C 82:3.
10. "To get salvation we must not only do some things, but everything which God has commanded." (DHC 6:223)
11. "Shim" names the hill from which Mormon was instructed to remove the cumulative Nephite records. (Mormon 1:3; 4:23) Shims are similar to laminates, both describing thin metal sheets.
12. Mormon 4:23.
13. Originally, Joseph made reference to the "horn" metaphor, although here he has been quoted by Brigham Young. see *Discourses of Brigham Young*, p. 470. See also *Journal of Discourses* 3:24; 8:354; 17:349 [Hereafter, J.D.] See also DHC 3:295.
14. D.H.C. 5:126-127; Proctor & Proctor, p. 119. In 1836, Joseph made up for the parson's thoughtlessness by relating his vision of the celestial kingdom in the Doctrine and Covenants. Alvin appeared to him there in glory while again noting the omission of Alvin's baptism during life. (See D&C 137:1-9).
15. PGP, Abraham. 3:23.
16. Proctor and Proctor, p. 121. *Inventing Momonism*, p. 120.
17. Micah 7:6.
18. Proctor and Proctor, p. 122.
19. 1 Nephi 5:14-16.
20. See *Collected Works of Hugh Nibley*, Vol. 5, Part 1, Chapter 5, p. 97.
21. 1 Nephi 3:3; Mosiah 1:4.
22. 1 Nephi 3:13.
23. 1 Nephi 3:25.
24. 1 Nephi 4:13.
25. John 11:50.
26. 1 Nephi 4:18.
27. 1 Nephi 4:7.

Chapter 10—p. 73-85
Painful Origins on Plates of Brass

1. DHC 5:297.
2. See 1 Nephi 13.
3. Proctor and Proctor, p. 58.
4. 1 Nephi 4:18-24. Note Joseph's ostensible purposes in characterizing the Old Testament record, preserved on "plates of brass," when actually referring to Tom Paine's book of Bible criticism. The word "brass" is commonly used to symbolize someone's

effrontery and that is exactly the view taken by America's religious conservatives towards Paine's book. Secondly, Israel had anciently been warned against faltering in obedience to the Lord: "And thy heaven that is over thy head shall be brass…." (Deuteronomy 28:23). Joseph made Laban's brass plates conform to "*hard, un-malleable*" revelation.

5. Proctor and Proctor, p. 72-76; 77, n4.
6. Mormon 1:7.
7. Joseph would explain that during his first vision his tongue had become bound so that he could not speak. (PGP, JS-H 1:15). Could his allusion be referring to the common wisdom of keeping one's heartfelt anti-religious opinions private?
8. Proctor and Proctor, p. 230-233.
9. Paine, p. 7, 146.
10. Ibid. 59-62.
11. Ibid. p. 66, 167-168.
12. Ibid. p. 183.
13. Ibid. p. 27, 56.
14. Genesis 6:5.
15. Romans 1:18-32. See also Paul Little, *Know What You Believe*, Victor Books, p. 87-98.
16. Paine, p. 42; Alma 32:27.
17. Paine, p.27.
18. Hebrews 10:10.
19. Leviticus 16:33-34.
20. Jacob 1:8. The "infinite atonement" is taught at 2 Nephi 9:7; 25:16; Alma 34:10-14.
21. Alma 34:11-12.
22. 2 Nephi 25:23. Joseph once stated, "To get salvation we must not only do some things, but everything which God has commanded." (DHC 6:223) He may have designed extreme perfectionism so that his followers might eventually realize the futility and frustration of (infinite) works.
23. Paine, p. 5, 13, 157.
24. John 19:30, 38, 20:14.
25. Mosiah 29:38.
26. D&C 101:78; see also 137:7-9.
27. Alma 36:21.
28. Proctor and Proctor, p. 74-75.
29. One evening's entry in his journal relates Joseph's method of study, "'I am going to study law, and this is the way I study it;' and then [Joseph] fell asleep." (DHC 5:307).
30. Joseph stretched law further than Voltaire in giving legal assistance. Not long before his martyrdom, he harbored a wanted fugitive, Jeremiah Smith, from justice, using his powers at the municipal bench to have federal warrants dismissed. He invoked Nauvoo's infamous, extra-legal powers for exercising *habeas corpus* (see DHC 6:416, 418, 420-423).
31. Here Candide's symbol name helps represent an autobiographical element. One who is candid (i.e., Candide) speaks words that are frank (i.e., franc, Francois? It was Voltaire's given name).
32. Jacob 7:27.
33. See Webster's, *A Compendious Dictionary of the English Language*, 1806 edition.

NOTES

Chapter 11—p. 86-97
Samuel, Jacob and Joseph: How Team Players Engineered the Great Media Coup

1. Joseph furnished both Ramah and Elkanah repetition in LDS scripture. Ramah refers to the hill now known as Cumorah, site of the repository of his golden plates. (Ether 15:11). Elkanah, Samuel's father, is transformed into the word Elkenah, one of the false gods mentioned in his Book of Abraham. (PGP, Abr. 1:6). The point is that Joseph appointed exceptional (if symbolic) acknowledgements to Samuel, the seer.
2. 1 Samuel 9:9; D&C 21:1.
3. 1 Samuel 8:1-8.
4. Mosiah 29:27.
5. Genesis 37:1-28.
6. Genesis 49:1-27.
7. Genesis 49:22-26.
8. 1 Chronicles 5:1-2.
9. Compare the blessings given by Moses at Deuteronomy 33.
10. Isaiah 28:10.
11. 2 Nephi 28:30.
12. 1 Nephi 1:2.
13. 1 Nephi 1:1; Faulring, p. 4.
14. 1 Nephi 2:22; see Genesis 37:6-8.
15. 1 Nephi 17:48; Genesis 37:18.
16. 1 Nephi 5:14.
17. 1 Nephi 16:18; Genesis 49:24; see also Psalms18:34.
18. 2 Nephi 3:3-7.
19. DHC 5:303; see Mark 5:30.
20. DHC 4:445.
21. Madsen, p. 106.
22. Deuteronomy 18:15.
23. Acts 3:20-22.
24. 1 Nephi 22:20.
25. Ibid., v.21.
26. 3 Nephi 20:23.
27. 2 Nephi 3:6, 9-11, 15.
28. Cf. Pratkanis and Aronson, Op. Cit., Chapter 17, "Self Sell," p.123, ff.
29. 2 Nephi 9:40.
30. 1 Nephi 13:24-29.

Chapter 12—p. 98-106
Zenos' Wild Allegory

1. 1 Nephi 19:10, 12, 16.
2. 1 Nephi 13:26-27.

❡ NOTES ❡

3. At least four men named Zeno achieved repute as ancient Greek philosophers. David Hume mentioned Zeno in his *Dialogues Concerning Natural Religion,* Part 1, published in 1779. Plato referred to Zeno in his dialogue, *Parminides.* Either book would have been available in Joseph's day.
4. E.g., 1 Nephi 11:21; 13:21-23; 15:21-27; 22:1-2.
5. Jacob 5:2.
6. Jeremiah 10:1.
7. Jacob 5:26, 46, 49, 66, 77.
8. Ibid., v. 25.
9. Ibid., v. 27.
10. Ibid. v. 7, 9.
11. Ibid., v. 10.
12. Ibid., v. 18.
13. Ibid., v. 32.
14. Ibid., v. 40-42.
15. Ibid., v. 49-50.
16. Ibid., v. 55-56.
17. Ibid., v. 14.
18. Ibid., v. 41, 47.
19. Ibid., v. 47.
20. Ibid., v. 48.
21. Ibid., v. 58.
22. Ibid., v. 61, 62, 64.
23. Ibid., v. 65.
24. Mosiah 4:26.
25. Jacob 5:66. The church's high council constantly excommunicated members, even those highest in the organization, "We have (reluctantly) been compelled to sever them from the Churches as withered branches" (DHC 6:228). "Nothing will have such influence over people as the fear of being disfellowshipped by so goodly society as this" (DHC 5:23).
26. Ibid., v. 72-73.
27. Ibid., v. 75.
28. Ibid.
29. Ibid., v. 76.
30. D&C 29:39.

Chapter 13—p. 107-111
Omni: One for All, All in Fun

1. PGP, JS-H 1:28.
2. Omni 1:9.
3. *Webster's New World Dictionary*, Second College Edition.
4. Omni 1:10.
5. Ibid., v.12, 19.
6. See *Webster's Dictionary: "Ki."*

7. Omni 1:23.
8. Genesis 35:17-18.
9. Judges 20:16.
10. Mosiah 1:2; 27:34.
11. Alma 17:35-38.
12. DHC 6:78.

Chapter 14—p. 112-121
Mosiah, the Prophet-Savior Combo

1. Mosiah 1:10.
2. Alma 1:14. Nephite law was referred to as the "law of Mosiah" (see Alma 11:1).
3. Mosiah 6:4; Luke 3:23.
4. Alma 10:19.
5. Matthew 10:5.
6. John 3:16; Mosiah 28:7.
7. DHC 6:500; see John 15:13.
8. DHC 6:411.
9. D&C 135:4; see Isaiah 53:7; Acts 8:32. See also DHC 3:228
10. Mosiah 21:28.
11. Mosiah 29:16-26. Mosiah terminated rule of kings, commanding the people to "do your business by the voice of the people."
12. Mosiah 13:15-24. Slight changes will be noted in arrangement of Abinadi's version of the Ten Commandments, nevertheless, because those commandments are specifically the subject of his sermon, his proposal for their future termination is more evident when he states, "The time shall come when it shall no more be expedient to keep the law of Moses." (v. 27). He isn't referring to other, collateral items of the law.
13. Matthew 5:17.
14. Romans 7:4.
15. Galatians 3:13.
16. Mosiah. Chapter 14.
17. Ibid. 15:2-3.
18. Isaiah 52:7; see also Isaiah 2:2-3.
19. Mosiah 15:14-18. Without making too much of this solemn subject it is fair to note that, during 1836, an obscure Christian ceremony had been revived, the washing of feet. Along with songs and prayers, the priesthood brethren spent hours in washing one another's feet. For reasons not readily apparent, this solemn ceremony failed to inspire continued practice. E.g., see DHC 2:430-431, 475-476.
20. Mosiah 17:15-18.
21. D&C 87:6 to further sample Joseph's curses, see also DHC 3:294; 4:587; 5:394; 6:244, 499.
22. Mosiah 11:20-23; 26-27.
23. Mosiah 11:28; 12:17.
24. Mosiah 13:9.

NOTES 285

25. DHC 5:517. Joseph may have borrowed the thought from Voltaire's *Candide*: "What does it matter whom you sup with, provided you make good cheer?" (see Chapter 27).
26. See Mosiah 17:12-13; B.H. Roberts, *Comprehensive History of the Church* 2:322 (hereafter, CHC).
27. Mosiah 17:20.
28. DHC 6:630.
29. Mosiah 18:17-18.
30. Ibid. 20:1-5.
31. Ibid. 23:30-35.
32. Ibid. 23:39.
33. Ibid. 24:4-6
34. Ibid. 24:9-11.
35. D&C 121:39.
36. DHC 5:287.

Chapter 15—p. 122-130
Zarahemla—One City, Two Tales

1. Mosiah 21:25.
2. Alma 22:28-32.
3. Helaman 6:10. Mulek's appearance in the Book of Mormon represents a quite grievous contradictory against the Bible record. According to the account in Jeremiah, all of King Zedekiah's sons were slain by invading Babylonians. (Jeremiah 39:6). To assert that Mulek somehow escaped registers another of Joseph's attempts for discounting biblical inerrancy. His task was to break down readers' reliance on the Bible using all reasonable means that couldn't be readily controverted. Here his reliance upon imaginative myth is prominent and effective.

Note especially how Mulek received his appearance in the Book of Mormon following the line-upon-line pattern: originally introduced at Omni 1:15, it isn't until Helaman 8:21 that the miracle of Mulek's survival is made explicit and his relationship to Zedekiah asserted. Joseph's dispute with the Bible is only given annotation by footnotes in the modern edition, and only those few who are willing to question any significance are likely to check references. Joseph's disputants are worn down by the sheer quantity of issues he raised, as each new contradictory requires laborious research to adjudicate.

4. Omni 1:12.
5. Omni 1:19, 24.
6. Mosiah 22:11.
7. Ibid. 24:25.
8. Ibid. 25:13.
9. Alma 27:10-15, 21-25.
10. Alma 56:25; Helaman 1:18-33.
11. Helaman 7:1-6; 13:12; 3 Nephi 8:8.
12. 3 Nephi 9:3; Revelation 18:10.
13. 4 Nephi 1:8.
14. Mormon 1:10.

15. 1 Nephi 12:20; 15:5; 2Nephi 5:25.
16. Matthew 14:36; See Matthew 23:5. Among the Jews, symbolic value of the garment's hem had been introduced in scripture; see Numbers 15:38-39. Garments were to be kept clean; see Genesis 35:2; Ecclesiastes 9:8.
17. E.g., 2 Nephi 9:44; Jacob 1:19; Mosiah 2:28; Mormon 9:35.
18. Helaman 9:31, "But behold, ye shall examine him, and ye shall find blood upon the skirts of his cloak."
19. Genesis 38:27-30.
20. George Arthur Buttrick, ed., *The Interpreter's Dictionary of the Bible*, Abingdon Press, 1962. "*Zarah*."
21. E.g., D&C 88:85; 112:33; 133:51; 135:5; DHC 4:45. Joseph's speeches occasionally referred to those whose "garments are not clean from the blood of this generation," thus invoking guilt among believers. Immediately prior to his journey to Carthage where he would achieve martyrdom, Joseph selected and marked a key Book of Mormon passage, as follows, "And now I [...] bid farewell unto the Gentiles; yea, and also unto my brethren whom I love, until we shall meet before the judgment-seat of Christ, where all men shall know that my garments are not spotted with your blood." (From Ether 12:38; see also D&C 135:4-5).
22. Korihor's sad tale is from Alma 30.
23. E.g., Omni 1:13; Alma 53:10, 12; 62:7; Helaman 6:4.
24. E.g., Mosiah 7:9, 13; Alma 26:9.
25. Faulring, p. 4. Hell suggested a different dimension for most Protestants of his day than for Joseph. He redefined hell simply as "a world of spirits" where all men await judgment and the resurrection. (DHC 5:425). According to him the torments of hell were self-inflicted, "a man is his own tormentor and his own condemner." (DHC 6:314). Similarly, the Book of Mormon concept of condemnation in the hereafter results from one's self-judgment: "And if they be evil they are consigned to an awful view of their own guilt and abominations, which doth cause them to shrink from the presence of the Lord into a state of misery and endless torment [...]." (Mosiah 3:25; see also Mosiah 2:38; 27:31; Alma 3:19; 12:14; 41:7).
26. Proctor and Proctor, p. 86, 134.
27. Critical attitudes towards the Smith family, especially with regard to Joseph, Jr., are documented through dozens of books and tracts that generally attempt discrediting Joseph's latter day work. Among them are Pomeroy Tucker, *Origin, Rise, and Progress of Mormonism*, 1867; O. Turner, *History of the Pioneer Settlement of Phelps and Gorham's Purchase and Morris' Reserve*, 1851; Wilhelm Wyl, *Mormon Portraits, Joseph Smith the Prophet, His Family and Friends*, 1886; and Eber D. Howe, *History of the Mormons*, 1840.
28. Marquardt and Walters, p. 131-133.
29. Brodie, p. 27-28.
30. O. Turner, p. 212-213, 400. Quote is from Marquardt and Walters, p. 4.
31. Hill, p. 47.
32. The quote has been taken from Hill, p. 45.
33. Alma 32:2-3.

NOTES

Chapter 16—p. 131-138
Alma, Part 1: Portrait of a Mormon Soul

1. Mosiah 27:8-17; Alma 36:6-24.
2. See Acts 26:13; PGP, JS-H 1:16.
3. Acts 9:1-9; 22:6-10; 26:13-16.
4. Mormon 7:9. "For behold, this is written for the intent that ye may believe that; and if ye believe that ye will believe this also…." In a roundabout way this quotation shows Joseph's confession of his purpose for having written the Book of Mormon. Because readers anticipate a much-needed confirmation of Bible truth, his book offers to supply that need—but with strings attached. In order to accept it as a "second witness," they must also buy into the balance of the book that does not confirm the Biblical account, but discounts, deprecates and contradicts it.
5. Mosiah 27:9-19; Alma 36:6-11.
6. Alma 36:6-9. The conundrum statement is repeated in verse 11, slightly changed: "If thou wilt be destroyed of thyself, seek no more to destroy the church of God."
7. Paine, p. 79.
8. Alma 31:5.
9. Faulring, p. 5. Joseph formed his conclusion after reading Hebrews 13:8 and Acts 10:34.
10. James 1:5, quoted in PGP, JS-H, 1:11.
11. Alma 32:27.
12. D&C 9:8.
13. Mosiah 29:42; Alma 2:16.
14. Alma 30:6, 43.
15. Ibid., v. 49. Joseph seems to have borrowed the words of the angel Gabriel when cursing Zacharias with dumbness because of his disbelief. See Luke 1:18-20.
16. Ibid., v. 51.
17. See Ezekiel 6:8-9.
18. Isaiah 53:7; Matthew 27:12, 14.
19. Alma 30:58-60.
20. Alma 6:7.
21. Alma 36:4.

Chapter 17—p. 139-148
Alma, Part 2: As Mormon As It Gets

1. D&C 88:5.
2. Alma 31:7.
3. Alma 37:2.
4. John 5:19.
5. Alma 46:6; see Hebrews 3:1.
6. Alma 45:22.
7. Alma 57:25.
8. John 17:12.

9. 1 Kings 16:31.
10. Alma 43:3-4.
11. Alma 40:3, 4, 5, 8.
12. Alma 40:19-21.
13. Joseph F. Smith, *Gospel Doctrine*, p. 309. See also Alma 39, chapter heading,.
14. Alma 63:10.
15. Joseph F. Smith, *Gospel Doctrine*, p. 108.
16. Bushman, *Beginnings*, p. 95.
17. Ibid, p. 77.
18. Alma 36:1; 38:1.
19. Alma 11:15.
20. Alma 38:2.
21. Ibid., v. 3-4.
22. Ibid., v. 7-8.
23. Ibid., v. 11, 14.
24. Ibid., v. 15.
25. Joseph Fielding Smith, *Doctrines of Salvation*, 3:252.
26. Judges 12:6.
27. CHC 1:130.
28. Alma 38:4.
29. Ibid., v.10.
30. Ibid., v. 12.
31. Cf. Alma 30:49-50, 58-59.
32. Alma 38:12.
33. Ibid., v. 14.
34. Ibid., v.15.
35. D&C 104:26. Code names were published through 1973, then removed.
36. Alma 37:23.
37. Kogos, Fred, *The Dictionary of Popular Yiddish Words, Phrases, and Proverbs*.
38. DHC 3:315; 328.
39. Alma 46:3; see also 1 Nephi 4:31; Alma 48:11.
40. Alma 46:9.
41. Alma 46:5; PGP, Abr. 3:23.
42. Alma 46:4.
43. William Marks had attained the highly rated position of President of the Nauvoo Stake, becoming one of half a dozen contenders in succeeding to the presidency of the church following Joseph's martyrdom. During 1853, he wrote, "I was also witness to the introduction (secretly) of a kingly form of government, in which Joseph suffered himself to be ordained king to reign over the house of Israel forever." (*Zion's Harbinger and Baneemy's Organ*, Vol. III, p. 52). See Brodie, p. 356, n.
44. Alma 51:34.
45. DHC 6:627.

❦ NOTES ❦

Chapter 18—p. 149-167
Alma, Part 3: Alma's Quasi-Chiasmi Find Their New Literary Heritage

1. DHC 4:461.
2. Paine, p. 19. His chiasmus reads: "That manufacturer of quibbles, St. Paul [...] makes there to be two Adams; the one who sins in fact, and suffers by proxy; the other who sins by proxy, and suffers in fact" (p. 24).
3. A collection of fun chiasmi, including several examples used here, are found in the book by Mardy Grothe, *Never Let a Fool Kiss You, and Never Let a Kiss Fool You.*
4. Matthew 6:22; 7:16-20; see 3 Nephi 13:22; 14:16-20.
5. 1 Nephi 1:2; Mosiah 1:4; Mormon 9:32.
6. Paine, p. 19.
7. See D&C sections 3, 10; DHC 1:20-28.
8. Howard F. Vos, ed., *Can I Trust the Bible?*, p. 122.
9. See Matthew 27:38—"Then were there two thieves crucified with him, one on the right hand, and another on the left."
10. See *Smith's Bible Dictionary*, "*cross.*"
11. Alma 36:10.
12. Ibid., v. 9, 11.
13. Ibid., v. 17.
14. Ibid., v. 10, 16.
15. See John W. Welch, "Criteria for Identifying and Evaluating the Presence of Chiasmus," *Journal of Book of Mormon Studies*, Foundation for Ancient Research and Mormon Studies, Vol. 4, Number 2. (1995). Welch's earlier studies include "Chiasmus in the Book of Mormon." *Chiasmus in Antiquity*, ed. J. Welch, (1981), pp. 198-210.
15. See Allan J. Christianson, "Chiasmus in Mayan Texts," *Ensign*, (Oct. 1988) pp. 28-31. Allan J. Christianson, "The uses of Chiasmus in Ancient Mesoamerica," (F.A.R.M.S., 1988), p.72.

Chapter 19—p. 168-176
A Hostile but Faithful Witness, Part 1: The Descent of Jesus Christ

1. Paine, p. 28, 62.
2. Matthew 27:51
3. 3 Nephi 8:14.
4. 3 Nephi 8:22.
5. Matthew 27:45; see also Luke 23:44-45.
6. 3 Nephi 9:1-22.
7. Matthew 23:37.
8. 3 Nephi 10:4-6.
9. Matthew 5:45-48.
10. 3 Nephi 12:47-48.
11. Paine, p. 176.
12. Matthew 14:19.
13. 3 Nephi 20:3, 5-7.

14. 2 Nephi 32:2.
15. E.g., 2 Nephi 31:4-5.
16. Mosiah 26:23.
17. Ether 12:27. Bible students are put off by Joseph attributing this ideal to God, contradicting the teaching at James, "Let no man say when he is tempted, I am tempted of God: for God cannot be tempted with evil, neither tempteth he any man." (James 1:13) Nevertheless, Joseph persisted in teaching that God worked on the wicked to "blind their minds," thus assuring their condemnation. (i.e., DHC 3:293)
18. DHC 5:140
19. Joseph spent his childhood among New Englanders, some having strong accents. To better appreciate pronunciation of Amulek's name, try imagining the character Popeye pronouncing the word.
20. Alma 34:15.
21. Paine, p. 27.
22. Alma 37:12; see also 1 Nephi 10:19; Alma 7:20.

Chapter 20—p. 177-189
A Hostile but Faithful Witness, Part 2: Spotting A Host of Dubious Gods

1. DHC 5:530 (P.S. Did you recognize chiastic structure in Joseph's quote?).
2. Alma 42:25.
3. Alma 26:20.
4. Although a strategy designed for the eventual disintegration of his church may seem disingenuous, Joseph's objectives as church builder were insignificant compared to his goal for transmitting enlightenment to future generations. Membership losses were intended as a catalyst in the learning process, and at one time, during the Kirtland period, he managed disenchanting at least half his apostles and church members. He took their apostasy in stride, established the mission to Great Britain, roughly doubling his supply of new members. Much of the church's success in England can be attributed to his caution to missionaries: "[...] adhere closely to the first principles of the Gospel, and remain silent concerning the gathering, the vision, and the Book of Doctrine and Covenants [...]." (See DHC 2:492).
5. Mormon 9:19, see v. 9-10, 15. While God's changeless nature is an accepted biblical teaching (e.g., James 1:17), Tom Paine also pressed the point of it in his book, p.183. (see also 2 Nephi 27:23; Moroni 8:18).
6. Jacob 7:13-20; Alma 30:43-60.
7. Joseph F. Smith, *Conference Report*, April, 1900, p. 40.
8. DHC 6:305 (Joseph appointed faith as the gospel's first principle. See A of F # 4).
9. Helaman 12:3. See also Mosiah 1:17
10. Helaman 12:1. The Book of Mormon is rife with evidence of the "Law of Rewards," a promise of prosperity for those who are faithful. See 1Nephi 2:20; 2 Nephi 1:9, 20, 31; Jarom 1:9; Mosiah 1:7; Alma 37:13; 49: 30, etc.
11. Alma 1:31.
12. D&C 82:10.
13. Mosiah 2:24.

14. Alma 20:2, 8, 20.
15. Karen Armstrong, *A History of God*, p. 117. Karen's book is to be recommended for extensive insights that inform and raise awareness about a complex, intriguing subject.
16. D&C 130:22.
17. See Bruce R. McConkie, *Mormon Doctrine*, "Light of Christ." Moroni 7:16.
18. See McConkie, *Mormon Doctrine*, "Jehovah."
19. Ether 3:14, 16.
20. *My Kingdom Shall Roll Forth, Readings in Church History*, Published by The Church of Jesus Christ of Latter-day Saints, Salt Lake City, Utah. 2nd ed. 1980, p. 76. This particular verse tends to be quite confusing to Mormons. Another doctrinal authority suggested Jared's visitor was neither Father nor Son, but the Spirit of Christ (see Bruce R. McConkie, *Mormon Doctrine*, "Spirit of the Lord.")
21. DHC 6:314. In King Benjamin's projection of judgment day, he explained, "And if they be evil they are consigned to an awful view of their own guilt and abominations, which doth cause them to shrink from the presence of the Lord into a state of misery and endless torment…therefore they have drunk damnation to their own souls." (Mosiah 3:24-25; see also Mosiah 2:38-39, 27:31; Alma 3:19, 12:14, 41:7).
22. D&C 76:23-24.
23. Bruce R. McConkie, *Mormon Doctrine*, "Eternal Lives."
24. Jeremiah 17:5.
25. Ether 3:6.
26. DHC 6:306.
27. Lucy once expressed this very thought in her biography of the prophet: "We considered ourselves as much…as did Adam and Eve." See Proctor and Proctor, p. 135.
28. R.W.B. Lewis, *The American Adam—Innocence, Tragedy and Tradition in the Nineteenth Century*, U. of Chicago Press. 1955, p. 5-6.
29. Journal of Discourses, 1:50 (hereafter JD). See also JD 2:6, 143; 3:319; 4:271; 5:31; 6:275.
30. Alma 42:3; also Alma 12:31. The cameo has been taken from the serpent's tempting advice to mother Eve at Genesis 3:5—"For God doth know that in the day ye eat thereof, then your eyes shall be opened, and ye shall be as gods, knowing good and evil."
31. D&C 27:1, 5, 11. Joseph reiterated and bolstered his teaching during a discourse to the twelve apostles. See DHC 3:385-388, and editor's footnote.
32. Daniel 7:22.

Chapter 21—p. 190-200
A Stratospheric Genealogy—Capped by Ether

1. The Jaredites and their historical records had been introduced at Omni 1:21-22 and Mosiah 21:27-28.
2. Russel Blaine Nye, *The Cultural Life of the New Nation*, p. 121.
3. "And the Lord said: Go to work and build, after the manner of barges which ye have hitherto built." Ether 2:16.
4. Ether 1:34.
5. Ibid 3:3.

6. Ibid. 3:2, 13-14.
7. Faulring, p. 4-6.
8. Fawn Brodie, *No Man Knows My History*, p. 366, 403.
9. DHC 4:461.
10. Ether 1:6-33.
11. The event is recorded in Genesis 11:3-9.
12. Proctor and Proctor, p. 39; 42, n2.
13. Ether 2:3.
14. Utah maintains its identity as the Beehive State, a legacy from Joseph Smith. Perhaps by coincidence, more Utah towns began as religious colonies than in any other state. Deseret's meaning seems to have been misread: above the beehive on Utah's state seal is the word "industry." While no teaching confers official status, today's Mormons continue promoting honey as a healthy snack food. Here, we'll engage it as a symbolic passage pointing to America's colonial past.
15. Proctor and Proctor, p. 58.
16. Tunbridge, Vermont, Town Records, Book A:188 (See H. Michael Marquardt and Wesley P. Walters, *Inventing Mormonism*, p. 58, n.19).
17. Brodie, p. 2.
18. Proctor and Proctor, p. 64.
19. Ibid. p. 63, 88-90
20. Hill, p. 45.
21. Ether, chapters 6 through 15 tell of more rebellion and kingdoms being overthrown than during the entire fall of the Roman Empire. More often than not, the conflict is between father and son or brother against brother. See 7:4, 8-9, 15; 8:2-3, 5; 9:5, 12, 27; 10:3, 14, 15, etc.
22. Faulring, p. 5.
23. Brodie, p. 4.
24. Proctor and Proctor, p. 91.
25. Ibid. p. 8.
26. Ibid. p. 7.
27. Ibid. p. 14.
28. Ibid. Chapter 10, pp. 47-50. Joseph borrowed this theme to make it appear as his original query. See PGP, JS-H 1:10.
29. Ibid. p. 18, ff.
30. Ibid., p. 20-21
31. DHC 7:470. William, her fifth son, wrote, "My mother, who was a very pious woman and much interested in the welfare of her children, both here and hereafter, made use of every means which her parental love could suggest, to get us engaged in seeking for our souls' salvation, or (as the term then was) 'in getting religion.' She prevailed on us to attend the meetings, and almost the whole family became interested in the matter, and seekers after truth." (See *William Smith on Mormonism*, p. 6, quoted from *Inventing Mormonism*, p. 120).

NOTES

Chapter 22—p. 201-207
Martyr's Journal, Part 1: A Pause for a Breath…Then Immortality

1. DHC 6:273.
2. DHC 6:540.
3. DHC 6:548.
4. DHC 6:592.
5. These events of June 22-23 are detailed more completely at DHC 6:548-550.
6. DHC 6:445; see also p. 463—Hyrum threatened to destroy the opposition press of the neighboring village at Warsaw.
7. Governors of Missouri, Illinois and Iowa had issued extradition orders in the summer of 1842. Joseph's months as a fugitive "in seclusion" are noted in DHC 5:89-179.
8. DHC 6:621-622; D&C 135:1.

Chapter 23—p. 208-216
Martyr's Journal, Part 2: Winning Position in a War of Words

1. Joseph Smith, DHC 5:529.
2. Doctrine and Covenants 93:36.
3. PGP, JS—H 1:10.
4. Faulring, p.4-5.
5. PGP, JS-H 1:56. See D. Michael Quinn's fine book, *Early Mormonism and the Magic World View*.
6. This instance of religious judgment hasn't yet fully dissipated after many generations. Benjamin Franklin, in his *Autobiography*, noted how, "[. . .] my indiscreet disputations about Religion begun to make me pointed at with Horror by good People, as an Infidel or Atheist." The Bible encourages disrespect towards non-believers, e.g., "The fool hath said in his heart, There is no God. Corrupt are they; and have done abominable iniquity: there is none that doeth good." (Psalms 53:1).
7. DHC 5:135.
8. Ether 15:29-32. Shiz and Coriantumr participate in giving brief recognition for two popular characters from Washington Irving's *Sketch-Book*. Shiz continues alive (momentarily) following the battle in which he is decapitated, mirroring the headless horseman from *The Legend of Sleepy Hollow*. Although Coriantumr won the battle, he fell into a deep sleep, "as if he had no life." Again the figure has been borrowed, this time from *Rip Van Winkle*, who slept for 20 years.
9. See Ether 14:17 through chapter 15.
10. D&C 38:13.
11. Ether 15:6, 19.
12. "Behold, you have not understood; you have supposed that I would give it unto you, when you took no thought save it was to ask me. But behold, I say unto you, that you must study it out in your mind; then you must ask me if it be right [...]." D&C 9:7-8.
13. Ether 14:8; see *Smith's Bible Dictionary*.
14. Ether 14:10-16.
15. DHC 5:355.

16. DHC 5:214, 340.
17. DHC 5:139. In the same work, Joseph declined revelation to his audience by declaring, "The design of the great God in sending us into this world, and organizing us to prepare us for the eternal worlds, I shall keep in my own bosom at present" (DHC 5:403). Generally he used literature indirectly to suggest his genuine perspectives.
18. DHC 4:479.

Chapter 24—p.217-223
Martyr's Journal, Part 3: Such a Short Lifetime, Only Nine Moons

1. Joseph Smith, DHC 5:259
2. Proctor and Proctor, p.350. Joseph's prophecy covered a period from January, 1838 until January, 1843, 17 months ahead of his martyrdom.
3. DHC 7:212.
4. J. D. 18:361.
5. D&C 58:27-28; see also DHC 2:6.
6. Mormon 2:2.
7. Ether 15:32.
8. Omni 1:21.
9. Daniel 9:2, 24.
10. J. Lawrence Eason, *The New Bible Survey*, p.341.
11. Quinn, especially p. 53-77.
12. DHC 6:365.
13. DHC 3:335.

Chapter 25—p. 224-230
The Polygamy Plot, Part 1: Essentials

1. 1 Kings 11:3.
2. Jacob 2:24, 27, 30.
3. See D&C 132:4—"For behold, I reveal unto you a new and an everlasting covenant; and if ye abide not that covenant, then are ye damned [...]."
4. B. H. Roberts, ed., DHC 5:xxix. See also preface to D&C 132.
5. "A bishop then must be blameless, the husband of one wife[...]. Let the deacons be the husbands of one wife [...]." 1 Timothy 3:2, 12.
6. E.g., see DHC 6:46; 2:247; 3:230.
7. D&C 135:4. DHC 6:555.
8. DHC 6:152, 164.
9. DHC 6:162-170, 238-240, 272, 278, 344-345, 348-350, 362, 436-446, 484.

Chapter 26—p. 231-248
The Polygamy Plot, Part 2: Opposition from a Chosen Few

1. DHC 6:484.
2. DHC 6:58.

3. Joseph's part in their dispute is preserved at DHC 5:284-285. See also Donna Hill, *Joseph Smith, The First Mormon*, p. 388.
4. DHC 6:279-280. See also p. 271.
5. DHC 6:239.
6. DHC 6:240.
7. DHC 6:522-523.
8. Joseph Fielding Smith, *Church History and Modern Revelation*, 4:182; DHC 6:457.
9. DHC 6:457
10. Originally excommunicated in May, 1842, Chauncey's weaknesses weren't exposed publicly until two years later when Joseph's timetable required discord be accelerated among the brethren. (DHC5:18; DHC 6:407). A similar embarrassment caught another member by surprise. In November, 1843, when the church's High Council charged Harrison Sagers with seduction, he, too, remembered hearing the Prophet condone illicit relationships. (DHC 6:81) Judgment against Sagers shows "Charge not sustained." A number of incidents might be found in which the suggestion had circulated in the church condoning promiscuous intercourse. (e.g. DHC 5:13, 42). Taking into consideration a number of examples suggesting moral relativism, it isn't so difficult to understand how members may have construed libertinism into Joseph's gospel.
11. E.g., DHC 6:46, 405, 410-411.
12. DHC 5:135.
13. DHC 4:445.
14. Alma 42:17.
15. 2 Nephi 2:23, 25.
16. DHC 5:526.
17. DHC 5:340.
18. DHC 5:214.
19. D&C 64:27-30.
20. DHC 5:140.
21. DHC 5:333; see also p. 332-334.
22. DHC 5:554.
23. D&C 132:26.
24. 2 Nephi 25:20.
25. D&C 4:2.
26. DHC 6:433-434.
27. DHC 6:445-446.
28. See PGP, Articles of Faith # 12: "We believe in being subject to kings, presidents, rulers, and magistrates, in obeying, honoring, and sustaining the law."
29. DHC 6:497.
30. *The Wasp*, April 16, 1842, (see Brodie, p. 288).
31. DHC 6:596
32. DHC 6:408.
33. D&C 132:1-4.

Chapter 27—p. 249-259
The Polygamy Plot, Part 3: Testing Games

1. Mosiah 23:21; see also Ether 12:6; Alma 32:36.
2. Spencer Kimball, "When Will the Earth Be Converted?" *Ensign*, Oct. 1974, p. 6.
3. Alma 45:14-15.
4. Madsen, p. 92. Orson F. Whitney, *History of Utah*, 4:282-284.
5. Whitney, *The Life of Heber C. Kimball*, p. 323-324. Evidently, Joseph tried this test on other married women, netting mixed successes. Notably, the Prophet got rebuffed by Sarah M. Granger Kimball, wife of Hiram S. Kimball. See Brodie, p.306, n.
6. DHC 5:412; *Discourses of Wilford Woodruff*, p. 97-98.
7. DHC 7:621 fn. Wilford Woodruff's weak response suggests Brigham's hesitancy in making the move: "I thought it would require a revelation to change the order of that quorum. [But] whatever the Lord inspires you to do in this matter. I am with you." In other words, it appears that the common view throughout the quorum was to have someone *else* propose the action. During the church's interregnum, Brigham's lead in the attempt at resuming the first presidency shows a spark of genius in recognizing that, without a leader to direct it, the church would begin losing its grip.
8. DHC 7:294, 621, 628.
9. DHC 7:288.
10. Brigham Young, *The Contributor*, vol.10:2, 1889. (Italics in original).
11. D&C 42:88—"And if thy brother or sister offend thee, thou shalt take him or her between him or her and thee alone; and if he or she confess thou shalt be reconciled."
12. Madsen, p, 87-88.
13. See Pratkanis and Aronson, *Age of Propaganda*, chapter 27, "The Committed Heart."
14. (Reported by Parley Pratt), *Millennial Star*, 55:585.
15. DHC 5:259. In the same work Joseph affirmed his denial of political affiliation, "The Lord has not given me a revelation concerning politics. I have not asked him for one. I am a third party, and stand independent and alone." (DHC 5:526).
16. E. g., see *The Reed Peck Manuscript*, p.25-26 (or Brodie, p. 217-218).
17. Rigdon later became a vocal critic of polygamy while making his bit to corner LDS member fallout. He bitterly denounced Joseph as a corrupted vessel.
18. DHC 6:46-49.
19. D&C 107:24.
20. See DHC 5:xxxii-xxxiii.
21. DHC 6:486, 494, 519. Hyrum wrote his letter on June 17. Joseph waited three days before writing his own message recalling the 12 to Nauvoo. Most of the 12 were unaware about the martyrdom until the second week in July, and didn't return to Nauvoo until August 6, 1844. See DHC 7:175.
22. DHC 6:607-608.
23. DHC 5:510.
24. DHC 5:517-518.

NOTES 297

Chapter 28—p. 260-266
Moroni, Last of the Mormons

1. Alma 54:7, 9.
2. "And now as Moroni had supposed that there should be men sent to the city of Nephihah, to the assistance of the people to maintain that city, and [. . .] therefore he retained all his force to maintain those places which he had recovered" (Alma 59:9-10).
3. "But behold, great has been the slaughter among our people; yea, thousands have fallen by the sword [...]." Alma 60:5.
4. Alma 59:12-13.
5. Alma 60:1-2.
6. Alma 43:16-17.
7. Mormon 8:3. The writer is Moroni, who has taken over his father's writings.
8. Examples of similarities immediately apparent include the fact that white and dark-skinned people are at war, differences in religion or philosophy are discussed, melodrama, themes of abduction, retributive justice, massacre, the powers of darkness, and the constrictions of one's cultural ties (i.e., "traditions of the fathers").
9. In the text, Alma is the character expressing his wish to speak as an angel, "with the trump of God," though he immediately acknowledged the sinfulness of such an exalted desire (See Alma 29:1, 3). From *Revelation* (Bible), the voice, "as of a trumpet," is the voice of God (Revelation 1:10-11; see also 1 Thessalonians 4:16). LDS scriptures contain no reference to Moroni's blowing a trumpet, therefore, his statue atop LDS temples is a fantasized expansion of his role. In one of his speeches, Joseph provided a parallel quote-clue suggesting how close was his relationship to Alma: "O that I had the language of the archangel to express my feelings once to my friends!" (DHC 5:362). Perhaps no less significant, Coriantumr is the only character in his book to be associated with blowing a real (rather than symbolic) trumpet. (see Ether 14:28).
10. Moroni 8:14. Readers must note a difference in attitude between Moroni's doctrine of "think wrong, go to hell," and the one found in the New Testament account of Jesus' Sermon on the Mount. His words: "[. . .] whosoever looketh on a woman to lust after her hath committed adultery with her already in his heart." (Matthew 5:28). Matthew encourages mental discipline in controlling one's lusts, although no scathing condemnation is exhibited, nor is it particularly implied.
11. Among critics of Mormonism there's a separate popular notion for the origin of the name Moroni. It is the name (same spelling) of a city 335 miles northwest of Madagascar, capital of Grande Comore, largest of the Comoro Islands (French territory) in the Indian Ocean. Again, however, random whimsy provides the sole support for Joseph having selected such a name. Due to the fact that Moroni produces onus within his writings, and thus gives insight into Joseph's method (his mind), I promote it as the preference selected by Joseph. Moroni ("More-onuses"), as a symbol, is literate and quite intelligent. More importantly, it features an organic relationship that connects the author, the book and LDS doctrine with the character he created.
12. Moroni begins his warnings about the "danger of hell fire" at Mormon 8:17-21; 31-41. See also Mormon 9:14, "…he that is filthy shall be filthy still…."

13. Moroni 10:9-16. The New Testament passage (1 Corinthians 12:8-10) reads,
    8. For to one is given by the Spirit the word of wisdom; to another the word of knowledge by the same Spirit;
    9. To another faith by the same Spirit; to another the gifts of healing by the same Spirit;
    10. To another the working of miracles; to another prophecy; to another discerning of spirits; to another divers kinds of tongues; to another the interpretation of tongues.

14. D&C 89 has been given the confusing label "The Word of Wisdom," when its intent seems related to laws of *health*. The section omits all suggestions for improving the mind, studying reason, logic, semantics, etc., that relate to wisdom. Members are promised wisdom through no greater mental exertions than by maintaining obedience to the commandments (see v. 18). Joseph took the same passage from I Corinthians, gave it some elaboration, then added it into his Doctrine and Covenants 46:17-26.

15. D&C 21:1.

16. PGP, JS-H 1:33.

In Conclusion—p. 267-274

1. Joseph explained, "The remnants are the Indians that now inhabit this country. (DHC 4:537-538).

2. Russel B. Nye, *The Cultural Life of the New Nation*, p.239.

3. DHC 2:268.

4. One example of genuineness in Joseph's egalitarian attitude has been preserved in his saying, "…equal rights and privileges is my motto; and one man is as good as another, if he behaves as well; and that all men should be esteemed alike, without regard to distinctions of an official nature." (DHC 2:403) But again, he said it while living his double life, and thus can often be made to appear hypocritical when placing his words in context with behavior.

5. Michael de Montaigne, *Essays*, "On the Cannibals."

6. *Dialogues of Plato*, "Apology."

7. DHC 5:297.

INDEX

A
Abiah, 87
Abinadi; 114-118, 219
    Martyr, 115
Abinadom, 109
Abraham, 7, 13, 186, 250
Abraham, Book of, 147
Acts, 94
Adam/Eve 44, 51-52, 78, 188, 203, 238
Adam-God doctrine, 187-189
Adieu, 84
Age of Reason, 74, 76
Alcohol, 193, 265
Alcott, Louisa, 23
Alice in Wonderland, 101
Alma, 29, 45, 81, 108, 119, 129, 131, 134, 135, 139-145, 152, 156, 161, 174, 179, 180, 219, 238
Amaleki, 108-109
Amalickiah, 147-148, 219, 256
Amaron, 108
America, 41, 115, 117, 123, 167, 177, 187, 191 194, 198, 209, 213
Ammaron, 28
Ammon, Ammonites, 33, 111, 119, 123, 179, 182, 219
Ammoron, 261
Amon (Egyptian god), 33, 111
Amulek, Amulet, 175, 209, 221
Amulon, 119
Ancient of days, 57, 63, 189
Angel, 1, 133, 161, 184, 246, 263, 265
Anti-Christ, 80, 135
Anti-Mormon, 206
"Any means necessary," 272
Apocalypse, 170
Apostate, Apostasy, 230
Apostles, x, 4, 33, 34, 103, 251, 254, 255
Armies of Israel, 11
Art, 118
Articles of Faith, 245
Assassination, 7, 148
Astrology, 209
Atonement, 77-80, 161-162
Authority, Authoritarian, 122, 123, 126, 130, 135, 199, 213, 227, 255

B
Babylon, 124; 150
Baneemy, 146
Baptists, baptism 103, 119, 121, 174
Baptisms for the dead, 68
Barges, 191
"Believe that, believe this," 132, 173
Benjamin, 110, 112-113, 123
Bennett, James Arlington, 254
Bias, 150

Bible, 27, 31, 32, 37, 38, 39, 40, 43, 74, 77, 91, 93, 96, 110-111, 116, 150; 155, 167, 194, 210, 229
Biography, ix, 2, 45, 47, 192, 193, 198
Birthright, 90
Bishop, 143, 227, 251
Bitter fruit, 105
Blacksmith, 39, 146
Blasphemy, 3, 241
Blessings, 90
Blood, 125, 126,; 206
Boggs, Liburn, 11
Boston, 75
Brainwashing, 14
Brother of Jared, 191
Burton, Richard, 267

C
Caesar, 203
Caiaphas, 71
Cain, 63
Calvin, John, 103
Campbell. Alexander, 254
Cancer, 209
Canterbury Tales, 250
Candide, 83-84 106
Carthage, IL, 113, 206, 228, 235, 246, 248, 255 257
Catholicism, 73, 101, 121, 160, 182, 185
Celestial kingdom, 34, 60, 181, 241, 272
Cervantes, Miguel, 269
Channeling, 155
Charon, 128
Chaucer, Geoffrey, 250
Chemish, 108
Chiasmi, Chiasmus, 149-167
    The Great Geographical Chiasmus, 154-155
    The Six-Chain-Linked Chiasmus, 161-166
    The Triple Crucifixion Chiasmus, 156-161
Children of God, 56
Cholera, 12, 235
Christians, Christianity, 39, 64, 69, 73, 79, 82, 89, 101, 103, 146, 166, 172, 183, 193, 194, 196, 198, 213, 223, 231, 268
Church of Christ, 239, 254
Cincinnati, OH, 204
Clavel, James, 272
Clues, codes, cues, prompts 6, 14, 20, 23, 24, 29-30, 64, 71, 72, 97, 110, 111, 112, 134, 141, 146, 147, 148, 194
Coffee, 202, 242, 265
Colonists, 194-195
Columbus, 41
Commitment, total, 14, 61, 67
Common Sense, 81
Coinage, 143
Cognitive dissonance, 180
Confession, 2, 21, 25, 96, 132, 137, 261, 174
Confusion, 194

Congregationalist, 76
Conrad, Joseph (quoted), 16
Conscience, conscious, 161, 184, 249
Conspiracy, 235
Constitution, U. S. 213, 247
Contrary, Contradictory, 1, 111, 218, 244
Controversy, 228
Conundrum, 133, 211
Cooper, James, F. 188, 260, 263, 269
Corianton, 138-142, 145, 161
Coriantumr, 123, 190, 210, 214, 220, 258, 260
Corinthians, 264-265
Council of Fifty, 147
Creed, 213
Critics, 1- 2, 7, 26
Cross, crucifixion, 157, 160
Cumorah hill, 29
Coriantumr, 123, 190, 210-214
Cult, 253
Curse, 136
Cynicism, 181

D

Damascus, 32, 132
Daniel, 189, 221
Darkness, 170
Dante, *Divine Comedy*, 54, 128, 269
Darwin, 187
David, 88, 224
DeGraaf, Regnier, 56
Deism, 74-79, 82
Democracy, 88, 114, 214, 262
Deseret, 194, 251
Deuteronomy, 94
Dialectics, 99
Dickens, Charles, 269
Dilemma, 135, 201
Diligence, 143, 145
Discernment, 79
Disinformation, 27
Doctrine and Covenants, 113, 120, 146
Double entendre, 53, 103, 214
Double mind, 180
Drama, vii; 272
Dunklin, Daniel, 11

E

Earthquake, 124, 170
Eclectic synthesis, 74
Egypt, Egyptian, 25, 32-33, 70, 84, 92, 107, 110 153
Elijah, 116
English, 84, 263, 265
Enos, 104
Ephraim, Ephraimite, 90, 144
Epilogue, 260
Equality, 80

Erie Canal, 191
Err, error, 19-20, 186
Esau, 97
Eternal progression (perfectionism), 78
Ethbaal, 141
Ether, 40, 107, 110, 190, 194, 199, 212
Ethics, 210
Evening and Morning Star, 10
Evolution, 104, 187
Exaltation, 2, 79, 91, 186
Excommunication, 105, 240
Experiment, 134-135
Extermination, 202
Ezekiel, 136

F

Fabricius, Hieronymus, 56
Faith, x;
　　Superfaith, 228, 229 (see True Believers)
Fall of man, 162, 188
Faith, x, 71, 103, 132, 134, 138, 209, 224, 249-251, 258
　　Superfaith (see True Believers), 250-251
Fate, 218
Father and Son, 43, 81, 115, 135, 145, 185-186, 192
Feet (metaphor), 116
Fire, 39, 118, 124, 146, 214
Fitzgerald, F. Scott, 272
Flattery, 147
Ford, Thomas, 204; 246
Foreshadow, 147, 206
Fornication, 140
Foster, Robert; Charles, 233-235
"Foxes spoil the vines," 239
Franklin, Ben, 25
Fraud, 128
Freedom, Free Agency, 4, 67, 218, 248
French Revolution, 85

G

Gazelem, 146, 256
Garden of Eden, 51, 59, 187
George III, 195
Genealogy, 92, 110, 199
Genesis, 37, 92, 113, 188, 193-195
Gentiles, 74, 101-102, 240, 255, 257, 259
Gilead, 212
Gilsum, NH, 198
God, (gods) 42, 44, 52, 93, 100, 130, 136, 148, 177-189, 271
　　Man's co-existence with God, 53, 77
Godhood, Godmaking, 41, 53, 59, 65, 103, 104, 185, 187, 241
"God would cease to be God," 179-180
Gold Bible 167, 169
Grace, 79, 199

INDEX

Grafting, 102
Grass, Gunter (quoted), 267
Greece, Greek, 32, 99, 128, 148, 167, 191
Guerilla survival techniques, 239
Guilt, guilt brokering, 125, 126, 143, 162, 205, 242, 264

H

Hale, Isaac, Elizabeth, 142
Halo effect, 256
Hancock County, IL, 92, 246
Harris, Martin, 146, 156
Hawthorne, Nathaniel, 126, 188, 269
Heaven, 11, 22, 34, 191
"Hebraic literary heritage" (see chiasmus), 152
Hebrews, 78, 167, 183
Helam, 119, 123
Helaman, 108, 125, 133, 138-140
Hell, 128, 191
Hellenism, 32
Hemingway, 23, 272
Higbee, Elias, 235
Higbee, Francis; Chauncey, 235-237
High Priest (see priesthood), 140
Holy Ghost, -Spirit, 103, 186
Homer (poet), 140, 269
Humiliation, humility, 138; 254
Hyde, Orson, 13
Hypocrisy, 130, 182

I

Idols, 263
Ignorance, 65, 177
Illinois, 5, 192, 206, 225, 228
Illusions, 124
Immigrants, 191
Independence, 189
Independence, MO, 9-11, 24
Innuendo, 66, 141, 229,; 236
Institute (LDS), 52
Innocent blood, 72
Intellectual, Intelligence, 13, 20, 27, 53, 96, 176, 178, 208, 212. Paradox. of, 64-65
Iroquois, 45
Irving, Washington, 269
Isaac, 250
Isabel, 141
Isaiah, 39, 91, 97, 100, 113, 116, 148
Ishmael, 44
Israel, 89, 97, 136

J

Jacob (Israel), 89, 90, 92
Jacob (Nephi's brother), 58, 84, 96, 97, 107, 108, 180, 227
Jacobins, 85
James, St. 34
James, Henry, 188
Jared, Jaredites, 110, 122-123, 191, 194, 210
Jarom, 108
Jehovah, 185
Jeremiah, 42, 100
Jershon, 123
Jerusalem, New Jerusalem, 4, 34, 41, 43, 57, 70, 92, 96, 99, 109, 152
Jesus (Christ), viii, 31, 34, 40-41, 64, 78, 80, 94, 100, 113, 124, 135-136, 153, 160-161, 167-176, 168-169, 173, 185, 203, 272
    Firstborn son, 139
Jezebel, 141
Joel, 87
John, (Apostle), 34
John (Baptist), 103, 173
Johnson, Aaron, 204
Johnson, Ben, 261
Jonah, 116
Joseph (Nephi's brother), 58, 89, 93, 96
Joseph of Egypt, 38, 92, 95
Joy, 238-239
Judaism, Judah, Jews, 32, 74, 89-90, 101, 110, 115, 125, 136, 150, 156, 259
Judas, 229
Judea, 174
Judges, Judgment, 87, 124, 130, 262
Justice, justify, 80, 162

K

Kennedy, John, 149
Kidnapping, 119
Kimball, Heber/Vilate, 251
Kings, kingdom, 87, 124, 130, 262
King James (English) Version, 19, 37, 169, 174
Kirtland, OH, 9-13, 217, 240, 254
Korihor, 135, 145, 180, 126-127

L

Laban, 70-72, 84, 86
Laman, Lamanite, 11, 18, 37, 54, 63, 65, 66, 86, 92, 105, 111, 119, 140
    Black skin (curse), 63
"Lamb to the slaughter," 113
"Large of stature," "large and mighty," 26, 147, 192
Lamoni, 111, 123
Last of the Mohicans, 260, 263
Law, 162, 179
    -of Marriage (polygamy), 224-225
    -of Obedience, Sacrifice, 60-61, 249
    -of Opposition, 20-22, 237-239
    -of Rewards, 143
Law, William; Wilson; Jane, 229, 232-233
Lebanon, NH, 75
LDS church, scholars, xi, 152, 166

Lehi, 22, 34, 41-44, 54-55, 63, 68, 86, 89, 93-94, 96, 104, 107,
    Dreams, visions, 46-47
    Murmurer, 41
Lemuel, 54, 86, 92
Liahona, 21
Lib, 213
Libertinism, 242
Liberty Jail, 218
Limhi, 104
"Line upon line," 90, 97-99
Logic, reasoning, 7, 17, 21, 133, 141, 211
Longfellow, Henry (quoted), 16
Longsuffering, 143
Lord of the vineyard, 100
Love, 145, 172
Loyalty, 89, 144
Luke, 100
Lutheran, 73

M

Mack, Solomon; Lydia Gates,. 198
Mack, Jason, 198
Mack, Lovina, 199
Mack, Lovisa, 198
Magic, 69, 178, 209; 221
Mahemson, 146
Male chauvinism, 264
Manasseh, 90
Marks, William, 229
Mary, (the Virgin) 31, 57, 103
Masonry, 59
Mayan, 167, 176
Master (vineyard), 100-106, 175
Matthew, 100, 151, 170
Melodrama, 135, 215
Melville, Herman, 23, 188, 269, 272
Mercy, 162, 175, 179
Messiah, Messianic figure, 41, 93-95, 115
Methodism, 3, 73-74, 121, 196
Michael, the Archangel, 188
Military, militarism; rank; strategy, vii, 261, 262, 271
Millennium, 260
Miracles, 77, 126, 140, 173, 180, 202
Missouri, 2, 5, 147, 192, 202, 225, 233, 235
Missionaries, 87, 103, 227, 233, 256
Mississippi, 204, 211, 233, 246, 257
Mob, Mobbing, 2
Montrose, IA, 204
Moons, 216, 221-222
Mormo, 30
Mormon, 4, 25-26, 107-108, 219
    Forest of, 29, 119
    Large of stature, 26; 37
    Learned, 25
    Named, 28-30

"quick to observe," 26
Mormon, Book of
    Abridgement, 42
    Absurdity, 141
    Allegory, 56, 97-106, 268
    America's earliest literary masterpiece, vii
    Ambiguity, 19-21
    "Another Testament of Jesus," 17; 168
    Anti-Christ, 41
    Autobiography, ix; 15, 23, 29, 75, 96
    Blasphemy, 33
    Blueprint, x, 118, 268
    Cameo (Bible), 88, 92, 94, 140, 188, 189, 264
    Caricature, 175
    Channel two, 17, 21-22
    Comedy, 100
    Contradictories, 1, 179
    Critics, 170, 194
    Dates, 40
    Dialectics, 99
    Double entendre, ix, 53
    Duality, 21, 269
    Egyptian, 25, 32-33, 70, 84, 92
    Façade, 69, 272
    Faults, 17, 20
    Fiction, 65, 193
    Foreshadowing, 147, 206
    Genius, x, 210
    Grammar, 24, 176
    "Great American Novel," xi
    Golden treasure, -Bible, 167, 169
    Hoax, x
    Homophones, 45
    Humor, ix, 19, 33-34, 269
    Hyperbole, 173
    Illusion, 133, 269
    Insult, 34, 176
    Intelligent, 15, 24, 270
    Irreverent, 33, 269
    Irony, 33, 111, 144, 170, 211, 272
    Keystone, 149, 193-194
    Linguistic façade, 18
    Literature, Literary qualities, ix-xi, 16-24, 36, 51, 65, 72, 148, 156, 220, 268
    Manuscript, 156
    Math, 41
    Melodrama, 215, 269
    Metaphor, 38, 52, 54, 65, 72, 75, 116, 125, 210, 214, 268
    Misdirection, 58
    "Most correct book," 149
    Myth, 272
    Nuance, 34
    Obscene, 269
    One-eyed View, 19, 22, 64
    Opposition, 15, 18, 20, 40
    Parable, 53, 170, 174, 210

INDEX

Paradox, 64-65, 99
Parallels, 14, 32, 47-48, 94, 118
Parody, ix, 32, 77, 82, 93, 111, 115-116, 140, 170, 176, 214, 269, 272
Philosophy, 35, 99, 106
Plagiarism, 170
Plates, brass, 44, 70, 72, 75, 92, 97, 99
Plates, gold, 4, 27, 28, 47, 82, 97, 107, 144, 209, 256, 263
Poetry, ix, 156
Polarized characters, 119
Politics, Political, 35
Propaganda, 272
Prosaic, 268
Published, 4
Pun, 190
Puritanical, 268
Religious thought, critique, ix; 35
Riddles, ix, 23, 111
Satire, ix, 167, 178, 194
Scripture, 17-18
Signatures, 36, 147
Stammering, Murmuring, 35, 43
Symbol, 14, 21, 42, 69, 113, 129, 160, 193-194, 204, 210, 212, 272
Symbol names, 22, 28, 37-38, 42, 44-45, 68, 72, 82, 84, 87, 89, 96, 104, 109, 110, 117, 120, 123, 125, 131, 136, 140, 142, 144, 147, 148, 191, 194, 211, 213, 214
Timeline, 40
Title page, 17
Translation, x, 17, 25, 35, 39, 47, 107
Mormon, place/forest of, 29
Mormons, Mormonism, LDS church, 77-78, 89, 102-106, 215, 220, 223-224, 237
    Bitter fruit, 105
    Chosen people, 239
    Cult, 237, 242
    Deniability, 239
    Double minded, 180
    Extermination orders, 201
    Fanatics, Zealots, 6, 9, 237, 255
    Humility, 65
    Inspiration, 218
    Jack Mormons, 243
    Libertinism, 242
    Missionaries, 5, 64
    Obedience, 60
    Organized, 4
    Perfection, 20, 52, 103
    Persecutions, -complex, 4, 103
    Polytheism, 184
    Popular movement, 215
    Pragmatic, 80
    Priesthood, 4, 61, 66, 102, 216
    Temples, ritual, work, 59-61, 79
    Total commitment, 61
True Believers, x, 33, 52, 250, 270
Moroni, 1, 4, 20, 25, 260, 264
Moses, 7, 13, 94, 113, 184, 186, 210
Mosiah, 88, 108, 110. 112-113, 123, 174
Mother hen parody, 170-171
Mulek, Mulekites, 101-123
Murder, 147, 241
Muslims, 72
Mystery, vii; 32, 57, 78, 80, 82, 192, 211

N

Nauvoo, IL, 5, 121, 147, 237, 244
    Dissidents, 242-244
    Expositor, 205, 232, 235, 244, 245, 246, 257
    Habeas Corpus law, 246
    House, 227, 234
    Legion, 205, 227, 233, 235, 246
    Martial law, 246
    Neighbor, 236
    University, 233
Nehor, 135
Nephi, Nephites, 14, 18, 19, 25, 26, 37-41, 42-43, 49, 57-58, 63, 69, 87, 92, 96, 98, 101, 105, 113, 124, 168, 173, 219, 260-263
    Blacksmith, 38, 65
    Bow of steel, 93
    Deception, 71
    Large of stature, 26, 38
    Leadership, 49
    Murderer, 71
    Protagonist, 37
    Ruler and teacher, 38
    Ship builder, 38
Nephihah, 261
Nephilim, Nephil, naphal, 37, 77
New and Everlasting Covenant, 20
New England, 113, 175, 196, 271
New Hampshire, 192, 198
New Testament, 31, 71, 94, 133, 169, 227
New World, 100-106, 109, 174, 191, 194
New York Tribune, 234
Nicknames, 89, 146
Nihilism, 191
Noah (king) 117, 119
Non-sequitur, 220
Norwich, VT, 43, 45

O

Objectivity, 134
Odyssey, The, 140
Ohio, 4
Old Testament, 97, 98, 103, 113-114
Ohio, 5, 202, 217, 225
Omni, 108, 109, 122
Omnipotent, -present, -scient, 93, 100, 103, 147, 182, 184, 213
Onidah, Oneida, 45

Onus, 142, 262, 264
Opposite, opposition, 5, 15, 22, 79, 132, 180, 191, 192, 196, 201, 202-203, 215, 228, 229, 233, 238, 239, 242, 248
Ordinance Concerning Libels, 244
Oregon, 257
Original Sin, 80
Orthodoxy, 37, 39, 126, 146, 194, 214
Overbearing, 145
Ovaries, Ovum, 54-56
Ovid (quoted), 190

P

Paine, Thomas, 26, 74, 76, 81-82, 133, 153, 168, 172, 175
Pagan, 32, 115, 121, 161, 183, 185, 263
Palestine, 212
Palmyra, NY, 3, 26, 29, 43, 45, 83, 127-129, 142, 191
Paul, St., 31-33, 81, 115, 132, 161
Parent-child wars, 197
Paternity, Paternalism, 130, 264
Patriarch, 71, 97, 110, 205, 224, 256
Pay-lay-ale, 61-62, 134
Pearl of Great Price, 131
Pelagoram, 146
Pentateuch, 114
Perfection, 20, 34, 77, 199
Persecution, complex, 172, 192, 212
Peter, St., 4, 34, 210
Pherez, 125
Philistines, 10, 87
Philosophy, ix, 99, 109, 122, 193, 220, 223, 238, 249, 268, 270, 271
Piety, 196
Pilgrims, 120
Pioneer, 269
Plagiarism, 115
Plan of Salvation, 53, 68, 162, 241
Poetry (see Chiasmus), 156
Politics, politicians, 119, 212, 123, 130, 147, 152, 178, 192, 199, 212, 214, 215, 246, 254
Polygamy, plural wives, 7, 37, 78, 103, 193, 225-226, 231,
    Celestial Marriage, 234, 241, 244, 247, 255
    Church law, 226
    Denials, 231, 236
    Easy-out, 226
    Spiritual wifery, 231
Polygamy plot, 223, 224, 230
Pontius Pilate, 136
Pratt, Parley, 254
"Praise to the Man," 94
Predestination, 218
Pre-Columbians, 167
Pre-existence, Pre-mortal 51; 64
Pre-figure (foreshadow), 147, 206

Presbyterianism, 3, 68, 69, 129
Priesthood, 123, 141, 239, 252
Prodigal Son, 161
Propaganda, 11, 22, 67, 70, 82, 88, 91, 96, 173, 178, 181, 199, 220, 238
Prophesies, self-fulfilling, 36, 215
Prophet, 153
Prosperity, 143, 178, 182
Protestants, 101, 114, 146, 160, 182, 185, 229
Puritanism, 229
Psychology, 80, 92, 132, 143, 215, 238, 242

R

Rachel, 110
Rationalizing, 242
Rattlesnakes, 12
Reason, 82, 96, 134, 183
Rebellion, 180
Religious scam, 49
Repentance, 103, 116, 162
Resurrection, 80, 141, 162, 168
Reuben, 89
Revelation, 124
Revolution, Revolutionary War, 74, 84, 198, 214, 269
Richards, Willard, 204
Riddle, Riddlemaster; viii, 23, 30, 128, 176, 194, 210
Rigdon, Sidney, 254-255
RLDS church, 225
Rockwell, Porter, 204-205
Rod of Iron, 53
Romans, 100

S

Salem, MA, 75, 81
Salt Lake City, UT, 251
Salvation, 141
Sam, 86
Samuel (Bible prophet), 87-88
Samuel the Lamanite, 64, 87
Sarah, Sarai, Sariah, 44-45, 47, 86
Satan, 53, 230, 241
Saul, 88
Schism, 203
Scarlet Letter, the, 126
Second-hand commandments, 224, 264
Second token of Melchizedek Priesthood, 61
Sectarian, 169, 194, 213
Seer, Seer stones, 12, 39, 88, 113, 146, 209, 212
Seezoram, 125
Self-righteousness, 122
Seminary (LDS), 52
Sermon on the Mount, 152, 169, 171
Servant, service, 100, 106, 144, 199
Seventh literary wonder of the world, 273
Seventy weeks, 221

INDEX

Sex, Sexual intercourse, 52, 140-141, 229, 235
Shadow God, 186-187
Shakespeare, 150, 261, 269, 272
Sharp, Thomas, 246
Sherem, 135, 180
Shibboleth, 144
Shiblon, 138, 142-145
Shim hill, 28, 65
Shiz, 190, 210, 215, 220, 246, 260
Sibling, 67, 668, 144, 257
Sidon, 137
Sin, 78, 79-80, 126, 174, 192, 197, 203, 236, 238, 242
Siren, Siron, 140-141
"Smith," (Bible) 39
Smith, Asael, 74, 196
Smith, Alvin, 66-68, 129
Smith, Don Carlos, 86
Smith, Emma Hale, 44, 142, 199, 204, 225-226
Smith family, 38, 49, 128, 192,
    Farmers, 129
Smith, Hyrum, 2, 68-70, 204-206, 233, 245, 256-258
    Co-Martyr, 258
    City Councilman, 256
    Patriarch, 256
    Proposed prophet, 258
    Slanderer, 245
Smith, Jesse (uncle), 72, 75-77, 86
Smith, Joseph, Jr.
    Author, vii-x, 36, 265
    Anti-Christ, 209
    Arrogance, 247
    Atheist, 271
    Biographers, 2
    Birth, 3, 30, 40-41
    Bravery, 2
    Bully, 229
    Charlatan, 202
    Charismatic, 24, 26, 222
    Christian, 14
    Commitment, ix
    Confessions, 2, 35, 148
    Conflict of interests, 89
    Controversialist, 228
    Discipline, 215, 228
    Double life, 204, 209, 211
    Dramatist, vii, 59
    Education, 26, 214
    Ego, 148, 234
    Enigma, 2
    Enlightened skeptic, 215
    Evening gatherings, 45-46
    Fugitive from justice, 219
    Genius, xi, 166
    Greek, Hebrew, German studies, 26-27
    History, Historian, 2, 135

Humanist, 271
Humor, 3, 35, 58, 61, 107, 111
Hypocrisy, 210
Ideology, 72
Ignorant, unlearned, x, 24, 26, 27, 35, 107, 161, 247, 272
Imagination, 166, 218
Immortal, 270
Imprisonment, 201, 245
Intelligence, ix, 27, 82, 101, 179, 218, 269, 272
Irrational, 132
Irreverent, 269
Judge, 5
King, 147
Large of stature, 26, 38
Levity, 35
Lieutenant General, vii, 5
Logic, 67, 220
Lunacy, 247
Make-Believe Martyr, viii
Mason, 83
Mayor, vii, 5, 205, 227, 244
Martyr, Martyrdom, viii, 6, 41, 49, 113, 193, 203, 211, 216, 228, 230, 234, 255, 258
Memory, 27, 40, 216
Messianic figure, 1
Middle-born, 43
Mobbed, 83
Money Digger, 142
Mysteries, Secrets, 115, 215, 225
Opposition, 201, 219
Osteomyelitis, 75, 81, 128
Paranoia, 232
Polarity, 202
Presidential Candidate, vii, 5, 245, 254
Prophet, prophecies, 2, 4, 217, 265
Psychology, 67, 72, 118, 148, 219
Psychotic, 271
Puzzle, vii, 14
Rebellious, 196
Registrar of deeds, 233
Revelation, 229
Riddlemaster, viii, 72
"Ruler and teacher," 38, 92
Sarcasm, 83
Scandal, 228
Scofflaw, 219
Seer, 12, 87
Self Promotion, 14, 36
Sinned outwardly, 241
Situation ethics, 237
Skeptic, 82, 271
Stolen property, 235
Tongues, Gift of, 265
Translator, x, 3
Treason, 147, 246

Trickster, 202
Tyranny, 232
Unethical business practices, 234
Visions, 81, 131-132, 134-135
Voltaire (as model), 83
Wrestler, 38, 219
Smith, Joseph F. 186
Smith, Joseph, Sr., 3, 26, 28, 43-44, 50, 74, 76, 129, 195-197
    Failures, 46
    Patriarch, 43
    Visionary, 46, 196
    Winebibber, 43
    Unambitious, 43
Smith, Lucy Mack, 3, 27, 45-50, 68, 74, 75, 128, 194
    Dominance, 45, 47, 197
    Memoirs, 47-48
    Mother, 47-48
    Pride, 47-48, 199
    Religious issues, 46, 47
Smith, Samuel, 86, 87, 128
Smith, Sophronia, 68
Smith, William, 86
Snow, Lorenzo, 39
Sober, 53, 143, 145
Socrates, 203, 271
Sodom and Gomorrah, 112
Solomon, 88, 224
Son of God, 57
Sophocles, 269
Spirit children, 139
Spirit of Christ, 184-185, 187
Spiritual death, 162
Standard works, 113
Stoicism, 99
Superstitions, 132, 189
Swift, Jonathan, 269

T

Tamar, 125
Tarsus, 31-32
Taxes, 196
Telestial kingdom, 34
Temples, 123, 140, 193, 227, 234, 258, 263
Ten Commandments, 71, 112-113
Terrestrial kingdom, 34
Tertullian, 228
Testing Games, 13, 229, 249-259
Texas, 202-257
Theology, 178, 189
"Think wrong, go to hell," 264
Tithes, Tithing, 102-103, 144, 228
Tobacco, 193, 228, 265
Tongues, 113, 265
Torah, 31
Total Commitment, 254

Tower of Babel, 191, 194-195
Traditions, 21, 44, 64, 213, 272
Tree of life, 47-48 51-59
Trinity, 80, 183-184
Truth, 21
True Believers, x, 250, 251, 253, 272
Twain, Mark, 51, 267, 269, 272
Typhoid, 128

U

Unconditional love, 172
Universalism, 71; 179
Unworthiness, 143, 145
Utah, 188, 194, 225, 243, 250, 251
Utica, NY, 45

V

Valiant, 53, 178
Van Buren, Martin, 233, 235
Vermont, vii, 3, 30, 40, 128, 192, 251
Vineyard, 100-106
Virgil (Greek poet), 54
Virgin, Virgin birth, 57-58, 77
Voice of the people, 88
Voltaire, 82-84, 106
Von Baer, Karl, 56

W

War, War of words, 3; 141, 198, 208, 213
Warrington, Benjamin, 245
Warsaw Signal, 246
Wasp, 246
Week per year prophecy, 221-222
Whitman, Walt (quoted), 188
Wight, Lyman, 218
Wine, 43, 71, 102-103
Women, 44
Wooley, Edwin, 250-251
Wisdom, Word of Wisdom, 102, 265
Woolf, Virginia (quoted), 25
Words of Mormon, 108
Work for the dead, 59

Y

Yosemite Sam, 100
Young, Brigham, 188, 218, 225, 244, 251-254
    Leadership, 253-254
    "Lion of the Lord," 252
    Rebuked by Joseph, 253
    Semi-literate, 252
    Stubborn, 253

Z

Zarah, Zarahemla, 80, 109, 121-130, 139, 173, 220, 261,
Zechariah, 148
Zedekiah, 40, 123

Zelph, 11
Zeno, Zenos, 97, 99-100, 189
Zion, Zion's Camp, 4, 8, 9-15, 24, 91, 118, 250
Zoramite, 139-140
Zombre, 146